American Yachts
in Naval Service

American Yachts in Naval Service
A History from the Colonial Era to World War II

KENNETH HOWARD GOLDMAN

McFarland & Company, Inc., Publishers
Jefferson, North Carolina

LIBRARY OF CONGRESS CATALOGUING-IN-PUBLICATION DATA

Names: Goldman, Kenneth Howard, 1947– author.
Title: American yachts in naval service : a history from the Colonial Era to World War II / Kenneth Howard Goldman.
Description: Jefferson, North Carolina : McFarland & Company, Inc., Publishers, 2021 | Includes bibliographical references and index.
Identifiers: LCCN 2020041428 | ISBN 9781476682600 (paperback : acid free paper) ∞
ISBN 9781476640747 (ebook)
Subjects: LCSH: Armed yachts—United States—History. | United States. Navy—History. | United States. Navy—Lists of vessels. | Warships—United States—History.
Classification: LCC V880 .G65 2020 | DDC 359.8/3—dc23
LC record available at https://lccn.loc.gov/2020041428

BRITISH LIBRARY CATALOGUING DATA ARE AVAILABLE

ISBN (print) 978-1-4766-8260-0
ISBN (ebook) 978-1-4766-4074-7

© 2021 Kenneth Howard Goldman. All rights reserved

No part of this book may be reproduced or transmitted in any form or by any means, electronic or mechanical, including photocopying or recording, or by any information storage and retrieval system, without permission in writing from the publisher.

Front cover: photograph of the *Sea Cloud* by the author

Printed in the United States of America

McFarland & Company, Inc., Publishers
Box 611, Jefferson, North Carolina 28640
www.mcfarlandpub.com

In memory of my father,
Lt. Robert W. Goldman, USNR (Ret.),
who sparked my interest in things nautical,
and for the peaceable citizens sailing the seas
for pleasure and profit, who stood and stand ready
to answer their nation's call to do more, with less, in harm's way.

Table of Contents

Preface   1

1. Beginnings   5
2. Minor Wars, Expeditions and Detours   18
3. A House Divided   27
4. War with Spain   59
5. The War to End War   83
6. World War Again   111

Epilogue   145
Appendix 1: Instructions to Commanders of Privateers   147
Appendix 2: The Trent Affair   150
Appendix 3: Yachts Acquired for Service in the War with Spain   151
Appendix 4: Yachts Over 100 Feet in World War I Naval Service, Including Shorter Vessels Named in Text   158
Appendix 5: World War II Yachts   169
Chapter Notes   183
Bibliography   197
Index   209

Preface

Even before there was a United States of America, there were those ready to pledge their lives and fortune to birth that nation. Farmers took payment in Continentals instead of English pounds. Common folk took up arms. Yachtsmen risked skin and treasure to catalyze a nascent Navy. From the American Revolution through the Second World War, in times of national need, yachts comprised an unofficial naval reserve, ready to shed their finery and take up arms. Whether gaining distinction in combat or serving as the nation's maritime eyes and ears, each dutifully filled its assigned niche. Theirs is a largely untold story, one that I literally stepped aboard.

After three hours of sleep in the Hotel Grande Bretagne in the heart of Athens, Greece, and a hurried breakfast, my wife and I settled into a taxi for a whirlwind sunrise tour of the city and its monuments. Our last stop was the port city of Piraeus, where we were in time for lunch at the seaside restaurant Tessera Adelphia. After convincing the waiter that we did indeed know what it was when we ordered retsina we settled in for a relaxing fresh-caught seafood meal. After baklava and coffee, we headed to the cruise ship terminal where we were met by an effusive, blond, blue-eyed woman spouting something in German. When she paused for breath my wife asked, "Sprechen sie English?" "Oh! You must be our two Americans!" was her welcoming response. The other 53 passengers comprised three Austrians and 50 Germans.

It was June 1995, and I was about to realize a childhood dream of sailing aboard a real square rigger, S/Y (sailing yacht) *Sea Cloud*, a four-masted diesel-electric auxiliary bark. German owned now, she was built, 64 years before, as E.F. Hutton's fifth yacht named *Hussar*. At the time, the irony of her current ownership was lost on me as we cruised among several of the Greek islands on a week-long trip to Kuşadashi, Turkey. It was only after our vacation that I discovered that *Sea Cloud* had once been USS *Sea Cloud*, a World War II naval auxiliary and hunter of German U-boats. If *Sea Cloud* had been in the Navy, what about other yachts and what about other wars? Those questions eventually led to the book that follows.

The earliest Dutch *jacht schepen* (hunting ships), from which we get the English "yachts," were fast vessels originally designed to hunt down pirates and smugglers. Their use in off hours was more in tune with what we now think of when hearing the term. That they were hunters to begin with fits nicely into their later use as naval auxiliaries. The renowned racing yacht *America*, from which the famous cup trophy is named, basically was a pilot boat in construction. A yacht, then, ultimately is defined by its use for private cruising or racing, whether or not it was built for that purpose. A working vessel could become a yacht, as it was with Cornelius Vanderbilt's eponymous *Vanderbilt* when he was aboard and so used her.

Though the definition is reasonably clear, assigning the yacht label to individual vessels can be less so. Early records are spotty and often incomplete, and naval acquisition prior to the Mexican-American War was haphazard. Knowing a yacht's name, at least prior to the 20th century, does not automatically clear your way to its particulars. The American Yacht List of 1896 reports seven named *Ripple*, eight *Rambler*, seven *Phantom* and ten *Edith*. The Annual List of Merchant Vessels of the United States, 1858 and 1860, respectively, show 20 named *Gipsey* or *Gypsy* and 17 *Syren*. The confusion is not just the bane of the historian; as *Hunt's Yachting Magazine* of 1852 pointed out, "Major Stirling, the owner of the *Triumvir*, has a schooner in frame at Ratsey's yard, Cowes, built after the plan of the *Gloriana*. The new schooner will measure about 110 tons, O.M. [Old Measurement, in use until 1849]. We have not heard what name she is to bear. We hope one perfectly new, for great inconvenience arises from several vessels bearing one and the same name." Through the years, others repeatedly dashed that hope. Joseph M. Cudahy had two yachts named *Innisfail*. J.P. Morgan had five named *Corsair*. During the American Civil War the Navy changed the name of the ship of the line USS *Alabama* to USS *New Hampshire* to avoid confusion with the Confederate cruiser CSS *Alabama*. No such accommodation, however, was reached to distinguish the Navy's USS *Miami* from the Revenue Marine's (later U.S. Coast Guard) USRC (Revenue Cutter) *Miami* during that same conflict.

A single vessel also often would sail under different names at different times. Some of the name changes were innocent, as when a yacht was sold from one yachtsman to another, and each subsequent owner attached his own appellation. Others were of a more nefarious nature, such as to disguise a blockade runner. Sometimes a capture was renamed when impressed into her captor's service.

Refits or conversion to naval service could change the listed tonnage, further complicating the attribution of service, both civilian and military, to a specific yacht. Tonnage itself varies according to which measuring system is employed, and often the formula is omitted in the reports. Measurement could be in tons burden (or burthen), an expression of a vessel's carrying capacity, the calculation of which was never clearly defined, or in tons displacement, a weight measurement. Gross tons measures the internal volume of a vessel, while net tons limits this to space allotted for cargo. Length could be "length over all," the longest measurement end-to-end including the bow sprit, or length at the waterline. The latter, of course, would vary if loaded or unloaded. Please note that in the pages that follow all amounts in dollars and pounds Sterling generally are values in the times given and are not adjusted to modern equivalents.

Neither is the supposed category of a vessel a definitive measure. A sloop could be a classification or a rig. A schooner could have any number of masts with fore-and-aft rig and even square topsails. It also could be a yacht or a merchantman. In various dispatches David Farragut refers to *Corypheus* as a schooner, her rig, while technically she was a steam auxiliary yacht.

In each case where there existed probable confusion, I have erred on the side of caution regarding what I have included. In each case that seemed suspect I have used at least two sources, after making sure, as far as is possible, that those sources were not merely repeating each other. And, yes, I did find unexpected mistakes in sources that should have been more accurate. Although one mistake does not invalidate everything in a source, that finding heightened my caution. History is, after all, a mystery that involves careful detection. Any given line of inquiry can open up others with a mere offhand mention. For example, the account of the Civil War capture of the sloop *Richard Vaux* by USS *Primrose* mentions the previous capture of the sloop *Flying Cloud* on 2 June 1863.

As this undertaking progressed, its potentially daunting scope became all too apparent. Without the Internet it might have proved impossible. The most important tools I had at my disposal were sources such as Google Books and Internet Archive, and the ability to keyword search the web, without which my ability to fully research my topic would have been sorely limited. Keywords saved me, I am certain, years of work and led me to sources that never would have occurred to me, such as the 1799 publication *Transactions of the American Philosophical Society, Held at Philadelphia, for Promoting Useful Knowledge*, which published David Bushnell's account of his Revolutionary War submarine, and the 1905 article "Catholics and the American Revolution," which provided insight into the beginnings of a Continental Navy.

As this nation's commerce evolved so did the nation's yachts, from their utilitarian beginning along the dual paths of racing competition and the floating palaces of conspicuous consumption. But whether awash with champagne or wreathed in cordite smoke, in time of need the American yacht has stood at the ready to augment the Navy.

1

Beginnings

From the time England's rebellious American colonies realized that words would not sway the mother country, that words must be backed up by action, the call to arms has included a call for vessels, both to protect the shoreline and to project that action off shore. The revolutionaries had to make do with what materiel was on hand, and nowhere in those clandestine armories was there a navy. In later wars, civilian ship owners would be called upon to augment the standing navy. At the outset of the American Revolution, such civilian vessels were the navy.

For nearly two centuries before the Declaration of Independence, wealthy Dutch merchants had been adapting light, fast, shallow-draft sailing vessels to private use from their designed purpose of chasing down coastal pirates or as dispatch vessels to personal excursion craft. These "yachts" (the name, as noted earlier, is shortened from the Dutch *jacht schepen*, meaning hunting or hunt ships) could vary from around forty feet in length to the hundred-foot length of a lower rated ship of the line.[1]

While the nascent sport of yachting gradually enticed the wealthy and the aristocracy of other nations, it had not yet significantly crossed "the pond" to the North American colonists. They, as yet, had little time for such costly leisure pursuits. The roles of ship owner and ship's captain often were combined in a single individual, whose workplace and domicile were likewise one and the same. Having the fastest vessel brought with it distinct economic advantage in the commerce of the day. Racing that vessel just for the reward of having one's name and vessel engraved on a silver cup would have felt like a waste of time to the practical ship owners.

Nevertheless, vessels termed yachts began to appear in the colonies as early as 1717. The Royal Governors of the Province of New York are recorded as using a yacht, prior to 1750, whenever business required their travel up the Hudson.[2] Nathaniel Hawthorne in his "American Notes," 12 August 1837, refers to a yacht owned by General Knox that he saw in 1797.[3] These vessels, few in number, largely were owned by wealthy Dutch settlers, who had brought their predilection for relaxing on their *jacht schepen* with them. Though the seed of American yachting had been planted, it did not grow into what we now consider the sport of yachting until the founding of the New York Yacht Club in 1844.

On the night of 16 December 1773 a protest meeting was called by Samuel Adams at the Old South Meeting House in Boston, Massachusetts, in culmination of the growing tension caused by the British Tea Act of 10 May 1773. Afterward, a large crowd of protestors, some disguised as Mohawk Indians, stormed out of the meeting and proceeded to Griffin's Wharf in Boston Harbor. There they boarded three English ships

Admiraliteits Jacht, c. 1640 (by Gerrit Groenewegen, 1789).

and destroyed their cargoes of tea. In response to this "Boston Tea Party," Parliament passed the Massachusetts Government Act of 20 May 1774, which effectively placed the colony in general and Boston in particular under martial law. The Siege of Boston began on 19 April 1775. Open hostilities against the Crown began in earnest with the Battle of Bunker Hill two months later on 17 June. The siege finally was broken by forces under the command of General George Washington, who seized the Dorchester Heights on 17 March 1776. Washington's artillerymen then turned the British guns, many captured from Fort Ticonderoga, on the British ships in the harbor.

The need for offshore protection had never been absent from the colonies. Merchant ships, while engaging in peaceful inter-colonial trade still had to protect themselves from Indians, buccaneers and freebooters. Now, they also had the formidable Royal Navy to contend with, in particular His Majesty's Frigate *Rose*, which had bottled up shipping in Naragansett Bay. On 12 June 1775, the General Assembly of the Crown Colony of Rhode Island and Providence Plantations created the first formal navy of the New World:

> It is voted and resolved, that the committee of safety be, and they are hereby, directed to charter two suitable vessels for the use of the colony and fit out the same in the best manner, to protect the trade of this colony.
>
> That the said vessels be at the risk of the colony, and be appraised, before they are chartered, by

1. Beginnings

Messrs. Joseph Anthony, Rufus Hopkins and Cromwell Child or any two of them; who are also to agree for the hire of the said vessels.

That the largest of the said vessels be manned with eighty men, exclusive of officers; and be equipped with ten guns, four-pounders; fourteen swivel guns, a sufficient number of small arms, and all necessary warlike stores.

That the small vessel be manned in a number not exceeding thirty men.

That the whole be included in the number of fifteen hundred men, ordered to be raised in this colony, and be kept in pay until the 1st day of December next, unless discharged before, by order of the General Assembly...

And that the lieutenant general, brigadier general and committee of safety, or the major part of them, have the power of directing and ordering said vessels; and in case it shall appear to them that the officers and men of said vessels can be more serviceable on shore, than at sea, to order them on shore, to defend the seaports in this colony.[4]

That same day, Governor Nicholas Cooke signed the order which also appointed Abraham Whipple commander of the sloop *Katy* and commodore of both vessels. (*Katy* was renamed *Providence* on 9 January 1776 when taken into Continental service.) This was not the same as a wealthy industrialist of a later century leasing his yacht to the government for the war effort for a dollar a year, but it definitely can be seen as the forerunner of such patriotic largess. It also is important to note that the resolution recognizes that said vessels remain private property and that Rhode Island would indemnify the owners for their loss. The order was immediately put into effect, and on the 15th, *Katy* chased ashore and destroyed *Rose*'s tender *Hope*. Captain Whipple previously had distinguished himself when he led the boarding party, on the night of 9–10 June 1772, that captured and then burned the grounded, British-armed schooner *Gaspé* that had been harassing both licit and illicit commerce on Naragansett Bay.

About the same time that Rhode Island was formalizing its navy, other colonies also began organizing their own forces afloat. Massachusetts in August commissioned *Machias*, *Liberty* and *Diligent*. Connecticut fitted out 12 vessels during the war. In July Pennsylvania organized a fleet of 10 sailing vessels and 30 boats to protect the Delaware River. Maryland and Virginia jointly patrolled the Chesapeake Bay. North Carolina stationed a small fleet off Ocracoke Inlet. Georgia had a small collection of galleys and commissioned a schooner in June. And South Carolina organized a fleet of 15 seagoing vessels, creating the most heavily armed navy of any of the colonies.[5]

Two months after Abraham Whipple received command of *Katy*, on 26 August 1775, the Rhode Island General Assembly went a giant step farther by passing a resolution directing its delegates to the Continental Congress to introduce legislation and "to use their whole influence, at the ensuing Congress, for building at the Continental expense a Fleet of sufficient force, for the protection of these Colonies, and for employing them in such a manner and places as will most effectively annoy our enemies, and contribute to the common defence of these Colonies."[6]

Samuel Ward, later governor of Rhode Island, carried out his brief on 3 October, but his motion was speedily tabled. Two days later, the Congress received intelligence that two ordnance-laden British transports had sailed from England to Quebec. Wouldn't it be better if that materiel could be diverted to the poorly supplied Continental Army? The Rhode Island proposal was taken up from the table. "The subject was brought up for consideration on October 7th. John Adams tells us that some thought the project 'the maddest idea,' that when John Rutledge, of South Carolina, moved the appointment of a committee to prepare a plan and estimate of a fleet, timid ones made the proposition a subject of such ridicule that Christopher Gadsden, also of South Carolina, had to protest against his associates doing so. Silas Deane, of Connecticut, advised Congress to give it 'serious debate.' He did not consider it 'romantic.'"[7] The overall sense, however, was that it was one thing to create a Continental Army to fight the Redcoats on the colonists' own turf and quite another to go against His Majesty's Navy on its own ocean. Samuel Chase, of Maryland, perhaps summed up the timid opposition, saying it was "the maddest Idea in the World to think of building an American Fleet." Even pro-navy members found the proposal too vague. It lacked specifics and no one could tell how much it would cost. Apart from arguing over details, there remained a majority of delegates, who hoped there still might be a reconciliation with England. They feared that a navy implied sovereignty and independence. The feeling was to pass the buck to the individual colonies to fit out armed vessels as they saw fit.[8]

For months, John Adams of Massachusetts had been campaigning for the raising of a Continental navy to "defend the seacoast towns, protect vital trade, retaliate against British raiders, and make it possible to seek out among neutral nations of the world the arms and stores that would make resistance possible."[9] Receipt of a letter from General Washington finally tipped the scales in Adams' favor. Events had impressed Washington with the immediate need for a navy, which could intercept and disrupt the seaborne supply line to the British troops that held Boston in thrall. He had taken matters into his own hands and, on behalf of the Continental Congress, he had assumed command of four fishing schooners in Massachusetts, which he had armed and renamed *Franklin*, *Harrison*, *Hancock* and *Lynch*.[10]

Capt. James Mugford of the Continental Schooner *Franklin* captured the British Transport *Hope*, 17 May 1776 (lithograph by L.W. Bradford & Co., 1854; NH 66510 courtesy the Naval History & Heritage Command Photographic Dept.).

1. Beginnings

Presented with this *fait accompli* and the news of the 5th, regarding the two British transports, the Congress at last agreed to acquire the means to attempt the capture of the arms carried by the British vessels. On Friday, 13 October they appointed a naval committee comprising Silas Deane, John Adams and John Langdon with the authority to take the first step in creating what eventually became the United States Navy:

> Resolved, That a swift sailing vessel, to carry ten carriage guns, and a proportionable number of swivels, with eighty men, be fitted, with all possible despatch, for a cruize of three months, and that the commander be instructed to cruize eastward, for intercepting such transports as may be laden with warlike stores and other supplies for our enemies, and for such other purposes as the Congress shall direct.
>
> That a Committee of three be appointed to prepare an estimate of the expence, and lay the same before the Congress, and to contract with proper persons to fit out the vessel.
>
> Resolved, that another vessel be fitted out for the same purposes, and that the said committee report their opinion of a proper vessel, and also an estimate of the expence.[11]

Two ships by themselves hardly constituted a Navy. "At the time the Continental Congress formally declared the United States independent of Great Britain, July 2, 1776, England had in commission one hundred and twelve vessels of war, carrying three thousand seven hundred and fourteen guns; and of this force, seventy-eight men of war, mounting two thousand and seventy-eight guns, were stationed on the coast of North America."[12] "The American Navy at the same time consisted of twenty-five cruisers, mounting four hundred and twenty-two guns; but only six of these vessels were built for war purposes, the others being merchantmen purchased and fitted out for the occasion."[13]

Necessity required reliance on private enterprise. On 23 March 1776, even before the formal declaration of independence from Great Britain, the Continental Congress issued its first Letters of Marque and Reprisal. These officially authorized private individuals and the colonies to fit out cruisers for the purpose of capturing or destroying any vessel sailing under the British flag. Within a fortnight they had designed a commission and promulgated instructions for commanding officers [see Appendix I]. This was a convenient way to increase naval force and bring additional pressure on an enemy without draining the nation's treasury. The incentive for a private citizen to face the concomitant risk to life and limb and the vessels themselves, apart from the value to the prosecution of the revolution, was prize money. This was the cash value of those British ships and cargoes, a bounty which went to the treasury and the owners, officers and crews according to a detailed schedule of shares after proper adjudication by a civil court of competent jurisdiction. An advertisement for seamen placed in the *Boston Gazette* of 13 November 1780 laid out the inducement to thus serve:

> An Invitation to all brave Seamen and Marines, who have an inclination to serve their country and make their Fortunes. The grand Privateer Ship DEANE, commanded by Elisha Hinman Esq., and prov'd to be a very capital sailor, will sail on a Cruise against the Enemies of the United States of America, by 20th instant. The DEANE mounts thirty Carriage Guns, and is excellently well calculated for Attacks, Defence and Pursute. This therefore is to invite all those Jolly Fellows who love their Country, and want to make their Fortunes at One Stroke, to repair immediately to the Rendezvous at the Head of His Excellency Governor Hancock's Wharf, where they will be received with a hearty Welcome by a number of Brave Fellows there assembled, and treated with what excellent Liquor call'd GROG which is allowed by all true Seamen to be the Liquor of Life.[14]

The object of issuing the Letters and the subsequent proceedings was to draw a clear line between legitimate naval action on behalf of the fledgling government and simple piracy on the high seas. The trade off to issuing Letters of Marque and Reprisal was that those vessels and crews so empowered operated on their own initiative absent any central direction. In other words, action was heavy on the tactics of the immediate situation and light on the coordinated strategy that might have achieved a greater, long-term effect for the overall war effort.

A major drawback to authorizing privateers versus commissioning civilian vessels into an official naval service was the lack of adequate communication and signaling. Though not very good in the age of sail even within the commissioned service, it essentially was nonexistent among the independent privateers. Although there were some sailors who could tell the nationality of a vessel by "the cut of her jib," even they could not be certain that the observed nationality of construction remained the nationality of operation at that point in time. The cry of "Sail Ho!" from the lookout could mean either make all sail toward the contact or come about. Even if a national flag flew from the masthead, it might be false rather than true, a decoy. Once the chase was on, especially between evenly matched vessels, the only way for the rabbit to increase speed was to jettison guns, water barrels, even spare spars. The hound could spend hours closing the potential enemy only to discover at the last that both rabbit and hound were countrymen. This was well illustrated in a later war when, on 16 January 1813, the American privateer *Anaconda* mistook the United States war schooner *Commodore Hull* for an enemy and fired a broadside into her before the mistake was discovered.[15] On 9 March of the same year, in the Chesapeake Bay, the American privateer *Argus* poured devastating fire into the American privateer *Fox*. Master-Commandant Arthur Sinclair of *Argus* related the incident in a letter:

> In consequence of silencing her I ceased my fire, believing that she had struck; but although she fired on me first, after being told who we were and never would answer who she was, yet so much did I fear that it was some of my impudent, headstrong countrymen that I took every opportunity to spare her, and try to find out who she was. I much fear they were all lost, as she could not have had a whole boat left, and we found pieces torn out of her by our shot ten or twelve feet long on the shore the next morning. I judge her to be upward of two hundred tons by the 9½-inch cable and the seven-hundred or eight-hundred weight anchors we got the next day.... I was sure she would sink, as we were within one hundred and fifty yards of her and I pointed myself seven long 18-pounders, double and treble shotted, just amidships between wind and water and could plainly hear the shots strike.[16]

As indicated in a letter from an Englishman residing in Grenada, dated 18 April 1777, despite the significant drawbacks, a valid comparison can be made between the effectiveness of the privateers of the American Revolution and the U-boat campaigns of two world wars:

> Everything continues excessively dear here, and we are happy if we can get anything for money by reason of the quantity of vessels that are taken by American privateers. A fleet of vessels came from Ireland a few days ago. From sixty vessels that departed from Ireland not above twenty-five arrived in this and neighboring islands, the others (it is thought) being all taken by the American privateers. God knows if this American war continues much longer we shall all die with hunger.[17]

On 6 February 1778, Alderman Woodbridge testified before the House of Lords:

> The number of ships lost by capture or destroyed by American privateers since the commencement of the war is seven hundred and thirty-three, of which, after deducting for those retaken and restored, there remained five hundred and fifty-nine, the value of which, including the ships,

cargoes, etc., amounted, upon a very moderate calculation, to £1,800,633 18s. That insurance before the war was two per cent to America, and two and a half per cent to North Carolina, Jamaica, etc. That insurance to America, Africa and the West Indies was now more than double, even with the convoy, and without the convoy, unless the ship was a ship of force, fifteen per cent. William Creighton, Esq., not only corroborated the alderman in the most material points, but added many new facts which had fallen within his own knowledge. He stated that losses suffered by the merchants in consequence of the captures made by American privateers to have amounted to at least £2,000,000 in October last, and that by this time they could not be less than £2,200,000.[18]

Though the general attitude remained that privateering is a military necessity if I resort to it, but it is piracy if you do it, there was an implicit "do unto others" agreement that gave at least official protection to those seamen. On the other hand, what if the issuing party was not universally recognized as the agency of a recognized, legitimate government? Were the colonies merely in criminal rebellion against their rightful government, or did they comprise a nascent nation with the concomitant established rights of nations and combatants to defend themselves by all legitimate means?

On 1 November 1775, the General Court of Massachusetts addressed that issue when they passed "An Act for Encouraging the Fixing out of Armed Vessels, to defend the Sea Coast of America..." which, in its preamble, laid out the legal case for the colonies to commission private vessels to take up arms against the British:

> Whereas the present administration of Great Britain, being divested of justice and humanity and strangers to that magnanimity and sacred regard for liberty which inspired their venerable predecessors, have been endeavoring thro' a series of years to establish a system of despotism over the American colonies and by their venal and corrupt measures have so extended their influence over the British parliament that, by a prostituted majority, it is now become a political engine of slavery; and whereas the military tools of these our unnatural enemies, while restrained by the united forces of the American colonies from proceeding in their sanguinary career of devastation and slaughter, are infecting the sea coast with armed vessels [sic] and daily endeavoring to distress the inhabitants by burning their towns and destroying their dwellings ... and making captures of provision and other vessels, being the property of said inhabitants; and whereas their majesties King William and Queen Mary by the royal charter of this colony ... did grant, establish and ordain that ... a majority of the council shall have full power ... for the special defence of their said province or territory, to assemble in a martial array and put in warlike posture the inhabitants of their said province or territory and to lead and conduct them and with them to encounter, expulse, resist and pursue by force of arms, as well as by sea as by land ... and also to kill, slay, destroy, and conquer by all fitting ways, enterprizes and means whatsoever all and every such person and persons as should at any time thereafter attempt or enterprize the destruction, invasion, detriment or annoyance of their said province or territory ... and whereas it is expressly resolved by the grand Congress of America, "That each colony, at their own expence, make such provision by armed vessels or otherwise ... as their respective assemblies ... shall judge expedient ... for the protection of their harbours and navigation on the sea coasts..."[19]

The United States gradually achieved recognition by other governments. On 16 November 1776, the brig *Andrew Doria*, flying the new American flag, on a mission to purchase arms, called on the island of St. Eustatius in the Dutch Antilles. On entering the harbor the vessel fired the standard salute to the host port officials. Governor Johannes de Graff ordered an answering gun fired, thereby being the first to give formal recognition with that salute to the new nation. This exacerbated the friction between Great Britain and the Netherlands. On 17 December 1777 the Sultan of Morocco formally declared his ports open to American ships, thereby becoming the first nation to recognize the United States. Although France had favorably regarded the American

Revolution, it did not formally recognize American independence until 6 February 1778, with the Treaty of Amity and Commerce and the Treaty of Alliance.

As far as the British government was concerned, however, captured American privateers were considered little better than pirates and were denied the better treatment of prisoners of war. They were treated more harshly even than French and Spanish prisoners. Light on calories and heavy on filth, they had to survive wearing the clothes they were captured in, eating meager rations that like as not were spoiled, and they were confined with a general lack of adequate sanitation. Estimates are that upwards of 10,500 men died in the British prison ships in Wallabout Bay, later site of the Brooklyn Navy Yard. David Sproats, the British official in charge of those prison ships, boasted that he had caused the death of more rebels than all the British armies in America,[20] and, as George Washington stated, "few or none of those prisoners belonged to the regular cruisers of the colonies, most of them being captured privateersmen."[21] British treatment of American privateersmen did not improve during the next war between the two countries. Mistreatment culminated with the "Dartmoor Massacre" on 6 April 1815, more than three months after peace was declared by the Treaty of Ghent, when the governor of Dartmoor Prison, Captain Shortland, who long had brooded on "fixing the damned rascals,"[22] ordered the guards to fire into the crowd of milling prisoners, more than 1,700 as of April 1813. Most of them were privateersmen. Seven were killed outright and 60 wounded. Charges were brought against Captain Shortland but were not proven.

"The total number of Continental vessels lost during the Revolution, by capture, wreck, etc., was twenty-four, carrying in all four hundred and seventy guns. The loss of the British Government war vessels was one hundred and two, carrying in all two thousand six hundred and twenty-two guns. About eight hundred vessels of all kinds were captured from the English by American cruisers, privateers and by private enterprise."[23]

One of those private enterprises (with much of the funding from the Connecticut colony), though only partially successful, and that indirectly, ushered in new age in naval warfare. On the night of 7–8 September 1776, a unique vessel, neither privateer nor private yacht but acting under the authority of General Washington, cast off the tow lines from two whaleboats and proceeded under its own power toward what is now Governors Island, south of Manhattan. The target was HMS *Eagle*, flagship of Admiral Richard Howe and the British fleet of four hundred vessels of all sizes blockading New York. The tiny American attacking vessel was named *Turtle* for its similarity to two turtle shells joined together. It was little more than a single man within a specially designed barrel that was capable of submerging for up to 30 minutes and, more importantly for Sergeant Ezra Lee (seconded by Brigadier General Samuel Holden Parsons) who was both captain and crew, returning to the surface before the air ran out. Designed by Yale University student David Bushnell, this first American operational submarine packed a punch consisting of a waterproof keg containing 150 pounds of gunpowder and a clockwork fuse. Upon setting the timer, Sergeant Lee, in his human powered submarine, had only 20 minutes to put as much distance as possible between him and the explosion. Lee slipped under *Eagle*, but the auger bit, which was to bore into the enemy hull and affix the mine, failed to penetrate. During a second attempt *Turtle* bobbed to the surface, attracting unwanted attention. Lee was forced to jettison the mine, which started the clock, and withdraw. Lee and *Turtle* escaped pursuit. The timer worked, and the mine detonated, throwing up a massive column of water. Though *Eagle* was undamaged, the action sufficiently unnerved Admiral Howe that he ordered the blockade moved farther from New York, thus relieving some of the pressure on the city. In October, Sergeant Lee and *Turtle* made an attempt on a British frigate anchored in the Hudson River. British ground forces had expanded their gains by then, and a sentry spotted the submarine while it ran awash. He raised the alarm, causing Lee to abandon the attempt. That same month, the British advanced up the river and sank the submarine's tender with *Turtle* aboard.

Bushnell continued his experimentation with mine warfare, immortalized by Francis Hopkinson in his contemporary poem, "British Valour Displayed or The Battle of the Kegs." Despite the levity of the poem, based on Bushnell's attack down the Delaware River in January 1778, his mines posed a serious threat to British vessels moored in American waters. Captain J. Symons, of His Majesty's Frigate *Cerberus*, described one such attack in a letter, dated August 1777, to Rear Admiral Parker:

> Wednesday night, being at anchor to the west of New London in Black Point Bay, the schooner I had taken was at anchor close by me astern. About eleven o'clock at night we discovered a line towing astern that came from the bows. WE immediately conjectured that it was somebody that had veered himself away by it and began to haul in. We then found that the schooner had got hold of it (who had taken it for a fishing line), gathered in near fifteen fathom, which was buoyed up by little bits of sticks at stated distances until he came to the end, at which was fastened a machine that was too heavy for one man to haul up, being upward of one hundredweight. The other people of the boat turning out assisted him, got it on deck, and were unfortunately examining it too curiously when it went off like the sound of a gun, blew the boat into pieces and set her aflame, killing three of the men who were in her stern; the fourth, who was standing forward, was blown into the water. Upon examining round the ship after this accident we found the other part of the line to the larboard side buoyed up in the same manner, which I ordered cut away immediately for fear or hauling up another machine.[24]

On 3 September 1783, the Treaty of Paris officially ended the war, and the impromptu fleet of privateers, which had so well served the fledgling nation, was suddenly out of business. The severely depleted treasury and the possibility that the allied colonies, now states, might go their separate ways meant that the remnants of the Continental Navy would soon disperse.

On 30 April 1789, the new Constitution went into effect, and the naval argument continued. Despite the value of seaborne operations to a successful outcome of the war, and the emerging threat to commerce posed by Barbary pirates, there was strong resistance among representatives to Congress to maintaining a standing military either ashore or afloat. Senator William Maclay of Pennsylvania summed up the opposition, "This thing of a fleet has been working among our members all the session.... It is another menace to our republican institutions."[25] Even those unafraid of establishing a new monarchy in the United States thought that one, the new nation did not have the wherewithal to launch sufficient ships to make any difference against an external threat, two, "it was a sacred duty as well as sound policy to discharge the public debt"[26] before taking on new debt, and three, the government could pay protection money to the Barbary pirates as older nations already were doing. The opposition lost in the House of Representatives by only two votes. It was not until 27 March 1794 that the legislature passed a law authorizing the construction of six frigates that an actual United States Navy was established. Meanwhile, a treaty was entered into with the Barbary States and the demanded tribute was paid.

Nevertheless, the price for "protection," as with any blackmail, even if it does not

Continental sloop *Providence* (oil by W. Nowland Van Powell; NH 85201-KN courtesy the Naval History & Heritage Command Photographic Dept.).

keep increasing, eventually becomes onerous. In the spring of 1801, the United States had had enough of the pirates' increasing demands. Soon after Thomas Jefferson's inauguration, Congress granted him the power to pursue whatever action was necessary to protect American seamen and commerce from the North African pirates. This first Barbary War was successfully prosecuted by the Navy and Marine Corps, and was concluded with a peace treaty signed on 10 June 1805.

Addressing the House of Commons on 1 March 1848, British Foreign Minister Lord Palmerston famously commented, "Therefore I say that it is a narrow policy to suppose that this country or that is to be marked out as the eternal ally or the perpetual enemy of England. We have no eternal allies, and we have no perpetual enemies. Our interests are eternal and perpetual, and those interests it is our duty to follow."[27] Nations have no permanent friends and no permanent enemies, only permanent interests. It was neither permanent friends nor permanent enemies, but permanent interests which dominated developments as the world transitioned from the 18th century to the 19th.

The Jay Treaty of 1794 cleared up lingering issues from the Treaty of Paris and improved commerce between the United States and Great Britain. France, however, saw this as a slight and a violation of the 1778 Treaty of Amity. President John Adams sent envoys Elbridge Gerry, Charles Pinckney and John Marshall to Paris to smooth things over, but the French Directory was less a government than a web of disputatious factions and intrigue, with Foreign Minister Charles Maurice de Talleyrand-Périgord the gray eminence at the center. French go-betweens failed in their extortionate demands and negotiations never really got started. America's former ally saw opportunity in this nation's lack of a navy to police its territorial waters. Ignoring America's neutrality, French cruisers and privateers freely preyed upon British merchantmen along the American coast and increasingly helped themselves to the occasional American vessel as well. Diplomacy failed. Charges that could not be backed up with adequate force availed naught. The situation reached a head when the United States abrogated all treaties with France on 7 July 1798, although it did not declare war. Nine days later Congress ordered construction of three more frigates. The smaller United States Navy amply proved itself against the French, losing only a single warship. Hostilities ceased on 30 September 1800 with the Treaty of Mortefontaine.

Relations between the United States and Great Britain existed more on sufferance than on amity. They remained reasonably cordial despite the contentious question of who was an American citizen and who a British subject, which eventually came to a head in the festering issues of naval deserters and impressment. The situation escalated into a one-sided action between the American frigate *Chesapeake* and the British ship *Leopard*. On 22 June 1807, the American frigate hove to on a ruse by the British captain. After Captain Barron refused to accede to the British demand that he hand over three of his crew, Captain Humphreys of *Leopard* opened fire. *Chesapeake* had put to sea with unsecured stores and impedimenta still crowding her decks and was able to fire but a single shot in answer to the British ship's several broadsides before the captain had to strike her colors. By 1812 over six thousand cases of American seamen impressed onto British warships were registered in Washington.[28] British commanders were equally cavalier with American cargoes and American neutrality, stopping American merchantmen, forcing them into a convenient port and seizing any lading they suspected of going directly or indirectly to England's enemies. It was a situation that could not be tolerated forever.

Despite the example of the quasi-war with France and the escalating hostilities with Great Britain, when the United States declared war with the latter on 18 June 1812, the United States Navy comprised 17 vessels mounting 442 guns manned and supported by 5,000 personnel. Of those, only eight vessels could get to sea in the first months of the war.[29] Great Britain, on the other hand, listed 1,048 vessels mounting 27,800 guns manned with total personnel of nearly 151,600.[30]

There were no American privateers at the outset of the war, but the tradition of civilians augmenting the Navy, whether for patriotism or profit or plaudits, resumed in earnest. Anything seaworthy from merchantman to fishing smack that could mount a gun was outfitted under a Letter of Marque and Reprisal. "The people of the eastern states are laboring 'might and main' to fit out privateers. Two have already sailed from Salem, and ten others are getting ready for sea. This looks well. From Baltimore there will, in a few days, be at sea, 12 or 15 of the fastest sailing, and best found and appointed vessels in the world, carrying from 10 to 16 guns each, and from 80 to 120 men."[31] A letter, dated 14 July 1812, added, "In sixty days, counting from the day on which war against England was declared, there will be afloat from the United States, not less than 150 privateers, carrying, on average, 75 men and 6 guns. If they succeed pretty well, their number will be doubled in a short time. Sixty five were at sea on the 16th inst. many others are probably out that we have not yet heard of."[32]

As happened in later wars, notably the "Hooligan Navy" of World War II, the smallest vessels capable of carrying and firing a cannon without capsizing, such as a long-tom swivel, or just an eager compliment of men armed with muskets and sabers, were the first to take to sea. Their size, however, effectively limited their operations to littoral waters, bays and inlets where pickings were rather slim. At the outset of the war, nearly any armament was sufficient to effect the capture of unarmed British merchantmen if these privateers could get close enough to board. As the British learned to take the threat seriously they armed their merchantmen, and transports usually traveled in escorted convoys. The early mosquito fleet was soon effectively out of business although it still was useful for logistics, surveillance and dispatch operations. Larger privateers soon followed and distinguished themselves against British privateers and men-of-war during the two and a half years of the conflict.

Among these light-weight privateers was at least one yacht, a vessel built neither for war nor for commerce but just for the pleasure of sailing. The Crowninshield family of Salem, Massachusetts, comprised a shipping dynasty with its own wharfs, warehouses and counting house. The ships of George Crowninshield & Sons (later George Crowninshield & Company, after the old man died) included the Revolutionary War

Ship *America* (formerly the British *Pompey*, captured during the Revolution) "Eight days from Grand Bank to the Channel of England, May 1789" (watercolor by Michele Felice Corné; NH 57016 courtesy the Naval History & Heritage Command Photographic Dept.).

prize *America* (ex–*Pompey*). They would later have three other ships named *America*. George, Jr.'s enchantment with affairs nautical expressed itself in wood and canvas in 1801 when he built the sloop *Jefferson* as his private yacht, arguably the first American sea-going yacht. She measured a trim 35 feet long, displacing 22 tons. George Junior was a sight to behold. A stocky five foot six inches tall, his hair braided into a pigtail, he wore custom-designed brocade waistcoats, a tall beaver-skin hat and Hessian boots with gold tassels.[33] No mere dandy, however, he could often be seen taking *Jefferson* out in foul weather to rescue the sailors from storm-foundered vessels in Massachusetts Bay. When the second war with Great Britain broke out in 1812, George Crowninshield was again ready to defend the common weal. With the added inducement of potential prize money, he obtained a Letter of Marque and Reprisal for his yacht. Mounting two guns, with a crew 30 men, under command of Captain John Kehew, *Jefferson* captured three British prizes in her only wartime cruise. She was too small and lightly armed, however, to continue as a privateer. *Jefferson* was the first of three Crowninshield vessels to sail under a Letter of Marque and Reprisal. One of them, *America*, their fourth vessel to carry that name and, at 114 feet, mounting 20 guns and a crew of 150 men, was more than three times the size of *Jefferson*. She was one of the most successful American privateers of the war, capturing, in five cruises, British ships and cargoes valued at $1,100,000.[34]

"In the War of 1812 five hundred and fifteen privateers were commissioned, as follows: one hundred and fifty from Massachusetts, one hundred and twelve from Maryland, one hundred and two from New York, thirty-one from Pennsylvania, sixteen from New Hampshire, fifteen from Maine, eleven from Connecticut, nine from Virginia, seven from Louisiana, and seven from Georgia, while fifty-five were from ports not designated. These vessels are known to have captured one thousand three hundred and forty-five craft of all kinds from the enemy."[35]

The war ended with the Treaty of Ghent the day before Christmas in 1814, and once again, the privateers were out of business. Vessels and crews were laid up or used in commerce as their situation allowed. Despite the United States' demand in later international negotiations that it be able to keep its options open, that banning the issuing of Letters of Marque and Reprisal would unfairly favor the European nations with their larger standing navies, the signing of the Treaty of Ghent effectively ended the U.S. Navy's reliance on civilian war auxiliaries. This hastened the transition to the formal acquisition and commissioning of civilian vessels under the Navy's flag when the need arose.

2

Minor Wars, Expeditions and Detours

When the Treaty of Ghent ended the War of 1812, the ad hoc privateering fleet was out of business. Vessels that could not profitably be used in commerce were laid up in storage or simply sent to the breaker's yard. Their fittings, spars and cordage were auctioned for whatever price they could bring, their crews mostly consigned to a more mundane life ashore. Some of the privateersmen, however, found it difficult to dispense with the adventure and ready profit, despite the danger, of their recent occupation. They turned to other profitable, though less honorable pursuits, like the slave trade. Speed and armament gave them an advantage, plus "it was customary for these vessels to sail from home ports, having on board alleged Brazilian, Spanish, French or Italian passengers, and when on the slave coast the crew went ashore and the 'passengers' took possession of the ship under a foreign flag, and a double set of ship's papers being made out in some instances."[1]

Unlike the end of the first war with Great Britain, the end of the second one did not bring with it the dissolution of the United States Navy. There were past wrongs to redress, a flag to be shown around the world and a burgeoning merchant marine to be protected. The United States and Great Britain had outlawed the international slave trade at the beginning of the 19th century. With the end of the war both American and British warships were freed to concentrate on the interdiction of Atlantic slavers off the coast of Africa and in the West Indies. Other significant U.S. Naval actions in this period included intimidating the Kingdom of Naples and Sicily (a Napoleonic client state) into finally paying a $2,000,000 indemnity demand for American vessels illegally seized while the United States was concentrating on Great Britain during the War of 1812, and suppressing pirates in the Indies, off Greece in the Mediterranean, at Quallah Battoo, Sumatra (Aceh Province), and at Matamoros, Mexico, in the Gulf. None of these actions required reliance on privateers. The Navy did, however, acquire and commission at least two private yachts, *Onkahye* and *Wave*, among lesser civilian vessels taken into service.

The United States had long been inconvenienced by the Seminole Indians in Spanish Florida. They sheltered runaway Southern slaves and not only traded with the British during the War of 1812 but even joined British military expeditions that thrust up into Georgia and Alabama in that conflict. After the war, the Royal Marines, who had been stationed in Fort Gadsden, turned over the facility to a group of runaway slaves. When the new garrison of the "Negro Fort" killed a group of American sailors, General

Andrew Jackson was sent down to redress the wrong and teach the Seminoles a lesson. This first Seminole War lasted from 1816 through 1818, and ended with the United States getting possession of Florida from Spain. Hostilities re-erupted in earnest in December of 1835, three years after the Treaty of Payne's Landing. A treaty in name only, it was a blueprint for Indian removal, to relocate the Seminoles to the Oklahoma Territory for the convenience of white settlers. Now president, Andrew Jackson sent in the Army, ultimately as many as two-thirds of the total available troops, along with units of the Navy and Marine Corps. The issue was not settled until August 1842. Meanwhile, the sloop-of-war *Vandalia* operated in close cooperation with the land forces. If any former yachts were also involved, they were not so identified.

Though a modest standing navy did exist, it was extended to its limit. "In 1830 the United States' Navy consisted of seven sail of the line, all of which were laid up in ordinary; seven frigates of the first class, of which three were in ordinary and four in commission; three frigates of the second class, of which one was a receiving-ship, one in actual service, and one in ordinary; fifteen sloops, of which two were in ordinary, and the remainder on different foreign stations; seven schooners, of which three were in employ as receiving-ships, one in ordinary, and two in commission. There were also five ships of the line and seven frigates in such a state of forwardness that they could be ready for sea in three months."[2]

To effectively prosecute in the Second Seminole War (1835–1842), the Navy found itself in need of additional hulls, especially barges for brown-water operations, transporting troops inland into the fecund Florida swamps, and fast dispatch craft that would facilitate communications and could rapidly deploy detachments of Marines and reinforcements along the lengthy Florida coastline. Considered the fastest vessel of her type, the 65-foot, centerboard, schooner-rigged racing yacht *Wave* admirably fit the Navy's requirements and was purchased outright in 1836. *Wave* was designed and built along pilot boat lines four years earlier by and for John Cox Stevens. Now mounting a single gun, USS *Wave* cruised the Florida coast in support of the Army ashore until 1840 when she was reassigned as a surveying vessel along the Eastern Seaboard under the command of Lieutenant J.R. Goldsborough. She likely was stricken from the Navy Lists and disposed of in 1846.[3]

As far back as 1816, John Cox Stevens and his brother Robert Livingston Stevens began their innovative exploration of naval architecture with their modified periauger design, *Trouble*, a two-masted, flat-bottom sailboat. Sixteen years passed between that beginning and their centerboard schooner *Wave*. With *Wave* now in the U.S. Navy, they turned their attention to the second of the Stevens' major racing yachts, the topsail schooner *Onkahye*, "dancing feather" in Algonquin. Laid down in 1839 and launched 1840 by William Capes in Williamsburg, New York, *Onkahye*, at 96 feet long and with a 22-foot beam, drew 12 feet, displacing 250 tons. To further his innovative bent, Robert designed *Onkahye* as a test bed for his ideas. These included the application of external ballast, sail slides, mast tracks, the addition of a second centerboard and, most daringly, an extremely thick keel and placement of the beam (widest point) aft of the midships line instead of closer to the bow.[4] Once again, the Navy took notice.

In 1843, the Navy purchased *Onkahye* and sent her to Gosport Navy Yard in Virginia for conversion to military service. There, her centerboards were replaced by a pair of bilge keels, she got her topsail rig, and her decks were strengthened to carry two cannons. On 11 July 1843, Lieutenant William C. Whittle took command of newly commissioned USS *Onkahye*. The schooner's first period in commission, spent as a dispatch vessel out of Charleston, South Carolina, lasted just short of eight months.[5]

✣ ✣ ✣ ✣

If your business was merchant shipping, efficiency was the key to profitability. A number of factors had to be weighed and balanced to achieve that goal for each vessel: maintenance schedules, crews, provisioning, gross register tonnage, sea-keeping ability and, above all, speed. The race went to the fleetest of sail, the sleekest of hull. This competitive spirit was not limited to the exigencies of commerce, it spilled over into the burgeoning pastime of recreational yachting. Two yachtsmen could barely say hello to one another before they were comparing yachts, planning a race and placing wagers. It was only natural that such ad hoc competitive camaraderie would lead to more formal arrangements. The sport and pastime of yachting had come a long way since 17-year-old John Cox Stevens built his small yacht, *Diver*, in 1802, of which he was "builder, captain, cook, and all hands,"[6] for racing and day sails. *Trouble*, *Wave* and *Onkahye* had followed *Diver*, and now, in 1844, Stevens' favorite builder, William Capes, launched his latest yacht, *Gimcrack*, named for the English thoroughbred stallion that won 27 of his 36 races. On 30 July of that year, just over a month after *Onkahye* was decommissioned, Stevens gathered fellow enthusiasts Hamilton Wilkes, yacht *Spray*; William Edgar, yacht *Cygnet*; John C. Jay, yacht *La Coquille*; George L. Schuyler, yacht *Dream*; James M. Waterbury, yacht *Minna*; Louis A, Depau, yacht *Mist*; James Rogers, yacht *Ida*; and George B. Rollins, yacht *Petrel* aboard *Gimcrack* to organize a club for the "systematic fostering of the noble art of yachting."[7] The New York Yacht Club was born. Its first commodore, by acclamation, was Mr. Stevens. That same year, William Capes built the schooner *Maria* for the Stevens brothers; the vessel went on to best the yacht *America*, of America's Cup fame, in 1851.

Meanwhile, the Navy was not done with *Onkahye* and recommissioned her on 10 April 1845. She saw duty, patrolling against pirates and slavers, carrying passengers and dispatches, in the Gulf of Mexico, the Caribbean and West Indies through the end of that year. On 9 January 1846, she was decommissioned and again laid up in reserve, this time for about 15 months. Back in active service on 22 April 1847, Lieutenant Otway H. Berryman commanding, she once again posted to the Caribbean, cruising the West Indies and off South America. On 22 November she put into Rio de Janeiro for two months and from there captured the fully laden slaver barque *Laurens* (some references refer to the slaver as *Lawrence*) on 24 January 1848. Continuing her patrols in the West Indies, *Onkahye* foundered off Caicos Reef, Turks and Caicos Islands, 21 June 1848 without loss of life. She holds the distinction of being the only converted sailing yacht to serve on distant station before the Civil War.[8]

Though the vessel was lost, the consequence of her capturing *Laurens* remained mired in litigation for nearly a quarter century. The matter, however, began straightforwardly enough. An Act of Congress passed on 10 May 1800, specifically concerning the slave trade, said, in part, that any vessel so employed, when taken by a commissioned United States vessel, "together with her tackle, apparel, and guns, and the goods and effects, other than slaves, which shall be found on board, shall be forfeited, and may

John Cox Stevens' yacht *Gimcrack*, 1844 (from *Yachting*, Vol. II, 1895).

be proceeded against in any of the district or circuit courts, and shall be condemned for the use of the officers and crew of the vessel making the seizure, and be divided in the proportion directed in the case of the prize."[9] The subsequent auction netted $4,720.02. Added to this tidy sum for the period was $18,992 in specie, found on board *Laurens* at her capture, bringing the total to $23,712.02. However, the Act of 10 May makes reference to "An Act for the Better Government of the Navy" of 23 April, instant, complicating the issue by stating that prize money, when the captured vessel is "of equal or superior force to the vessel or vessels making the capture, shall be the sole property of the captors: and when of inferior force, shall be divided equally between the United States and the officers and men making the capture."[10] This issue was eventually settled in favor of Berryman and his fellows, but was there anything to actually distribute?

By law, all monies received by marshals and prize agents had to be deposited into the United States Treasury not later than 60 days after receipt. Marshal Ely Moore, who took charge of *Laurens* when she berthed in New York, set up a personal bank account and embezzled the cash found aboard the vessel. Lieutenant Berryman was not one to give up easily. By the time the matter reached the new Court of Claims in 1857, all Treasury had was the auction money, which, less ongoing expenses, came to $1,672.69. The Court of Claims ruled that the government was liable for the full amount despite its employee's defalcation. The judgment, however, did not lay the matter to rest. Since the full amount never was deposited into the Treasury, it required an act of Congress to appropriate the prize money from funds not otherwise allocated. Such a bill was repeatedly introduced and then tabled. Lieutenant Berryman died in 1861. Finally, on 28 May 1872, 24 years after *Onkahye* captured *Laurens*, "An Act for the Relief of the Children of Otway H. Berryman, Deceased, and Others" passed and payment in the amount of $20,664.69 was made to the survivors and heirs of the men of USS *Onkahye*.[11]

✣ ✣ ✣ ✣

Occasionally, a yacht ended up on the other side of the maritime fence. Such was the case of the schooner-rigged yacht *Wanderer*. She was designed by W.J. Rowland for Colonel John D. Johnson, wealthy Louisiana sugar planter, to be the largest, fastest yacht up to then. *Wanderer* was built by Thomas Hawkins at his shipyard in Setauket, Port Jefferson Harbor, Long Island, New York, and was launched on 19 June 1857. At 106 feet long, 25½-foot beam and 9½-foot draft she displaced 300 tons. A contemporary newspaper account called her "a beauty, with spacious decks and low bulwarks…. Her bow is very long and very sharp … even when pressed down to her bearings [by the wind], there is nothing to impede her progress…"[12] "Interiorly her accommodations were of the most costly and luxurious character, her cabin presenting the appearance of a magnificently furnished parlor."[13] Colonel Johnson spent an enjoyable season at his summer place near Islip, New York, showing off his new toy on the waters off Long Island. As the weather changed he decided to head down to the Caribbean and provisioned his yacht accordingly. This included an armory of firearms, cutlasses and boarding pikes and two 6-pounder deck guns,[14] presumably as protection from pirates.

Colonel Johnson took a long detour from his voyage to race and otherwise display his epitome of the yacht builder's art in Charleston, South Carolina, and Savannah., Georgia. While in Savannah, he was introduced to bombastic, yet gracious planter and entrepreneur Charles A.L. Lamar. That the two men socialized is established, what they might have discussed in private is not recorded. At length, Colonel Johnson took his leave and sailed down to Havana, Cuba. Eventually he headed up to New Orleans and thence back to New York on 11 April 1858. Much to the surprise of everyone, Colonel Johnson proceeded to sell *Wanderer* to fellow Southerner and yacht club member William C. Corrie for $12,000, less than half of the $25,000 she cost to build.[15] It was under "Captain" Corrie that *Wanderer* slipped over to the dark side.

Captain Corrie proposed to take a group of friends and enthusiasts on an extended voyage to see some of the world. The nature of the vessel's provisioning and modifications, however, caused more than a few raised eyebrows in Setauket. To begin with, there were the specially made galvanized water tanks being fitted. Their 15,000 gallons capacity would supply far more water than the guests and crew could possibly consume themselves. The locals immediately were mistrustful of the new, "foreign-looking" crew that was brought aboard. When the schooner *Charter Oak* arrived off Port Jefferson with *Wanderer*'s provisions, including a large store of barter beads, knives, gaudy cloth and rum,[16] Surveyor of the Port S.S. Norton suspected she was being outfitted as a slaver. He hightailed it to New York City and explained his suspicions to U.S. Marshal Isaiah Rynders. The latter was convinced, and the two men set out for Port Jefferson in the steam revenue cutter *Harriet Lane*. The law first captured the lighter and towed her into port, then she went after *Wanderer*, now heading to sea under full sail. *Harriet Lane* had the advantage of steam power and overhauled the yacht, which yielded to the former's second hail. Under arrest, *Wanderer* and *Charter Oak* accompanied *Harriet Lane* back to the port of New York. When Marshal Rynders and his colleagues came on board to investigate, Captain Corrie had a plausible alternate explanation for each of their concerns. He pointed out that there was nothing on board that was not listed on

Topsail schooner yacht USS *Wanderer*, the penultimate slaver (NH 109128 courtesy the Naval History & Heritage Command Photographic Dept.).

the manifest. Mere speculation on the evidence of "eavesdroppers, who hung around [his] windows," regarding what his vessel might do in future hardly was proof of proscribed activity. Therefore, it was he, in effect, who was the aggrieved party. His partner Charles Lamar even went so far as to have their lawyers file a damage claim for "eight days' detention," in the amount of $1,320, which apparently was paid.[17]

Free of legal entanglements, Corrie and *Wanderer* cleared for Charleston and from there to St. Helena by way of Port of Spain, Trinidad. The British at St. Helena may have had their suspicions about the true intent of the voyage, but, absent proof, they cleared *Wanderer* to proceed to the African coast. At Punta de Lehna, near the mouth of the Congo, she ran into a potentially serious obstacle, the steam paddle packet HMS *Medusa* on anti-slavery patrol. The burgee of the New York Yacht Club helped allay any doubts *Medusa*'s officers may have had about Corrie's intentions and occasioned vessel-to-vessel social calls and pleasantries. Meanwhile Corrie bided his time. Eventually, *Medusa* left to chase a suspicious vessel, leaving *Wanderer* alone. At last away from observation, the crew quickly stripped the yacht of her trappings of leisure and prepared her to receive some six hundred slaves in a vessel that, Corrie had joked to the marshals in New York, "wouldn't carry ten niggers."[18] Charles Lamar had another, cynical name for those unfortunates. In a letter dated 24 May 1858, to "Thomas Barrett, Esq., Augusta," he wrote, "I have in contemplation, if I can raise the necessary amount of money, the fitting out of an expedition to go to the coast of Africa for a cargo of African apprentices *to be bound for the term of their natural lives....*"[19] The italics are his.

The heavily laden slaver was spotted by the 18-gun sloop-of-war USS *Vincennes* as she left the coast of Africa. Despite the burden of her illicit human cargo and of the extra water, her racing genesis stood her in good stead. She easily outran her pursuer. On 28 November 1858, after a six-week voyage, *Wanderer* made Jekyll Island, Georgia, with two-thirds of her original cargo. There, under arrangements set up by Corrie's partner in crime, Charles Lamar, the naked, emaciated surviving slaves were offloaded and spirited away. The crew was paid off and scattered. Forged papers reflected *Wanderer*'s return from St. Helena but nothing of her time in Africa. When the authorities arrived most of the physical evidence was gone, but nothing could disguise the distinctive smell of a slave ship. Captain Corrie was arrested on 22 January 1859, Charles Lamar about the same time. The incident briefly became a cause célèbre. Even Congress took up the matter. However, the principals had not been caught red handed. Ultimately, the lack of conclusive evidence of personal guilt and some well-placed bribes and connections won out. The partners were released without punishment, but *Wanderer* was condemned and sold at auction by the court.

Aside from the unconscionable, illegal and immoral misuse of the yacht *Wanderer*, William Corrie had besmirched the name of the New York Yacht Club by engaging in his nefarious deed while sailing under the club's flag. The board therefore resolved:

> Whereas, the fact is officially stated that a cargo of upwards of three hundred negroes from the coast of Africa has been landed in Georgia from the Wanderer; and whereas the vessel thus designated is comprised in the list of yachts forming the New York Yacht squadron: it is unanimously resolved that the name of the yacht Wanderer be erased from the list, and that William C. Corrie, proprietor of said yacht and member of this Club, primarily for his deliberate violation of the laws of the United States, but more especially from his being engaged in a traffic repugnant to humanity and to the moral sense of the members of this association, be, and hereby is, expelled from the New York Yacht Club.[20]

New York Yacht Club Regatta—1869 (Currier & Ives). Popular Graphic arts collection, Library of Congress, Prints & Photographs Division).

And what of Charles Lamar? Unabashed by the proceedings against him, he made the winning bid of $4,001 at the auction[21] and, in the spring of 1859, he sent *Wanderer* back to the west coast of Africa on another slave run![22] During the next two years, ownership of the vessel changed again and, "on one occasion, the ship was stolen and taken to sea on a piratical and slaving voyage. Near the coast of Africa, the first mate led a mutiny and left the pirate captain at sea in a small boat before bringing the ship back to Boston on Christmas Eve 1859 and turning her over to authorities there."[23]

✦ ✦ ✦ ✦

Even before the American Civil War, steam power was poised to supplant wind-driven sails in war and commerce, despite the latter mode's beauty and grace. Steam engines meant the yacht so possessed of it was no longer prey to the vagaries of King Aeolus' breath and could go wherever and whenever her owner desired. A genetic layer of involvement between sailor and environment was threatened by the change. Perhaps a feeling amongst the general public, doubtless not shared by serious yachtsmen, that the age of sail was passé, that the machine was the future, made another species of human smuggler and pirate opt for a more leisurely, incognito past. Spurning the full-steam-ahead future, 47 years after *Wanderer's* second slave run, another group of "businessmen" looked to sail when choosing a craft on which to smuggle Chinese immigrants to America in violation of the Chinese Exclusion Act of 8 May 1882. The vessel so misused in the autumn of 1906 was the schooner-yacht *Frolic*, built at Islip, Long Island in 1879 by Alonzo Smith for Philadelphia financier and member of the New York Yacht Club, J. Gardner Cassatt. His brother Alexander was president of the Pennsylvania Railroad, and his sister Mary was an important Impressionist painter. *Frolic* measured 56½ feet long with a 16-foot beam, displacing 26 tons. She had a flush deck with no cockpit. Crucial to her later foray into smuggling and clandestinely landing illicit passengers was her draft of only seven and a half feet.[24]

In December 1902, *Frolic's* current owner, Herbert H. White, who had often welcomed aboard good friend and future Supreme Court Justice Louis D. Brandeis for summer sails, engaged in a complex rental-to-purchase deal with Herbert F. Colby for the vessel. This arrangement allowed several years to intervene while Colby made payments and before actual title was transferred. By 1906, Colby seized the opportunity presented by prospective charter John C. Lehnmann, whose intention was anything but a pleasure cruise. There was profit to be had in smuggling legally excluded Chinese immigrants to the United States from Canada. Previously, Lehnmann had chartered the schooner-yacht *Bonita* from C.E. Stevens, of the Boston Yacht Club, and had offloaded a cargo of smuggled Chinese immigrants at Marblehead, Massachusetts. When Stevens got his yacht back, he found evidence of the charter's real purpose. He declined a second charter to Lehnmann and then alerted the Chinese Inspection Service of the Treasury Department, forerunner of the Immigration and Naturalization Service.

Lehnmann turned to *Frolic* where Colby was more receptive and apparently eager to participate. Shortly thereafter, White received a letter from Colby's wife, "who said that her husband had gone for a cruise to the Labrador coast which Mrs. Colby thought would prove a very profitable one. Upon the Captain's return, she said, he would make further payments on the rental of the yacht."[25] By the time the authorities knew what was going on, *Frolic* had already left Placentia Bay, Newfoundland, on 21 September 1906, with her human cargo. As reported in *The New York Times* of 1 October, "From

Cape Henry, Va., to Deer Island, Me., every revenue cutter stationed in those waters and every life saver at every life-saving station has been ordered to be on the lookout for the schooner yacht *Frolic*, which is understood to have on board thirty-three Chinamen that the skipper and his associates are trying to land in this country."[26]

After easily evading her would-be pursuers for more than two weeks, *Frolic* was apprehended at Providence, Rhode Island, after a local discovered two disheveled Chinese asleep on the wharf and alerted law enforcement. The two crew members still aboard were arrested, and 17 of the illegals were captured. Later John Lehnmann joined those already in custody and freely confessed. Colby escaped.[27] *Frolic* did not fare so well.

White, still the nominal owner, sued for the return of his yacht from government impound, but Rhode Island District Judge Brown ruled against him on 15 November 1906: "Upon the foregoing facts I am of the opinion that, while title to the vessel did not pass to Colby and remained in White, Colby had such possession and control of the vessel as to authorize him to appoint E.A. Junkins as master. As it is agreed that said Junkins knowingly and in violation of the statutes landed certain Chinese persons at the port of Providence, the schooner Frolic is subject to condemnation. The claim of Herbert H. White [is] dismissed."[28]

3

A House Divided

At the close of the Crimean war in February 1856, Count Walewski, president of the Congress of Paris, sought to go beyond the immediate concerns of the peace negotiations and proposed the creation of a uniform maritime law to control the actions of belligerents at sea. Of primacy in his simple statement of principles was the abolition of privateering:

> The plenipotentiaries, considering that the maritime law in time of war has been for a long time the subject of unfortunate controversies, that it is advantageous, in consequence, to establish a uniform doctrine on a point so important, have issued the following solemn declaration:
> 1st Privateering is and remains abolished;
> 2nd The neutral flag protects the enemy's goods, except contraband of war;
> 3rd Neutral goods, except contraband of war, are not subject to seizure under the enemy's flag;
> 4th Blockades, to be binding, must be effective; i.e., maintained by force sufficient to render approach to the enemy's coast really dangerous.[1]

With the devastation wreaked on His Majesty's shipping by American privateers in two wars in mind, Lord Clarendon, plenipotentiary for Great Britain, readily agreed. All of the seven nations and states attending (the United Kingdom, Austria, France, Prussia, Russia, Sardinia, and the Ottoman Empire) concurred, and the Declaration of Paris was signed on 16 April 1856. The members believed that these principles would be universally accepted by the world's governments and included such belief in the document along with a pledge to so promote general participation.

The signatories' assessment was mostly correct, with three notable exceptions: Spain, Mexico and the United States. All had relatively weak navies which had to patrol and protect very long coastlines. President Franklin Pierce, for the same reason Lord Clarendon, was in favor of the Declaration, but was opposed to unconditionally surrendering a naval option that figured significantly in both the creation and maintenance of the United States. He was, however, willing to compromise if the Declaration's first proposition were modified to protect private property from seizure. A letter, dated 28 July 1856, from Secretary of State William L. Marcy to the Comte de Sartiges, laid out Pierce's position: "The President, therefore, proposes to add to the first proposition in the 'declaration' of the Congress of Paris, the following words: 'and that the private property of the subjects or citizens of a belligerent on the high seas shall be exempted from seizure by public armed vessels of the other belligerent, except that it be contraband.'"[2]

The British weren't so ready to open that loophole, and negotiations stalled. Finally, in March 1857, President-elect James Buchanan, more concerned about the likely adverse impact on the nation's maritime strength in time of need, ordered the negotiations

28   American Yachts in Naval Service

suspended. It should also be remembered that the issuance of Letters of Marque and Reprisal was a time-honored way to allow the official employment of private vessels without expense to the issuing government.

The situation changed on 13 April 1861 when the Confederate batteries in Charleston, South Carolina's harbor, under the overall command of Brigadier General Pierre G.T. Beauregard, opened fire on Fort Sumter. Abraham Lincoln had been in office fewer than six weeks. On the 15th, President Lincoln issued a proclamation to call up 75,000 troops. Two days later, Jefferson Davis, president of the Confederate States of America, invited Southern ship owners and captains to apply for Letters of Marque and Reprisal for operations against vessels of the United States. Davis's proclamation required successful applicants to post a bond of at least $5,000 per vessel, $10,000 should said vessel's crew number greater than 150 men. He, however, refrained from issuing any of those documents until being duly authorized by the Confederate Congress, which met in special session on the 29th and passed such legislation on 6 May.[3]

Knowing that the Confederacy had no navy to speak of, therefore it would have to rely heavily on sanctioned privateers, U.S. Secretary of State William H. Seward, a week after Davis' proclamation, instructed his ambassador to the Court of St. James in London to inform the British that the United States was now ready to unconditionally accept the terms of the Declaration of Paris. This, of course, would more seriously affect the South than it would the North, with its far superior navy. Both the British and the

Confederate privateer *Savannah*, Letter of Marque no. 1 (Library of Congress, Prints & Photographs Division).

French could see through the argument. If the United States had signed the Declaration before the South seceded, all of the States, North and South alike, would be bound by the treaty, since at the time of the Declaration the Confederate States were part of the Union. Furthermore, not only did they brush off the United States' convenient change of heart and characterization of the Confederates as "rebels" and "pirates," they recognized the Confederacy as a belligerent force, if not yet an officially recognized separate nation. They reasoned that President Lincoln had, in effect, already given tacit recognition of the South by his formal proclamation of Southern blockade on 19 April. The United States could not have it both ways and sign away the rights of a now separate government, and the United Kingdom comfortably straddled the fence.[4]

Situations change and evolve. An argument that once seemed to be appropriate, may ironically come back to bite the speaker. In the House of Representatives, on 12 January 1848, then Representative Abraham Lincoln, speaking on the constitutionality of the war with Mexico, said:

> Any people anywhere, being inclined and having the power, have the *right* to rise up and shake off the existing government, and form a new one that suits them better.... Nor is this right confined to cases in which the whole people of an existing government may choose to exercise it. Any portion of such people that *can may* revolutionize, and make their *own* of so much of the territory as they inhabit. More than this, a *majority* of any portion of such people may revolutionize, putting down a *minority*, intermingled with, or near about them, who may oppose their movements. Such minority was precisely the case of the Tories of our own Revolution. It is a quality of revolutions not to go by *old* lines, or *old* laws; but to break up both, and make new ones [emphasis original].[5]

In 1836 the strongest voices for disunion came from the North as the abolitionist movement gathered momentum. Delegates to the May 1844 American Anti-Slavery Convention in New York resolved: "That secession from the United States Government is the duty of every Abolitionist, since no one can take office or deposit a vote under its Constitution without violating his anti-slavery principles." Furthermore, "That the Abolitionists of this country should make it one of the primary objects of their agitation to dissolve the American Union."[6] Events gradually caught up with rhetoric. This was the second time the New England states threatened secession. The first coalesced in the Hartford Convention of 1814–15, over grievances related to the continuing War of 1812, and concern over the Congressional imbalance given the slave states by the three-fifths compromise in the Constitution. On 16 October 1859, John Brown attempted to spark a slave revolt with a raid on the federal armory at Harper's Ferry, Virginia. Just over a year later, on 20 December 1860, the South Carolina legislature passed a bill of secession, and the die was cast. But there was, as yet, no Southern navy.

"Lieut. Haralton [USN] addressed the 'Southern officers of the U.S. navy' a warm appeal, under the date of Jan. 14, 1861, to resign and accept commissions from their States. His earnest appeal to the officers, 'to bring with you every ship and man you can, that we may use them against the oppressors of our liberties,' received no response, and not a United States vessel was delivered up by a Southern officer."[7]

With the commencement of hostilities on 12 April 1861, the Union administration adopted several measures to immediately augment the Navy. Primary among them, according to James Russell Soley, Assistant Secretary of the Navy, 1890–1893, was "to buy up everything afloat that could be made of service—a measure which was impossible for Mr. Mallory (CSA Secretary of the Navy) to imitate because in the Confederacy there was nothing afloat to buy, and no money with which to purchase."[8]

Three months after the surrender of Fort Sumter, the U.S. House of Representatives, in a rush to increase the strength of the Federal Navy, passed a resolution "authorizing the Secretary of the Treasury to employ a sufficient force to protect the commerce of the United States from Confederate privateers. The object of the act was to send out privateers to capture those of the Confederacy that were annoying U.S. commerce."[9] A cogent argument against issuing such Letters of Marque and Reprisal, however, was the unintended, adverse consequence of enacting the bill: "A bill to authorize the President, during the continuance of the civil war, to grant Letters of Marque and Reprisal, was introduced at the session of 1861-'62, but failed in consequence of the position taken in opposition, that Letters of Marque could only be granted against an independent state, and that their issue might be regarded as recognition of the Confederate States. It was also objected that the bill if passed would be regarded as an admission of weakness on the part of the Federal Navy, and as conflicting with the position that privateering, as conducted by the Confederate States, was piracy."[10] Lincoln, apparently swayed by the counterargument in Congress, refrained from issuing Letters of Marque and Reprisal, thus effectively ending the expedient of sanctioning civilian vessels with civilian crews to operate as United States warships. This did not, however, preclude commissioning by charter or outright purchase private vessels into the U.S. Navy itself.

The Confederacy, feeling no such constraint, had to build a navy from scratch. The Montgomery, Alabama *Mail* of 29 May 1861 reported: "We learn that there are now quite a number of privateers in the service of the Confederate government cruising off the Gulf and Atlantic coast, all well armed and manned—dispatches having been received in the city showing that hundreds of others are fitting out at various points for the same purpose."[11] Although more or less true, there was a significant element of wishful thinking in that report. Large cargo vessels mostly were owned by Northern shipping companies, making for a shortage of Southern hulls suitable for open ocean

Confederate blockade runner CSS *Advance*, later USS *Frolic II* (oil by R.G. Skerrett, 1899; NH 61882 courtesy the Naval History & Heritage Command Photographic Dept.).

operations and able to carry sufficient armament. Still, smaller vessels were useful to harry Federal vessels in coastal waters. The individual states as well as the Confederate government set about remedying the situation by confiscating Federal vessels that happened to lie within southern ports as the various states seceded and by outright purchase of both Southern- and Northern-owned hulls.

Three of the earliest Confederate privateers granted Letters of Marque and Reprisal were the schooner *Savannah*, the brig *Jefferson Davis* and the schooner *Petrel*. Their histories indicate the inadequacy of privateers. *Savannah* left Charleston, South Carolina, on 2 June 1861 under T. Harrison Baker. The next day she captured the brig *Joseph* of Philadelphia. Emboldened by such early success Captain Baker, that same day, made all sail toward a distant target. Too late, the tempting "merchantman" resolved herself into the U.S. Navy brig *Perry*. *Savannah* could not outrun *Perry* and, carrying but a single gun, was forced to strike her flag after a 20-minute exchange of gunfire. A prize crew took *Savannah* to New York where she was condemned and sold at auction.[12]

Petrel, the former United States Revenue Cutter *Aiken*, now under Captain William Perry, departed Charleston on 28 July 1861, 18 days after receiving her commission as a privateer. That same day the United States Navy frigate *St. Lawrence* engaged and sank her.[13]

On 18 June 1861, the brig *Jefferson Davis* received her commission. Armed with five 60-year-old British guns, under the command of Louis M. Coxetter, she began her privateering career ten days later on 28 June. Although much more successful than her above compatriots, taking nine prizes in seven weeks, ultimately only two of

Destruction of the Confederate privateer *Petrel* by U.S. frigate *St. Lawrence*, 1861 (Library of Congress, Prints & Photographs Division).

those vessels, the brigs *John Welsh* and *Santa Clara*, made it into Savannah, Georgia, for adjudication. Of the other seven, the schooner *Enchantress* was recaptured by USS *Albatross* while making for a Southern port; the bark *Alvarado* ran aground and was burned to prevent her recapture by USS *Jamestown*; the brig *Mary E. Thompson*, schooner *Windward* and ship *Mary Goodell* were released with prisoners on parole; Coxetter burned the army ship *John Carver* and her cargo of anthracite at sea; and the schooner *S.J. Waring* was recaptured by her black cook, William Tillman. Told by his captors that he was now the property of the Confederate States of America and that he would be sold back into slavery once they reached Charleston, Tillman took up an axe in the middle of the night of 16–17 July and killed three of the five-man prize crew. With the help of the two remaining of the original crew and *S.J. Waring*'s passenger he captured the remaining Rebels and took command of the vessel. This motley crew then managed to work the vessel up the coast to New York where Tillman was hailed a hero. This was particularly ironic since privateer *Jefferson Davis* had been captured by USS *Dolphin* in 1858 as the slaver *Echo*. *Enchantress* too was saved by her black steward. Taken a few weeks after *S.J. Waring*, she was recaptured when her steward, Jacob Garrick, managed to alert the passing USS *Albatross*. While running into St. Augustine, Florida, in mid August, *Jefferson Davis* grounded and was destroyed without loss of life.[14]

Though the privateers had limited success, they were followed by far more successful, purpose-built commerce raiders like CSS *Alabama*, CSS *Shenandoah* and CSS *Florida*. Nevertheless, there was little chance that the Confederacy could significantly disrupt Northern shipping to the point it would tip the balance of the war in the South's favor. Preying on Northern maritime commerce, though tactically useful, was strategically less important than it was to maintain the South's commercial presence on the high seas.

> Had the Confederacy instead of the United States been able to exercise dominion over the sea; had it been able to keep open its means of communication with the countries of the Old World, to send its cotton abroad and to bring back the supplies of which it stood so much in need; had it been able to blockade Portland, Boston, Newport, New York, the mouth of the Delaware and the entrance of Chesapeake Bay; had it possessed the sea power to prevent the United States from dispatching by water into Virginia its armies and their supplies, as the United States was blockading and intercepting everywhere its supplies, it is not too much to say that such a reversal of conditions would have reversed the outcome of the Civil War.[15]

But to establish that "dominion over the sea" the North first had to have the ships to render the blockade "effective," as required, if other nations were to respect it. Just how many ships remained an open question. The initial recommendation was sheer guesswork. The actual answer would not be known until the final tally at war's end, but at least it was a start.

> "The Navy Department, at first, selected some of the most prominent and trusted shipping merchants in New York, and consulted with them … in regard to the purchase and fitting out of vessels.... [O]ne of the most eminent of these advisers gave it, as his opinion, that it would require [fifty] sailing vessels to complete the blockade.... [I]t actually required nearly six hundred vessels—most of them steamers—to seal up our coastline" of approximately 3,500 miles, with many inlets and shallows and places to hide.[16]

The age of sail was passing. Secretary of the Navy Gideon Welles and President Lincoln had a bit more foresight than did the New York experts as is evident in Welles' letter to Commodore Samuel L. Breese at the New York Navy Yard, sent just over a week after Confederate guns opened up on Fort Sumter:

> By order of the President of the United States you will forthwith procure ten steamers capable of mounting a 9-inch pivot-gun, with light draft, about nine or twelve feet, having particular reference to strength and speed. You will consult with Commodore Foote, the naval constructor, and such other persons as are capable of giving information and advice. Charter on the best terms possible for three months, with the option of the government purchasing them within that time at a stipulated price; these vessels to be immediately removed to the navy or private yards, with the necessary alterations and equipments to render them efficient for the service required.[17]

Even as the Union Navy was gearing up to meet the challenges brought on by the rebellion, there was a need for all types of vessels, capable of being armed, to back up the warships. On Tuesday, 30 April 1861, the members of the New York Yacht Club voted to offer their yachts to assist in the US Navy in any way it deemed appropriate.[18] Among those vessels was the wood-hull schooner *Hope*, owned by Thomas P. Ives of Rhode Island, co-owner of Brown and Ives, a vast shipping and manufacturing empire founded in 1796. Built by Henry Steers of Greenpoint, Long Island, New York, the 85 foot, 134-ton yacht was capable of 10 knots. Accepting the proviso that Ives remain her captain, the United States Revenue Marine commissioned USRC *Hope* into service on 24 May 1861 under newly minted Lieutenant T.P. Ives and assigned her to blockading duty off Patuxent, Maryland. That arrangement only lasted until 22 November of the same year after Ives requested her return and his own discharge from the Revenue Marine. Lieutenant Ives, however, exchanged Navy blue for Army blue. Now Captain Ives, he served under General Burnside, who, taking advantage of his captain's yachting expertise, eventually placed him in command of the United States steamer *Picket*. It is likely that Ives' change of mind about *Hope* was prompted by a realization that war service would likely take a heavy toll on his yacht, because, immediately upon his yacht's return, he turned around and sold her to the U.S. Navy for $13,000.[19]

USS *Hope* was commissioned in New York on 14 December 1861. Armed with one 20-pounder Parrott rifle and under the command of Acting Master M.S. Chase, she took up station with the South Atlantic Blockading Squadron, based at Port Royal, South Carolina. Despite her initial duties as a dispatch and supply vessel for naval assets to the south, on 27 January 1863, while patrolling off Charleston, she captured the schooner *Emma Tuttle* laden with saltpeter for Confederate gunpowder. *Hope* took a second prize, the sloop *Racer*, off Bull's Bay, South Carolina, on 1 August 1864. After the fall of Savannah in December 1864, *Hope* was no longer required for blockade duty. The Navy refitted her for diving and salvage operations, clearing sunken obstacles to navigation in the Savannah River and later in Charleston harbor. *Hope* was decommissioned on 6 September 1865 and was sold the following month to T. Morley for $5,050.[20]

In the runup to the 1860 presidential election, James Gordon Bennett's *New York Herald* strongly opposed Abraham Lincoln. Lincoln, however, had won, and Bennett was just as strongly pro–Union. In 1861, Bennett invited journalist (later war correspondent, later still railroad baron) Henry Villard to dine with him and his son James, Junior. The elder Bennett enlisted Villard to be his emissary, to assure Mr. Lincoln that henceforth the *Herald* would throw its support behind him. On his son's 16th birthday, 10 May 1857, Bennett gave him the 77-ton centerboard sloop, *Rebecca*. His son, and his 22-man crew, raced well enough that year that the New York Yacht Club elected James, Jr., their youngest member. Now, the elder Bennett wanted Villard to go to Washington and offer *Rebecca* for service in the Treasury Department. In exchange, Bennett wanted his son commissioned in the Revenue Marine,[21] probably hoping to cultivate some discipline in his rambunctious son. Villard met with Secretary of State William H. Seward and apparently did his work well. Seward contacted Lincoln, who in turn sent the following note:

> To Salmon P. Chase, Hon. Sec. of Treasury, Executive Department
>
> Dear Sir May 6, 1861
>
> The Secretary of State this moment introduces to me Mr. James Gordon Bennett, Jr. who tenders to the U.S. service, a fine Yacht of 160 tons burthen. If you allow him an interview, which I ask for him, he will talk with you about putting some other vessels of the same class, into the service. We send this subject to you because we believe these vessels may be made most available in the Revenue service.
>
> Yours truly, A. LINCOLN[22]

Nothing more is heard about *Rebecca*, but Junior was commissioned a third lieutenant. At that same dinner in New York with Henry Villard, the elder Bennett also had discussed his son's newest yacht, the recently launched schooner *Henrietta*. It was that vessel, accepted 19 June 1861 and armed with two 6-pounders and one 12-pounder guns, which saw service in the war, under 20-year-old 3rd Lieutenant Bennett, Jr. USRC *Henrietta* spent an uneventful several months patrolling Long Island

U.S. Revenue Cutter *Henrietta* (NH 59584 courtesy the Naval History & Heritage Command Photographic Dept.).

3. A House Divided

Sound, New York, before she was reassigned to Port Royal, South Carolina, where she arrived on 19 February 1862. On 4 March *Henrietta* participated in the Navy's capture of Fernandina, Florida. Seeing no further value in the vessel's retention, *Henrietta* was decommissioned on 29 April.[23] Less than a month later, on 11 May, 3rd Lieutenant Bennett, Jr., resigned his commission and sailed his yacht back to New York. On 11 December 1866, *Henrietta*, in competition with yachts *Fleetwing* (George and Franklin Osgood) and *Vesta* (Pierre Lorillard, Jr.) sailed from Sandy Hook, New Jersey, in a transatlantic race to Cowes, Great Britain. Bennett won, traveling 3,135 miles in 13 days, 21 hours and 55 minutes.[24]

As early as 1836, in *The Three Cutters*, a work of nautical fiction, the author, Captain Frederick Marryat, Royal Navy, saw the value of a ready fleet of vessels, with well-trained crews, to fill out the navy in times of trial:

> Of all the amusements entered into by the nobility and gentry of our island there is not one so manly, so exciting, so patriotic, or so national, as yacht sailing. It is peculiar to England, not only from our insular position and our fine harbours, but because it requires a certain degree of energy and a certain amount of income rarely to be found elsewhere. It has been wisely fostered by our sovereigns, who have felt that the security of the kingdom is increased by every man being more or less a sailor, or connected with the nautical profession.[25]

Although the Confederacy had few blue water options at the outset, it did not lack for yachts and yachtsmen. While the Rebel government secretly arranged to have warships built in British yards, they sought to enlist whatever was afloat in Southern ports. Antebellum New Orleans was a thriving commercial and cultural center, but it was hot, humid and subject to outbreaks of yellow fever during the summer. Many of the well heeled who could get away for those months to the Gulf Coast resorts sought the luxury of the Pass Christian Hotel in Pass Christian, Mississippi, and the fine sailing on Lake Ponchartrain. As was the case in New York five years earlier, when and where yachtsmen congregated, impromptu racing was sure to follow. Hotel manager R.H. Montgomery organized the first formal regatta on 21 July 1849, and the Southern Yacht Club was born. Thomas Smith Dabney, owner of Burleigh Plantation in Virginia, was elected its first president. As Dabney's daughter Sophia Dabney Thurmond later remembered the time, "Many gentlemen at Pass Christian owned fast-sailing yachts, and during the season, fortnightly regattas were held, in which the entire population felt deeply interested, as almost everyone owing a yacht entered in for the race."[26]

Of the summer 1854 regatta, a contemporary governess wrote:

> The grand regatta of the Southern Yacht Club came off today and created fine sport with a beautiful breeze prevailing. The steamer Mobile came from Biloxi with a large array of ladies and gentlemen, accompanied by a fine band of music, to witness the race, which added to the excitement. The race was for 15 miles which sailed around a triangle of seven and one-half miles. The prize for the first class was a silver pitcher, to the second, two silver goblets, and for the third, a silver cup. The boats [18 yachts] were placed in position at 12 o'clock. A gun fired as a signal for them to get underway. The first boat finished the course in two hours, 20 minutes, and 14 seconds.[27]

Three years later, the club relocated to New Orleans. In April 1860, the club scheduled its annual regatta for 27 June. Concern and preparation for the impending war meant only four boats entered, being the *J.W. Balfou, Adena, Benecia Bay,* and *Phantom,* and the commodore canceled the event.[28]

Before forces under the command of Major General Benjamin Butler captured and occupied New Orleans in May 1862, "many of the club members joined the Confederacy,

Southern Yacht Club, New Orleans, Louisiana, c. 1890 (Detroit Publishing Co. Collection, Library of Congress, Prints & Photographs Division).

quite a few performing yeoman service on vessels of an extemporized navy. Their yachts were utilized during the war, some as blockade runners, and others pressed into service as supply carriers, etc."[29] Yacht racing on Lake Ponchartrain was not resumed until after the Civil War.

Frederick Marryat also commented on the money required in order to acquire and maintain a yacht. The British vessels he saw as potential naval auxiliaries were, for the most part, well appointed with all the comforts expected ashore and therefore at sea. Naval architect William Picard Stevens, looking back on the development of the pastime, noted a difference on the other side of the pond: "The yacht owner in America appears to understand only one thing—the speed attained by his vessel."[30] The emergence of the steam yacht began to facilitate the pursuit of both ends. In wartime, however, speed and shallow draft were exactly what both sides required in the naval conflict. The North needed to police the myriad inlets and bays where a privateer or blockade runner could hide and to speed communications along the 3,500 mile front. For the South, those self-same characteristics, at least initially, allowed its privateers and blockade runners to hide in those same waterways.

The later purpose-built blockade runners and cruisers are of concern in this work only in how their existence affected the conscripted and enlisted yachts. Sorting out which vessels actually were yachts is complicated by the various services of the two sides, occasionally bestowing the same name on different vessels, for example USS *Miami*, a side-wheel double-ender gunboat, and USRC *Miami*, a schooner-rigged screw-steamer. The listings themselves, which might describe a yacht by its rig alone, can sow further confusion, and many Confederate naval records were lost when Richmond burned in 1865. Nevertheless, there remain enough verifiable examples to illustrate the contribution of yachts during the hostilities.

The first officially recognized American steam yacht was William H. Aspinwall's *Firefly*, launched in 1854. President of the Pacific Mail Steamship Company, Aspinwall fairly early saw that steam power for pleasure boating would allow more luxurious furnishings without worrying too much about their weight's affect on the vessel's speed. The advantage of steam overall, of course, was that one could post a schedule, no longer having to rely on the arbitrariness of the wind for motive power. Built by Smith & Dimon of New York, the 98-foot *Firefly*'s original configuration included a center-mounted paddle wheel in an iron box. This proved unworkable and she was refitted with two side wheels. After several years service for his commute between work in New York City and his home on Staten Island, Aspinwall sold *Firefly* to the United States Coast Survey.[31] While engaged in her normal duties, under Lieutenant Fontleroy, off the coast of South Carolina, *Firefly*, in company with the schooner *Petrel*, was seized by secessionists on 29 December 1860.[32] Under her new masters, *Firefly* served as tender for the Confederate ironclad CSS *Savannah*. Both were scuttled to prevent capture by Union forces on 21 December 1864 at Savannah, Georgia.

Not every "yacht" started life as a yacht. The term applies more to a vessel's use than to a particular type. The United States Revenue Cutter *Harriet Lane* was built by William H. Webb directly for the Treasury Department. Launched from Bell's Shipyard in New York harbor on 19 November 1857 at a cost of $140,000, she was sold to the U.S. Navy 10 September 1861 for $15,000.[33] A side-wheel steamer with a brigantine rig, capable of making 14 knots, she was the only steam vessel in the Revenue Service at the start of the Civil War. At roughly 675 tons and 180 feet long, her initial battery consisted of one 32-pounder pivot gun, four 24-pounders and one 12-pounder.[34] "Her berth deck was seven feet below the main. Abaft the shaft was the captain's cabin and stateroom, beneath which was a magazine. Next were the officers' ward room, staterooms and lockers, under which was another magazine. Midships were the machinery and coal bunkers. Forward were staterooms, the galleys and quarters for the crew, below which was a third magazine."[35]

The cutter was briefly transferred to the Navy in late 1858 to engage in a little gunboat diplomacy to back up diplomatic discussions between U.S. Special Commissioner James B. Bowlin and Paraguayan dictator Carlos Antonio Lopez. In addition to discussing a maritime commercial treaty Bowlin was there to demand a formal apology and reparations for Paraguay's unprovoked 1855 bombardment of the side-wheel gunboat USS *Water Witch* while the steamer was conducting a survey of the Rio de la Plata basin.[36] Both were forthcoming.

Named after President James Buchanan's niece, the defacto First Lady during his presidency, *Harriet Lane* rates a place here because she performed double duty as the presidential yacht. In September 1860, she was placed at the disposal of His Royal Highness Edward Albert, Prince of Wales, for a trip to Mount Vernon and a ceremony at the grave of George Washington.[37]

During the War Between the States, however, the ship and her crew had no time for ceremonial pursuits. Arriving off Charleston, South Carolina, on 11 April 1861 she

USS *Harriet Lane* (oil by Clary Ray; NH 57514 courtesy the Naval History & Heritage Command Photographic Dept.).

fired the first naval gun of the Civil War, the 32-two pounder in charge of Lieutenant W.D. Thompson,[38] across the bow of the merchant steamer *Nashville*. Hoisting the American flag, *Nashville* escaped to later see service as a Confederate privateer. *Harriet Lane* withdrew two days later when Fort Sumter fell. In August she participated in successful amphibious operations against Forts Clark and Hatteras on the Outer Banks of North Carolina.[39]

> Upon the organization of the West Gulf Squadron under Commodore Farragut for the reduction of Confederate ports in Louisiana and Texas, because of her light draft, she was chosen for the work and her batteries were strengthened as follows: one four-inch rifled Parrott gun as pivot on the forecastle deck; one nine-inch Dahlgren gun on pivot forward of the foremast; two eight-inch Dahlgren Columbiads and two twenty-four-pound brass howitzers on ship carriages, aft; and cutlasses and small arms for ninety-five men. She was commanded by Commander [Jonathan M.] Wainright and Lieutenant Commander Edward Lea, and was used as the flag ship by Commodore Farragut until January 20th, when he transferred his flag to the Hartford.[40]

Assigned as flagship to Captain David Dixon Porter's Mortar Flotilla at Key West, her arrival was delayed by damage inflicted by the Rebel shore battery at Shipping Point, Virginia. Upon completing repairs, while proceeding to Florida waters, she captured the Confederate schooner *Joanna Ward*. She next participated in the capture of Forts Jackson and St. Philip at New Orleans. In early May 1862 she took on transport duties ferrying Brigadier General L.G. Arnold's garrison troops across Pensacola Bay. She next saw action in the river assault on Vicksburg, Mississippi, which failed because the Union Army brought insufficient force to bear on the landward side. After blockade duty in Mobile Bay, *Harriet Lane* was instrumental in the successful seaborne bombardment and capture of Galveston, Texas, on 3 October 1862.[41]

Harriet Lane's luck changed on New Year's Day, 1863, when Rebel forces retook

Galveston and captured the ship. Worse than the loss of the ship and the deaths in action of both captain and executive officer was that "among other papers in the chart room of the Harriet Lane the Confederates found a complete copy of the code of the United States signal service, which when copied and distributed among the signal corps of the Confederacy proved of inestimable value in subsequent engagements when orders were transmitted by signal flags."[42] Until transferred to the Confederate States War Department on 31 March 1863, *Harriet Lane* remained under the jurisdiction of the Confederate Army's Marine Department of Texas until 1864 when she was stripped down and converted into the blockade runner *Lavinia*. On 30 April 1864 she slipped past the Union pickets to deliver a cargo of cotton to Havana, Cuba. Spanish authorities, however, interned her for the duration. In 1867 Spain returned her to the United States Government, which in turn sold her. Converted into the freighter *Elliot Richie*, she met her end "in a gale off Pernambuco, Brazil, on 13 May 1884."[43]

✣ ✣ ✣ ✣

The 115-foot, 225-ton schooner-rigged screw steamer yacht *Lady LeMarchant* was built by Robert Steele & Company on the River Clyde, Great Britain, in 1852 for shipping magnate and businessman Arthur Leary, one of the New York Four Hundred social elite. Her hull was of teak planks over oak frames. From the spring of 1855 through the end of 1856 she operated as a packet to the Canadian Maritime Provinces. On 28 January 1862, Arthur Leary sold his yacht to the United States Revenue Marine for $25,000. She was fitted out in New York, armed with one 24-pounder and one 12-pounder howitzer and re-christened USRC *Miami*.[44]

In short order, *Miami* returned, for a time, to her yacht roots. On 19 April of the same year she steamed down the Potomac from Washington to US Army Headquarters at Aquia Creek, Virginia, about halfway between Washington and the Chesapeake Bay. Her passenger list included President Lincoln, Secretary of the Treasury Salmon P. Chase, Secretary of War Edmond M. Stanton, Rear Admiral John A. Dahlgren, USN, and Brigadier General Egbert L. Viele. The next day Major General Irvin McDowell, commander of the Army of Northeastern Virginia, joined them in conference. Two weeks later, the president and his party proceeded to Fort Monroe at Hampton Roads, Virginia, arriving about nine o'clock the next night.[45]

The next morning, Lincoln went on board to tour USS *Monitor*, still on station after the history-making battle between her and CSS *Virginia* (ex–USS *Merrimac*) two months earlier. Chase and Stanton accompanied him. *Monitor*'s paymaster William Frederick Stanton recalled the visit in a letter to his wife Anna, written immediately after the visit:

> As the boat which brought the party came alongside every eye sought the Monitor but his own. He stood with his face averted as if to hide some disagreeable sight. When he turned to us I could see his lip quiver & his frame tremble with strong emotion & imagined that the terrible drama in these waters of the ninth [eighth] & tenth [ninth] of March was passing in review before him.... He examined everything about the vessel with care, manifesting great interest, his remarks evidently shewing [*sic*] that he had carefully studied what he thought to be our weak points & that he was well acquainted with all the mechanical details of our construction.... Most of our visitors come on board filled with enthusiasm & patriotism ready, like a bottle of soda water, to effervesce the instant the cork is withdrawn, but with Mr. Lincoln it was different. His few remarks as he accompanied us around the vessel were sound, simple, & practical, the points of admiration and exclamation he left to his suite.[46]

Lincoln had more on his mind than imagining the clash of ironclads. He was there to personally command the beginning of the Peninsular Campaign, and *Virginia* still remained a viable threat. On 11 May, *Miami* stood offshore in gunnery support of the landing of Union troops at Ocean View, Virginia.[47] Shortly thereafter, Norfolk surrendered. CSS *Virginia* never came down the James River to interfere and was scuttled by her crew off Craney Island. Lincoln, who previously had returned to Fort Monroe to await the outcome, boarded USS *Baltimore* for the return to Washington. *Miami* returned to general duties off New York.

On 7 December 1863 Confederate sympathizers, posing as passengers, seized the six-hundred-ton screw steamer *Chesapeake* 20 miles north-northeast of Cape Cod, Massachusetts. Fleeing a gale they sheltered at Shelbourne Harbor, Nova Scotia. Word got back to the Federal Navy, and Lieutenant J.F. Nickels, USN, in command of the gunboat USS *Ella and Annie*, was sent after *Chesapeake*. Nickels caught up to his quarry at Mud Cove, Sambro Harbor, Nova Scotia, on the 17th. This second Chesapeake Affair (the first one was in the War of 1812) threatened a diplomatic breach with Great Britain as a blatant violation of British neutrality. *Chesapeake* was ordered to Halifax for adjudication. The diplomatic saber-rattling calmed to insignificance when the malefactors were legally judged to have acted as pirates, not as agents of a belligerent nation, and were therefore fair game.[48]

In March 1864, *Miami* was dispatched to Halifax to convoy *Chesapeake* back to New York where her charge was returned to her owners. On 14 November of that year, *Miami* was transferred to Newport, Rhode Island. She underwent a refit there in October of the following year and was laid up at Staten Island for nearly the whole second half of 1867 before resuming operations, this time out of Wilmington, Delaware. In 1871, the Revenue Service sold *Miami* to Mason, Hobbs & Company of Philadelphia for $2,149.[49]

✳ ✳ ✳ ✳

The 106-foot, 300-ton yacht *Wanderer* re-entered the stage of martial events when the former slaver arrived in Key West, Florida, from Havana, Cuba, on 5 April 1861. Exactly one week later Confederate shore batteries opened their bombardment of Fort Sumter. Unfortunately for her owners in Savannah, Key West remained a Union naval base throughout the war despite that the rest of the state had joined the Confederacy at the beginning of the year. Fearing that her Southern registry would result in her enlistment as a Confederate privateer, Lieutenant Tunis Augustus Craven, commanding USS *Crusader*, voiced his suspicions to Secretary of the Navy Gideon Welles on 14 May:

> [O]n consulting with the U.S. district attorney I am satisfied that no libel can be sustained against the vessel. [Nevertheless] ... my investigation has brought to light the fact that this schooner is to be sold to certain parties in New Orleans at a high price, to be fitted out as a privateer. I have therefore detained her as a vessel which can be used for no valuable purpose except as a cruiser or dispatch vessel. As a privateer she would be most formidable ... has the reputation of being a remarkably fast sailer, and is ready for sea. Armed with one long 24-pounder, and with a crew of 25 men, this vessel may be disastrously destructive to our shipping in the West Indies, and there was a general feeling of relief expressed among ship-masters in Havana when it was learned that I had seized the Wanderer.
>
> While aware that I have no legal grounds for detaining the vessel, I do not feel justified in permitting her to escape to the rebels, and the only way in which that result can be prevented is by the U.S. Government becoming purchasers or charterers. She can be bought for $15,000,

and without expense or alteration can be fitted out as a dispatch vessel or as a serviceable light cruiser.[50]

Three days later, Lieutenant Craven confiscated *Wanderer*. Before June was out, the yacht, armed with one 20-pounder Parrott rifle and two 24-pounder Dahlgren howitzers, joined the Gulf Blockading Squadron, serving primarily as a tender and dispatch vessel. She was not yet, however, an official "United States Ship." That U.S. Navy designation would not come her way until nearly two years later when the Philadelphia prize court finally condemned the yacht as a lawful prize and sold her to the Navy for $1,125—considerably less that Lt. Craven's estimate.[51]

Despite *Wanderer*'s new role, controversy continued to follow her wake. On 30 November, while on normal patrol, *Wanderer* stopped the British schooner *Telegraph* coming out from Key Vaccas, Florida (Confederate territory). Lieutenant James H. Spotts, commanding *Wanderer*, acting in accordance with his orders, detained *Telegraph* and her complement for suspiciously deviating from their filed course which had cleared the vessel for Abaco in the Bahamas. *Wanderer* escorted *Telegraph* back to Key West, whence the latter had departed two days earlier to investigate the suspicious activity. The deviation turned out to be an innocent, though ill-advised, detour for firewood and baggage, and, on 6 December, *Telegraph* was released to proceed. Nevertheless, British Minister to the United States Lord Richard Lyons, after receiving a complaint from the British Counsel at Key West, in early March 1862, demanded an explanation from Secretary of State Seward. An exchange of letters seems to have laid the matter to rest.[52]

On 20 January 1862, *Wanderer* was reassigned to the newly formed East Gulf Blockading Squadron. She resumed her original duties, operating between Tortugas, Florida, and Havana and Cape San Antonio, Cuba. Her blockade duties throughout the year off both coasts of Florida resulted in no further captures. New Year's Day, 1863, saw *Wanderer* back in Key West to replace the copper plating on her hull. On 25 March, her luck changed. In concert with the schooner *Ezilda*, she captured the sloop *Ranger* off Cedar Keys, Florida, and on 17 April, off Egmont Key, she captured the schooner *Annie B.*, laden with cotton. The end of April saw *Wanderer* back in Key West for a major refit, then return to squadron duties until 15 July when she returned for conversion to a hospital ship. This proved portentous when the June-July 1864 yellow fever epidemic felled her entire crew, with one fatality. She languished there as a guard ship for the remainder of the year. At war's end, Rear Admiral Cornelius K. Stribling, commanding the East Gulf Blockading Squadron, advised that *Wanderer* was too deteriorated to be of further use to the Navy, and on 28 June she was sold at public auction at Key West to Packer & Watson.[53]

The tired, former racing yacht, slaver and Union gunboat was reduced to hauling lime to New York and then cocoanuts from Honduras. On the return voyage from Honduras she ran aground on Cape Henry, Virginia. Abandoned to her fate, she was subsequently refloated and repaired and sold to S.S. Scattergood of Philadelphia in January 1869. Back in the fruit trade, *Wanderer* operated between Philadelphia and the West Indies until she died on the rocks at Cape Maisi, Cuba, on 21 January 1871, in a gale.[54]

✢ ✢ ✢ ✢

The former status symbols and playthings of the North's wealth-aristocracy, converted yachts were proving their value to the prosecution of the war. Once the smoke

USS *Vanderbilt* in port during the Civil War (NH 42188 courtesy the Naval History & Heritage Command Photographic Dept.).

of combat had cleared and glasses could be raised to the fallen, a grateful government could take notice—especially if one of said vessels was larger and faster than a second class screw frigate, and a gift to boot. Due notice and thanks were tendered by Congress on 28 January 1864, just over 14 months before Robert E. Lee's Army of North Virginia surrendered at Appomattox Court House:

> WHEREAS Cornelius Vanderbilt, of New York, did, during the spring of eighteen hundred and sixty-two, make a free gift to his imperilled country of his new and staunch steamship "Vanderbilt," of five thousand tons [sic] burthen, built by him with the greatest care, of the best material, at a cost of eight hundred thousand dollars, which steamship has ever since been actively employed in the service of the republic against the rebel devastations of her commerce; and whereas the said Cornelius Vanderbilt has in no manner sought any requital of this magnificent gift, nor any official recognition thereof:
> Therefore,
> *Resolved by the Senate and House of Representatives of the United States of America in Congress assembled*, That the thanks of congress be presented to Cornelius Vanderbilt for this unique manifestation of a fervid and large-souled patriotism.
> Sec. 2. *And it is further resolved,* That the President of the United States be requested to cause a gold medal to be struck, which shall fitly embody an attestation of the nation's gratitude for this gift; which medal shall be forwarded to Cornelius Vanderbilt, a copy of it being made and deposited for preservation in the library of congress.[55]

When secession turned from politics to combat, Cornelius Vanderbilt immediately sought to express his support of the Union in concrete terms by offering his eponymous side-wheel steamer *Vanderbilt* to the Navy. Gideon Welles turned him down. At 333 feet long, 47½-foot beam and displacing 3,360 tons,[56] *Vanderbilt*, thought Welles, likely would be too expensive to fit out and maintain, especially since "everyone knew" the war would not be a long one. As for the expense, the $800,000 ship would end up costing the Navy $221,433.86 for alterations and repairs during her service from 1862 to 1873.[57]

Everything changed on 8 March 1862 when the ironclad CSS *Virginia* (ex–USS *Merrimac*) sortied down the James River and wrought havoc among the Union ships assembled at Hampton Roads. For the moment, USS *Monitor*, fighting *Virginia* to a draw on the 9th, held the threat in check, but if anything happened to her, even a simple mechanical failure, there was nothing capable in the U.S. Navy arsenal for a realistic Plan B. Secretary of War Edwin Stanton had none of his naval counterpart's qualms. Results were what mattered and hang the cost. The financials could be worried about after victory was attained. On 17 March, Stanton escorted Commodore Vanderbilt to the White House to meet with President Lincoln. Could Vanderbilt do it? Would even his vessel be able to stop *Virginia*? "I replied to him that it was my opinion that if the steamship Vanderbilt was there properly manned, the Merrimac would not venture to come out; or if she did, that the chances were ten to one that the Vanderbilt could sink and destroy her. No vessel had been, or could be, made by the rebels that could stand the concussion or stand before the weight of the Vanderbilt."[58] By "concussion" he meant the full mass of his ship behind an added steel ram, traveling at her top speed of 14 knots. Focused at the point of a ram, the impact would have been devastating to *Virginia*—had that encounter ever taken place.

At the time, however, they could not know that circumstances would dictate that *Virginia* had finished her role and would be scuttled to keep her from Union hands. One question remained before their discussion could go from the abstract to the concrete. Lincoln asked how much Vanderbilt wanted for his vessel. "The Commodore bridled at the implication that he was one of the 'vampires' who profited from the war. He said he would donate the Vanderbilt to the Union navy, provided he could control its preparations for battle." Lincoln agreed and directed Stanton to draft the orders granting Vanderbilt, a private citizen, "full discretion and authority as you may deem fit."[59] A week later, "Vanderbilt's Yacht," armed with two 100-pounder Parrott rifles, 12 nine-inch Dahlgren smooth bores and one 12-pounder, backing up her new ram, under the naval command of Commodore Louis Goldsborough, sortied from New York.[60]

Laid down in 1856 and launched a year later, "Vanderbilt's Yacht" was built by Jeremiah Simonson of Greenport, Long Island, New York. She was to be the flagship of Cornelius Vanderbilt's North Atlantic Mail Steamship Line, carrying passengers, at least the first class ones, in accommodations to rival those of a fine hotel, albeit on a somewhat smaller scale, between New York and Le Havre, France. As was the case with *Harriet Lane*, *Vanderbilt* was, per se, not built to be a yacht although she occasionally served that purpose when the Commodore was aboard. A reporter, in "The Staten Islander" of 20 May 1853, waxed effusive over the furnishings of the Commodore's previous steam yacht, *North Star*, on her maiden voyage in 1853. The article reflects the opulence built into the emerging class of steam yachts and gives some idea of what this newest, largest ship must have been like before her conversion to a naval vessel:

> ...the main saloon is splendidly fitted up with all that can tend to gratify the eye and minister to luxurious ease. The state-rooms, which lead to it from either side, are fitted up in the first style of the upholsterer's art.... This saloon is of beautiful satin-wood, with just enough rosewood to relieve it.... The furniture of the main saloon is of rosewood, carved in the splendid style of Louis

XV, covered with a new and elegant material of figured velvet plush, with a green ground filled with bouquets of flowers. It consists of two sofas, four couches, six arm-chairs. Connected with this saloon are ten state-rooms, superbly fitted up, each with a French *armour le gles* [*armoire à glace*], beautifully enameled in white, with a large glass door ... forty by sixty-four inches. The berths are furnished with elegant silk lambricans [lambrequins] and lace curtains. Each room is fitted up with a different color, namely, green and gold, crimson and gold, orange, &c. The toilet furniture matches with the hangings and fittings, by being of the same colors, and presents a picture of completeness not often met with. The saloon and state-rooms are kept at a pleasant temperature by one of Van Horn's steam heaters, which occupies the centre of the cabin. It is a beautiful specimen of bronze trellis-work, with marble top, and has richly burnished gilding. The tapestry carpet is one of gorgeous pattern. Forward of the saloon is a magnificent dining-saloon.... The walls are covered with a preparation of ligneous marble, polished to a degree of mirror-like brightness.... The panels are of Naples granite, the style of Breschia jasper, and the surface of yellow Pyrenees marble. The ceiling of the room is in panels painted white, with scroll-work of purple, light green and gold, surrounding medallion paintings of Columbus, Webster, Clay, Calhoun, Washington, Franklin and others, together with various emblematic conceptions.... The china is of ruby and gold finish, and the silver ware of the finest kind.... A fine entrance saloon, leading from the deck, conducts, by an elegantly adorned staircase, to the main saloon. The reception saloon has a circular sofa capable of seating some twenty persons, and is covered with crimson plush. Over the stairway is a good painting of Mr. Vanderbilt's summer villa at Staten Island, which was placed there, without his knowledge, by the polite attention of his artist friend.[61]

North Star made but one voyage as a yacht prior to her entering commercial passenger service.

USS *Vanderbilt*'s next assignment, under the command of Commander Charles H. Baldwin, was to seek out and destroy the Confederate merchant raider CSS *Alabama*, which was far too successful preying on Northern shipping. For over a year, the chase would take her to the West Indies, the eastern coast of South America, the Cape of Good Hope, St. Helena, Cape Verde, the Canary Islands, Spain and Portugal.[62] Always, however, Baldwin seemed to be one step behind or one ahead of his quarry. That latter situation did on one occasion disrupt the plans of *Alabama*'s Captain Rafael Semmes. Arriving at Simon's Town, South Africa, on 12 September 1863, Captain Semmes discovered not only that his adversary had left the port the previous night, but "that huge old coal box the Vanderbilt, I found, had exhausted the supply of coal at Simon's Town, having taken in as much as eight or nine hundred tons. Commodore Vanderbilt, as he is called, had certainly presented a mammoth coal-consumer to the Federal Government, if nothing else. I was obliged, in consequence, to order coal for the Alabama, around from Cape Town."[63] In January 1864, Baldwin gave up the chase and headed back to the New York Navy Yard for an overhaul.

The cruise, however, had not been entirely without reward or incident. While in the West Indies, *Vanderbilt*, under Baldwin's command, served as flagship for Commodore Charles Wilkes' Flying Squadron. On 25 February 1863 a sail was sighted off St. Thomas, Virgin Islands. Though the merchant steamer was under British colors, even neutral vessels were subject to confirmation that they did not carry contraband destined for a blockaded belligerent. Wilkes ordered Baldwin to stop the vessel and investigate. The boarding party found her to be the side-wheel steamer *Peterhoff*, which, according to her documents was en route from London to Matamoras, Mexico. A large portion of her cargo consisted of 36 cases of artillery harness in sets for four horses, with two riding-saddles attached to each set; 14,450 pairs of "Blucher" or army boots; also "artillery boots"; 5,580 pairs of "government regulation gray blankets"; 95 casks of

USS *Kearsarge* sinks the commerce raider CSS *Alabama*, 19 June 1864 (oil by Xanthus Smith; National Archives photograph K-29827).

horseshoes of a large size, suitable for cavalry service; 52,000 horseshoe nails; considerable amounts of iron, steel, shovels, spades, blacksmiths' bellows and anvils; nails; leather; and assorted medical supplies including a thousand pounds of calomel, large amounts of morphine, 265 pounds of chloroform, and 2640 ounces of quinine.[64] This coupled with the proximity of Matamoras to Brownsville, Texas, just across the Rio Grande from each other, indicated a strong probability that those items were in reality bound for the Confederacy. Wilkes ordered *Peterhoff* seized and Baldwin sent her to New York under a prize crew.

Conceived as an opulent imperial yacht for Tsar Nicholas I, the 210 foot, 412 ton, iron hull, side-wheel steamer *Peterhoff* was built by C.J. Mare & Company at Blackwall, England, and launched in October 1850. Instead of service in royal splendor, however, she got off to an unlucky start on her maiden voyage from London to St. Petersburgh, Russia, under the command of James Boniland. A navigation error in the midst of a hurricane caused her to run upon the rocks at Ösel Island at the entrance to the Gulf of Riga, when making for Dagö Island in the Gulf of Finland. Although the passengers and crew were rescued, the vessel was believed a total loss and became the property of the insurers. *Peterhoff* weathered the winter where she lay until spring when she was salvaged and repaired to eventually enter merchant service. At the time of her capture she was commanded by Stephen Jarman and registered to Joseph Spence of Pile, Spence, & Company, City of London.[65]

The capture became a minor cause célèbre in the British Parliament, not least due to the involvement of Rear Admiral Wilkes, who had previously roiled the waters between the United States and Her Majesty's Government over the Trent Affair in late 1861. M.P. Seymour Fitzgerald, speaking in Parliament, made it clear what they thought of "Commodore Wilkes, whose name was well known in this country some months ago as being borne by a man who had committed a greater outrage upon the English flag, and done more to embroil the two countries, than any other man living...."[66] The *New York Times* reported, dateline London, Saturday, April 18, 1863, "The British Lion lashing himself into a rage is an edifying spectacle.... [T]he capture of the Peterhoff, and the course taken by the American Minister, are raising such a storm as the Government will find it very hard to resist.... John Bull's choler rises. 'A pretty pass,' he cries, 'if I cannot send a steamer to a neutral port without the permission of the Yankee Minister!' ... Lord RUSSELL, it would appear, is for peace Lord PALMERSTON, however, is for whatever the British public requires, and is always ready for a row."[67]

Judge Betts, presiding over the prize court, issued his judgment. *Peterhoff* was condemned as a legitimate prize. Despite the owners duly filing an appeal to the Supreme Court, the U.S. Navy was able to buy the yacht for her appraised value of $80,000.[68] Tempers quieted down in Great Britain. In 1866, the United States Supreme Court finally issued its ruling, reversing the prize court's judgment. Their rationale was, in part, that by treaty with Mexico, navigation of the Rio Grande was to be shared and unimpeded except by written declaration otherwise. Furthermore, the administration in Washington had been allowing exceptions to the announced blockade. Ergo, the blockade was porous, not effective as required under the 1856 Declaration of Paris. *Peterhoff* was free.[69] But by then it was too late. Assigned to the North Atlantic Blockading Squadron on 20 February 1864, she survived just over two weeks when, stationed

USS *Monticello* (wash drawing by Clary Ray, c. 1900). She sank USS *Peterhoff* (former British blockade runner) in a collision off North Carolina, 6 March 1864 (NH 60661 courtesy the Naval History & Heritage Command Photographic Dept.).

off New Inlet, North Carolina, USS *Peterhoff* collided with USS *Monticello* 6 March and sank.[70]

On 16 April 1863, *Vanderbilt* captured the British blockade runner *Gertrude* off Eleuthera Island, Bahamas. With a cargo that included 250 barrels of gunpowder, there was no question this time that it was a legitimate stop. The New York prize court condemned the vessel and, on 4 June, the U.S. Navy purchased the 156-foot, 350-ton, iron-hulled screw steamer from the court for $45,000. USS *Gertrude* went on to capture the blockade runners *Warrior* and *Eco*, and the schooner *Ellen*, as well as salvaging the 50 bales of cotton jettisoned by the blockade runner *Denbigh* to lighten ship during her escape.[71]

Vanderbilt's next significant action was one of mercy rather than war. It is best described in a letter from O.J. Truter, General Consul of the Netherlands for all the British Possessions in South Africa, to his American counterpart Walter Graham, Esq., Consul of the United States for Cape Town, dated 8 September 1863:

> Sir: Having only returned from a week's tour into the country late last night, I learned this morning from my vice-consul how readily Commander Charles H. Baldwin, of the U.S. corvette *Vanderbilt*, had rendered assistance to the Dutch bark *Johanna Elizabeth*, Captain Junius, when the latter vessel was in distress from the loss of topmasts, yards, and sails, and a broken rudder, off L'Agulhas, by towing her to the entrance of False Bay, a distance of 100 miles, thus enabling her to reach and safely anchor in Simon's Bay on the evening of the 1st instant.
>
> I beg through you to express to Commander Baldwin my acknowledgments for the aid thus rendered by him to a Dutch merchant vessel in distress, and to assure him that the readiness with which that assistance was granted, and the disinterestedness evinced by Commander Baldwin in waiving all claims to salvage, are not only highly appreciated by the master of *Johanna Elizabeth* and myself, but will be duly brought to the notice of his Netherlandic Majesty's Government.[72]

Vanderbilt again ran afoul of British sensibilities when, on 30 October 1863, she captured the British bark *Saxon* at Angra Pequena, Cape of Good Hope. Although her cargo of wool was not contraband per se, its origin was at issue, being alleged to have come from the Northern bark *Conrad*, which previously had been captured by the commerce raider CSS *Alabama*. The affair was further complicated when, during the capture, Acting Master's Mate Charles Danenhower of the prize crew accidentally shot and killed Chief Mate James Gray of *Saxon*.[73] "On the 7th March [1864] Judge Betts, in the District Court at New York, decreed the restitution of the vessel and cargo free of all costs, charges, and expenses, reserving for future consideration the question of probable cause of seizure. Lord Lyons was subsequently informed that Her Majesty's Government saw no reason to complain of this sentence."[74]

After putting into New York in January 1864, *Vanderbilt* was reassigned to patrol off Halifax, Nova Scotia, to interdict blockade runners. Aside from being an imposing presence and probable deterrent she failed to take any prizes. After the war she served as a receiving ship at Portsmouth, New Hampshire, before being transferred to Commodore John Roberts' Pacific Squadron, showing the flag at major South American ports on her way to round the Horn. Her last yacht-type duty involved returning Queen Emma of Hawaii to Honolulu from San Francisco. In 1873, after lying in ordinary at Mare Island, San Francisco, she was sold to Howe & Company, who converted her to a three-masted clipper, renamed *Three Brothers*. In this incarnation, *Vanderbilt* passed through several owners until sold for scrap at Gibraltar in 1899.[75]

✤ ✤ ✤ ✤

Scant information survives about the 94-ton schooner yacht *Dart*'s civilian days beyond that she was likely employed most often as either a packet, or a pilot boat. On the Fourth of July 1861, off Galveston, Texas, she ran afoul the screw steamer USS *South Carolina*, of the Gulf Blockading Squadron. At the time of her capture, *South Carolina*'s captain, Commander James Alden, believed his capture to be essentially worthless to the Navy. After sending her ashore to release her passengers Alden had second thoughts. Four days later, he contacted squadron commander Flag Officer William Mervine to suggest arming her with a single 12-pounder gun and a crew of 12 to scout the shore between the Rio Grande and the southwest pass of the Mississippi, where her shallow draft of nine feet would enable exploration of virtually every inlet along the way. That the formalities of libeling the vessel and having her condemned at a prize court were conveniently ignored apparently bothered no one. Soon she was on station, accompanied by sloops *Aid* and *Shark*.

On 3 August, *Dart*, under the command of Master's Mate William M. Wheeler, was sent to probe the defenses of Galveston Harbor. To that end, she fired several shots, doing minimal damage ashore. On 24 September, she proved her worth by capturing the schooner *Cecilia* in ballast, carrying 14 passengers bound for Berwick, Louisiana. The passengers were landed instead at Vermilion Bay, and *Cecilia* received her own howitzer to join *Dart* as tenders to *South Carolina* and USS *Huntsville*.

Dart scored again on the evening of 30 September-1 October, when she captured the 30-ton schooner *Zavala*, carrying 247 bales of tobacco, six passengers and eight mysterious sealed boxes. Wheeler failed to inventory the boxes and clearly state their contents to his superiors. Commander Cicero Price, aboard *Huntsville*, dug a little deeper and learned the boxes contained $10,000 worth of quinine, badly needed by Confederate troops along the mosquito infested Gulf. Price contacted the squadron commander:

> I am of the opinion he [Master's Mate Wheeler] must have compounded with the party interested for the landing of the quinine, by accepting presents of articles which they had no further control of or he any right to accept. In addition, he is charged with having rifled the prize of various articles [including considerable liquor]; and also with having been grossly intoxicated for several days, and also part of his crew. This I am assured of, both by the sober part of the crew, as also two prisoners, whom I detained for several days on account of their insubordination.[76]

The requested court-martial did not take place, but Wheeler was dis-rated and sent to New York. *Dart*'s brief naval career ended just over three months from her capture when she was dismantled by sailors from the screw frigate USS *Niagara*, off the southwest pass of the Mississippi, between 19 and 21 October 1861 and turned over to the Union Army.[77]

❖ ❖ ❖ ❖

The 82-ton schooner yacht *Corypheus*, under the command of Acting Master Alden T. Spear, was with *Harriet Lane* in the Battle of Sabine Pass, when Confederate forces captured the latter in the course of retaking Galveston, Texas, on New Year's Day, 1863. In that action, as reported by Rear Admiral David G. Farragut to the board of inquiry: "The attack commenced on shore about 3 a.m. by the enemy upon our troops, which were defended by the *Sachem* and *Corypheus* with great energy; our troops only replying with musketry, having no artillery."[78]

Half a year earlier, on 13 May 1862, under different colors, CSS *Corypheus* was cut out by a cutter from USS *Calhoun* in Bayou Bonfuca, Louisiana. Condemned by the Key West prize court, she was purchased by the Union Navy for $14,724.05, armed with one 30-pounder Parrot rifle and one 24-pounder howitzer, and assigned to tender duty for the bark USS *Arthur*. *Corypheus* began her life in a Northern shipyard in Brook Haven, New York, in 1859. Below the Mason-Dixon Line when war broke out, General M. Lovell, CSA, ordered her seized and outfitted as a gunboat to patrol Lakes Borgne and Ponchartrain, Louisiana.

Less than a month after the Stars and Stripes replaced the Stars and Bars at *Corypheus'* masthead on 12 June, Lieutenant J.W. Kittredge, commanding *Arthur*, sent the former yacht alone against the battery at Corpus Christi Bayou. The action drove out the 150 Confederate defenders and resulted in denying 180 miles of Texas coastline to Southern trade. The day after, 10 July, *Corypheus* sealed the deal by capturing the nine-ton sloop *Belle Italia*. She repeated her success a month and two days later by participating in the capture of the armed schooner *Breaker* and the scuttling of *Hannah* and *Elma* by their fleeing crews. Moving into Aransas Bay, she captured the blockade running schooner *Water Witch* of Jamaica, denying the South her vital cargo of gunpowder. In between those naval engagements, her guns were again active against Southern forces at Corpus Christi. In that action she took a shot through her magazine, on 16 August, while providing close-in littoral artillery support to Lieutenant Kittredge's 30-man raiding force. Though her battery significantly aided repelling successive infantry and cavalry counterattacks, Kittredge and seven of his force ultimately were captured.[79]

After the action at Galveston at the turn of the new year, *Corypheus* spent most of the next two years patrolling Lake Ponchartrain interdicting small-craft traffic between New Orleans and points along the coast as well as raiding tanneries and salt works. In November of 1864 she went to Pensacola, Florida, for repairs, thence to the area around Mobile, Alabama, until sold on 15 September 1865 for $1,380.[80]

※ ※ ※ ※

The 25-ton *Teazer*'s star burned brightly and famously for a time before she literally succumbed to the flames. Her fame began in 1852 after her new owners, Messrs. Smith and Tobitt of Great Tower Street, London, acquired her from T. Bartlett, Vice Commodore of the Royal London Yacht Club.[81] An enthusiastic article in *Lippincott's Magazine* of 1882 relates her place in the yachting history books:

> What more can man desire in his hours of leisure than to bound with swift courser's speed over the foam-crested billows of old ocean, or to rest at ease "in safety moored" within the protecting arms of any one of our countless beautiful harbors? The ideal yacht is not a mere racing-machine, any more than the ideal man is a champion pedestrian. It is not a thing of canvas and boards eagerly clutching after cups and trophies, as Gaspard struggled for gold. The yachtsman who treats his craft merely as an expensive toy fails to obtain the real pleasure appurtenant to its possession. For him "yachting" is but the synonyme [sic] of extravagance, another form of excitement, a pleasure most substantially enjoyed by proxy. As a lay figure for marine architects, the racing yacht has its uses and its proper field. But it is the cruising yacht—the stoutly-built, able, roomy boat—which best develops yachting and gives it practical use and precedence over other sports. Owing to its insular position and the stormy seas in which the yachtsman has to sail, the English yacht must be primarily a sea-going boat.... English yachts have circumnavigated the globe, sailed around Land's End and Good Hope, cruised the length and breadth of the Mediterranean and the Baltic, explored the icy regions of the North, and wintered in the tropics. In 1852, the little Teazer, of but twenty-five tons' burden, went to the West Indies and back.[82]

Under the command of Captain W.H. Froud, *Teazer* set sail for Jamaica on 13 March 1852 and ran into a gale off Cape Espichel, Portugal, which forced her to put in for repairs. A month later, she resumed the outward bound voyage, arriving, without further mishap, on 3 June. After laying over only three days to replenish stores, he turned her head back to England. Near continuous bad weather prolonged her return to 58 days but she returned in good order.[83]

So much for acclaim. *Teazer* next attains official notice in admiralty court in an insurance dispute: *The Teazer; Offer v. Gray, Q.B., July 7, 1853*. "Policy on yacht void owing to misrepresentation and concealment as to the yacht being employed as a trading vessel."[84] History then appears silent regarding this doughty vessel until she reappears, in 1862, as a footnote in the Peninsular Campaign of the American Civil War. Based on *Teazer*'s oceangoing capability, her previous commercial ventures and that she next appears at Newcastle Ferry, Virginia, an established tobacco port, one can reasonably surmise she was engaged in blockade running. In any event, her fate was sealed, as related by the chaplain of the 1st Regiment, Connecticut Volunteer Heavy Artillery:

> Monday, May 26th.... Company E, under Captain Rockwood, marched to Newcastle Ferry with orders to destroy all means of crossing the [Pamunkey] river from that point down, until he communicated with the gunboats. At Newcastle Ferry, Captain Rockwood burnt the ferry-boat and captured four row-boats, in which he embarked half his detachment, and proceeded down the river, the other half moving along the bank in support. About two miles down, Captain Rockwood captured four row-boats, and about four miles (by river) found a ferry called Basset's Landing, and twelve boats, one of them a small yacht called the Teazer, said to have been used at Yorktown.[85]

So ended the yacht *Teazer*, put to Rockwood's torch, although she was not the vessel Captain Rockwood imagined. The craft that accompanied the ironclad ram CSS *Virginia* at Yorktown in the Battle of Hampton Roads was the screw steamer CSS *Teaser*, a Virginia tugboat taken into the Confederate Navy when Virginia seceded. Shortly after *Teazer* (with a Z) was burned, *Teaser* (with an S) was captured on the Fourth of July by USS *Maratanza*. CSS, later USS, *Teaser* was arguably the first aircraft carrier, serving as hangar and launch pad for a tethered observation balloon that gave Rebel troops ashore a bird's eye view of their enemy's positions.[86]

✤ ✤ ✤ ✤

Long-time resident of New Orleans and cotton entrepreneur John G. Robinson was a founding member of the Southern Yacht Club at Pass Christian in 1849. That same year, his sloop yacht *Pilgrim* won the first Gold Challenge Cup in the September regatta. He repeated his victories in three consecutive years, 1857, 1858 and 1859, which entitled him to keep the trophy.[87] Three years later he was engaged in a far different race, of much higher stakes, with his schooner yacht *Gipsey* (also *Gypsy*). Despite being a British subject, his business interests and loyalties lay with his domicile in the Confederacy.

> CUSTOM-HOUSE, COLLECTOR'S OFFICE, New Orleans, June 6, 1861.
>
> Hon. L.P. WALKER, Secretary of War, Richmond, Va.:
>
> > SIR: Referring to my report of the 3d instant, I have the honor to inform you that Mr. John G. Robinson, a wealthy English gentleman, who has resided many years in this city, has placed his fine yacht Gypsy, of about sixty tons burden, under British colors, and sails this day with a carefully prepared chart indicating the track of the Windsor Forest in search of that vessel. He goes

James River, Virginia. 100 pounder gun on Confederate gunboat *Teaser*, captured July 4, 1862, by USS *Maratanza* (Library of Congress, Prints & Photographs Division).

ostensibly on a fishing or pleasure party, taking all the risk of capture, but for no other object than the hope of being able to give this vessel timely warning to make a port of safety. Mr. Robinson, at my suggestion, entered with zeal and alacrity upon the attempt to accomplish this object without the expectation of fee or reward in any shape, but from pure devotion to the Confederate States. I cannot doubt that this noble and patriotic service will call from the Department an expression of its appreciation commensurate with the risk incurred and the interests involved; but I beg to add that as a British subject I am satisfied that it would be more agreeable to him that whatever expression the Department should think proper to make should be of a private character, and not made public.

Very respectfully, your obedient servant,

F. H. HATCH, Collector.

P. S.—Mr. Robinson will also include the Bamberg in his search.

F. H. H.[88]

British merchantman *Windsor Forest* had departed Liverpool, England on 27 April 1861 with a cargo of arms and munitions. She missed her rendezvous with the Confederate schooner *Adela*, commanded by civilian captain Horace L. Hunley, who later would design and lose his life aboard his eponymous submarine *H.L. Hunley*. *Windsor Forest* had already sought safety in New York after being alerted to nearby Union warships by a passing vessel.[89] It was a brazen maneuver considering the merchantman's intended mission, but the ship of a neutral openly entering a Northern port would not arouse undue suspicion. The British ship *Bamberg*, also carrying arms and munitions for the Confederacy, made it into Havana, Cuba, falsely flying American colors. Her cargo was surreptitiously unloaded and transhipped to Southern ports.[90]

Remaining in Confederate service, Robinson next employed *Gipsey* as a blockade runner. That career ended just before the new year when Lieutenant Read, USN, commanding USS *New London*, intercepted her off East Pascagoula, Louisiana, on 28 December 1861. Flag Officer William W. McKean, USN, Commanding Gulf Blockading Squadron, aboard USS *Niagara*, reported the event to Secretary of the Navy Gideon Welles:

> [*Gipsey*] was discovered inside of Horn Island Pass, was chased and overtaken in the neighborhood of Pascagoula, when the crew deserted and set fire to her; the fire, however, was extinguished before she had sustained much injury. She is of about 50 tons, and was built for a yacht, and is said to be remarkably fast. Her cargo consisted of cotton of superior quality; it will be shipped on board the storeship *Supply*.[91]

Gipsey was immediately appraised and taken into service with the Union Navy in the Gulf of Mexico. The libel case only later reached Judge Samuel R. Betts sitting on the Circuit Court, Southern District, New York, for adjudication. He handed down his decision in March 1862:

> ...the proofs being clear that the yacht was seized in attempting to evade the blockade of the port of New Orleans, the strong presumption, from the written letters and memoranda found on board the vessel, being that she and her lading were both enemy property ... it is considered by the court that sufficient authority is shown for the condemnation of the said vessel and her cargo as prize of war.... Judgment of forfeiture is accordingly given in favor of the libelants.[92]

Subsequently, *Gipsey* seems to have disappeared from the Civil War record. Not so, however, John G. Robinson, who had more than one yacht up his sleeve. His sloop *Mary Baker* might not have been the fastest racer of the Southern Yacht Club, but she was fast enough to slip past the Gulf Blockading Squadron of 1861 and become a prime example of the ongoing commercial relations between British merchants in Nassau and the South. Neutrality did not mean foregoing commercial opportunity. Customs officials in Nassau went so far as to compile a list of Southern successful blockade runners to promote "the importance of the trade that has recently grown up, and which, if properly fostered, may attain much wider proportions.... It is a notable circumstance that the arrivals from Southern States are far more than those from the North, with which our intercourse is free and unrestricted."[93] Of those listed arrivals, *Mary Baker* delivered a cargo of rice from Savannah on 8 November 1861.

The blockade gradually tightened, but, as the expression goes, the devil was in the details. Two of Robinson's schooners, *Alcyon* and *General Worth*, were seized by Federal authorities at New Orleans, on 21 March 1863, and their cargo, 238 bales of cotton, was likewise seized and sold at auction. The proceeds, $88,260, were held by the United States government. This time, Robinson had a valid basis to protest. On 4 May 1862, Benjamin Franklin Butler, Commanding General of the Department of New Orleans, cognizant of the distress afflicting the local population, issued General Orders, No. 22, which stated:

> ...all cargoes of cotton and sugar shall receive the safe-conduct of the forces of the United States, and the boats bringing them from beyond the lines of the United States forces may be allowed to return in safety ... *provided* they bring no passengers except the owners of said boat and of the property so conveyed, and no other merchandise except provisions, of which such boats are requested to bring a full supply for the benefit of the poor of this city.[94]

3. A House Divided

On 16 February 1863, Special Agent of the Treasury Department and Acting Collector of Customs for the Department of New Orleans, George S. Denison, issued an order that essentially reiterated General Butler's earlier order. Furthermore, Denison's order was approved by Rear Admiral David. G. Farragut. Robinson died in 1869, his claim still in limbo. William G. Ford, Robinson's executor, filed suit before the Mixed Commission on British and American Claims in March of 1872. On 24 September 1873, the commission awarded Robinson's English heirs, his brother and sister, $29,638 to be paid to the British government for distribution. The two American heirs got nothing[95]

❈ ❈ ❈ ❈

Not much remains in the public record about the sloop-yacht *Richard Vaux* beyond the record of her capture as a likely blockade runner. That she would find herself in that position appears counterintuitive because her likely namesake was the founder of a respected Philadelphia Quaker family. Born in 1751, Richard Vaux emigrated from London to Philadelphia shortly before the War for Independence and established a lucrative mercantile business. Loyalist sympathies forced his return to England, but he maintained his Philadelphia contacts during his absence. His younger brother James meanwhile, sided with the revolutionaries and established a farm, Vaux Hill, on three hundred acres near Valley Forge, Pennsylvania. During the conflict, in 1777, George Washington actually did sleep there. So did General Howe, though obviously not at the same time. Richard returned in 1783, and the family became prominent in trade, philanthropical and civic pursuits. Another Richard, Richard's grandson, a Philadelphia lawyer and mayor of the city just before the name Fort Sumter was indelibly etched into the American consciousness, remained active in local politics for the duration.[96]

On 20 July 1863, off Blakistone Island, Maryland, in the Potomac River, the sloop-yacht *Richard Vaux* became a prize of USS *Primrose*, Acting Master William T. Street, commanding. Her cargo of scrap iron and rags could easily be construed as contraband, her lack of an official captain on board, failure to obtain the required pass and clearance, and trading stops at several points along the river, which divided northern and southern states, taken together was sufficient evidence at the time to suspect illicit dealings with the Confederacy.[97] The prize court agreed with the libel and condemned the yacht *Richard Vaux*, which it valued at $380.[98]

❈ ❈ ❈ ❈

American by continent if not by country, *Sylphide* is another yacht that played a small part in the War Between the States. A schooner of 57 tons, she was built in Shelburne, Nova Scotia, Canada, in 1851.[99] As is the case with *Richard Vaux*, the public record seems limited to the circumstance of her capture by USS *Virginia* [not to be confused with CSS *Virginia*, ex–USS *Merrimac*] on 9 March 1864. USS *Virginia* was herself the captured blockade runner *Noe-Daquy*.[100] *Sylphide* was flying a peculiar black-white-black horizontal stripe, swallow-tail flag when taken after a brief chase and a number of shots put over her and across her bow. The boarding party from *Virginia* found her papers not to be in order as she was stopped outside the normal shipping lane that would have taken her from Tampico, Mexico, to Havana, Cuba, her avowed course. Her lack of a national flag and cargo of salt, bagging, bale rope, coffee, cigars, and bundles of flat and bar iron were also suspicious. What was not on the manifest, however, was even more damning: 20,000 percussion caps. Acting Volunteer Lieutenant Charles

H. Browning, commanding *Virginia*, put a prize crew aboard and sent *Sylphide* to the prize court in New Orleans for adjudication.[101] Judge Durell agreed with the libel and at the United States Marshal's sale *Sylphide* and her cargo brought the government $3,050.69.[102]

❖ ❖ ❖ ❖

On 3 August 1864 Commodore C.K. Stribling, as agent for the Navy Department, purchased the 58-foot, 12½-knot screw steam yacht *Fairie* for $10,000 from the Central Sanitary Fair in Philadelphia.[103] Therein lies a tale unique among the yachts involved in the maritime conflict.

The United States Sanitary Commission was a civilian relief organization authorized by President Lincoln and Secretary of War Simon Cameron on 13 June 1861, in order to provide for the general comfort of the Union soldiers and the best care available for their wounded and sick comrades, in support of official government agencies.[104] To carry out such a broad agenda, without government financial backing, required extensive private sector fund raising, which naturally included special events. The most ambitious of those affairs was the Great Central Sanitary Fair held in Philadelphia, Pennsylvania, on 7–28 June 1864. The event had the draw of a world's fair. Its main exhibition hall contained 200,000 square feet of display space. Thinking on a grand scale did not stop at the gate. The executive committee appointed a "Committee on

Certificate for the Great Central Fair for the United States Sanitary Commission held in Philadelphia, June 1864, where the custom-built steam yacht *Fairie* was sold to the Union Navy (Library of Congress, Prints & Photographs Division).

Ship-builders" to build a full-rigged ship to be sold at the fair. William Cramp, owner of Cramp's Shipyards, chaired the committee and "immediately set about constructing a steam yacht, a perfect model for beauty and speed. He furnished the hull and fittings, which were of the handsomest and most complete kind, and the machinery was provided by Messers. Neafie & Levy. The cost of this vessel to these two liberal firms was about ten thousand dollars,"[105] the Navy's purchase price. Renamed *Emerald*, she served as a noncommissioned ferry at the Portsmouth Navy Yard at Kittery, Maine, from 1864 to 1883. Total cost to the government for repairs and maintenance throughout her career was an additional $14,168.63.[106]

* * * *

On 3 May 1851, the schooner yacht *America*, arguably is the most famous yacht of all time, slid down the ways at the New York shipyard of William H. Brown. She was designed by self-taught naval architect George Steers for a syndicate led by New York Yacht Club Commodore John Cox Stevens. The 94-foot (measured on deck), 170-ton yacht cost Stevens and his partners, Hamilton Wilkes, George L. Schuyler, James Hamilton, J. Beckman Finlay and Edwin A. Stevens, $20,000. *America* was designed for one purpose: speed. Stevens and his partners expected to make back their costs and turn a tidy profit by wagering on her races.[107] *America*'s radical hull design and raked masts looked good on paper, but how would that translate into the vagaries of competition? As Lord Anglesey put it after inspecting *America* at Cowes on the Isle of Wight, "If she be right, then we are all wrong."[108]

Though built for speed, she was, after all, a yacht, and as such included a certain minimum of comfort, especially for an Atlantic crossing to where the action was. As reported by yachtsman J.F. Loubat:

> The fore cabin is 21 ft. by 8 ft., with 14 berths (seven on either side) for the crew, besides state-cabins for the master and mate. The galley ... is apart between the fore and after cabins.... The fore-cabin is ventilated by a circular skylight, 3 ft. in diameter. Between the galley and main cabin there are two large state-rooms; there are also two other state-rooms, a pantry and wash-room. The cockpit, as it is termed, is a circular opening abaft, of 30 ft. circumference, from which is the entrance to the main cabin. On the starboard side is the bath-room, and on the opposite is a clothes and wine-room; and under the cockpit is the sail-room. The main cabin, or saloon, is fitted with sofas, of mahogany and velvet, corresponding furniture, with a splendid carpet. Lockers extend the whole length of the cabin, with plate-glass panels. The internal decorations are Chinese, white and gold, with mahogany reliefs.[109]

Less than a month after her launching, *America* turned her head from New York to England with a stop, on 12 July, at Le Havre, France, in order to attend to any irregularities that showed up on this, her shakedown, cruise. After a general refit and a fresh coat of black paint, she dropped anchor off the Solent on the evening of 30 July to await the morning tide and clear weather for her arrival at the Royal Yacht Squadron at Cowes. The new day brought with it Britain's top-rated racing yacht, the cutter *Laverock*, ostensibly to escort *America* in. However, she instead proceeded to circle *America* in an obvious challenge. Commodore Stevens, to his later regret, took the bait and gave his skipper, Captain Dick Brown, his head. Even though the schooner was laden with stores and was not ready to race, by the time they arrived off the Royal Yacht Squadron, *America* was several hundred yards ahead. Obviously, British hubris did not prevent an equal measure of caution. *Laverock*'s welcoming gesture was, in effect, a reconnaissance. As a result, though the English opened their homes and clubs to the challengers, they snapped shut their purses. British yachtsmen refused to take any wagers. It was not until the British press chided their countrymen's timidity that *America* was invited to sail in an open race. The course was 53 miles around the Isle of Wight, to be held on 22 August, for a trophy known as the 100 Guineas Cup.[110] *America* won, over 17 other entries, in 8 hours, 34 minutes. Henceforth, the trophy became known as the America's Cup. The schooner *Titania* presented the only other challenge, and she lost by almost an hour.[111]

With his cash cow giving powdered milk instead of cream, Stevens sold his yacht for £5,000 to Irish peer Lord John de Blaquiere, who cut down her rig and raced her for a time. He then turned around and sold her to Henry Montagu Upton, 2nd Viscount Templeton, who renamed her *Camilla*. Eventually tiring of yachting and his new toy, Templeton abandoned *Camilla* on the mud flats at Cowes, in 1858. A forlorn sight, she sat there deteriorating until shipbuilder Henry Sotheby Pitcher bought her for junk in 1859. Pitcher's expertise told him there was more there than scrap value. He restored the yacht and sold her to Henry Edward Decie of the Royal Western Yacht Club, in July 1860. Decie, aware of the political situation across the Atlantic, also saw profit to be made and sailed her to Savannah, Georgia, in the spring of 1861. After the attack on Fort Sumter, Decie put into Montgomery, Alabama, where he sold *Camilla* to the Confederacy, as a blockade runner, for $60,000. He, however, remained in command, running the blockade several times.[112]

In a memo to Gideon Welles, Flag Officer S.H. Stringham, Commander Atlantic Blockading Squadron, filled in some of the details:

> From a source entitled to credit I learn that the commander, Decey [sic], of the yacht Camilla (formerly America), went to Montgomery, and afterwards, about June 1, sailed from Savannah with two ordnance officers (Lieutenant North and Colonel K.C. Anderson) to Europe, to, it is supposed, procure rifled cannon and bring back the commissioners of the Confederate States. It is probable the yacht has gone to Liverpool, as the agent in Savannah is Andrew Low, a branch of the house of Isaac Low & Co., of Liverpool. The yacht is very fast, and will probably attempt to run the blockade, passing into some shallow inlet on the Southern coast with the British flag flying.[113]

As Union forces approached Jacksonville, Florida, in early spring 1862, *Camilla* found herself bottled up in St. John's River. Fearing her capture by the Yankees, the Confederates sank her in Daw's Creek. Their action proved futile when a Union boat expedition up the river found her on 18 March and later raised her. On 19 April, USS *Ottawa* towed *Camilla* to Port Royal for repairs, where she was armed with one 12-pounder rifle and two 24-pounder smooth bores. Under her original name, *America*, Acting Master Jonathan Baker commanding, joined the South Atlantic Blockading Squadron.[114] It wasn't until almost a year later, 19 May 1863, that *Camilla* was officially condemned by the New York prize court and purchased by the Navy Department for $700.[115]

America made her first capture on 13 October when she stopped the schooner *David Crockett* en route to Bermuda with a cargo of turpentine and rosin. Even more significant was her assist, on 29 January 1863, off Charleston, South Carolina, in capturing the iron screw steamer *Princess Royal* with her cargo of rifled artillery, small arms, ammunition, and steam engines for ironclads being constructed at Charleston. On the night of 18–19 March, *America* initiated action which led to the destruction of the British steamer *Georgiana*, with a cargo of rifled cannon for the Confederacy. On 31

March, *America* made her final capture, the blockade running British topsail-schooner *Antelope*, before her redeployment to the United States Naval Academy. Despite her nominal role as a training vessel, *America* still found herself in more active service, sent out, though unsuccessfully, after the commerce raider CSS *Tacony* in June and the Northern blockade running schooner *Medford*.

So ended *America*'s active involvement in the Civil War. From 1866 to 1869, the yacht was laid up at Annapolis until sent to the Washington Navy Yard for a complete refit back to her racing trim. On 8 August 1870 she again competed, against 18 other entries, for the racing cup that now bore her name. This time, however, she came in fourth. 1873 saw *America* struck from the Navy List and sold, on 20 June, to Major General Benjamin Butler for $5,000, who, when he could spare time from politics, enjoyed racing and cruising. In 1917, 24 years after General Butler's death, his heirs decided to part with the now little-used, deteriorating vessel and put her up for sale.[116]

Likely inspired by *America*'s historical significance, Charles Henry Wheelwright Foster contracted to purchase the yacht through his company. In 1921, he transferred the schooner to the America Restoration Fund, a non-profit chaired by Charles Francis Adams, III, skipper of *Resolute*, which would have defended the America's Cup in 1914 and successfully did so in 1920, for major restoration. Adams personal pedigree was no less impressive: great-grandson of President John Quincy Adams, great-great

Yacht *America*, c. 1910. She has kept her second topmast, added in 1863 at Boston Navy Yard (Detroit Publishing Co. Photographs, Library of Congress, Prints & Photographs Division).

grandson of President John Adams, Secretary of the Navy under President Hoover, as well as great-great grandson of Secretary of the Navy Benjamin Williams Crowninshield, who served under Presidents James Madison and James Monroe.

Upon completion of the restoration work, Foster arranged, through the Eastern Yacht Club, to sell *America* to the Government for the sum of $1.00. Secretary of the Navy Edwin C. Denby accepted delivery of the schooner at the United States Naval Academy, Annapolis, Maryland. The Navy began a second major overhaul of her in 1941, but after the Japanese attack on Pearl Harbor, Hawaii, the Navy halted all work on nonessential repair and construction projects. A blizzard on 29 March 1942 piled enough snow atop the shed housing the yacht that it collapsed, destroying both. The headline to a *New York Times* article at the time of *America's* sale back to the Navy proved unintentionally prophetic: "Famous Old Yacht America Gets Ovation as She Leaves Boston on Final Journey." And so she sat until the end of the war when she was stricken from the Navy List on 11 October 1945 and burned.[117]

✳ ✳ ✳ ✳

Tactically, yachts played an important role on both sides of the conflict. The overall naval situation, however, meant their contribution to the Northern effort, especially to the blockade of the Southern ports, was the greater of the two. But, was the blockade itself truly successful? When first proposed by "Old Fuss and Feathers," 75-year-old Lieutenant General Winfield Scott, it was dismissed as both unworkable and unnecessary, since "everyone knew" the war would be over in a few months. Besides, a blockade would take months to establish and likely years to be effective. It was derisively dubbed the "Anaconda Plan" when a line drawn on a map to limn the 3,500 mile extent of such an action was likened to a monstrous constrictor, slowly strangling the South.

At first, the anaconda was the proverbial 98 pound weakling. Although exact numbers are unknown, estimates indicate actual interdiction at 10 percent in year one. Three years later, in 1864, the success rate was closer to 67 percent, even accounting for the purpose-built blockade runners. Antebellum Southern cotton exports averaged three million plus bales per year for 1858–1860. This dropped to only 500,000 bales total during the blockade period.[118] Converted yachts significantly added to the effectiveness of the blockade. "The number of prizes brought in during the war was 1,149, of which 210 were steamers. There were also 355 vessels burned, sunk, driven on shore, or otherwise destroyed, of which 85 were steamers; making a total of 1,504 vessels of all classes. The value of these vessels and their cargoes, according to a low estimate, was thirty-one millions of dollars."[119] It would appear that Old Fuss and Feathers was right all along.

4

War with Spain

When Confederate guns began their bombardment of Fort Sumter on 12 April 1861 the Federal Navy possessed 42 ships. During the course of the War Between the States that small beginning grew to comprise 671 vessels at the end of hostilities. This made the United States Navy the largest navy, at least in number of bottoms, in the world.[1] At the outset of the rebellion, Federal naval strength consisted of 7,600 men in active service. This increased to 51,500 men at its close. During this period, the Navy constructed 208 vessels and purchased another 418, "of which three hundred and thirteen were steamers."[2] Additionally, the Federal Navy captured or destroyed 1,504 vessels which were in some form of service to the Confederacy. During the War of 1812, 517 American privateers took 1,428 vessels in service to the enemy.[3]

The late conflict expanded United States naval operations around the globe and made the Federal Navy a force to be noticed on the international stage. The nation, however, was exhausted by the conflict and its treasury was much depleted, which meant the Navy's role was to be a walk-on rather than a permanent fixture. Even before the last Confederate forces laid down their arms in June of 1865, Secretary of the Navy Gideon Welles received the draw-down order: "to exhibit the policy and measures of the department in effecting at the earliest moment, in view of returning peace, a reduction of naval expenditures, while providing for the prompt re-establishment at any time of our great naval power in all it efficiency to meet the exigencies of any possible crisis in which its services may be invoked to maintain the rights or vindicate the honor of the country."[4]

The latter promise proved to be wishful thinking on Welles' part. Peace moved the military out of the public consciousness and reasserted the Founding Fathers' distrust of a standing military. Gradually reduced to ineffectiveness, the Navy faded from the global stage and deteriorated to the point at which rapid remobilization in time of crisis was impossible. In his report to Congress a year later, Welles described a force reduced to 278 vessels carrying 2,351 guns, of which only 115, carrying 1,029 guns, were in commission on active duty. The most powerful ship in the fleet was the 3,360-ton USS *Vanderbilt* with her two 100-pounder Parrot rifles and her 12 nine-inch Dahlgrens. The state of the Navy was actually even worse than the total numbers would suggest. Sixty-one of the 278 were ironclads either laid up or not completed, 19 were uncompleted steamers, two were old line-of-battle ships, and 81 were wood hull vessels, including those laid up, repairing, fitting out and for sale.[5] The decline continued during 1867 with an aggregate force reduction of 40 vessels carrying 482 guns.[6] Stagnation and attrition continued so that Secretary of the Navy William E. Chandler lamented that the situation was worse even than the low number, 37, of available cruising war vessels in 1882 would indicate:

> These vessels are creditable in their appearance, commodious in their quarters for officers and seamen, well adapted for ordinary naval exercises, and useful for displaying the national flag upon the seas and in the harbors of the commercial world. But they are of low speed; their engines are not modern ... and their steaming, maneuvering, and destructive powers are inferior to those of the present ships of war of other navies. It is not the policy of the United States government to maintain a large navy, but its reputation, honor, and prosperity require that such naval vessels as it possesses should be the best human ingenuity can devise and modern artificers can construct. Our present vessels are not such, and cannot be made such.... With not one modern high-powered cannon in the Navy, and with only eighty-seven guns worth retaining, the importance of action for the procurement of naval ordnance seems apparent, if the Navy is to longer survive.[7]

That same year Commander George Dewey assumed command of the 20-year-old sloop-of war USS *Juniata*. The prestige of command was, however, somewhat tempered by the overall state of the Navy, as he noted later in his autobiography:

> Naval science had gone ahead rapidly and we had stood still. While Europe was building armored battle-ships and fast cruisers, we were making no additions to our navy. We had no sea-going commerce to protect. [The bulk of American import-export commerce at the time was aboard foreign-flagged bottoms.] With the coming of steel hulls and steam this had all passed to England and France, and that rising sea-power, the German Empire.... Our antiquated men-of-war had become the laughing-stock of the nations. Their only possible utility was as something that would float for officers and men to cruise in in time of peace and be murdered in by a few broadsides in time of war. We had appropriations only for running expenses and repairs, none for building new ships. Italy, Spain and Holland were each stronger on the sea than the United States.[8]

Secretary Chandler and the administration of President Chester Alan Arthur would work to change this deplorable situation. The Navy Appropriations Act of 3 March 1883, under the heading "Increase of the Navy," authorized the expenditure of $1,300,000 for the construction of three steel-hull cruisers and a dispatch vessel as recommended by the new Naval Advisory Board.[9] These "ABCD" ships (protected cruisers USS *Atlanta*, USS *Boston*, USS *Chicago* and dispatch-gunboat USS *Dolphin*) would begin the transition to a modern navy. Considerable time, however, passed between authorization and commissioning: *Dolphin*, in December 1885 (from 1899 to 1908 *Dolphin* variously served as the presidential yacht); *Atlanta*, in July 1886; *Boston*, in May 1887 and *Chicago*, not until April 1889.[10] It was a slow process for a navy that could be called to action at any time.

Long before William Randolph Hearst, publisher of the *New York Journal*, and Joseph Pulitzer, publisher of the *New York World*, fought their circulation war over events immediately precedent to the war with Spain, intercourse between that government and the United States often was strained. Those relations reached the tipping point at 9:40 p.m. on 15 February 1898 in Havana Harbor, when USS *Maine* mysteriously exploded and sank. In addition to humanitarian and political considerations between those nations, Spanish possession of Cuba and Puerto Rico was of strategic naval concern as Cuba commanded the major approaches to the Gulf of Mexico. This became an even more important consideration with renewed interest in the Panama Canal after failure of the French effort. Yet the importance of Cuba and the Isthmus of Panama had been stressed from the earliest days of the republic. As Alfred Thayer Mahan summarized:

4. War with Spain

Start of the Goelet Cup Race, 5 August 1887. Real estate magnate Ogden Goelet commissioned silver trophy cups for the winners of New York Yacht Club races for sloops and schooners from 1882 until his death sixteen years later (Detroit Publishing Co. Collection, Library of Congress Prints & Photographs Division).

> Extension of national control had for its chief motive the exclusion of European influences.... This tradition passed on to Cuba; it would have been impossible for the United States to acquiesce in the transfer of the island to a strong naval state. Even Jefferson regarded as desirable to include it within our schemes of national extension.... The force of circumstances, however, pushed the active interests of the United States beyond Cuba to the Isthmus [Panama]. This was immediately consequent upon the development of the Pacific coast, accelerated by the conquest of California from Mexico, and by the discovery of gold ... [and] it became clear when she [the United States] too had political and commercial interests on the two coasts...[11]

In 1823, at the behest of Ferdinand VII and under the direction of the Quadruple Alliance of Great Britain, France, the Netherlands and Austria, France invaded Spain to restore the absolute monarchy. Despite the thousands of miles that separated the United States from this latest European conflict, President James Monroe was concerned about the possible ramifications in the Americas. His Secretary of State, John Quincy Adams, expressed in a letter of 28 April 1823, to Hugh Nelson, Minister Plenipotentiary to Spain, what became the basis of the Monroe Doctrine:

> In the war between France and Spain, now commencing, other interests, peculiarly ours, will in all probability be deeply involved. Whatever may be the issue between those two European powers, it may be taken for granted that the dominion of Spain upon the American continents, north and south, is irrevocably gone. But the islands of Cuba and Porto Rico [sic] still remain nominally, and so far really, dependant upon her, that she yet possesses the power of transferring her own

> dominion over them, together with the possession of them, to others. These islands, from their local position are natural appendages to the North American continent, and one of them (Cuba) almost in sight of our shores, from a multitude of considerations has become the object of transcendent importance to the commercial and political interests of our Union. Its commanding position, with reference to the Gulf of Mexico and the West India seas; ... its safe and capacious harbor of the Havana, fronting a long line of our shores..., give it an importance in the sum of our national interests with which that of no other foreign territory can be compared, and little inferior to that which binds the different members of this Union together.[12]

Thirty-one years later, acting under the instructions of Secretary of State William L. Marcy, after the customs seizure in Havana Harbor of the American packet *Black Warrior*, the Ministers to England (James Buchanan), France (John Y. Mason) and Spain (Pierre Soulé) met at Ostend, Belgium, to formulate a plan for the acquisition of Cuba from Spain at a sum not to exceed $120,000,000.[13] This Ostend Manifesto, of 18 October 1854, even went so far as to threaten force to seize the island

> if Spain, dead to the voice of her own interest, and actuated by stubborn pride and a false sense of honor, should refuse to sell Cuba to the United States, then the question will arise, What ought to be the course of the American Government under such circumstances? ... Does Cuba, in the possession of Spain, seriously endanger our internal peace and the existence of our cherished Union? Should this question be answered in the affirmative, then, by every law, human and divine, we shall be justified in wresting it from Spain, if we possess the power...[14]

Focusing on that last caveat, "if we possess the power," it was just as well that President Franklin Pierce did not endorse Marcy's initiative.

On 31 October 1873, another marine incident threatened war between the United States and Spain when the Spanish paddle-steamer gunboat *Tornado* gave chase to her American-registered sister ship *Virginius*, while the latter was ostensibly off the south coast of Cuba in support of local insurgents. *Tornado* finally captured *Virginius* in international waters and took her and her crew to Santiago, Cuba, where her captain, Joseph Fry, a former U.S. Navy officer, and 53 of her crew were executed by order of General Juan Burriel. The remaining 102 crewmen were rescued by the British sloop of war *Niobe*.[15] This was a clear *causus belli*, but the state of the U.S. Navy at that juncture meant the only broadsides to be fired would be done so by American newspapers. The Navy was still in its period of active decline, and the nation had forgotten the incisive observation by President George Washington in his eighth annual message to a joint session of Congress on 7 December 1796:

> To an active external commerce the protection of a naval force is indispensable. This is manifest with regard to wars in which a State is itself a party. But besides this, it is in our own experience that the most sincere neutrality is not a sufficient guard against the depredations of nations at war. To secure respect to a neutral flag requires a naval force organized and ready to vindicate it from insult or aggression. This may even prevent the necessity of going to war by discouraging belligerent powers from committing such violations of the rights of the neutral party as may, first or last, leave no other option.[16]

The build-up of the New Navy, begun under President Arthur, continued under subsequent administrations with appropriations for more and more technologically advanced ships. But, as seen with the ABCD ships above, the transition from blueprint to commissioned man-of-war in peacetime was a matter of many years. As Captain A.P. Cooke lamented in 1888:

> Some day we must meet an enemy prepared to fight, who will not wait for us to get ready,—and what are we going to do about it? ... We have at present no power of expanding an establishment

4. War with Spain

[the U.S. Navy] barely sufficient for peace purposes, into a navy prepared for war. We should, at least, always have the means of sending forth a fleet with alacrity, and in sufficient strength to hold possession of our own waters.[17]

It wasn't until 1893 that William Gardner, member of the Society of Naval Architects and Marine Engineers, formulated a plan to address Captain Cooke's complaint, a method that would create a ready reserve of smaller, faster vessels that could be rapidly converted to naval use—especially as torpedo boats. At the very least, this auxiliary fleet could serve in coastal defense, freeing up the Navy's warships for offensive action. He proposed:

> The man desiring to have a yacht built shall submit to the Navy Department the complete drawings of the vessel as a yacht and as a torpedo-boat, with a specification of the changes and additions necessary to make the conversion.
>
> The Department can consider the merits of the boat for war purposes. In accordance with their decision an amount shall be allowed the owner sufficient to make it an inducement for him to build such a boat.... The materials and work to be under Government inspection, and the hull and machinery to be regularly inspected in order that they may not deteriorate.
>
> In return for the bonus given, the Government shall have, in case of war, the right to take the boat so long as they shall need her or to buy her outright, paying a proper consideration for use or purchase. In case the boat is sold in the United States, the sale to be conditional upon Government agreement. In case she is sold out of the country a rebate to be paid the Government, depending on the length of time the boat has been built, before such sale shall be effective....
>
> Such a course would be a benefit both to the Government and to the yacht owner. The Government would soon have a large fleet of desirable boats at call, the designs and merits of which they would be familiar with. The owner would have a boat, the materials, workmanship and strength of which he could feel assured were all right.[18]

Two years later, Assistant Secretary of the Navy William McAdoo reiterated that proposal, "while few yachts are so constructed as to be of much use in time or war, yet the possibilities are such that, by mutual agreement between yacht owners and the government when the plans are under consideration, they may be constructed to answer the double purpose of yachts in time of peace and naval auxiliaries in time of war."[19]

That such a proposal ever was put into effect is doubtful. The detailed description of the conversion of the steam yacht *Mayflower* as a naval auxiliary in the *Brooklyn Daily Eagle* of 3 April 1898 would seem to bear that out.[20] It is difficult to imagine that such a proposal would appeal to the yachtsmen of the period, but the likelihood of abuse is far easier to imagine. That is not to asperse the patriotism of the American yachtsmen, who had amply demonstrated that patriotism when called upon in the past. It merely reflects the individualism of the titans of industry and the unlikelihood of their willing acceptance of government oversight. The situation, however, apparently was different when commercial interests were the issue. Reporting on the Navy's acquisition, as auxiliary cruisers, of the ocean liners *St. Louis* (3rd USS *St. Louis*), *St. Paul* (USS *St. Paul*), *City of New York* (USS *Harvard*) and *City of Paris* (USS *Yale*), the *Chicago Tribune* of 11 October 1897 noted that, "the four large first class cruisers already are fully armored in accordance with specifications furnished by government experts...."[21]

Right up to the explosion in Havana Harbor which sank USS *Maine*, as Congressman Robert G. Cousins (Republican from Iowa) put it shortly after the war, "There were thousands of people in the country willing to sleep in the back pews while wisdom and patriotism were urging the necessity of a larger navy, and there were even those who,

USS *Mayflower* underway, sometime between 1900 and 1917 (National Photo Co. Collection, Library of Congress, Prints & Photographs Division).

apparently awake, contended with much noise against the evolution of an American sea-power."[22]

Assistant Secretary of the Navy Theodore Roosevelt, never one to mince words, declared what it would take to birth a world-class navy: "I should welcome almost any war, for I think this country needs one."[23] Like a festering carbuncle, events and bellicose rhetoric were coming to a head. A year later, Roosevelt would have his war. Just over two months after Spain surrendered, Congressman Cousins delivered a speech, in part, that might very well have preceded President McKinley's declaration of war as an example of the political fervor of the time:

> Although sympathizing with every struggle that has been made for the achievement of liberty and self-government, it has never been the policy or practice of this nation to meddle with the management of other powers or to menace their authority as exercised among their own dependencies. The United States would not have thought of interfering with the Spanish government except for the injuries we had sustained and the serious and continuous detriment which we suffered by reason of its uncivilized, inhuman, and unlawful acts. It is the right of every nation to defend itself and to protect its own. More than that, it is morally bound to do so. The causes of the interference of this nation with the barbarous practices of Spain involve the history of continuous crime which that power had been committing in our immediate vicinity contrary to and in violation of the law of nations and of civilization, and which finally brought about and culminated in the horrible disaster which took the lives of two hundred and sixty of our seamen, for which the kingdom of Spain should have at once realized and recognized its responsibility and

accountability if it were not utterly incapable of such realization by reason of its long-continued, ignominious and criminal career, presenting at last to the eyes of the world the spectacle of its bankrupt and creditless condition, not only financially, but morally. That history of continuous criminal oppression and the threatening situation then existing in the island of Cuba and its material and disastrous effects upon our people and their interests had been clearly set forth in the message of our President and in those of his predecessors.[24]

On 20 April 1898, President William McKinley signed the Congressional Resolution authorizing military intervention in Cuba. On the 26th, the Kingdom of Spain declared a state of war was in existence between it and the United States. Congress, on the 27th, declared that a state of war had been in existence since the 22nd. On the 28th, McKinley stated that the United States would abide by the Declaration of Paris, banning privateering.[25] Ironically, the declaration of war included an amendment, proposed by Senator Henry M. Teller (Republican from Colorado), "that the United States hereby

Yachts *Viking* (left) and *Thespia* (USS *Hist*) are readied for Navy service, April 1898 (National Archives photograph 19-N-19-16-12).

disclaims any disposition of intention to exercise sovereignty, jurisdiction, or control over said island [Cuba] except for pacification thereof, and asserts its determination, when that is accomplished, to leave the government and control of the island to its people."[26]

Anticipating the commencement of hostilities, the Navy had earlier purchased the steam yacht *Mayflower*. She underwent conversion at the Brooklyn Navy Yard and was commissioned the previous month, on the 24th. The day before the president signed the declaration of war, Congress authorized the Naval Board on Auxiliary Cruisers to purchase the yachts *Viking*, *Restless*, *Illewarra* [sic], *Thespia*, *Hiawatha*, *Ituna* and *Au Revoir* for conversion to gunboats. That same day, "Vice Commander Harrison B. Moore of the Atlantic Yacht Club [offered] the Government his new yacht *Marietta*, one of the finest and swiftest American yachts."[27]

Patriotic fervor was not, however, universal. The Navy needed fast patrol vessels, and, when volunteers were insufficient, they resorted to conscription. Such was the case with J. Pierpont Morgan's *Corsair II*. The yacht was his pride and joy. Furnishings and ornamentation were comparable, though admittedly a bit more cramped, to what could be found in his estates on land. Beyond extending terrestrial comforts to the marine environment, a close secondary purpose was to impress down to the smallest detail all who came aboard. There were "little places to put your watch at night, sponge hooks in the bathrooms, real fireplaces, wardrobes in every room, full sets of Corsair china, glass, silver and linen, a storage room for trunks, and steam heat. You cannot imagine anything more splendid in the way of construction, or tasteful decoration."[28] Morgan already was on record as adamantly opposed to war with Spain, so it was a double blow, one which he strongly protested, when the U.S. Navy, on 23 April 1898, appropriated his beloved yacht for $225,000.[29] Built by Neafie and Levy of Philadelphia in 1891 and able to drive her 786 tons displacement at a top speed of 17 knots, *Corsair*, renamed USS *Gloucester*, went on to distinguish herself in combat under Lieutenant Commander Richard Wainwright, late of USS *Maine*. She was part of the American fleet that devastated the Spaniards at the Battle of Santiago on 3 July 1898, and she single-handedly captured Guanica, Puerto Rico. In company with USS *Wasp* (ex–steam yacht *Columbia*) she captured and held Arroyo, Puerto Rico, until relieved by the Army. Post-war, from 1899 to 1902, *Gloucester* operated as a training vessel at the United States Naval Academy. Later duties included a similar function with the Massachusetts and New York Naval Militias, until called up to do her part in the Great War, patrolling New York Harbor. Her naval career ended when the Navy sold her on 21 November 1919.[30]

Despite Morgan's hesitation, nationalism was the order of the day. The competition between William Randolph Hearst and Joseph Pulitzer to inflame public outrage about Spanish atrocities in Cuba and, later, the sinking of the *Maine*, and to thereby increase circulation of the *New York Journal* and the *New York World*, is legendary. What is not so well known is how deep ran Hearst's jingoism and his willingness to risk more than mere printer's ink. As Hearst's "Special Correspondent" James Creelman articulated, "There are times when public emergencies call for the sudden intervention of some

Opposite top: **J. Pierpont Morgan's steam yacht *Corsair II* ready for war in 1898 as USS *Gloucester*. She continued to serve through World War I (NH 53746 courtesy the Naval History & Heritage Command Photographic Dept.).** *Opposite bottom:* **Morgan's yacht *Corsair II*, 1893, prior to her naval conversion (Detroit Publishing Co. Collection, Library of Congress, Prints & Photographs Division).**

U.S.S. GLOUCESTER

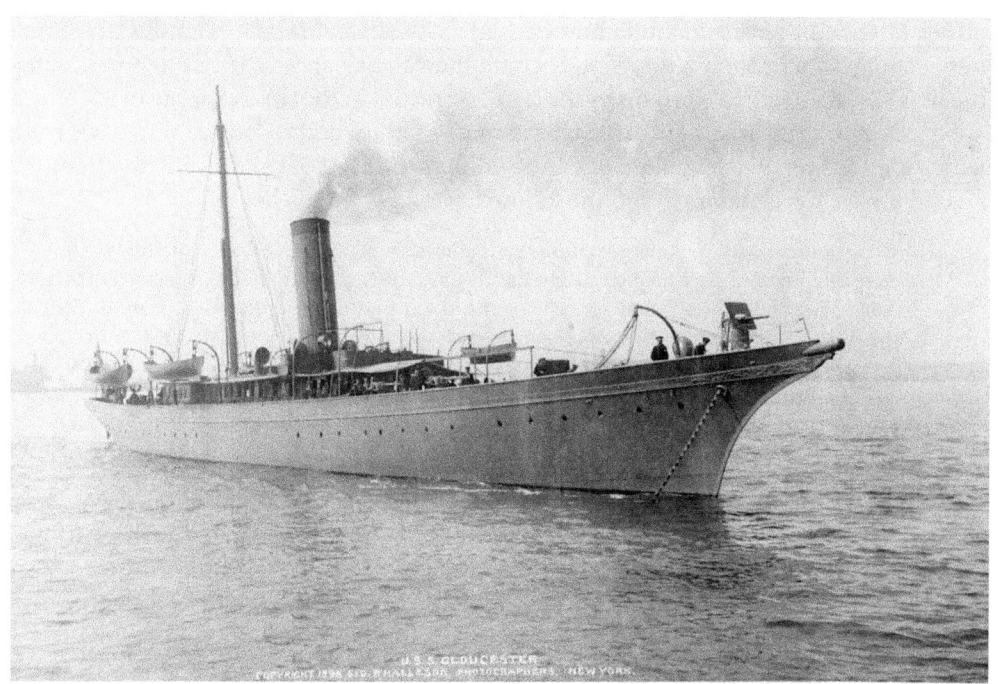

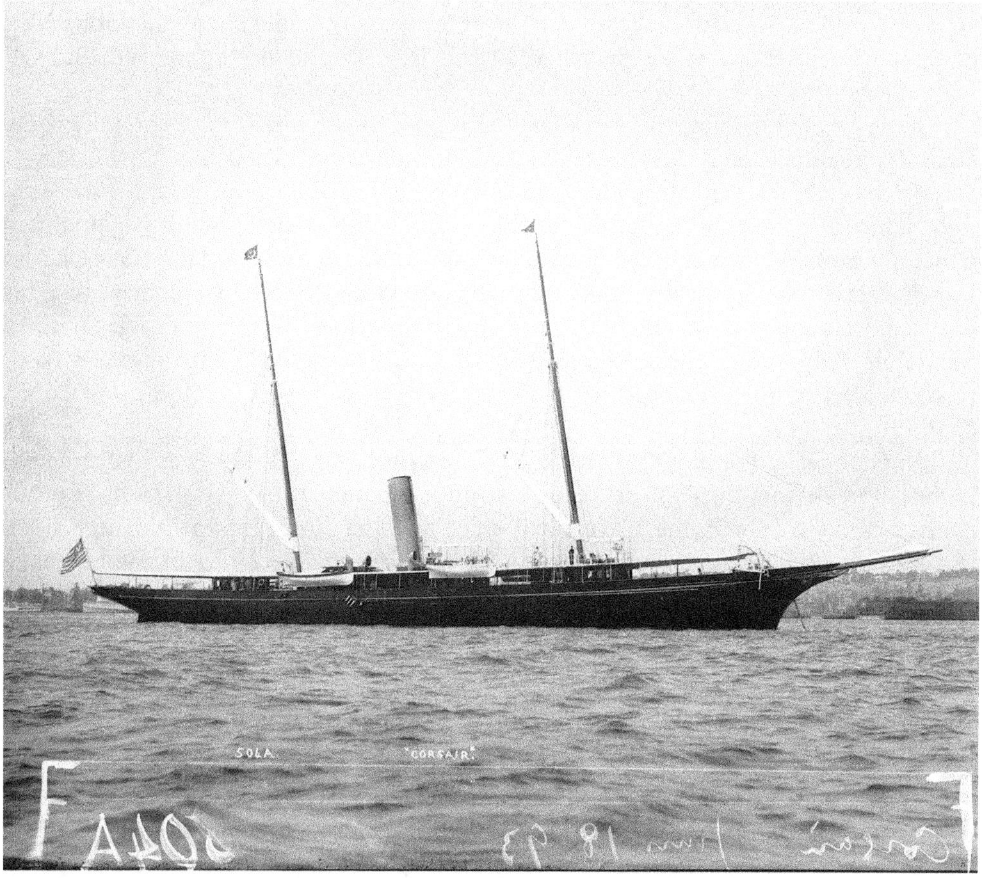
SOLA
"CORSAIR"

power outside of governmental authority. Then journalism acts."[31] Despite the future implications should such a doctrine become the rule, Hearst, as interested in making the news as reporting it (perhaps even more interested in the former), was ready to act. When Dewey expressed concern that Admiral Manuel de la Cámara's Spanish fleet, with superior firepower, would reach the Philippines ahead of reinforcements from the United States, Creelman received the following letter from his boss:

> I wish you would at once make preparations so that in case the Spanish fleet actually starts for Manila we can buy some big English steamer at the eastern end of the Mediterranean and take her to some part of the Suez Canal where we can sink her and obstruct the passage of the Spanish warships. This must be done if the American monitors sent from San Francisco have not reached Dewey and he should be placed in a critical position by the approach of Camara's fleet. I understand that if a British vessel were taken into the canal and sunk under the circumstance outlined above, the British Government would not allow her to be blown up to clear a passage and it might take time enough to raise her to put Dewey in a safe position.[32]

Contrary to what Hearst seemed to assume, Secretary of the Navy John Davis Long was not asleep at the helm, and he was not about to risk another war with Great Britain. Aware that Admiral Cámara's fleet was approaching the Suez Canal, he ordered Rear Admiral William T. Sampson to detach the battleships USS *Iowa* and USS *Brooklyn*, and the armored cruiser USS *Oregon*, with their support vessels, to prepare to directly attack the Spanish coast. Long then had agents in Paris leak this plan to the Spanish in order "primarily to alarm Spain and to cause the recall of Camara, and secondarily to awaken Europe to the fact that the republic of the western hemisphere did not hesitate to carry war, if necessary, across the Atlantic."[33] The American plan worked, and Cámara turned back.

Hearst went on, in late May of 1898, to propose to personally raise and fully equip a cavalry regiment at his own expense. After McKinley turned him down, Hearst abruptly switched service branches and offered his 138-foot steam yacht *Buccaneer*, fully manned, armed and equipped, to the Navy. In return, he asked to be appointed either her captain or executive officer. On 4 June, Acting Secretary of the Navy Charles H. Allen accepted the vessel, but he informed Hearst that the latter would have to apply for a commission through regular channels. By the time Honorary Ensign William Randolph Hearst received his commission the war had ended.[34] For the newly commissioned yacht, however, her pending service would not be her first foray into Cuban affairs.

In October of the previous year, *Journal* reporter Karl Decker was instrumental in the jailbreak from the Casa de Recojidas and subsequent escape from Cuba of Evangelina Cosio y Cisneros, the 18-year-old niece of Cuba's insurgent president.[35] Then, in February 1898, Spanish authorities in Havana seized *Buccaneer* in the mistaken belief that she had ferried Karl Decker back to Cuba. Reporter Julian Hawthorne was the real passenger, assigned to write a hit piece on the deplorable conditions of the concentration camps, ostensibly established to protect non-combatants from the insurgency. No longer having the supposed grounds for seizing the vessel, the customs officials came up with another infraction and fined Hearst $500 for the return of his yacht.[36]

Hearst had acquired *Buccaneer* in 1897. Built by Atlantic Iron Works of Boston in 1888 for Oliver Burr Jennings of Standard Oil, the 160-ton yacht's original name was *Unquowa*. She measured 138 feet long by 20 feet in the beam and drew nine feet, three inches draft. The Navy armed her with two 6-pounder, four 2-pounder and one 1-pounder guns and placed her under the command of Lieutenant H.W. Hines, with a complement of 31. She spent the summer of 1898 patrolling the waters off Key West, Florida. USS *Buccaneer* was decommissioned at the New York Navy Yard in early September of that year and was returned to William Randolph Hearst on the 12th of that month.[37]

✤ ✤ ✤ ✤

In all, more than two dozen luxury yachts shrugged off their lavish habiliments to don navy blue (actually, navy gray). Just how drastic was the change in dress is exemplified by a period description of Howard Gould's *Niagara*, which, though of the period, was not sold into naval service until the United States entered the Great War. Gould's second *Niagara* (his first was a racing sloop) was designed W.G. Shackford and built by Harlan & Hollingsworth of Wilmington, Delaware. She was a steel-hull, twin-screw bark, 272 feet length over all, 36 feet across the beam, drawing 18 feet draft and displacing 2600 tons. Launched 19 February 1898, Gould took delivery in late August. In later Navy trials she was clocked at just over 14 knots, with her shafts turning outward.[38] Inward, she was designed for luxury rather than speed.

After going aboard, Frank Leroy Blanchard, writing for *The Metropolitan Magazine*, waxed effusive for 26 pages about what he saw:

Howard Gould's steam auxiliary bark *Niagara*, 1898 (Detroit Publishing Co. Collection, Library of Congress, Prints & Photographs Division).

It is the interior ... that arouses the greatest enthusiasm among those who have been on board.... The dining saloon, a magnificent apartment 36×24 feet in size, is finished in hand-carved quartered oak and decorated with old Renaissance tapestry. At one end is an open fireplace enclosed with slabs of delicately tinted Mexican onyx, above which rises an elaborately carved mantel of oak bearing in bold relief a representation of Diana standing, spear in hand, ready for the chase. Directly opposite the fireplace rests an upright piano in a massively carved oak case which matches the rest of the apartment. Three tapestry panels in the top complete its decorations. On four sideboards of stout oak curiously carved are displayed the owner's elaborate dinner service in gold and silver. Ten large porthole windows and two skylights of tinted glass flood the saloon with sunlight during the day, and at night scores of electric bulbs half hidden in the ceiling diffuse a soft mellow glow over the apartment...

The library ... is reached from the dining saloon by a wide archway, and from the social hall on the deck above by a broad stairway, the balustrade of which is one of the best examples of black walnut carving produced during the year.... One of the newel posts supports an artistic group of bronze figures which holds aloft a tropical bush in whose branches glow lamps burn. The library is finished in American black walnut with hangings of Venetian red. Around the walls stand bookcases filled with over 600 volumes.... At one end are two covered glass cases containing a well selected complement of arms, such as revolvers, cutlasses, rifles, and swords, to be used in case of emergency....

...the chief object of interest ... [is] the state apartments. This suite, located on the port side, is a dainty dream of loveliness in ivory and rose of the Louis XVI period. The draperies about the portholes, the royal canopy of rich silk above the couch of spotless white, the velvet carpet upon the floor, into which the feet sink without a sound, are of a delicate shade of rose, in which garlands and bows of ribbon are worked in graceful design. The commodious dressing room is brilliantly illuminated from the ceiling by glow lamps set in tulip shaped opalescent glass shades. A large, full length, three-leaved folding mirror is an accessory of this room which every woman can appreciate. Leading from this room is a private hall connecting with the boudoir, a chastely elegant apartment corresponding to the dressing room in general tone effect. The globes of the electric lamps are half open roses of opalescent glass. Wall cabinets of French plate glass, on whose crystal shelves gleams a dainty china tea service; a beautiful writing desk of the Louis XIV period; a long, low divan piled high with silken cushions, and, above it, an Oriental canopy, from which hangs a colored glass lantern of novel design.... A bath room all in ivory and rose tiles ... completes the suite....

Forward ... are four guest chambers, each nearly 12 feet square and finished in a different kind of wood, and each provided with a private bath room.... On the lower deck are three more guest chambers of the same character, though finished in different woods, and, like them, provided with private bath rooms. Each is furnished with a brass bed, a bureau with a large plate glass mirror, a wall writing desk, and a cedar lined clothes closet.

The ... social hall on the upper deck, 16 feet wide and 32 feet long, [is] finished in African mahogany and upholstered in dark green. Wide windows, consisting of single panes of heavy plate glass, furnish plenty of light and afford an excellent opportunity for observation in rainy weather. A concert orchestrion, equivalent to a band of eighteen pieces, furnishes music for dancing or plays the latest songs and instrumental compositions.... Around the skylight ... growing foliage and running plants are arranged in such a manner as to give a conservatory or garden effect. Just abaft this hall is the smoking room, in old oak, fitted with big easy chairs and comfortable lounging divans covered with soft Venetian leather.... A second social hall, 18 feet square, is located on the lower deck....

In addition ... there are rooms for Mr. Gould's private secretary, doctor, valet, and personal servants; an apothecary shop, a photographer's room, a fully equipped steam laundry, a refrigerating plant capable of turning out 400 pounds of ice a day and cooling 1,500 cubic feet of space to a temperature of 34 degrees Fahrenheit; a hospital, and a room for fishing tackle and camping outfit.

The Niagara's electric plant ... runs the big orchestrion in the social hall, cooks steaks in the kitchen, warms the rooms, lights cigars, operates the laundry machinery, heats my lady's curling tongs, carries messages over the telephone wires, summons the servants, and cools the air with whirling fans....[39]

4. War with Spain 71

Yacht *Niagara*'s Welte Philharmonic pipe organ, 1914 (from Welte & Sons catalogue, 1914).

Despite the desirability of acquiring these palatial yachts, it was easier and less expensive to start with a hull not yet adorned with deck houses and below-decks finery. The Navy purchased as yet unnamed Hull No. 295 in June 1898 from her builder John Roach & Company of Chester, Pennsylvania. Though never outfitted in *Niagara*'s opulence, the steam yacht's livery did end up more attractive than utilitarian military. Her "magazine" stored vintage wines instead of ordnance, and the pop of champagne corks substituted for the roar of deck guns. On 18 August of that year, Hull No. 295 finally had her name. Measuring 123 feet, eight inches at the waterline and displacing 152 net tons, the newly commissioned USS *Sylph*, the Navy's third of that name, was assigned to the Washington Navy Yard where she became the presidential yacht for William McKinley. Though capable of making 15 knots, she generally kept to lesser speed as she mostly made excursions down the Potomac River and in the Chesapeake Bay. Excursions along the Atlantic Seaboard, however, allowed her skipper to open her up. *Sylph* ended her service as presidential yacht with the end of Woodrow Wilson's term in office. Though no longer an official presidential perquisite, she remained available to the Secretary and Assistant Secretaries of the Navy and made pleasure cruises for patients of the Naval Hospital. Presidents Theodore Roosevelt and William Howard Taft used her in a less official capacity for sightseeing excursions. Her illustrious passenger list included the King of Belgium and the Crown Prince of Sweden. On 17 July 1921 she was reclassified as Patrol Yacht 5 (PY-5) but continued to operate as before until being decommissioned on 27 April 1929 and sold, in November, to Frank B. Glair of Brooklyn, New York.[40]

✢ ✢ ✢ ✢

President Theodore Roosevelt and Admiral "Fighting Bob" Evans aboard USS *Mayflower*, 1907 (Library of Congress, Prints & Photographs Division).

Stiletto, of 1883, was a special case. Once steam had proved itself a reliable propulsion system the pastime of the leisurely sail gradually gave way to the desire for speed. It soon became apparent that the sheer weight and broad beam of the comfortable, stable, sea-going pleasure palaces made those vessels incompatible with the quest for speed. "A story is told of Mr. [Matthew Chaloner Durfee] Borden returning to New York in Little Sovereign, being overhauled and passed by one of the Winchesters. Turning to his captain, he said, 'Don't stop at the Yacht Club landing, but continue on to Seabury's yard so I can order a faster yacht.'"[41] *Stiletto* was yacht designer N.G. Herreshoff's answer to that demand. At 94 feet long over all with a 26-foot, three-inch beam and weighing in at 568 gross registered tons, she was built to demonstrate his design for a high-speed steamer. With her narrow hull design and novel three-drum boiler, she was capable of making 23 knots. It wasn't only the yachting community that was impressed. The Navy purchased her in 1887 for conversion to a torpedo boat. She served in that configuration as an experimental vessel until 1911.[42]

✢ ✢ ✢ ✢

The Navy purchased *Dorothea* on 21 May 1898 for $187,000 from the estate of Philadelphia railroad magnate Thomas McKean. She had been launched only five months earlier at the William Cramp and Sons yard in Philadelphia. In under two weeks she was commissioned. On 14 June 1898, she steamed out of the Philadelphia Navy Yard under the command of Lieutenant Commander W.J. Bernette, ordered to patrol the waters between Key West, Florida, and Havana, Cuba. At war's end, after an uneventful tour of duty, *Dorothea* was laid up for three years, after which she was called upon as a training vessel for the Illinois Naval Militia. Eight years later she was transferred to the Ohio State Militia until called back to full active service on 20 April 1917 after America joined the European conflict. The Great War found her again patrolling in southeastern waters and the Gulf of Mexico. On 8 January 1918 *Dorothea* served as a training vessel for Cuban officers, and she served out that year and part of the next under the command of the military governor of Santo Domingo. The Navy decommissioned *Dorothea* on 23 June 1919 and sold her five months later.[43]

✢ ✢ ✢ ✢

The "top-down" effort to modernize and expand a Navy inadequate to project and protect American interests found its counterpart in the "bottom-up" push to create a reserve force of well-trained civilian sailors, with a ready flotilla of auxiliary vessels, to augment the regular navy in time of national emergency or war. Washington Curran Whitthorne, former Adjutant General of the Confederate Army and now Democratic Senator from Tennessee (after a full presidential pardon from Andrew Johnson), introduced, on 17 February 1887, a bill "to create a Naval Reserve of auxiliary cruisers, officers and men from the Mercantile Marine of the United States."[44] Opposition from commercial interests helped kill the bill. A second attempt a year later also failed. But the seed had been sown and it took root in the Commonwealth of Massachusetts.

On 17 May 1888 Massachusetts passed an act creating the nation's first naval militia, a reserve force that would be capable, in time of state or national need, of assuming coastal and harbor defense duties, thereby freeing the regular navy to concentrate on offensive action at sea. Creating this weekend navy on paper was one thing; actually putting it in operation took almost two years. Soon other states established their own naval militias, each under the command of that state's governor and unified under the purview of the Assistant Secretary of the Navy.[45]

It wasn't until 1908, however, that the Navy Department considered the State Naval Militias to be a truly useful reserve force.[46] Initially, the members came to those reserve units already possessed of seagoing and small vessel handling ability. Naval discipline, signals and gunnery were another matter. This could be addressed thanks to the Navy's yacht-buying spree going into the war with Spain. Most of those yachts did their job largely unheralded as dispatch or section patrol vessels. Many, like *Dorothea*, continued to serve after hostilities as training vessels attached to the various State Naval Militias. [See Appendix 3.] A few proved themselves valuable assets in combat.

※ ※ ※ ※

Hermione was designed by George L. Watson and was built in 1889 by Fleming and Ferguson of Paisley, Scotland, for James and Richard Allan, owners of the Allan Line Steamship Company. She passed through several hands before the Navy purchased her, on 2 April 1898, from the estate of politician and chocolate manufacturer Henry Lillie Pierce for $50,000. The vessel took both her name and theme of her furnishings from Shakespeare's "The Winter's Tale."

> All the figures in the play: Mamillius, Camillo, Sicilian gentlemen, etc. are represented. Some carved in wood, others cut in the glass of the "ports." The saloon is furnished in mahogany and oak, the overmantel work is mahogany. There are eight staterooms for passengers, two of them being double berths. There are three berths done in olive wood. Four of the staterooms are provided with hot and cold baths, under the floor, and two over the floor. The vessel has electric light, generated and stored into accumulators, sufficient to supply for 24 hours without use of the engine. There is an electric launch, 27 feet long, and, should anything get wrong with this electrical apparatus on board the steamer, the machinery of the launch would generate sufficient electricity of the demand.[47]

Hermione's state of the art electrics and a power plant and design that could drive her 545 tons displacement at a sustained top speed of 14 knots made her ideal for naval

USS *Hawk* (ex–*Hermione*), c. 1900 (Detroit Publishing Co. Collection, Library of Congress, Prints & Photographs Division).

service. Even her decorating theme could be thought to foreshadow the yacht's new role. In Act 4, Scene 4, of the play, Camillo pronounces, "A cause more promising ... a wild dedication ... to unpath'd waters, undream'd shores, most certain..." Commissioned as USS *Hawk* on 5 April, Lieutenant J. Hood commanding, *Hawk* was ready to join Admiral Sampson's North Atlantic Squadron's blockade of Cuba on the opening day of hostilities. In early June she intercepted the Spanish freighter *Alphonso XII*, en route to Cuba, and sent her to the bottom. A month after the war's end, *Hawk* was decommissioned at Norfolk, Virginia. In two years, however, she was back in service, this time with the Ohio Naval Militia for the next nine years. In August 1909, *Hawk* transferred to the New York Naval Militia, operating out of Buffalo until 21 May 1919 when she was laid up in the reserve fleet. On 16 April 1922, the Navy again had need of her for training on the Great Lakes. This lasted until 14 February 1940. Eleven days later, the Navy sold *Hawk* for scrap to the Indiana Salvage Company of Michigan City, Indiana.[48]

✦ ✦ ✦ ✦

Eugenia, another Scottish built steam yacht, was built by Hawthorne and Company of Leith in 1897 for Philadelphia financier Joseph Gardner Cassatt. On 9 June of the following year, the Navy purchased the 315-ton schooner-rigged, single-screw steamer for $40,000, and commissioned the renamed USS *Siren* 15 days later under

F. Augustus Schermerhorn's steam yacht *Free Lance*, 1896 (Detroit Publishing Co. Collection, Library of Congress, Prints & Photographs Division).

the command of Lieutenant John M. Robinson. While assigned to the North Atlantic Squadron, blockading Cuba, from 25 July to 12 August 1898, she captured the Norwegian ship *Franklin* with a contraband cargo. Five days later, on 7 August, in company with the converted yacht USS *Viking*, *Siren* captured another Norwegian flagged blockade runner, the *Brezen*. A month after the war ended the Navy was done with her, and she was decommissioned on 24 September 1898. *Siren's* service was not done, however. On 22 June 1899 she joined the Virginia Naval Militia. Sometime after that the Navy again called her up, and *Siren* served in the far less glamorous capacity of tender to a receiving ship, ironically named *Franklin*, at the Norfolk, Virginia, Navy Yard until struck from the Navy List on 30 August 1910.[49]

Siren's companion on 7 August 1898, *Viking*, was built in 1883 in Chester, Pennsylvania, by John Roach and Company for oilman Horace A. Hutchins. He sold his 218-ton yacht to the Navy on 22 April 1898 for $30,000. Under the command of Lieutenant Henry Minett, USS *Viking* joined the North Atlantic Squadron off Cuba three days after *Siren*. Aside from her joint effort with *Siren*, *Viking's* duties consisted primarily in ferrying communications and passengers between ships. The Navy decommissioned her on 22 September 1898. Subsequently, she was briefly reactivated before finally being transferred to the War Department on 9 December 1899.[50]

✤ ✤ ✤ ✤

Petty officers with Gatling gun aboard USS *Free Lance*, January 1898 (Detroit Publishing Co. Collection, Library of Congress, Prints & Photographs Division).

4. War with Spain

Henry Morrison Flagler, industrialist and founding partner of Standard Oil, was an avid yachtsman. His second yacht *Columbia* successfully defended the America's Cup in 1881. His third yacht would be a steamer, the *Alicia*. He invested $113,000 in her construction and outfitting by Harlan and Hollingsworth of Wilmington, Delaware, in 1890. With war with Spain looming on the horizon, the Navy, on 6 April 1898, purchased the 301-ton, 15-knot *Alicia* for $117,500 and armed her with three 6-pounder and two 1-pounder guns. Commissioned on 12 April under her new name USS *Hornet*, Lieutenant James M. Helm in command, she joined the North Atlantic Squadron, which was deploying to blockade Cuba. On 30 June, in company with USS *Hist* (ex-steam yacht *Thespia*) and the armed tug USS *Wompatuck*, and under the guns of the Spanish fort at Manzanillo, *Hornet* captured the blockade runner *Nickerson* and sank a Spanish gunboat and an armed sloop. *Hornet*, however, was disabled in the action and *Wompatuck* took her under tow. Eleven days later *Hornet* was back on station with her same two companions to cut the telegraph cable that communicated between Havana and Manzanillo. A week later, she was back in heavy action off Manzanillo, which resulted in the sinking of nine Spanish ships and four armed pontoons. After her wartime service, USS *Hornet* was decommissioned on 18 October 1898 and lent to the North Carolina Naval Militia, where she served until 1902. After a brief turn as tender to the receiving ship *Franklin* at Norfolk Navy Yard, *Hornet* was sold on 12 July 1910 to N.S. Sterns of New Orleans.[51]

✦ ✦ ✦ ✦

Built in 1895 by William Cramp and Sons of Philadelphia, the 472-ton *Thespia* was owned by millionaire grain merchant David Dows, Jr., when the Navy purchased her, three days before war was declared, for the sum of $65,000. The Navy armed her with three 3-pounder guns and four 1-pounders, commissioned her on 13 May as USS *Hist*, under Lieutenant Lucien Young. *Hist* joined *Hornet* and *Wompatuck* only the day before their abovementioned action at Manzanillo, where she was hit 11 times but suffered no casualties. The fireworks came a day early for *Hist* that year as she joined the fleet off Santiago, on 3 July, when the Spanish made a major, unsuccessful, attempt to break the blockade. That day the Spanish lost the destroyer *Furor*, the torpedo boat *Plutón*, and the armored cruisers *Infanta María Teresa*, *Almirante Oquendo*, *Vizcaya*, and *Cristóbal Colón*. Subsequently, *Hist* and *Wompatuck* engaged in cable cutting operations, and she participated in the bombardment of Santa Cruz on 20 July. *Hist* was decommissioned and laid up on 2 February 1899. In 1902, the Navy again had need of *Hist* and recommissioned her for patrol and dispatch duties in the Caribbean. On 4 March of that year she was reassigned to assist in the testing of new submarines in Long Island Sound. Though decommissioned on 3 May 1907, she was back in harness five months later as tender to the 2nd Submarine Division. USS *Hist's* final assignment came on 6 October 1908 when she returned to the Caribbean as a supply and dispatch vessel for the Cape Cruz-Casilda surveying expedition under Commander Armistead Rust. *Hist's* last decommissioning came on 18 May 1911, and she was sold in November of that year.[52]

✦ ✦ ✦ ✦

The seventh USS *Wasp* was birthed by William Cramp and Sons of Philadelphia in 1893 for Joseph Harvey Ladew, Sr., partner in Fayerweather & Ladew, one of the largest leather manufacturers worldwide. She slid down the ways as the 630-ton, 16½-

Gunner at 37 mm gun on USS *Hist*, 1898 (National Archives photograph 19-N-14187).

knot steam yacht *Columbia*, named after Ladew's alma mater. Anticipating war with Spain, the Navy purchased her from her owner on 26 March 1898 for $95,000 and armed her with four 6-pounder guns and two Colt machine guns. Under her captain, Lieutenant Aaron Ward, she joined the Cuban blockading squadron off Havana on 7 May. Five days later, *Wasp* diverted from blockade patrol to join up with a small convoy that included SS *Gussie*, carrying two companies of troops. *Gussie* landed about half of them at Cabañas at 1500 hours. Their advance stalled when the Spanish counter-attacked 15 minutes later, driving them back toward the beach, where *Wasp* provided close-in covering fire for their extraction. *Wasp* resumed blockading duties off various parts of Cuba, with occasional runs to Key West, Florida. On 21 July *Wasp*'s lookouts observed the Spanish cruiser *Don Jorge Juan* at anchor in Nipe Bay. *Wasp* made signal to the accompanying tug USS *Leyden* and initiated an attack. The gunboats *Topeka* and *Annapolis* followed *Wasp* in, and in one hour the Spanish cruiser lay on the bottom. *Wasp* spent the remainder of the war on station off Puerto Rico and was decommissioned on 27 September. On 15 December, however, she was back at sea, this time with the Florida Naval Militia until 21 June 1899. *Wasp* continued with miscellaneous duties until serving a nine-year tour with the New York Naval Militia. The First World War saw USS *Wasp* in the 3rd Naval District, patrolling off the Eastern Seaboard. After postwar duty at Annapolis, Maryland, she was finally decommissioned on 1 December 1919 and was sold on 20 September 1921.[53]

✤ ✤ ✤ ✤

The fourth USS *Eagle* was another Harlan and Hollingsworth steam yacht. The 434-ton displacement, 177-foot *Almy* was built in 1890 for prominent New York attorney Frederic Gallatin. He sold her to the Navy on 2 April 1898 for a modest $10,000, possibly due to her age and relatively slow 12 knots top speed. Armed with two 6-pounder rapid-fire guns and commissioned on 5 April, Lieutenant W.H.H. Southerland commanding, the renamed USS *Eagle* was quickly dispatched to the North Atlantic Squadron, ready to blockade Cuba when war was declared. On 22 July, *Eagle* captured the Spanish freighter *Santo Domingo*. The remainder of her tour was less exciting. Postwar, *Eagle* was destined to remain in the Caribbean both as a survey vessel and as a gunboat supporting ongoing Marine Corps operations protecting American interests. This general duty continued during World War I as a unit of the American Patrol Detachment, Atlantic Fleet. *Eagle*'s Navy career ended with her decommissioning on 23 May 1919 followed by her sale on 3 January 1920.[54]

※ ※ ※ ※

Industrialist Matthew Chaloner Durfee Borden's yacht *Sovereign* was the second yacht he contributed to Naval service, after his *Stiletto*. She began life in 1896 at the John N. Robbins yard in South Brooklyn, New York. Her 212-foot waterline length could cut through the waves at a top speed of 14 knots, and her 775-ton displacement supported a deckhouse that contained chartroom, deck saloon, galley, a lavatory, deck

Drying laundry on the forestay aboard USS *Scorpion* (ex–*Sovereign*), 1900 (Detroit Publishing Co. Collection, Library of Congress, Prints & Photographs Division).

storeroom and access to the engine room. Enclosed below deck, going from stem to stern, were the crew's quarters, officers' quarters, 10 staterooms surrounding a mahogany dining room, a mahogany main saloon, the furnishings of which included two sofas, two sideboards, an organ and a piano. Next came the pantry, a companionway and a bathroom. The engine and boiler spaces preceded the full-width owner's suite, followed by four more staterooms, a bathroom, the after saloon and yet two more staterooms.[55] The Navy was interested and purchased her for $300,000 on 7 April 1898. Outfitted with four 6-pounder guns, with a ship's complement of 90, the renamed USS *Scorpion*, the Navy's fourth of that name, was commissioned on 11 April 1898, under the command of Lieutenant Commander Adolph Marix.

On blockade with the Flying Squadron off Cuba, she racked up the sea miles but saw only limited action at the Daiquiri landings and at Manzanillo harbor, where, on 11 July, she participated in a one-sided action that destroyed all Spanish vessels remaining in the harbor. Born to provide luxury for the few, USS *Scorpion*'s real value would come in the next century when she provided succor for the many. In between *Scorpion* underwent full conversion to a gunboat, going into the yard on 14 January 1899. The new gunboat's first assignment, in spring 1900, was in support of the Isthmian Canal Commission, investigating and surveying proposed canal routes. On 1 July 1902 she was reassigned to North Atlantic Squadron in various capacities that occasionally took her back to the Caribbean. A change of venue took *Scorpion* to Constantinople on 4 December 1908 to serve as station ship. The end of the month, however, saw her dispatched to Messina, Italy, engaged in relief efforts for the survivors of the 7.5 earthquake and subsequent 40-foot tsunami that devastated the area on the 28th.

After nearly two years in Trieste undergoing extensive repairs she returned to Constantinople and six months later was again involved in humanitarian aid, this time to Turkish earthquake victims. The first and second Balkan wars, 1912 and 1913, saw *Scorpion* assisting American evacuees and guarding American interests. When the United States officially entered the now global war on 11 April 1917, she was interned at Constantinople. After the war, *Scorpion* was back assisting refugees in that part of the world. By 27 October 1927 the Navy was through with the 31-year-old former yacht, and two years later sold her for scrap.[56]

※ ※ ※ ※

In 1896, James and George Thomson, of Clydebank, Scotland, built the commodious steam yacht *Mayflower* for New York real estate tycoon and avid yachtsman Ogden Goelet. On 27 August 1897, after a two-month illness, Goelet died aboard his beloved yacht while anchored at Cowes, Isle of Wight.[57] His twin-screw steamer was capable of 17 knots despite her 2,690-tons displacement. In January of 1898 his heirs accepted an offer for the yacht from King Leopold of Belgium. Somehow the deal went sour. Three months later, the Navy expressed serious interest to the tune of a $430,000 purchase price from the Goelet estate on 19 March. With her large displacement, overall length of 318 feet, 36½-foot beam and 18½-foot draft she was the largest of the yachts acquired for the impending war, and the Navy took full advantage of her size. *Mayflower*'s refit at the Brooklyn Navy Yard included arming her with two 5" guns for a main battery, six 6-pounders on each side as broadside batteries, two Colt 6 mm machine guns and two torpedo tubes. Her assigned complement numbered 171.[58]

Under the command of Commander M.R.S. MacKenzie, USS *Mayflower*, the second Navy ship of that name, joined up with Admiral Sampson's North Atlantic Squadron blockading Cuba on 20 April at Key West, Florida. En route to Havana, *Mayflower* captured the Spanish sloop *Santiago Apostal* and several smaller vessels. On 11 May, she stopped another *Mayflower*, this one a British merchantman attempting to run the blockade. MacKenzie ordered a prize crew aboard and sent her to the States for adjudication. Three days later, the Spanish first class cruiser *Alphonso XII* [not to be confused with the freighter *Hermione* stopped] and two gunboats attempted to sortie from Havana Harbor but were driven back under the protecting guns of Morro Castle by *Mayflower's* aggressive assault. Despite the former yacht's impressive armament, *Alphonso XII* normally would have outgunned the American, but her six 6.4" guns had been removed to augment the shore batteries at Torreón de Chorrera and Regina, guarding Havana. Ironically, *Alphonso XII* had been in Havana Harbor when USS *Maine* exploded, where she played a major role in rescuing and caring for the survivors. *Alphonso XII* remained bottled up in Havana Harbor for the remainder of the war, and *Mayflower* resumed general blockading duties.

Her guns now silent, *Mayflower* nevertheless saw plenty of action after the war. After a refit for special service, her new captain, Commander Duncan Kennedy took her to Puerto Rico in 1900, where she served as headquarters for the new American government. In 1902 *Mayflower* served briefly as Commodore Dewey's flagship in the Asiatic Fleet. November 1903 saw her off Panama in support of the revolution, which would enable American control of what would become the Panama Canal Zone. Decommissioned on 1 November 1904 for another refit, she was recommissioned 25 July 1905 as the new presidential yacht. Her first major duty in that role was to play host for President Theodore Roosevelt's peace negotiations which ended the Russo-Japanese War and earned T.R. a Nobel Peace Prize. Except for a time out as a dispatch vessel off Santo Domingo in 1906, *Mayflower* served as presidential yacht until decommissioned 22 March 1929 as an economy move by President Hoover. After being heavily fire damaged at the Philadelphia Navy yard 24 January 1931, the Navy sold her 19 October of that year to an agent of Chicago financier Frank P. Parish. His plans to restore her to her prewar glory collapsed along with his fortune, and he fled the country to avoid prosecution for mail fraud and assault on two government witnesses. Successive owners, each with a different plan for *Mayflower*, nevertheless kept her afloat. On 31 July 1942, the War Shipping Administration recognized she still had value and purchased her from Broadfoot Iron Works of Wilmington, North Carolina, and renamed her USS *Butte* before turning her over to the Coast Guard on 6 September of the following year. The Coast Guard decided to retain her original name and assigned USCGC *Mayflower* to patrol the Atlantic coast hunting for U–Boats. Decommissioned in 1946, she was sold 8 January 1947 for use as an Arctic sealer, but another fire aboard precluded that career. Yet another owner, Collins Distributors, Inc., repaired her and renamed her SS *Malla* of Panamanian registry. Subsequently fitted out at Genoa, Italy, allegedly for the Mediterranean coastal trade, she instead snuck out from Marseilles with a clandestine cargo of 1,200 Jewish refugees, most of whom were from SS *Exodus*, and landed them at Haifa, Palestine, on 7 April 1948. She transported another 1,100 refugees in June. In January 1949 *Malla* transferred to Israeli registry. She finally went to the breaker's yard in 1950.[59]

The final yacht of concern here was neither under construction during the war with Spain nor did she see service in the United States Navy. Boston copper mining magnate Albert S. Bigelow's yacht *Pantooset* rounds out this chapter inasmuch as Commodore Bigelow sold her for $270,000, on 18 May 1907, to the Cuban Government when he retired from yachting. Delivered to Bigelow on 10 June 1902 by Bath Iron Works of Bath, Maine, at a cost of $350,000, *Pantooset* measured 212 feet long, from the end of the snub bowsprit over her clipper bow to her elegant fantail, with a beam of 27 feet four inches and a draft of 13 feet. She was capable of moving her 538 gross tons at a speed of 15 knots. Stripped of her elaborate furnishings, armed with four guns and re-christened *Hatuey*, she entered naval service as flagship of the Cuban Coast Guard and, on 4 June 1910 became the first warship of independent Cuba to call on New York.[60]

✻ ✻ ✻ ✻

An armistice between the United States and Spain ended the war on 12 August 1898. The two sides made it official with the signing of the Treaty of Paris on 12 December of that year. Though the guns now were silent, the rhetoric was not. Jingoism, and its partner militarism, did not easily fade. Now another "ism," imperialism, entered the arena of debate that surrounded the issue of naval preparedness. Journalist, newspaper editor and former Civil War general, Carl Schurz, acknowledged the external realities while still pushing for restraint:

> Not we ourselves, but our rivals and possible enemies will decide how large our armies and navies must be, and how much money we must spend for them. And all of that money will have to come out of the pockets of our people, the poor as well as the rich…. But set your policy of imperialism in full swing, as the acquisition of the Philippines will do, and the time will come, and come quickly, when every American farmer and working-man, when going to his toil, will, like his European brother, have "to carry a fully armed soldier on his back."[61]

Representative Robert G. Cousins (Republican from Iowa) argued convincingly for a standing navy, in essence echoing George Washington's warning, "To secure respect to a neutral [American] flag requires a naval force organized and ready to vindicate it from insult or aggression."

> It is not necessary to compliment the men who had the foresight to advocate and to accomplish the development of our sea-power. The world has already witnessed, and history verifies their wisdom. It will not be contended for a moment that the situation in the United States requires as large a standing army as in other countries, but we do contend that reasonable foresight and prudence would authorize a sufficient standing army to protect our interests and properties, to preserve our institutions, to maintain peace and order, and to protect the liberties of our citizens.[62]

At least from these two examples it would appear that the two sides were not irreconcilably apart. How the debate ultimately would affect the naval modernization begun under the Arthur Administration remained to be seen.

5

The War to End War

In a few short months in 1898, the United States Navy established itself as no longer just the new kid on the block, perhaps to be acknowledged but then largely ignored. It proved itself a naval force to be reckoned with in Asia and South America. Over and above the victory over Spanish colonialism the population in general congratulated itself on their altruistic reasons for risking American lives and treasure. They saw the nation as a beacon of global democracy and morality and a bulwark against oppression. As John Ireland, Archbishop of St. Paul, Minnesota, put it: "To-day we proclaim a new order of things. America is too great to be isolated from the world around her and beyond her. She is a world-power, to whom no world-interest is alien."[1]

New York Senator Chauncey Mitchell Depew was no less jingoistic but also saw the more practical fallout of America's new presence: "...a war has been fought and won ... to add incalculably to American enterprise and opportunity by becoming masters of the sea ... [to] ride the waves and direct the storm."[2] A year later, Massachusetts Senator Henry Cabot Lodge reiterated Depew's sentiments:

> by throwing our weight into the scales we may be able to keep those vast regions and those teeming millions, not only open to our trade and commerce, but open to the light of Western civilization.... The master of Manila can make terms with every power in the East, and those vast markets must be held open in the interest of our industry and our commerce, of our farmers and our working men, to the free competition of mankind, a contest in which the genius of American enterprise need fear no rival.[3]

There was, however, another dimension to America's victory. Senator Albert J. Beveridge from Indiana missed the irony that the United States had suddenly become the very thing that it opposed in Europe in principle, an imperialist nation, when he enthused that the American people were now,

> by virtue of their power, by right of their institutions, by authority of their heaven-directed purposes—the propagandists and not the misers of liberty. It is a glorious history our God has bestowed upon His chosen people, a history whose key-note was struck by Liberty Bell; a history heroic with faith in our mission and our future; a history of statesmen who flung the boundaries of the Republic out into unexplored lands and savage wildernesses; a history of soldiers who carried the flag across the blazing deserts and through the ranks of hostile mountains, even to the gates of sunset.[4]

The chest-thumping braggadocio did not impress William Jennings Bryan, who, as the flush of victory began to fade, saw fit to question the scruples of America's new-found possessions and what would be the judgment of history: "Whether the Spanish war shall be known in history as a war for liberty or as a war of conquest; whether the principles of self-government shall be strengthened or abandoned..."[5] Even Archbishop Ireland saw the inherent dilemma in the same speech quoted above when he quoted General Ulysses S. Grant: "I look forward to an epoch when a court, recognized by all nations, will settle international differences, instead of keeping large standing armies, as they do in Europe."[6]

Perhaps Czar Nicholas II had been keeping abreast of all the American soul searching and saw an opportunity. Perhaps not. Perhaps he truly was influenced by the increasing destructive power nations could wield to devastate their adversaries. In any case, in the midst of the national ambivalence in the United States, he saw an opportunity and commanded his foreign minister, Count Muravieff, to issue an invitation to the major world governments, to wit:

> The economic crisis, due in great part to the system of armaments *a l'outrance* and the continual danger which lies in this massing of war material are transforming the armed peace of our days into a crushing burden which the peoples have more and more difficulty in bearing. It appears evident that if this state of things were to be prolonged it would inevitably lead to the very cataclysm it is desired to avert, and the horrors whereof make every thinking being shudder in advance. To put an end to these incessant armaments and to seek the means of warding off the calamities which are threatening the whole world—such is the supreme duty to-day imposed upon all states. Filled with this idea, his majesty has been pleased to command me to propose to all governments whose representatives are accredited to the imperial court the assembling of a conference which shall occupy itself with this grave problem.[7]

The immediate global response was mostly favorable, as exemplified by an editorial in the Charleston, South Carolina, *News and Courier*: "If it shall only put an end to the increase of armies and navies, and thus leave free for peaceful industries and sciences the immense sums that would otherwise be absorbed in safeguarding the nations against each other, it will bring untold blessings upon mankind and render immortal the name of Nicholas II."[8] Others remained far less sanguine. The Chicago *Journal* referred to "the czar's Quixotic suggestion"; the Toronto *Globe* called it "a generous illusion"; and the Portland, Maine, *Argus* wondered "is the czar sincere?"[9]

The czar's "conference" convened at The Hague on 18 May 1899. The United States participated albeit with reservations regarding restrictions on weapons not yet developed and the overall affect on national sovereignty. Secretary of State John Hay's instructions to the American Delegation set out the limits to American enthusiasm:

> The first article, relating to the non-augmentation and future reduction of effective land and sea forces, is, at present, so inapplicable to the United States.... In comparison with the effective forces, both military and naval, of other nations, those of the United States are at present so far below the normal quota that the question of limitation could not be profitably discussed.... The second, third, and fourth articles, relating to the non-employment of firearms, explosives, and other destructive agents, the restricted use of existing instruments of destruction, and the prohibition of certain contrivances employed in naval warfare, seem lacking in practicability.... It is doubtful if wars are to be diminished by rendering them less destructive, for it is the plain lesson of history that the periods of peace have been longer protracted as the cost and destructiveness of war have increased.... The eighth article, which proposes the wider extension of good offices, mediation and arbitration, seems likely to open the most fruitful field for discussion and future action.[10]

Then came the kicker. "Nothing contained in this Convention shall be so construed as to require the United States of America to depart from its traditional policy of not intruding upon, interfering with, or entangling itself in the political questions or policy or internal administration of any foreign State; nor shall anything contained in the said Convention be construed to imply a relinquishment by the United States of America of its traditional attitude toward purely American questions."[11]

Before delegations from the international community could meet for the second Hague Convention in 1907, war broke out between Russia and Japan. On 27–28 May 1905, in the Sea of Japan near Tsushima, Admiral Togo's mixed fleet destroyed Admiral Nebogatov's Russian battleships in a classic engagement reminiscent of those of the line-of-battle ships of the age of sail. It would have done Horatio Nelson proud. The outcome continued the naval emphasis on preparation for big fleet engagements, and the public debate became one of flexibility versus concentration of firepower.

Less than three weeks after the Battle of Tsushima, Captain Alfred Thayer Mahan, USN, argued in *Collier's* for many smaller, faster battleships. This would permit deployment adaptability which would preclude any ships of a defeated enemy from escaping.[12] Commander Bradley A. Fiske, USN, writing in rebuttal in *The Proceedings of the United States Naval Institute*, argued that first one had to defeat one's enemy and that concentration of firepower and armor in fewer massive battleships was the best way to ensure that victory.[13] The Republican Party chose its side and their 1908 campaign platform came out strongly for naval expansion: "The Navy of the United States is an instrument of peace. Regarded as an insurance against war and the consequent enormous losses…, it is the cheapest insurance in which our nation can invest."[14] And heavier, bigger-gunned battleships were the best riders on that insurance policy.

Naval warfare, however, already was on the cusp of change. Technologies of the air and the depths would forever alter the situation on the briny. Writing scarcely four years after Tsushima, Victor Lougheed, in *Vehicles of the Air*, mused:

> Fancy for a moment the disillusionment to come when in some great conflict of the future a splendid up-to-date battleship fleet of the traditional order, with traditional sailors, traditional admiral, and traditional tactics, finds itself beset in midseas by a couple of great, unarmored, liner-like hulls, engined to admit of speeds and steaming radii as will permit them to pursue or run away from any armored craft yet built, and designed with clear and level decks for aeroplane launching…. Then picture the terribly one-sided engagement that will ensue—the thousands of tons and millions of dollars' worth of cunningly-fashioned mechanism all but impotent against the unremitted, harrying, and reinforced attacks from aloft…[15]

Vehicles beneath the waves had already made great strides since David Bushnell's *Turtle* attacked HMS *Eagle* in 1776, and Horace Lawson Hunley's eponymous CSS *H.L. Hunley* sank the screw sloop-of-war USS *Housatonic* in 1864. The submarine and countermeasures against it would continue to evolve through two world wars and beyond. Much has been written about the torpedoing of RMS *Lusitania* by U-20, on 7 May 1915. That incident, however, took place in the war zone. Kapitänleutnant Hans Rose in U-53 brought the reality to the Eastern Seaboard of the United States. On 7 October 1916, U-53 steamed into Newport, Rhode Island, and was assigned a berth. Kptlt. Rose then paid a courtesy call on the commandant of the Naval Station, after which he invited American naval officers to tour his boat. The next day, he proceeded beyond the three-mile limit and set about to work, sinking the British merchant ships *Stephano, Strathdine, West Point*; the Dutch steamer *Blommersdijk*; and the Norwegian *Christian Knudsen*. All the neutral American warships could do was stand by to rescue survivors.[16]

At the start of the Great War, defensive measures against the submarine menace lagged well behind the latter's offensive capability. The most effective countermeasures

German submarine U-53 at Newport, Rhode Island, 1916 (Bain News Service Collection, Library of Congress, Prints & Photographs Division).

were eyes and ears and enough vessels to spread those organs across the greatest area possible. To that end, Secretary of the Navy Josephus Daniels proposed:

> The naval coast defense reserve shall be composed of those persons who may be capable of performing special useful service in the Navy or in connection with the Navy in defense of the coast and who obligate themselves to perform such service with the Navy in time of war or national emergency.
>
> Persons may enrol in this class for service with coast-defense vessels … in various ranks or ratings corresponding to those of the Navy for which they shall have qualified under regulations prescribed by the Secretary of the Navy: *Provided*, That the Secretary of the Navy may permit the enrollment in this class of owners and operators of yachts and motor power boats suitable for naval purposes in the naval defense of the coast; and is hereby authorized to enter into contract with the owners of such power boats and other craft suitable for war purposes to take over the same in time of war or national emergency upon payment of a reasonable indemnity…[17]

As Assistant Secretary of the Navy Franklin Delano Roosevelt later observed: "The present war is showing that the submarine is a weapon that has an important bearing on the final result. As developed by the Germans, there is at present a decided menace to England's ability to keep itself and allies supplied with food. One of the most effective methods to overcome this menace has been found to be small surface craft armed to destroy a submarine."[18]

President Woodrow Wilson might have won reelection because "he kept us out of war," but public opinion was changing to outrage over Germany's resumption of unrestricted submarine warfare on 1 February 1917, after more than a year's hiatus.

The public clamor for action was no more evident than within the younger generation. This was exemplified when, on 26 February 1917, Professor of Latin and assistant crew coach Mather Abbott announced the formation of a naval unit at Yale University. Its members would be trained and ready for eventual enrollment in the Government Coast Defense Service in the event of the United States entering the European war.[19] That same day, *The Brooklyn Daily Eagle* reported, "Forty yachts and motor boats from the New York district alone already have been enrolled by the Naval Training Association in the 'Mosquito Fleet' intended to operate as a part of the coast patrol ... under the auspices of the Navy Department ... officially known as the 'Naval Coast Defense Reserve.'"[20]

※ ※ ※ ※

While future military and naval matters remained in flux, America's average Joe and Jane were more focused on the doings of the wealthy elite. The most anticipated social event of the 1900 Winter Season was the pending nuptials of Louisa Pierpont Morgan and Herbert Livingston Satterlee. A prominent corporate attorney, Satterlee also was manager of the Seawahanka Yacht Club and a lieutenant in the New York Naval Militia. From December 1908 to March 1909, he would serve as Assistant Secretary of the Navy under President Theodore Roosevelt. Appropriately, the wedding gift from his fellow officers was a loving cup fabricated from a shell from a Spanish warship sunk at the Battle of Santiago, Cuba. Twenty-five hundred invitations went out for the ceremony itself, and J.P. Morgan had a special extension built from his mansion's conservatory into the adjacent vacant lot to hold the reception guests. On the happy day, 15 November, New York's Finest, afoot and on horseback, kept back the crowd of onlookers that thronged both sides of the street outside St. George's Episcopal Church and nearby Stuyvesant Park.[21]

It was, as Mark Twain dubbed it, "The Gilded Age." As the American economy grew, the number of people with the wherewithal to indulge themselves increased along with it. In 1850 the United States Census listed a mere 19 millionaires. By the time Confederate guns opened fire on Fort Sumter, a little over a decade later, their number had risen to four hundred. By 1892 their ranks had swelled to more than tenfold to 4,047.[22] "Between 1869 and 1910, the value of American manufacturing rose from $3 billion to $13 billion. The steel industry produced just 68,000 tons in 1870, but 4,200,000 tons in 1890. The central vehicle of this surge in economic productivity was the modern corporation."[23] What hitherto had been a largely agrarian and small business based nation was transforming into an urban based corporate industrial powerhouse, and the capitalists were poised to reap the benefits. In a sermon delivered on 15 November 1900 Episcopalian Bishop William Lawrence defended the amassing of great wealth by stating that "it is only to the man of morality that wealth comes.... Godliness is in league with riches."[24]

It remains a matter of conjecture what the Massachusetts bishop might have said when newspapers of the day reported socialite Mamie Fish's notorious dogs' birthday dinner, which she co-hosted with fellow wag and prankster Harry Lehr, in honor of the latter's wife's Pomeranian Mighty Atom. Marion "Mamie" Graves Anton Fish was the wife of Illinois Central Railroad tycoon Stuyvesant Fish. Mamie's own dog was decked out for the occasion in a $15,000 diamond studded collar, and the one-night party, including a special birthday cake, for one hundred dogs and their humans was reported to have cost $50,000.²⁵ This at a time when the average working man, by the most optimistic of estimates, earned less than $500 per year.²⁶

In 1899 economist Thorstein Veblen propounded his "Theory of the Leisure Class," in which he observed, "Conspicuous consumption of valuable goods is a means of reputability of the gentleman of leisure."²⁷ Owning a yacht, the more opulent the better, was a well-established symbol of one's financial success, and the new industrial tycoons were not to be left behind. The New York Yacht Club listed only four steam yachts among its members in 1870. Twenty years later that number had grown to 71.²⁸ Sailing yachts had a graceful elegance, but by nature they required a leisurely schedule if they were not being raced. The steam engine freed the yachtsman from the vagaries of the wind and meant that one's home on the waves could also serve as a convenient way to hassle-free commute from one's landed estate to an office in the city. There remained, as yet, the drawback of size. Whether an auxiliary means of propulsion or its sole means, steam power required an engine room, a boiler room and a sizeable coal bunker to give the vessel any reasonable range, which combined generally took up a third of its waterline length. It also dictated a minimum size for one's yacht that could still shut out the merely wealthy. A relatively short-haul steam motor launch hardly projected the desired social status. A sea change, however, was in the offing.

In 1883, Rudolf Diesel built an eponymous prototype engine. Two years later, Gottlieb Daimler and Wilhelm Maybach fitted a one-cylinder gasoline engine of their design to a two-wheel vehicle and created the motorcycle. Adding two more wheels in 1886, they gave birth to the automobile. That same year, they repeated their engine experiments on the Neckar River, which flows through the state of Baden-Württemberg, Germany. The result, a 15-foot skiff became the first motor boat.²⁹ An oil fueled or gasoline engine was considerably smaller than its steam counterpart, there was no need for a boiler room and liquid fuel could be stored anywhere in the hull at the convenience of vessel's design. Additionally, said fuel gave greater range for the same volume it occupied. Yachts could now be considerably cleaner and either smaller, but still elegantly appointed, or the same size and be even more palatial.

The new technology, however, did not really catch on until, in 1912, Thomas Fleming Day, editor of *The Rudder* magazine, demonstrated the reliability of the gasoline engine by navigating his 35-foot motorboat from New York to Russia.³⁰ Nevertheless, steam was, and still is [today the Navy uses nuclear fission to boil the steam], a reliable source of motive power. Though the yachting community might have hesitated to abandon steam, they were not so loathe to dispense with the soot and ash and dust of coal. Mid May 1912 saw the launching of dry-goods wholesaler Peter Winchester Rouss' 225-foot, 399-ton yacht *Winchester* at the Yarrow Yard in Glasgow, Scotland. Her twin oil-fired boilers generated the steam for twin Parsons turbines, which could drive her at a top speed of 32 knots. Speed and comfort made for an easy commute between his Oyster Bay country house and his office in New York City.³¹ What worked in a vessel as large as *Winchester* was even more adaptable to smaller, less opulent, less pricey day or weekend excursion vessels, and today's cabin cruiser was born.

※ ※ ※ ※

In his State of the Union address of 7 December 1915, President Wilson laid before the Senate and House of Representatives a naval expansion program that would create a United States Navy second to none. He pushed:

...for the Congress to adopt a comprehensive plan for putting the navy upon a final footing of strength and efficiency and to press that plan to completion within the next five years. We have always looked to the navy of the country as our first and chief line of defense; we have always seen it to be our manifest course of prudence to be strong on the seas. Year by year we have been creating a navy which now ranks very high indeed among the navies of the maritime nations. We should now definitely determine how we shall complete what we have begun, and how soon.[32]

There remained, however, a vocal faction content with a "little Navy." The Battle of Jutland between the British Grand Fleet and the German High Seas Fleet, 31 May to 1 June 1916, changed enough minds that Navy Secretary Josephus Daniels was able to push Wilson's proposal through the legislature and make it the major section of the Naval Appropriations Act of 29 August 1916—but not soon enough. The proposed capital ships would not be ready until well after the Armistice.

In assessing America's woeful lack of preparedness for the recently ended world war, a U.S. Senator demanded to know why the naval expansion, especially in destroyers, had not begun in time for the ships to be ready in 1917. To which Vice Admiral William Sowden Sims, commander of the United States fleet in European waters, replied, "If we could have imagined that the Germans would do what they did do we could have prepared for it and built destroyers galore, if we could have persuaded Congress to give us the money. Nobody had any experience with this kind of war at all, and nobody could

Secretary of the Navy Josephus Daniels (third from right, others unidentified) aboard USS *Sylph* (third Navy ship of that name), 1919 (Harris & Ewing Collection, Library of Congress, Prints & Photographs Division).

be savage enough in his disposition to know what the Germans would do, and therefore to prepare for it..."[33]

There was a partial alternative that, due to the ultimate nature of the marine conflict, was far more useful to the United States than would have been any number of big-gun battleships. Four weeks before the epic Battle of Jutland commenced, Navy Secretary Daniels anticipated a more immediate need for small, fast vessels capable of a variety of missions, and, as *The New York Times* reported, "the Secretary announces that the department has approved a plan to mobilize the motor power boats owned by Americans for patrol purposes."[34] The Naval Appropriations Act of 24 May 1916 made it official. Ultimately the Navy would conscript 1,597 civilian vessels,[35] of which nearly a third were yachts, motor yachts and motor boats. They would serve along both coasts

George W.C. Drexel's steam yacht *Veglia*, commissioned USS *Alcedo* (SP-166), off New York City, August 1917. The topmasts have been removed for her wartime configuration (NH 57785 courtesy the Naval History & Heritage Command Photographic Dept.).

and the Caribbean and both sides of the Atlantic in various capacities including going head to head with German U-boats.

On 5 November 1917, newspaper publisher George W.C. Drexel's 275 foot, 981-ton yacht *Veglia*, commissioned USS *Alcedo* (SP-166) just over three months earlier, flagship of the North Sea Patrol Squadron, fell prey to a torpedo from Oberleutnant zur See Ernst Steindorff's UC-71. She sank in eight minutes and became the first American warship lost in the war.[36]

Custom tailored suits and gleaming brightwork were about to give way to bell bottom trousers and hulls of Navy gray. Less than seven months before UC-71 sent *Alcedo* to the bottom, *The Brooklyn Daily Eagle* observed the tenuous situation that presented itself but still managed to sound a note of hope:

> When shining brass and ivory white give way to the dull gray of warships on yachts..., when upholstery and silverware are stored and guns are brought on board, the world gets some idea of how little we shall have to depend on the Navy's fighting ships for a deep sea patrol along the Atlantic coast.... [A] junior navy of power boats is shown to be available for guns that can sink a submarine and for steady work in hunting the German terrors if these appear off our coast.[37]

At the outbreak of the war there was precious little in the surface arsenal to counter the U-boat threat other than eyes and ears. The existing numbers of armed vessels could, in practice, only threaten a surfaced submarine. There was no sonar, crude underwater hydrophones were unreliable, and small depth bombs truly were a hit-or-miss affair.

Q-ship (U-boat decoy) schooner *Robert H. McCurdy*, 1918 (NH 46475 courtesy the Naval History & Heritage Command Photographic Dept.).

Despite Secretary Daniels' ideal to acquire only vessels of one hundred feet and longer, capable of making 26 knots, and able to mount at least a single 3-pounder gun,[38] the Navy snapped up pretty much anything that was not commercially critical, mostly for assignment to section patrol (SP). The little sailing sloop *Eliza Hayward* (SP-1414) could at least operate as a training vessel out of Norfolk, Virginia. The same task went to the 1899-built, 117½-foot, 118-ton, ketch-rigged auxiliary schooner USS *Anemone IV* (SP-1290). Acquired under a free lease 3 October 1917 at Fort Townsend, Washington, she did not have far to go. Though never actually commissioned, the Navy assigned her to the Naval Training Station, Seattle. The three-masted schooner *Helvetia* (SP-3096) and four-masted schooner *Robert H. McCurdy* (SP-3157) found their calling as U-boat decoy ships. In theory, a U-boat would surface to use its deck gun and not waste a torpedo on what appeared to be an easy target and would itself become easy prey to a lurking American submarine. No U-boats took the bait.[39]

USS *Tech Jr.* (SP-1761) might only be a 20-foot motor boat, but she could make a dandy navy yard taxi or dispatch boat, as could USS *Itty E* (SP-952) at 25 feet and an alacritous 35 knots. The 58-foot *Get There* (SP-579) did just that, operating as an admiral's barge in New York Harbor. H.P. Davidson's *Shuttle* (SP-3572) lived up to her name in naval service, shuttling personnel between the Washington Navy Yard and ordnance facilities at Indian Head, Maryland, and Machodoc Creek, Virginia. USS *A-1* (SP-1370) was a 31-foot-long houseboat that kept watch off Southern California.[40]

The Richards' motorboat *Get There*, 1916 (NH 96133 courtesy the Naval History & Heritage Command Photographic Dept.).

USS *Get There* (SP-579) alongside the battleship USS *Indiana* in New York Harbor, c. 1918 (NH 102949 courtesy the Naval History & Heritage Command Photographic Dept.).

Occasionally, however, the Board of Appraisal could be over hasty in its acquisitions. Case in point is USS *De Grasse* (ID-1217), acquired from J.L. Redmond, 7 June 1917, while she was still under construction by George Lawley and Son of Neponset, Massachusetts. At just over 81 feet long, the wood hull, steam turbine yacht was armed with one 3-pounder gun and one machine gun. Capable of 14½ knots, she looked to be a worthy asset. Trials at the Boston Navy Yard, however, proved her unfit for naval operations, and she was disarmed and returned to her owner four days before the Armistice.[41]

If *De Grasse* was a disappointment, the slightly longer, at 89¼ feet and displacing 340 tons USS *Hermes* had a far more glamorous career. Built in 1914 by W.F. Stone of Oakland, California, for German shipping company Jaluit Gesellschaft of Hamburg, the diesel auxiliary schooner was confiscated in Honolulu when the United States declared war on Germany. Though unarmed during her Great War service, she, and her complement of 31, under the command of Lieutenant John T. Diggs, were assigned anti-submarine patrol out of Pearl Harbor, Hawaii. Since any U-boat out there would have been woefully off course, and there wasn't much she could do if she found one, her primary duty, in reality, was cataloging the islands' bird species for the Biological Survey Commission in Washington, D.C. On 23 January 1919, *Hermes* was decommissioned and transferred to the Hawaiian Territorial Government. Nine months later, she found herself back in the Navy as a stores ship and general auxiliary vessel until sold, 21 October 1926, to the Lanikai Fish Company, who eponymously renamed her. *Lanikai* was sold three more times before being purchased in 1937 by Metro-Goldwyn-Mayer for a major role in the motion picture "The Hurricane," starring Dorothy Lamour and John Hall. For the next two years *Lanikai* served as the official MGM yacht. On 6 April 1939, the studio sold her to E.M. Grim of the Luzon Stevedoring Company of Manila, Philippine Islands, bringing *Lanikai* one step closer to serving in a second world war.[42]

Real life, however, is unlike a Hollywood movie in which the boring bits are skipped over to advance the story and keep the viewers' interest. Even in wartime, mundane routine, tedious duties and, throbbing engines that seemingly counted out each passing idle second far outnumbered the adrenaline rush of the call to General Quarters, the chest pounding blast from a fired deck gun, the excitement of spotting a thin periscope and its feather wake, or the near unbearable tension of navigating in a fog-obscured convoy when one could barely see the bow of one's own fragile yacht let alone the looming bulk of an escorted freighter which might have zigged when it should have zagged. Section patrol more often than not sailed in tandem with ennui. Most of the conscripted yachts provided eyes and ears that made any lurking U-boat skipper's job more difficult along the American Eastern Seaboard. How many enemy attacks were thwarted in the offing by the mere presence of section patrol vessels is impossible to know, but, despite the coverage, Kapitänleutnant Hans Rose's success prior to the American war declaration would be repeated.

The merchant U-boat *Deutschland* had already made two well-publicized, successful commercial runs to the then neutral port of Baltimore, Maryland, when she returned, unheralded, to the East Coast as the submarine cruiser SM U-151. It was the night of 28 May 1918, off New York City. Her captain, Korvettenkapitän Heinrich von Nostitz und Jänckendorff, could see the lights of Broadway from his conning tower. For three days, in sight of Fire Island, the U-boat trolled for undersea telegraph cables to cut. Earlier, she had laid a floating minefield in Delaware Bay. Now she was free for more direct hunting and on 2 June she sank three steamers and three schooners for a total of 14,518 tons. In the 94 days of U-151's patrol she had logged 10,915 miles and had sunk 23 ships of 61,000 tons in aggregate, plus another four ships of 10,000 or 12,000 tons from the mines she had sown.[43]

Undetectable by underwater microphones, mines were a particularly insidious form of passive attack. The only way to be certain a given passage was safe was to stream paravanes and sweep for the infernal devices. (Towed from the bow, paravanes would cut a submerged mine's anchor cable, sending it to the surface where it then could be destroyed.) The wood hull, steam yachts USS *Pawnee* (SP-699) (ex–*Monoloa II* and the Navy's third USS *Pawnee*) and USS *Seneca* (SP-427) were outfitted with the necessary sweep gear and went to work in the spring of 1917 in the First and Third Naval Districts[44], respectively. The 150 foot, 157-ton, 18-knot *Seneca* was the senior of those two, having been built in 1888, 10 years before the Spanish-American War. The 130-foot, 302-ton steam yacht USS *Sylvia* (with no SP number), however, was the oldest of the champagne fleet. Built by A. Stephan & Sons of Glasgow, Scotland, in 1882, she patrolled off Key West, Florida, in the Spanish-American War. She repeated her performance, this time off Norfolk, Virginia, 27 years later, standing guard against a different European enemy. The 101-foot USS *Elfrida* (SP-988), built by Harlan & Hollingsworth of Wilmington, Delaware, was another Spanish-American War veteran who was called back to serve her country. She was assigned section patrol in the Fifth Naval District. All four did their job apparently without incident.[45]

Expectation of incidents on the West Coast, other than tangling with a whale, had

Screw yacht USS *Sylvia* at anchor, c. 1898 (L45–272.02.02 courtesy the Naval History & Heritage Command Photographic Dept.).

USS *Bayocean*, summer 1918 (NH 100108 courtesy the Naval History & Heritage Command Photographic Dept.).

to have been next to zero. Nevertheless, anything was possible. Built in Portland, Oregon, in 1917, and prophetically named *Patrol*, the 120-foot auxiliary schooner joined the Navy almost immediately. Commissioned USS *Rainier* (with no SP number) and armed with two 4" guns, she was ordered south to patrol off Southern California and Baja, Mexico. USS *Bayocean* (ID 2640) was a wood-hull, diesel-powered yacht that spent her civilian life as a taxi from Bayocean, Oregon (the Atlantic City of the West coast), to Portland. After being acquired by the Navy, she remained in familiar waters while on patrol. Originally built in 1897 for F.S. Fowler of New York City, USS *Vergana* (SP-519) was a steel-hull, auxiliary schooner. Heeding Horace Greeley's advice, she eventually went west to sunny California, purchased by Hollywood writer-director Wilbert Melville of Los Angeles. *Vergana* next headed north, purchased by stationer and printer Charles H. Crocker of San Francisco, where, upon donning Navy gray, she remained on patrol assignment for the duration.[46]

Perhaps taking her cue from the Confederate tug CSS *Teaser* and its observation balloon, USS *Mohican* took on a hydrogen kite balloon to peek over the usual horizon and thereby expand her visible search area for lurking, surfaced U-boats. Built in 1890, as the steam yacht *Lady Godiva*, by Laird Brothers of Scotland, her name was *Mohican* when the Navy acquired her under a free lease from Robert Perkins of New York City. She was renamed SP-117 in April 1918 to avoid confusion with the still in commission, 1883-built steam sloop-of-war USS *Mohican*. The 144-foot armed yacht sported two 6-pounders and two machine guns should she spot her quarry.[47] To some extent this balloon tactic continued into the Second World War with the use of Goodyear blimps to provide eyes over merchant convoys. Although *Mohican*, and 25 years later the blimp, provided some comfort to the merchant sailors that they were being watched over, it was far more practical to find an effective way to locate a submerged submarine.

Eyes over the surface were one thing, but submarines still could effectively hide beneath the waves. There, one needed ears. In 1912, Reginald A. Fessenden, working for the Submarine Signal Company of Boston, Massachusetts, designed an underwater transducer (hydrophone) that could listen for the sound generated by a submerged U-boat's propeller. Work also advanced in Europe and America on an echo ranging system (ASDIC or Sonar) that could locate submerged vessels themselves. French physicist Paul Langevin demonstrated the first such system in 1918, but the first one that allowed searching from a moving vessel was not tested until 1919.[48] Clara B. Stoker's 211-foot steam yacht USS *California* (SP-249, ex–*Hauoli*) spent her war service on section patrol and ferrying passengers to and from convoys in the Third Naval District. The Navy changed her back to her original name on 18 February 1918, and, just under a year later USS *Hauoli* was placed at the disposal of Thomas Alva Edison as a test bed for his research on hydrophonic detection of submerged submarines.[49]

The 157½-foot, 375-ton USS *Aramis* (SP-418) was built for Goodrich Rubber Company vice president Arthur Hudson Marks in 1916 and was one of the first yachts outfitted with a marine diesel engine. Initially she was assigned net patrol duty in the Third Naval District, but on 9 January 1918 *Aramis* was reassigned to New London, Connecticut, to conduct underwater listening tests of the new "K-Tubes" under the direction of Lieutenant Commander Chester W. Nimitz, future fleet admiral. She did this until running into a submerged debris field the last day of February and breaking off a screw blade. While undergoing repairs, Elmer A. Sperry (the inventor himself) came aboard to recalibrate the yacht's gyrocompass. After repairs and refit, *Aramis* returned to patrolling off New York harbor. On 13 August she acquired a U-boat contact on her K-Tubes, but propeller and engine noise from her companion USS *Hauoli* drowned out the signal and the U-boat escaped.[50]

The oil-fired 146½-foot USS *Gem* (SP-41) was involved in a different, more passive, approach to the U-boat problem. From 12 December 1917 she was primarily engaged in camouflage defense research. Other research assignments included testing colloidal fuel (pulverized coal) and the Bates Automatic Course Indicator, work that continued until she was returned to her owner, William Ziegler, Jr., in January 1919.[51]

In a few instances the Navy acquired the yachtsman as well as his yacht. One can reasonably expect that the crew took somewhat better care of their vessel when her owner retained command. James W. Aker of New York City was commissioned an ensign in the United States Naval Reserve Force. He went active with his 124-foot yacht, USS *Florence* (SP-173, ex–*Quickstep*) in April 1917, when he lent her to the Navy on a free lease. After wartime service patrolling the Third Naval District, *Florence* was decommissioned 22 February 1919 and returned to her owner.[52]

Lieutenant Maxwell Wyeth, USNRF, lent his 140⅓-foot yacht USS *Emerald* (SP-177, ex–*Emrose*) to the Navy on 23 July 1917. Owner and yacht were assigned section patrol in the Fourth Naval District. One month after the Armistice *Emerald* was returned to her owner, who was awarded the newly established medal, the Navy Cross, "For distinguished service in the line of his profession as commanding officer of the yacht *Emerald*, owned by Lieutenant Wyeth and placed by him at the disposal of the Government upon the declaration of war. Under his command the *Emerald* was one of the most efficient boats of the fourth naval district, performing very strenuous work on patrol, convoy, and in mine sweeping duty."[53]

William Kissam Vanderbilt II, Lieutenant (Jg), USNRF, retained command of his yacht USS *Tarantula* (SP-124), the Navy's second of that name. Both were assigned

Motor yacht *Tarantula*, dressed with flags, 1912 (NH 82946 courtesy Naval History & Heritage Command Photographic Dept.).

to the Third Naval District, until he was reassigned on 1 October 1917. That was the last time he would walk the decks of his beloved 129-foot steamer. Just 15 days before the Armistice, *Tarantula* came off second best in a collision with Royal Holland Lloyd Line's SS *Frisia*, and she sank eight miles off Fire Island, New York.[54]

For armed yachts operating off the Atlantic Seaboard, the submarine danger did not only originate from Berlin. Often used to escort United States' subs on sea trials, section patrol yachts and their charges occasionally operated a little too closely, and the result could be a lot more than scraped paint. Operating in the Third Naval District, on 5 October 1918, the steam yacht USS *Mary Alice* (SP-397, ex–*Oneta*, ex–*Bernice*) was accidentally rammed and sunk by submarine O-13 she was escorting. Ultimately, however, 13 proved a lucky number for the yacht's crew, all of whom were rescued by the submarine.[55] USS *Felicia* (SP-642) was built in 1898, a year after *Mary Alice*. Though now in U.S. Navy livery, a coat of gray paint could not completely obscure her previous civilian luxury. Deckhouses and decks were of polished mahogany. The after deckhouse social hall was "a handsomely furnished apartment." Five guest rooms and the owner's stateroom were ivory and gold beneath the gray. Her furnishings for entertaining included an electric ice maker and an electric piano. Doubtless the piano was removed in the course of her military conversion. History seems silent on the fate of the ice machine. On 30 August 1918, in heavy fog off Montauk Point, Long Island, New York,

Racing yacht *Pilgrim*, 1893, before her many modifications (Detroit Publishing Co. Collection, Library of Congress, Prints & Photographs Division).

Felicia played host to an unwanted guest when she collided with a friendly submarine. As a result, the yacht was laid up for repairs for the duration and finally was sold on 25 March 1920.[56]

The 120-foot, 98-ton USS *Pilgrim* (SP-1204) wasn't so much a pioneer as she was a living history of yacht propulsion. *Pilgrim* started life in 1893 as a sailing yacht, designed for a Boston racing syndicate to compete for the America's Cup. She lost to *Vigilant* to represent the United States that year, but the latter went on to defeat the British *Valkyrie*. Sold in 1894, her new owner Lamont G. Burnham, Esquire, of Boston, converted *Pilgrim* to a steam auxiliary. In 1907, Burnham sold the yacht to the Boston Floating Hospital, a charitable organization, founded by the Rev. Rufus B. Tobey to provide a fresh sea air, low anxiety environment in which volunteer physicians could administer to disadvantaged mothers and children. The Floating Hospital for Children continues to operate to this day as an adjunct to Tufts University. Sold twice more, in 1913 Hugh C. Jones of Beaufort, North Carolina, converted her to gasoline power. In 1916, he sold *Pilgrim* to the decidedly unglamorous Beaufort Fish Scrap and Oil Company. It was from them that the Navy leased the yacht for section patrol in the Fifth Naval District. After the war, *Pilgrim* went back to her owner to engage in menhaden fishing. Two more owners later, *Pilgrim* was abandoned in 1935 and eventually was towed to Harkers Point, Harkers Island, North Carolina, filled with concrete and sunk as a breakwater.[57]

Like *Pilgrim*, Wilson Marshall's 185 foot, three-masted auxiliary schooner *Atlantic* was built for speed. Launched in 1903, she briefly attained a top speed of 20 knots during her sea trials. In 1905 she took up the Transatlantic Kaiser Cup challenge and won

Wilson Marshall's steam auxiliary schooner *Atlantic II*, 1903 (NH 95757 courtesy the Naval History & Heritage Command Photographic Dept.).

handily, making the 3,006 miles crossing from Sandy Hook, New Jersey, to Lizard Light, Cornwall, United Kingdom, in 12 days, 4 hours, 1 minute and 19 seconds. The record stood for 75 years. The win itself turned out to be a double victory over Kaiser Bill and his "$5,000 solid gold trophy." Both *Atlantic*, commissioned USS *Atlantic II* (SP-651) and Marshall's son Wilson Marshall, Jr., a lieutenant in the 22nd Aero Squadron, went off to war. The yacht had a rather uneventful service as a net guard ship and a submarine chaser tender in the Fifth Naval District before eventually serving in the Second World War with the United States Coast Guard. Marshall's son, however, did not survive the war, killed in a crash on Salisbury Plain, England, on 27 April 1918. As a result, Marshall's Kaiser Cup trophy became a hated reminder of why his son had died, so he donated it to raise funds for the Red Cross. The trophy was auctioned off, re-donated and re-auctioned several times, before, at a Red Cross rally held at the Metropolitan Opera House in New York City, anyone who donated five dollars could come on stage to witness the cup's destruction. The mangled remains were then sent to a jeweler to be melted down and sold to raise yet more money for the Red Cross. Upon testing the metal for purity, the jeweler found it to be almost pure—pure pewter—worth about 35 dollars. Kaiser Bill's shabby ruse, however, had backfired because the fools gold cup had ended up raising $125,000 for the Red Cross.[58]

※ ※ ※ ※

As the chorus to George M. Cohan's 1917, immensely popular song went, "Over there, over there. / Send the word, send the word over there / That the Yanks are coming, the Yanks are coming..." so too did the Navy Department know that as important as it was to secure American territorial waters, wars are not won by defensive measures alone. Force had to be projected "over there," if America and her allies were to achieve victory.

In 1899 Trenor Luther Park took delivery of his brand new, 186 foot, 390-ton, steam auxiliary, 3-masted topsail schooner *Sultana* for a honeymoon trip around the world with his new bride Julia Hunt. The vessel's size, hundred tons of coal capacity and fresh water condensers made her ideal for deep water travel, and no expense was spared on her fittings and accommodations: interior paneled with quartered oak, decorated in Italian Renaissance style in cream, gold, and blue. In 1907, Mary Harriman, widow of railroad tycoon and naturalist Edward Henry Harriman, purchased *Sultana* from the Park estate. In May 1917 she turned it over to the Navy on a free lease. USS *Sultana* (SP-134), now armed with four 3" guns and manned by 62 souls, served in the United States patrol Squadron out of Brest, France. She was returned to Mrs. Harriman on 17 February 1919.[59]

Eight years before *Sultana's* launch, the Cleveland Shipbuilding Company of Cleveland, Ohio, completed the schooner-rigged steam yacht *Wadena* for financier Jeptha Homer Wade II, whose grandfather Jeptha Homer Wade founded Western Union. This yacht also was designed and furnished to cruise the world while, accommodation wise, her owner's family would never have to leave home. The owner's stateroom, on the starboard side, was paneled with elaborately carved mahogany. It was furnished with a double bed, commodious bureau and closet, reading desk and washstand, and a porcelain-lined bathtub, with hot and cold taps of course, nestled beneath the floor. Perhaps hinting of the yacht's naval service to come, his daughter's stateroom, done in white mahogany and blue tapestries, on the port side, was reached by passing the gun case, which was "well filled with cutlasses, revolvers, rifles and shotguns, which may come in handy down in the South Seas." Acquired by the Navy on 25 May 1917, USS *Wadena* (SP-158) added two 3" guns, two .30 caliber machine guns and a rack of "depth bombs" to her arsenal before heading, not to the South Seas, but to convoy American-built submarine chasers to France en route to joining the United States Patrol Squadron operating out of Gibraltar. She was decommissioned in May 1920 and sold that July 12.[60]

USS *Isabel* (SP-521), built in 1917 for John N. Willys, as in Jeeps, earned her USS designation almost before she slid down the ways at her launching. Her design specifications included building in qualities that would make her quickly adaptable to naval service. Her twin Parson's turbines and twin screws were capable of driving her 245-foot length, displacing 930 tons, at nearly 29 knots. Despite her obvious desirability, the Navy expressed zero interest in the yacht until after war was declared, then the Navy paid $611,553 for the nascent warship. Armed with four 3" guns and four torpedo tubes, USS *Isabel* was the only converted yacht commissioned as a destroyer. Under Lieutenant Commander Harry E. Shoemaker, *Isabel* left for France, 28 January 1918, on coastal convoy duty, during which, on four separate occasions, she encountered German U-boats. In company with the destroyer USS *Reid* (DD-21) on 18 March, the two ships were credited at the time with sinking a U-boat. Under a new captain, *Isabel* continued convoy escort duty for the duration. 14 May 1919 saw her cruising the Mississippi River from New Orleans to St. Louis, Missouri, and back to further Navy recruiting efforts. *Isabel's* next assignment posted her, on 18 September, to Rockaway Beach, Long Island, New York, as tender to the seaplane flotilla that included Curtiss flying boat NC-4, the first airplane to cross the Atlantic Ocean, just four months earlier. The Navy decommissioned *Isabel* at the Philadelphia Navy Yard on 30 April 1920, but that would not be the end of the yacht's naval career.[61]

J.P. Morgan's 304 foot, 1600-ton *Corsair* (SP-159), his third yacht of that name, and Colonel Oliver Hazard Payne's slightly smaller 302-foot, 1823-ton *Aphrodite* (SP-135) were in at the start of America's involvement in more than just name. The two converted yachts were two of the 22 vessels escorting the 14 transports of the first convoy carrying the first troops of the American Expeditionary Force to France. Each yacht was armed with four 3"/50 caliber guns. The heavily escorted convoy was broken into four groups, the first three of which departed New York on 14 June 1917 and the fourth three days later. USS *Corsair*, assigned to Group No. 1, in company with the armored cruiser USS *Seattle*, the auxiliary cruiser USS *De Kalb* and destroyers USS *Wilkes*, *Terry* and *Roe* protected the transports *Saratoga*, *Havana*, *Tenadores* and *Pastores*. USS *Aphrodite* joined the scout cruiser USS *Birmingham*, the cruiser transport USS *Henderson*, and the destroyers USS *Fanning*, *Burrows* and *Lamson* to escort the transports *Momus*, *Antilles* and *Lenape* of Group No. 2. All of the heavily protected convoy groups safely arrived in France.[62]

It was not unusual for several of the converted yachts to operate together. Under normal circumstances it would have occasioned a gala regatta when *Margaret* (SP-527, ex–*Marjorie*, ex–*Eugenia*), *Helenita* (SP-210), *May* (SP-164), *Rambler* (SP-211), *Utowana* (SP-951) and *Wenonah* (SP-165) got together. The circumstance, however, was not normal on 4 November 1917, and each of those yachts now bore "USS" in front of her name. France needed more than the American Expeditionary Force's doughboys if they were to stand against the German U-boat threat, and American industry geared

USS *Wenonah* in heavy seas en route from Bermuda to the Azores, November 1917. Photographed from USS *Margaret* in convoy. At least bad weather, an intractable foe above the waves, also kept the U-boats at bay (NH 48479 courtesy the Naval History & Heritage Command Photographic Dept.).

up to address the problem. On that day in November, each of the now armed yachts had in tow a new 110 foot, newly designed submarine chaser destined for the French Navy. Though of the latest design, those doughty vessels had insufficient range to make the crossing under their own power, and their tows had their own problems. *Helenita*, *Margaret*, *Utowana* and *May* all experienced mechanical difficulties which kept the flotilla from reaching Hamilton, Bermuda until 9 November. For now, that was as far as *Helenita* and *Utowana* got. The two disabled yachts were replaced by the converted yachts *Artemis* (SP-593, ex–*Cristina*), *Cythera* (SP-575) and *Lydonia* (SP-700). When the voyage resumed, *May* had *Wenonah* under tow. Before long, *Margaret* broke down yet again and had to be towed by *Cythera*. The sea state did not make things any easier, but despite the stormy passage all of the vessels reached Horta, Fayal Island, the Azores, on 5 December.[63] Although this episode demonstrated the value of utilizing converted civilian vessels in order to free up limited naval resources, it also pointed out the limitations to pushing these luxury craft beyond their original, more glamorous than strenuous, designed purpose.

Helenita and *May* were assigned back to the States for section patrol duty off the Atlantic Seaboard and in the Caribbean. *May* proved her value on 19 August 1918 when she was dispatched in response to the distress call from SS *Westward Ho*, which had been torpedoed and abandoned by her crew. The offending U-boat had departed before finishing the job, and *May* found the merchantman still afloat, despite the gaping hole in her bow. Lieutenant Thomas Blau, USNRF, led a salvage party aboard, which managed to stabilized the ship and start the pumps. *May*'s captain, Lieutenant Commander Charles Clifford Windsor, then ordered *Westward Ho* taken under tow, stern first. They proceeded thus for 315 miles to safely deliver both ship and her cargo. Both Blau and Windsor subsequently were awarded the Navy Cross for their efforts.[64]

Margaret would go on anti-submarine patrols out of the Azores when she was not laid up for the repairs. Numerous breakdowns continued to plague her skipper, Lieutenant Commander Frank Jack Fletcher, who would go on to command an aircraft carrier task force in the Second World War. *Rambler* operated out of the Azores before transferring to the Breton Patrol out of Brest, France.[65]

Lydonia and *Wenonah* performed convoy escort duty between Gibraltar and Bizerte, Tunisia. On 8 May 1918, in concert with British destroyer HMS *Basilisk*, *Lydonia* attacked and sank UB-70 in a 15 minute attack after the U-boat torpedoed the British SS *Ingleside*. For this action, Lieutenant Commander R.P. McCullough, commanding *Lydonia*, was awarded the Navy Cross. *Wenonah* too had her run in with Germany's sharks of steel, though the outcome was not nearly so satisfying. On 23 July 1918, while escorting a convoy from Gibraltar to Genoa, Italy, one of her charges, SS *Messidor* was torpedoed and sunk. After dropping a depth charge, more to scare away the U-boat than as an actual attack, *Wenonah* attended to rescue operations for the survivors before taking station astern of the convoy. Early the next morning lookouts spotted a flare up ahead, and the yacht raced forward to find SS *Rutherglen* settling by the stern after being torpedoed. *Wenonah* made an attack but her depth charge failed to explode. She next turned to rescuing survivors and took 38 aboard. That night *Wenonah* made another run at the enemy with another dud depth charge. At this point each merchant captain seemed to decide for himself the safest course to avoid further U-boat attack. The resulting chaos and danger of collision became a greater enemy than any lurking German submarine. Tension remained high even after order was restored. Late that night and again early the next morning *Wenonah* fired her 3" gun at a porpoise masquerading as a surfacing U-boat. After the war the Navy transferred *Wenonah* to the United States Coast and Geodetic Survey for service on the West Coast. On 15 May 1929, she passed into private hands. Renamed *Stranger* and subsequently *Blue Water*, a private citizen acting for the Canadian Government circumvented American neutrality and quietly purchased her for the Canadian Navy and HMCS *Wolf* was commissioned on 2 October 1940.[66]

Artemis and *Cythera* stayed in the Mediterranean Theater. *Cyrthera* survived the war and was returned to her owner William L. Harkness on 19 March 1919. On the last day of December 1941, she would again answer her nation's call to duty in a Second World War. Reclassified PY-26 (Patrol Yacht) she entered service on 3 March 1942. Just two months later, while coming to the aid of the torpedoed Soviet tanker *Ashkhabad*, off North Carolina, two more torpedoes from Siegfried von Forstner's U-402 found their mark. *Cythera* sank before her depth charges could be made safe. The torpedo devastation and ensuing detonation of her depth charges left only two crewmen to be rescued. They were taken aboard the U-boat and spent the remainder of the war in Germany.[67]

Although assigned to North African convoy escort duty, the problems that dogged the submarine chaser regatta of November-December 1917 continued to plague *Artemis* and her captain, Lieutenant Commander Stanton L. Hazard. The repairs from that episode kept her in Gibraltar until 28 January 1918 when she took station with a convoy assembling off Bizerte. The next day the crew went to General Quarters when Kapitänleutnant Wilhelm Canaris' SM U-34 torpedoed British steamer SS *Maizar*. The U-boat escaped and *Artemis* picked up 16 of *Maizar's* survivors. Canaris eventually would rise to the rank of Admiral, and, in 1935, he became head of the Abwehr, the Third Reich's military intelligence service.

Condenser problems sent *Artemis* limping to Algiers for repairs, but her engines failed and she had to be towed in. The balky condensers continued to plague the yacht,

USS *Cythera*, March 1942. She was torpedoed and sunk two months later (NH 83392 courtesy the Naval History & Heritage Command Photographic Dept.).

sending her to Gibraltar for repairs between breaks for convoy escort duty. On 2 June 1918 her captain, as of 29 March, 1st Lieutenant Charles Frederick Howell, USCG, received word that his ship's name had been changed three months earlier to USS *Arcturus*. The new name did not bring her any more luck with her power plant, which failed during a gale just five days before the Armistice. His ship taking on water from an unknown leak in the engineering spaces, dead in the water and in danger of foundering in the storm-tossed sea, her third captain, Lieutenant Frederick William Maennale, USNRF, ordered his crew to stand by to abandon ship. The radioman sent out an S.O.S. and the ship's position. But Lieutenant Maennale was in no hurry to lose his command, and the men continued to fight back the impending doom. Gradually, *Arcturus*' luck changed. By the time the cable ship *Amber* and the tug *Crucis* were able to rendezvous with the stricken yacht her crew had effected sufficient repairs to restart her engines and make it, under her own power, to Lisbon the next day. In December *Arcturus* started for home and again her condensers failed. On Christmas Day USS *Surveyor* took the yacht in tow and they made New York on the 28th. After decommissioning on 5 May 1919 and transfer to the U.S. Coast and Geodetic Survey, for eight months, she resumed her original name and passed through three owners before ending up at the Tropical Fruit and Steamship Company of Honduras. While in their employ *Artemis* burned and sank in February 1927.[68]

The collision danger that *Wenonah* found herself in when her nervous convoy scattered under a persistent U-boat threat was very real and potentially deadly. USS *Wakiva II* (SP-160) had been a carefree, palatial world traveler for her owner, major Standard Oils shareholder and world renowned harness racing horse breeder, Lamon Vanderburgh Harkness. The Navy acquired her from his son and heir Harry on 20 July 1917. The nearly 240-foot yacht, with a main battery of four 3" guns, had already established herself as an effective U-boat hunter with one probable kill on 28 November 1917 and in subsequent encounters driving off the surfaced predators before they could claim one of the yacht's charges. On 21 May 1918, under her third captain, Lieutenant Commander Ezra Griffin Allen, USN, *Wakiva II* was escorting an eastbound convoy from Brest, France, in dense fog. It was only by listening to the various whistles of the ships in convoy that the ships' captains could keep position. Stress was high and the likelihood of error was even higher. At 0310 on the 22nd, aboard *Wakiva II* the whistle from SS *Wabash* sounded too close aboard. Before the former's lookouts could react, the screech of rending steel drowned out all other sounds as *Wabash's* bow tore a mortal wound down to her keel into her escort's starboard quarter, just abaft the mainmast. Two of the yacht's crew were killed outright. The ships ground together then pulled apart, and *Wakiva II* began to settle by the stern. Several of her crew, who were not regular Navy, sprang into action, heedless of their own safety. Chief Gunner's Mate Oliver P. Cooper ran to safe the depth charges on her stern. Electrician 2c Charles E. Kirkpatrick risked going down with his ship by staying in the radio room sending out an S.O.S. until the last possible moment. Chief Boatswain's Mate Thomas Olson rigged out the motor whaleboat, then, with the captain, made sure everyone alive was up on deck. Machinist Mate 1c Charles A.A. Smith stayed below to start the pumps until he realized it was futile. The yacht's boats pulled clear 20 minutes after the impact, and six minutes later *Wakiva II* was gone. *Wabash* rescued the survivors.[69]

✣ ✣ ✣ ✣

The depth bomb, or depth charge, was the only real weapon against a submerged enemy submarine, but knowing where and when to deploy it was largely guesswork. Occasionally, however, it could pose a greater danger to the hunter than to the hunted. This was especially true of the earlier, mechanically detonated devices in which the firing pistol was tethered to a float by a line equal to the depth at which the charge was thereby set to explode. Extreme care was required because, once the charge was armed, a good yank on the lanyard would be enough to set it off.

In 1914, Pusey & Jones of Wilmington, Delaware, built the 243 foot, 1,265-ton steam yacht *Nokomis II* for Horace E. Dodge. The Navy acquired her on 1 June 1917 and dropped the Roman numeral.[70] Chief Carpenter's Mate E. Artimas Chastain, aboard USS *Nokomis* (SP-609), was aware of the depth charge danger when he literally dove into action to save his ship and comrades, earning the Navy Cross. His citation reads:

> For extraordinary heroism and devotion to duty while serving on the U.S.S. Nokomis. On the night of January 11, 1918, while that vessel was at sea a wave broke over the stern, smashing the depth bomb launching device. The bomb was hurled on board and the bomb float which was detached started forward in the wash water. Chastain threw himself down on the float holding it and remaining buried in water until assistance reached him, when the bomb was secured, this preventing the bomb from firing and detonating the other bombs.[71]

Nokomis survived that incident and the war in the Breton Patrol Squadron, being reassigned as a survey ship in the Caribbean until she was laid up in 1938. The yacht was recommissioned in 1942 for service in the Second World War, but in 1944 the Navy determined *Nokomis* could better serve that war effort as a source of scrap steel.[72]

Aboard USS *Christabel* (SP-162) a similar action by reserve officer Ensign Daniel A.J. Sullivan garnered him the Medal of Honor:

> For extraordinary heroism as an officer of the U.S.S. Christobel [*sic*] in conflict with an enemy submarine on May 21, 1918, when, as a result of the explosion of a depth bomb dropped near

Converted steam yacht USS *Nokomis* (SP-609), 1916 (Harris & Ewing Collection, Library of Congress, Prints & Photographs Division).

the submarine, the Christobel was so badly shaken that a number of depth charges which had been set for firing were thrown about the deck and there was imminent danger that they would explode. Ensign Sullivan immediately fell on the bombs and succeeded in securing them, thus saving the ship from disaster which would eventually have involved great loss of life.[73]

On 17 December 1917, in the middle of a raging storm in the Bay of Biscay, lookouts aboard the 200 foot, 600-ton armed yacht USS *Remlik* (SP-157, ex–*Candace*) spotted a surfaced U-boat. The yacht's captain, Lieutenant Commander I.C. Johnson, ordered General Quarters and immediately rang up her top speed of 14 knots while changing course to intercept the German. Lookouts aboard the U-boat spotted the approaching hunter, and the submarine submerged before *Remlik* could open fire. Now, the storm was in control of the situation. The heavy sea prevented the U-boat for getting a torpedo firing solution, but it also prevented *Remlik* from making a depth charge run against her adversary. At maximum shaft revolutions, the yacht could only make two knots against the gale. The U-boat escaped in the relative calm below the surface. Above, it was anything but calm for *Remlik*. A following wave crashed over the fantail, smashing a depth charge box and sending an armed bomb rolling about the storm-tossed deck. Chief Boatswain's Mate John MacKenzie reflexively sprang into action and sat on the errant depth charge until his ship could be brought about to allow a more permanent solution. For his selfless action preventing an explosion that likely would have sent *Remlik* to the bottom with all hands, MacKenzie also was awarded the Medal of Honor.[74]

The surface gun duel that *Remlik* attempted was less hit-or-miss than a depth charge run, but a U-boat was a small target which could pull the plug and dive at any moment. The upside for the hunter, however, was this created a brief window of from 45 to 90 seconds during which the U-boat could not shoot back.[75]

On 15 August 1917, Lieutenant Commander Howard H.J. Benson, commanding the steam yacht USS *Noma* (SP-131), reported the first actual fire fight with any German submarine:

> At 2: 17 P.M. in position Lat. 47° 40' N. Long. 5° 05' W. sighted a suspicious object bearing about 245° (per standard compass), distance about 6,000 yards. Object was made out to be a submarine on the surface heading about 320° psc. A discharge was being emitted by the submarine, very much like smoke and was very misleading. Submarine was evidently charging her batteries. At 2:20 P.M. went to "general quarters" and closed in on submarine. At 2:24 P.M. opened fire with port battery, distance about 4,000 yards. Fired ten shots. Submarine fired three shots at this ship, one striking about 500 yards ahead of the ship and the other two shots well over and on the quarter. At 2:27 P.M. the submarine submerged. Proceeded to vicinity of submarine, but did not see her again. At 2:35 P.M. resumed our course.[76]

Six days earlier, the 1899 converted steam yacht USS *Vedette* (SP-163, ex–*Virginia*), a second *Vedette* in the Navy, went to General Quarters and raced to attack the U-boat that had just torpedoed her charge SS *Hundvaago*. *Vedette* never got to fire her guns as, obscured by the sinking merchantman, the U-boat escaped. A day later *Vedette* did fire on a suspicious vessel in the distance. Luckily, she missed, as her target turned out to be a French patrol boat.[77]

John Diedrich Spreckels' million dollar, 226 foot, 589-ton steam yacht *Venetia*, "one of the most palatial and luxurious yachts that has plied Pacific waters ... scene of many brilliant social functions" was acquired by the Navy on 4 August 1917. USS *Venetia* (SP-431) transited the Panama Canal on 6 November for final outfitting of four 3' guns, machine guns and depth charge tracks at the Philadelphia Navy Yard. After towing a submarine chaser to France, *Venetia* assumed convoy duties. On 11 May 1918,

USS *Noma* making heavy rolls on World War I patrol. Note the depth charges on her fantail (NH 44876 courtesy the Naval History & Heritage Command Photographic Dept.).

lookouts aboard were startled to suddenly see a torpedo cross her bow then continue on to a fatal result, exploding in SS *Susette Fraisinette*. Her captain, Commander Lewis B. Porterfield, sounded General Quarters and searched over an hour for the enemy submarine, finally spotting UB-52 on the surface well away from the convoy. Her guns manned, *Venetia* drove at her full 13 knots to engage the U-boat. Alert to the approaching American, Oberleutnant zur See Launburg decided not to risk a surface gun duel and pulled the plug. *Venetia* switched gears and commenced a depth charge attack, dropping 13 bombs in the space of two hours. Launburg escaped—this time. Twelve days later, HM submarine H-4 came across UB-52 in the Adriatic Sea and sank her. On 4 April 1919, the Navy returned *Venetia* to her owner. The yacht subsequently passed to three more owners before a date at the breaker's yard in 1968. She saw no further military service[78]

On 10 May 1917, the U.S. Navy commissioned William Vincent Astor's 15-year-old yacht *Noma* and posted her owner, an ensign in the New York Naval Militia, as a junior officer in the yacht's 80 man complement. USS *Noma* left New York for Europe, on 9 June 1917, in company with armed yachts *Christabel*, *Harvard*, *Kanawha II*, *Sultana* and *Vedette*. Now in France, Ensign Astor was re-assigned as naval port officer at Royan

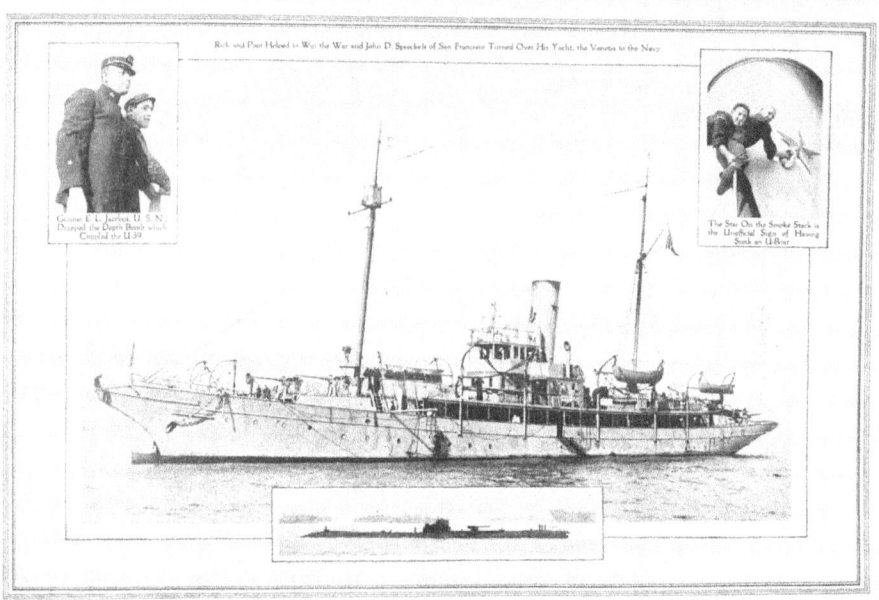

Newspaper clipping showing converted yacht USS *Venetia* with inset of the German submarine U-39 she was credited with disabling (NH 76700-KN courtesy Naval History & Heritage Command Photographic Dept.).

before being transferred again as a junior officer aboard the armed yacht USS *Aphrodite*. On New Year's Day 1918, Astor was promoted to Lieutenant (Jg). Seven months later, he made full lieutenant. Lieutenant Astor's final blue water assignment was unusual for an American naval officer. Instead of hunting U-boats he was to serve aboard the mine laying German submarine U-117, which was responsible for sinking or damaging 24 ships, totaling 58,304-tons, including damaging the 18,000-ton battleship USS *Minnesota*. Surrendered at the end of the war, her new assignment would be to raise money for bonds along the Atlantic coast. But first, she had to get there, in company with other surrendered U-boats, UB-88, UB-148, UC-97 and the submarine tender USS *Bushnell* (AS-2), which comprised the jokingly christened Ex-German Submarine Expeditionary Force.[79]

Over the next several years most of the Navy's yachts were transferred to other service, sold or returned to their owner. The 140-foot steam yacht USS *Onward* (SP-311), after patrolling the 5th Naval District, was transferred to the U.S. Coast and Geodetic Survey before finally being sold in April of 1921. Renamed *Thelma Phoebe* she became a rum runner until, two years later, she, and her quarter of a million dollars cargo of illegal booze, ran aground on Fishers Island off Sandy Hook, New York. By the time the Coast Guard arrived her cargo had been spirited away by the locals.[80]

The 1893-built, 185-foot steam yacht USS *Yankton* (ex–*Penelope*), after previously serving in the Spanish-American War and circling the globe with the Great White Fleet before taking up convoy escort duties out of Gibraltar, found herself still at war even after the Armistice. On 23 February 1919, Rear Admiral N.A. McCully flew his flag from *Yankton*'s masthead at Murmansk when he took command of American forces fighting the Bolsheviks in northern Russia. The effort failed and, after several months in England, the armed steam yacht returned to New York where she was decommissioned 27 February 1920 and sold over a year later in October. 1923 saw *Yankton* back in federal custody, albeit under less honorable circumstances, having been seized in New York with a cargo of illegal rum. Unlike what happened with *Thelma Phoebe*'s illicit cargo, there were no thirsty islanders to abscond with the goods. Eventually, *Yankton* took up more law-abiding commercial service until she was scrapped in 1930.[81]

✣ ✣ ✣ ✣

When textile industrialist and heir William Slater spent $300,000 for his 243-foot, 804-ton steam auxiliary three-masted bark *Eleanor* in 1894, she was the largest, most elegant yacht of her day. Tiffany & Company designed her luxurious interior. As noted earlier, several of the yachts included a small arms armory in their original fit. That was not good enough for Slater, who planned to spend a year and a half circumnavigating the globe with his wife and children aboard. To ensure their safety should they encounter pirates, he had the Colt Armory install three 800-rounds-per-minute electric Gatling guns on the deck. When the family left New London, Connecticut, that October, in addition to the ammunition for the machine guns, the yacht carried 75 cases of champagne.[82]

On 23 April 1917, the Navy leased her from her then owner, New England banker George F. Baker, Jr., and commissioned her USS *Harvard* (SP-209, ex–*Wacouta*, ex–*Eleanor*). She survived the war to go back to her owner, who eventually sold her to European commercial interests. Surviving a second world war, she was still working the waters around Greece as late as 1948.[83]

John D. Spreckels was less than thrilled when the Navy returned his yacht *Venetia*, and he did not sugar coat his displeasure. He claimed he would be out of pocket to the tune of $100,000 to restore his yacht to her original condition. The Navy counter offered $76,331.83. Spreckels took back his yacht, reserving the right to file suit for damages in the Court of Claims in Washington. Whether he considered the bad press such a lawsuit would inevitably bring him or he simply simmered down, he apparently took the Navy's offer, since there appears to be no record of such a legal action.[84]

The war over, it once again was time for the Navy to stand down. After all, this had been the war to end war.

6

World War Again

SALE OF U.S. NAVAL VESSELS (Motor Boats and Yachts)—
Sealed proposals will be received at the bureau of Supplies and Accounts, Navy Department, Washington, D.C., until 12 o'clock noon, 27 August, 1919, when they will be publicly opened, for the purchase of the Motor Yacht ATLANTIS S.P. 40, now at New York; Motor Boat COYOTE S.P. 84, now at Chicago, Ill.; Steam Yacht SISTER S.P. 822, now at New Orleans, La.[1]

The Great War was over, the marauding U-boat was no longer a threat, and the German djinn had been forced back into its bottle. It followed that the Navy no longer needed, nor had the budget to support, the many civilian vessels it had drafted into the war effort, and the inevitable draw down could begin. A year later, the pendulum had swung so far in the opposite direction from war preparedness that the Navy Department was also advertising the desirability of converting small warships into civilian yachts. "In addition to gunboats, cruisers, yachts and other miscellaneous vessels which are now offered for sale, there are approximately one hundred fifty (150) submarine chasers.... The catalog emphasizes the adaptability of these boats for use as yachts."[2] By 1935 only two converted yachts, USS *Nokomis* (PY-6) and USS *Isabel* (PY-10) were still in commission,[3] although the aging USS *Mayflower* (PY-1 and former presidential yacht) would eventually be reacquired by the Navy for service in the next war.

After the global catastrophe of the World War, the consensus was that it was inconceivable there could be a next one. After the often misguided, self-serving and historically disastrous attempt at sorting out the immediate post-war and future global political situation in 1919, steps were taken to make war more difficult to pursue and more humane should it erupt regardless. Beginning with the Washington Naval Conference of 1921, there followed a series of international attempts, under Presidents Wilson, Coolidge, Harding and Hoover, to limit armaments and to make war itself a crime. As President Coolidge defined the problem:

> We have been attempting to relieve ourselves and the other nations from the old theory of competitive armaments. In spite of the arguments in favor of great military forces, no nation ever had an army large enough to guarantee it against attack in time of peace or to insure victory in time of war. No nation ever will. Peace and security are more likely to result from fair and honorable dealings, and mutual agreements for a limitation of armaments among nations, than by any attempt at competition in squadrons and battalions.... I can see no merit in any unnecessary expenditure of money to hire men to build fleets and carry muskets when international relations and agreements permit the turning of such resources into the making of good roads, the building of better homes, the promotion of education, and all the other arts of peace which minister to the advancement of human welfare.[4]

While the diplomats and officers argued about formulae for warship parity in aggregate tons displacement and caliber of guns, the civilian population was ready for those "good roads." There seemed to be a need for speed, as if one could run away from the recent horror. The Volstead Act, which introduced the age of Prohibition, ironically fueled the Roaring Twenties by adding a frisson of lawlessness that ramped up a general good time. The longer one partied, the further behind the war seemed to be. The generation of survivors was like a dog that has been leashed too long and is finally released to run. It was a great inflating bubble, which eventually would burst—but not quite yet. The need for speed had its partial expression in the boating arena. In addition to more powerful marine engines, such as the 300 horsepower Sterling Viking, many aircraft engines, like the 1917 Liberty L-12, could be adapted to marine use to create what amounted to a water-borne, shallow-draft sports car, generally 28 to 32 feet long, which might also speed a shipment of illicit spirits past local law enforcement. Alcohol wasn't the only business that was booming, so was business itself. As the stock market rose, many brokers with newfound wealth could move farther away from Wall Street, to the "country," where their suburban mansions could be connected to their office by a fast commuter yacht. These later craft typically ran to 75 feet long and up to 30 knots.[5]

Just as Henry Ford's assembly line made automobiles accessible and then ubiquitous in the 1920s, Christopher Columbus Smith, who built his first boat at age 13, started a boom in motor boating. Chris-Craft's sleek mahogany runabouts and cruisers became synonymous with the sport. "By 1936, the family cruiser had become the backbone of the U.S. motorboat industry. These cruisers would become the backbone of the World War II Auxiliary and Coast Guard Reserve small boat fleet."[6] But first, the

Christopher Columbus Smith at the helm of one of his Chris-Craft runabouts (courtesy Chris-Craft, Inc.).

population needed a bit of encouragement, as was given in an editorial that appeared in the April 1920 issue of *Motor Boating*:

> A great many more people would become owners of motor boats if the public could be brought to understand that the purchase of a motor boat of anything like sensible design and honest construction does not represent a mere expenditure of money but rather is a safe investment.... If you buy a house for $5,000—which used to be possible—live in it for five years and take reasonable care of it, the property will be worth as much, or practically as much, as it cost.... If you buy a motor boat ... for the same amount, use her every season for five years, put her into shape every spring and see that she is laid up properly in the fall, you can get nearly what she cost after five years pass.... With a boat of this kind you actually can have a summer home for your family, a place to entertain guests at a cost no more than that of a little bungalow.[7]

So long as the banks were solvent and the stock market was booming, and you weren't a farmer, miner, or factory worker, who could take issue with that? After all, this was a period of incredible growth as wartime industry switched full throttle to produce consumer goods. The gross national product of the United States rose from $70.2 billion in 1919 to $101.4 billion 10 years later (in 1929 dollars). In the same period, the number of households that owned a radio rose from 60,000 to 10,000,000, and the number of millionaires, as shown by tax returns, rose from 65 to 513. Yet, 42 percent of the population continued to survive below the poverty line, and five percent of the population controlled a full third of the nation's wealth.[8]

And those five-percenters knew just how to enjoy their wealth. For the multimillionaires of the 1920s the world cruise was the ultimate pastime, an event that also kept their prominent position in the society pages. Unlike the $5,000 "bungalow" posited by *Motor Boating*, these ocean-going mansions were opulently furnished, staffed with cooks and maids—often their own doctor—and could comfortably accommodate more than 15 guests. As bigger and better yachts were built, competition increased in yachting circles. When industrialist Julius Forstmann spent two million dollars for his 333-foot *Orion* in 1929, he got what the *Milwaukee Sentinel* described as the "Biggest, Most Luxurious Private Yacht in the World":

> ...large and spacious rooms panelled in rare woods ... open through French windows onto a promenade deck over six feet wide ... sun room..., a music room..., and a dining room.... There is a service pantry and a galley adjoining the dining room. All of these rooms, with the exception of the service quarters, are separated from each other by twelve-foot glass panelled doors which, when thrown open, give one the impression of being in a single immense room. Forward of this suite are the owner's private quarters consisting of a large bedroom, ladies' dressing room, two baths, morning room and private writing room. A private staircase leads from this suite at a spacious, light green and white tiled swimming pool on the power deck.... On the boat deck ... there are the smoking room, gymnasium, library, observation room and additional suites for guests, ... each with bath attached.[9]

And, of course, since Forstmann planned on an around-the-world voyage, there was an infirmary staffed by an on-board doctor. Though capable of making 16½ knots, at her more sedate cruising speed of 12 knots *Orion* had a range of almost 24,000 miles. The full crew numbered 54.

About six weeks after Forstmann took delivery of his new yacht, the Wall Street Crash of 29 October 1929 presaged the Great Depression. One week later, *Orion* left on a seven-month-long around-the-world cruise. Despite the rapidly deteriorating global economy, the yachtsmen's race for bragging rights, for the biggest most opulent vessel, was unabated. Forstmann's *Orion* did not hold the ranking of world's biggest yacht for very long. In 1930, J.P. Morgan spent $2,500,000 for his 343-foot yacht *Corsair IV*. The following year saw stock broker Edward Francis Hutton invest $1,500,000 in his latest *Hussar*, later *Sea Cloud*. Although only 316 feet long, this elegant four-masted bark turned heads wherever she went. That same year Emily Roebling Cadwallader set the new benchmark at 446 feet with the launch of her over $4,000,000 *Savarona III*. On average, the monthly operating expenses for these symbols of consumption ran to $20,000.[10]

Back in the real world the economy continued to falter. Housing starts fell 80 percent between 1929 and 1932. In that same period 5,000 banks went belly up.[11] In 1929, the United States Steel Corporation had 224,980 full-time employees on its payroll. By 1932 that number had dropped precipitously to 18,938, and in April of the following year the number was zero. All remaining employees were part-time.[12]

In his fireside chat of 7 April 1932, President Franklin Delano Roosevelt recognized the plight of the jobless workers when he said, "These unhappy times call for the building of plans that rest upon the forgotten, the unorganized but indispensable units of economic power, … that build from the bottom up, … that put their faith once more in the forgotten man at the bottom of the economic pyramid."[13]

But what about that middle-class poor soul having difficulty maintaining his small yacht while awaiting the promised prosperity around the corner? Four months after F.D.R.'s fireside chat *Motor Boating* magazine posited its own Forgotten Man in an editorial pep talk:

> The Forgotten Man has become a mysterious but verbally important figure in our quadrennial attack of political epilepsy. The farmer thinks he is the one who has slipped from the minds of our wise and patriotic political overlords … but how about the motor boat owner? Surely he has long been in the legion of forgotten men…. He has not clamored to be relieved every few minutes, although his need of help has been keen. Most motor boat owners are small business men or workers for moderate salaries…. Thousands of families have found living on their boats a sure and delightful cure for financial and mental troubles. Many of them will continue the marine life when prosperity turns that vaguely located corner, going to bigger and better boats as the pressure of penury is relieved and their needs expand…. The Forgotten Man is not so badly off—if he owns a boat.[14]

Whether this allegedly forgotten motor boater could keep his small cabin cruiser, let alone live on it during the Great Depression, remained an open question. That he actually was forgotten was not exactly true. United States Code 46, Section 57105, of 29 June 1936, reiterated the power of the Secretary of the Treasury to "acquire a vessel, by purchase or otherwise, if … the Secretary of the Navy has certified … that the vessel is suitable for economical and speedy conversion into a naval or military auxiliary or otherwise suitable for use by the United States Government in time of war or national emergency."[15]

On 18 September 1931, Japan invaded Manchuria in violation of the Kellogg-Briand Pact outlawing war, signed 21 August 1928. If it was meant as an American response, the belated restatement of civilian vessel acquisition authority was not much of a threat. Precious little else was done before the Japanese bombed and sank the gunboat USS *Panay* on the Yangtze River on 12 December 1937. It wasn't until the unthinkable, another world war, had already begun in Europe that the President and Congress finally committed to the expansion and modernization of the Navy, with the 11% Naval Expansion Act of 14 June 1940 and the Two-Ocean Navy Act of 19 July 1940.[16]

Although the acts of congress focused on the types of vessels that could not readily be converted from those in civilian service, battleships, aircraft carriers, cruisers and destroyers, the Navy had not forgotten the need for smaller patrol craft. The April 1938 issue of *MotorBoating* reported that "the Navy is making a check of thousands of small commercial craft and yachts to determine their possible usefulness in an emergency [or war]. Questionnaires have been sent to many owners and arrangements made for inspection of numerous craft of 15 tons or more."[17] That was only the beginning. Rear Admiral Thomas Malloy, USCG, noted in a speech on small boat safety that there were roughly 300,000 pleasure boats cruising federal waters alone. Recalling the role of formerly civilian vessels in World War I, he noted that "should a similar crisis arrive in our national life again, your boats and your experience will be needed."[18] On 24 April 1939, Representative Schuyler Otis Bland introduced Bill No. 5966 to create the volunteer Coast Guard Reserve. By the end of the following year the Reserve comprised 3,000 members who owned 2,700 boats, organized into 150 flotillas.[19]

Though nominally neutral, the United States was becoming increasingly involved, albeit peripherally, in the naval portion of the European war. By the 22nd anniversary of the armistice that silenced the guns of the first World War, the Navy neared completion of an auxiliary vessel acquisition that totaled 350,000 tons. In the latter half of 1940 this included 18 yachts, "seven of which were given to the Navy by wealthy persons who either wished to aid the defense program or rid themselves of expensive upkeep charges."[20] During fiscal year 1941 alone, 237 vessels "were taken over for conversion to auxiliary, district and patrol craft."[21]

✦ ✦ ✦ ✦

German U-boats increasingly interfered with neutral American shipping. On 21 May 1941, 750 miles west of Freetown, Sierra Leone, Kapitänleutnant Wilhelm Zahn's U-69 torpedoed and sank SS *Robin Moor*, after allowing her passengers and crew to abandon ship. That summer, Alfred Stanford, commodore of the Cruising Club of America, anticipated the need for small craft to patrol American shipping lanes and provide the eyes and ears the Navy was ill prepared to furnish itself. He suggested that yachtsmen could establish a civilian coastal picket patrol of auxiliary (having a gas or diesel engine) sailing yachts that could cordon the entire Eastern Seaboard while maintaining visual contact with the previous and next vessels in the chain. The initial official response to these sails against the Reich was, "Thanks, but no thanks." Then, on 7 December, aircraft and midget submarines of the Imperial Japanese Navy attacked the U.S. Navy base at Pearl Harbor, Hawaii. Sixteen days later, Kapitänleutnant Reinhard Hardegen's U-123 left Lorient, France, for New York. Operation Drumbeat was underway. Ironically, on the night of 13 January 1942, off Montauk Point Light, lookouts aboard U-123 spotted a two-masted sailing yacht.[22] Had the picket patrol been in effect, that yacht might have spotted the surfaced submarine and raised the alarm. It wasn't until an act of Congress in June 1942 that the Coastal Picket Patrol, under the United States Coast Guard Temporary Reserve, became operational. Officially christened the Corsair Fleet, the decidedly unmilitary collection "of college boys, adventurous lads of shore villages, Boy Scouts, beachcombers, ex-bootleggers and rum runners, [and men otherwise classified 4-F,] almost everyone who declared he could reef and steer, and many who couldn't...."[23] gave rise to the unofficial name, the one that stuck, "The Hooligan Navy."

Coast Guard Temporary Reserve "Hooligan" sailor on the lookout for German submarines (National Archives photograph 170602-G-XX000–040).

Ernest Hemingway had his own plan to protect Caribbean waters from marauding U-boats. He and his less-than-sensible friends would load up his 38-foot cabin cruiser *Pilar* with rifles, hand grenades and ample alcohol. Upon sighting a U-boat, his innocent-looking fishing boat would dash full speed ahead at a surfaced submarine. The plan was that before its crew could react Hemingway and friends would throw grenades down the open hatches. Yo-Ho-Ho and a bottle of—make that a case of—rum. Hemingway did claim an actual sighting, never confirmed, but, luckily for him, never got close enough to test his plan, or it might have been his own death in the afternoon.[24]

The official pickets, however, had their own odd moments. Gunnery practice more often than not consisted of firing a worn-out World War I .50 caliber machine gun in an attempt to burst an inflated condom tossed overboard. A depth charge rolled over the side would more likely sink the yacht that dropped it than bring up a U-boat. The real weapons of the Hooligan Navy were the eyes and ears, and noses (one cold smell a surfaced U-boat's diesel exhaust) of the crews, and the radio to report a contact.

One night out of Nantucket, Massachusetts, soundman Charlie Grean, aboard the 146-ton, 112-foot auxiliary schooner *Valor* (CGR-3080, ex–*Hardi Biaou*) reported suspicious sounds on his hydrophones. The skipper, convinced they had detected a U-boat, reported the same to the destroyers escorting a nearby convoy. One of their number sped toward the reported contact, where she made an unproductive depth charge run. Satisfied the threat no longer was immediate, the destroyer captain broke off to return to his charges. *Valor*'s crew was ready to congratulate themselves on foiling a U-boat attack on the convoy, but, when the churned ocean calmed, once again Grean picked up the motor sounds. At about the same moment, another crewman came topside to report a problem with the motor on their refrigerator. That is what Grean heard. They had been chasing themselves.[25]

The 68-foot yawl *Edlu II* (CG-68007) had better luck than *Valor*. Patrolling off Montauk Point, New York, on 15 September 1942 she stumbled across a surfaced U-boat scarcely one hundred yards away. Armed with only a .38 caliber revolver and a Lewis machine gun, she came about and headed straight for the submarine. Startled by this pipsqueak's bravado, and not knowing her lack of serious armament, the German skipper ordered a crash dive and disappeared.[26]

By May 1943, the tide was turning in the Battle of the Atlantic. Improved countermeasures and increased numbers of escorts were sinking U-boats faster than the Kriegsmarine could replace them, and the German crews were going out with less experience. On October first of that year, the Navy deemed the Coastal Picket Patrol superfluous, and it was ordered disbanded.[27] Though it is impossible to prove a negative, it is, perhaps, reasonable to infer a valid contribution by those doughty seamen and their essentially unarmed sailboats. The fact that they were out there paying attention doubtless convinced some U-boat skippers to remain submerged longer, running on slower speed battery power. That alone could have saved both ships and merchant mariners.

✤ ✤ ✤ ✤

Even more yachts, the kind of craft associated with real wealth and extravagance, were lent to the Navy or acquired by outright purchase. Acquisition of these craft began before the attack on Pearl Harbor and proceeded in earnest in the first half of 1942. These, for the most part, larger yachts were well and truly armed and were commissioned into specific classifications: patrol gunboat (PG), patrol yacht (PY), coastal patrol yacht (PYc) and yard patrol (YP). Still others fell into the miscellaneous unclassified category (IX).

The largest of the converted yachts were the patrol gunboats, which displaced from 1400 to 3200 tons and measured 226 feet to over 330 feet long. These mostly diesel powered motor yachts could make 13 to 17 knots, with a classification average speed of 15 knots. The naval complement varied from as few as 81 to 279. Their main battery varied from the single 3"/50 caliber dual purpose mount aboard USS *Hilo* (PG-58) to the four 3"/50 dual purpose mounts on USS *Vixen* (PG-53). USS *Plymouth* (PG-57) carried one 4"/50 as well as two 3"/50s, and USS *Nourmahal* (PG-72, ex–WPG-122) sported a main battery of two 4"/50s in 1945. The larger four inch guns increased the range by 1,300 yards beyond the three-incher's 1,600 yards, and, at 33 pounds, the larger projectile eclipsed that from the smaller gun by 20 pounds.[28]

These big sisters of the Hooligans often too did their duty in boring obscurity, although often in more interesting climes. The 226 foot, 1,434-ton USS *Beaumont* (PG-60, ex–*Carola*, ex–*Chalena*, ex–*Reveler*) patrolled the Hawaiian Sea Frontier between Pearl Harbor and Midway Island on weather station duty, without firing her guns or

USS *Nourmahal* (PG-72) at Guantanamo Bay Naval Base, Cuba, c. 1943. She later became USCGC *Nourmahal* (WPG-122) (National Archives photograph 26-G-4431).

dropping her depth charges in anger.[29] The over 240-foot, 1,768-ton USS *San Bernardino* (PG-59, ex–*Vanda*) performed similar duties around Oahu, Midway, Johnston, Canton and Palmyra Islands. Both were decommissioned in early 1946.[30] USS *Nourmahal* too performed weather station duty, this time out of Boston, Massachusetts, but had a far more interesting prewar life.

The nearly 264 foot, 2,250-ton (in 1941) diesel yacht *Nourmahal* was built by the Krupp Germaniawerft in Kiel, Germany, in 1928 for William Vincent Astor, whose father went down with RMS *Titanic*. In addition to its social duties, the yacht frequently went on philanthropic voyages. Although capable of making nearly 14 knots, at the more leisurely eight she had a range of 23,500 miles. This ambit served her in good stead when, in the spring of 1930, Astor and experts from the New York Aquarium, American Museum of Natural History and Brooklyn Botanic Garden made an expedition to the Galapagos Islands that would have made Charles Darwin jealous. They returned with specimens of reef fishes, penguins, tortoises, iguanas, and a varied botanical collection for the Brooklyn Botanic Garden. Several repeat expeditions to the Galapagos occurred throughout the 1930s. Cleaned up and aired out from her biological adventures, *Nourmahal* was an elegant hostess. In the Bahamas, on 27 March 1935, Astor and his yacht entertained President Franklin Delano Roosevelt, the Duke and Duchess of Kent and Governor Sir Bede and Lady Clifford on board. This wasn't the first time the president had been aboard. Two years earlier, on 15 February 1933, Giuseppe Zangara attempted to assassinate President-elect Roosevelt in Miami, Florida. Chicago Mayor Anton Cermak, seated next to Roosevelt, was mortally wounded, but FDR was whisked to safety aboard *Nourmahal*.

The Coast Guard acquired Astor's yacht on 21 March 1940 for conversion to an anti-submarine gunboat bristling with depth charge tracks and projectors as well as her pair of four-inchers and six 20-millimeter guns. She transferred into the Navy on 3 March 1941; however, the yacht's only run-in with the enemy was back in 1939, when Astor and Theodore Roosevelt's son Kermit sailed to the Marshall Islands. Speculation was they were looking for evidence of Amelia Earhart's fate. Possibly that was a cover to assess local Japanese strength. Whatever was the truth, the Japanese turned them back. *Nourmahal* was laid up in the James River Reserve Fleet on 18 July 1948 and was subsequently sold for scrap in 1964.[31]

✤ ✤ ✤ ✤

Although the steam yacht *Delphine* and the diesel powered yachts *Orion* and *Aras II* had their elegant brightwork and paneling stripped or painted Navy gray, there still was plenty of brass to polish. Purchased from woolen manufacturer Julius Forstmann on 13 November 1940, *Orion* was renamed USS *Vixen* (PG-53), the fourth *Vixen* in the Navy. She was one of the largest and most heavily armed of the converted yachts at just over 333 feet long, displacing almost 3100 tons and sporting a main battery of four 3"/50 dual purpose guns. Her graceful lines and pedigree apparently were the deciding factors in her employment. On 23 May 1941, Rear Admiral Richard S. Edwards, Commander, Submarines, Atlantic Fleet, broke out his flag at *Vixen*'s masthead. Seven months later, on 20 December, Edwards' flag came down to be replaced eight days later when she became flagship of four-star Admiral Ernest J. King. On 17 June 1942, King transferred his flag to USS *Dauntless* (PG-61), the Navy's second *Dauntless*. After a refit, *Vixen* piped aboard a new admiral, Royal E. Ingersoll, Commander-in-Chief Atlantic Fleet. *Vixen* welcomed aboard her fourth admiral on 15 November 1944 when Admiral Jonas H. Ingram relieved Ingersoll as CinCLANT. *Vixen* was decommissioned on 24 May 1946 and sold 21 January 1947 to an Egyptian tour company who renamed her *Regina Maris*.[32]

The steamer USS *Dauntless* (PG-61, ex–*Delphine*) was less impressive than *Vixen* when Admiral King, Commander-in-Chief, United States Fleet (CinCUS), broke out his flag, but she had the advantage of being at Washington, D.C. Horace Elgin Dodge's 258-foot, nearly 1000-ton *Delphine* almost did not survive to see wartime service. Dodge died before his $2,000,000 yacht was launched, in 1921, by the Great Lakes Engine Works of Ecorse, Michigan. His widow Anna took delivery. In 1926, *Delphine* caught fire and sank in the Hudson River, where she remained for 667 days before being refloated and restored to suit Anna. "The dark and elaborately carved mahogany paneling was ripped out and [she was redecorated] … throughout in an understated,

USS *Vixen* (fourth Navy ship of that name) (PG-53) off the Philadelphia Navy Yard, 11 April 1944 (NH 91116 courtesy the Naval History & Heritage Command Photographic Dept.).

modern, and more feminine manner. Beamed overheads were covered with flat white painted panels, and everything was made simpler and less ornate." So she was when the Navy acquired her on 21 January 1942. Renamed USS *Dauntless*, the yacht remained in Washington until decommissioned 11 May 1946.[33]

✣ ✣ ✣ ✣

Wood pulp and Oxford Paper Company magnate Hugh J. Chisholm took delivery of his new, 1800-ton, diesel powered, steel-hull yacht *Aras II* at the beginning of 1931. The Navy acquired her just over a decade later in anticipation of official United States involvement in World War II and immediately began her conversion from symbol of wealth to one of sea power. "[T]eak and mahogany joinerwork was ruthlessly ripped out, thrown overboard into a waiting dump truck, and deposited in a dump. In its place, panels of asbestos were installed, creating a resolutely plain interior. In the dining salon, only the marble [fireplace] mantle survived."[34] Armed with two 3"/50 dual-purpose mounts, eight machine guns, two depth charge tracks and a Y-gun, the newly christened USS *Williamsburg* (PG-56) arrived at Halifax, Nova Scotia, the day before the Japanese attack on Pearl Harbor. The ship was assigned the arduous duty of convoy escort out of Reykjavik, Iceland. Until mid–May 1942, she also served as the headquarters of Rear Admiral James L. Kaufman. On 31 March 1943 Rear Admiral Donald B. Beary, Commander, Fleet Operational Training Command, Atlantic Fleet, broke out his flag from the masthead. After the war and another conversion, *Williamsburg* was promoted from carrying mere admirals to serve the overall commander in chief of the armed forces, replacing USS *Potomac*, on 5 November 1945, as presidential yacht for Harry S Truman and later Dwight D. Eisenhower. Struck from the Navy List on 1 April 1962, she was transferred to the National Science Foundation as an oceanographic research vessel and renamed *Anton Brunn*. She was damaged beyond economical repair while in drydock in 1968.[35]

✢ ✢ ✢ ✢

On 13 January 1943, USS *Niagara* (PG-52), USS *Hilo* (PG-58) and USS *Jamestown* (PG-55) were all reclassified as motor torpedo boat tenders, becoming AGP-1, 2 and 3 respectively.

The 279-foot diesel yacht *Caroline* was built in 1931 by the Bath Iron Works of Bath, Maine, for Eldridge H. Johnson. He sold her to William B. Leeds, who renamed the yacht *Moana*, which was her name when the Navy acquired her on 28 November 1941 and renamed her USS *Hilo*. She and her brood of PT boats supported the Buna-Gona campaign in New Guinea and participated in the Battle of the Bismark Sea, 2–4 March 1943. Three months later she was stationed at Mios Woendi, code name "Stinker," in the Schouten Islands where she served as command ship for PT boat operations, 7th Fleet. From 12 November 1944, *Hilo* operated in Leyte Gulf, where she survived a kamikaze near miss on 16 November. *Hilo* was decommissioned on 3 March 1946.[36]

USS *Williamsburg*, newly designated as Presidential yacht, anchored at Charleston, South Carolina, 13 November 1945 (NH 107693 courtesy the Naval History & Heritage Command Photographic Dept.).

Diesel yacht *Hi-Esmare*, built by the Bath Iron Works in 1929, displaced 1,922 tons. The Navy acquired her on 16 October 1940 from Mrs. H. Edward Manville and, at first, converted her into coastal minelayer CMc-2. In November she was reclassified patrol gunboat PG-52 and commissioned USS *Niagara*, the seventh Navy vessel to carry that name. After the attack on Pearl Harbor, her mission changed yet again when she became a PT-boat tender. *Niagara* was stationed at Noumea, New Caledonia, when she received her new classification, AGP-1, on 13 January 1943. Subsequently, she and her brood were active off Tulagi and Guadalcanal. On 7 April 1943, while moored on the Maliali River, Solomon Islands, *Niagara* and minesweeper USS *Rail* (AM-26) came under Japanese air attack. The Americans shot down six of the nine aircraft without suffering damage to themselves. En route to New Guinea, she again came under air attack on 22 May. This time, *Niagara*'s luck ran out. She was damaged by near misses and mortally wounded by a direct hit on her forecastle. With fires raging out of control and her ammunition cooking off, there was nothing to do but abandon ship. Two of her charges, PT-146 and PT-147, braved the inferno to come alongside and rescue her entire crew. Then PT-147 stood off and launched a torpedo, which finished what the Japanese had started. *Niagara* went down in less than a minute.[37]

USS *Jamestown* (PG-55) began her naval life in similar fashion to that of *Hilo* and *Niagara*. She was built in 1928, by Pusey & Jones Corporation of Wilmington, Delaware, as the second *Savarona* for Emily Roebling Cadwallader, granddaughter of John A. Roebling of Brooklyn Bridge fame. At that time, *Savarona* was the largest, most luxurious yacht in the word.[38] Mrs. Cadwallader sold her yacht to financier and mining engineer Colonel (an honorary Red Cross title) William Boyce Thompson a year later. After selling her second *Savarona*, Emily Cadwallader commissioned a third yacht of that name, built by Blohm & Voss of Hamburg, Germany, in 1931. At 446 feet length overall, she was even grander than her predecessors. She can be seen interior and exterior, plying the North Sea in the German film *Gold* of 1934, starring Hans Albers and Brigitte Helm. As for *Savarona*, the second, Colonel Thompson renamed her *Alder*. Ten and a half years after his death, on 6 December 1940, his daughter donated *Alder* to the Navy, who commissioned her USS *Jamestown* on 26 May 1941. Prior to the declaration of war *Jamestown* served as a training vessel at the United States Naval Academy. After refitting as a motor torpedo boat tender, she made supply runs to Tulagi and Guadalcanal in August 1942, and her PT-boats saw action in "Iron Bottom Sound." Given her AGP-3 classification on 13 January 1943, she continued to operate in the Solomon Islands, Bismark Archipelago and New Guinea, heading to Leyte Gulf early February 1945. *Jamestown* was decommissioned 6 March 1946.[39]

✤ ✤ ✤ ✤

On 4 November 1941, William Kissam Vanderbilt II donated his diesel yacht *Alva* to the Navy. Built in 1931 by the Krupp Germaniawerft of Kiel, Germany, *Alva* weighed in at 1500 tons for her over 264 feet length. Although heavily armed with one 4"/50 and two 3"/50 dual purpose mounts, the newly commissioned USS *Plymouth* (PG-57) was initially assigned inshore patrol in the 5th Naval District out of Norfolk, Virginia. Later orders assigned her to convoy escort duty between Guantanamo Bay, Cuba, and New York City. While off Elizabeth City, North Carolina, on 4 August 1943, *Plymouth*'s soundman picked up a suspicious contact on his hydrophones. Lieutenant Ormsby M. Mitchel, Jr., USNR, in command, ordered the helm on an intercept course.

6. World War Again 123

USS *Jamestown* (ex–*Savarona II*) tending PT boats at New York, October 1941 (19-N-25720 courtesy the Naval History & Heritage Command Photographic Dept.).

The contact proved to be Kapitäenleutnant Hans Hornkohl's U-566. Instead of running, Hornkohl attacked, firing a single torpedo which struck *Plymouth* on her port side abaft the bridge. The massive explosion rolled the yacht onto her starboard beam ends, then back to a permanent list as flames engulfed the forward half of the yacht. *Plymouth* went down in two minutes. Eighty-five of her 155-man complement were rescued.[40] Curiously, the Vanderbilt family's previous yacht *Alva* was also ill-fated. On 24 July 1892, the steamer SS *H.F. Dimock* accidentally ran her down and sank her off the Nantucket Shoals.[41]

※ ※ ※ ※

USS *St. Augustine* (PG-54) began life in 1929 as 272-foot, 1722-ton, turbo-electric powered yacht *Viking*, built for George F. Baker by the Newport News Shipbuilding & Dry Dock Company. Norman B. Woolworth later purchased the yacht and renamed her *Noparo*. He in turn sold the yacht to the Navy on 5 December 1940. Commissioned USS *St. Augustine*, the converted yacht was also lost escorting a convoy from New York to Guantanamo Bay, Cuba. On 6 January 1944, southeast of Cape May, New Jersey, she was accidentally rammed amidships by the merchant tanker *Camas Meadows*. *St. Augustine* sank in five minutes, taking 115 of her 185 man crew with her.[42]

※ ※ ※ ※

The PY classification of converted yachts designated those that were somewhat smaller than the PGs, running from 500 to 1400 tons for their 154- to 245-foot lengths. Average speed was a few knots slower except for USS *Crystal* at 18 knots and USS *Isabel* that, with her dual Parsons steam turbines, clocked in at a blazing 28 knots. Despite their smaller size, they carried a similar main battery of one or two 3"/50 dual purpose mounts and depth charge tracks.

Emily Roebling Cadwallader's first *Savarona*, built in 1926 by Newport News Shipbuilding and Dry Dock Company, was acquired by the Navy 16 March 1942 for conversion to a patrol yacht. She had sold the 174 foot, 607-ton yacht to her son a year after the vessel's construction. He in turn sold the vessel two years later to James Elverson, Jr., owner of the *Philadelphia Inquirer*, whose estate subsequently resold her the same year to Eugene F. McDonald, Jr., founder and president of the Zenith Radio corporation. By the time *Savarona* was enlisted in the Navy, classified PY-29, her appellation was *Mizpah* (Hebrew for watchtower), which the Navy left unchanged. After providing convoy escort between New York and Key West, Florida, for two years, USS *Mizpah* was reassigned as navigation schoolship, Amphibious Training Base, Little Creek, Virginia. Her final wartime assignment was as flagship, Destroyer Force, Atlantic Fleet from 28 May 1945 to her decommissioning 15 January 1946.[43]

✤ ✤ ✤ ✤

USS *Coral* (PY-15) began life as the 207-foot steam yacht *Sialia*, built in 1914 for James K. Stewart, partner in the Stewart-Warner Speedometer Company, by Pusey & Jones Company of Wilmington, Delaware. Keeping his yacht in the automotive realm, Stewart sold her, on 20 January 1917, to Henry Ford for $250,000. With American involvement in the Great War looming on the horizon, Ford sold the yacht to the Navy just shy of six months later. After her wartime service the Navy sold USS *Sialia* (SP-543) back to Ford on 13 April 1920. Ford renamed his yacht *Yankee Clipper*. She was rebuilt and lengthened seven and a half feet in 1925 and subsequently went through a series of owners before the Navy once again required her service. Her engines were replaced with diesels, and, on 27 February 1941, she was commissioned USS *Coral* and assigned various training, inshore patrol and service duties along the Eastern Seaboard and in Guantanamo Bay, Cuba. Less than two-and-a-half years after her commissioning, *Coral* was decommissioned and then abruptly recommissioned 15 days later, on 27 August 1943, to escort a convoy to Norfolk, Virginia. Decommissioned again a fortnight later, this time her service truly was over. The Navy sold her 15 July 1947.[44]

✤ ✤ ✤ ✤

The converted steam yacht USS *Cythera* (PY-26) also served in the First World War on section patrol as SP-575. She was reacquired by the Navy on the last day of December 1941. Two months after her recommissioning, USS *Cythera* was torpedoed and sunk by U-402 [see chapter 5]. A second USS *Cythera* (PY-31) was commissioned after the Navy acquired the diesel yacht *Vita* roughly a month after the first *Cythera*'s loss. The 800-ton *Vita* began life as *Argosy*, built in 1931 by the Germania Werft of Kiel, Germany, for C.A. Stone. In 1934, Stone sold *Argosy* to Thomas O.M. Sopwith, English aviation pioneer, founding partner of the Sopwith Aviation Company (builder of the famous World War I biplane fighter the Sopwith Camel) and competitive yachtsman. He kept her for three years. At some point before the Navy got her, *Argosy* was renamed *Vita*. Throughout the war, *Cythera*'s main assignments were with the Underwater Sound Laboratory in the 3rd Naval District, New York, in 1944 and the Antisubmarine Development Operational Detachment, Atlantic Fleet at Port Everglades, Florida, in 1945. *Cythera* was sold the following year and then sold twice more, each time being renamed.[45] Her name was *Abril* when purchased by the Bergson Group with funds raised through performances of Ben Hecht's play *A Flag is Born*. Her mission was to run the British blockade of Palestine with a cargo of Jewish refugees. Her new name was SS *Ben Hecht*. Elliott Roosevelt volunteered to serve as captain, but he was dissuaded by his mother Eleanor, who feared the British would fire on the vessel. On 9 March 1947, HMS *Chieftan* intercepted the former yacht and sent aboard 40 Royal Marines to effect her capture. *Chieftan* towed the vessel to Haifa, Palestine, and the 600 Jewish refugees aboard were then interned in Cyprus. After the State of Israel was established, SS *Ben Hecht* was converted into an Israeli Navy gunship and renamed INS *Maoz*. *Maoz* was decommissioned after the Suez-Sinai War of 1956 and was sold to Italy, into civilian service, under yet another name, *Santa Maria del Mare*.[46]

✧ ✧ ✧ ✧

As was USS *Coral* (PY-15), the 191 foot, 500-ton diesel yacht *Trudione* was ordered by an automotive innovator. In this case he was Ross W. Judson, founding partner of the Continental Motor Manufacturing Company. *Trudione* was launched by the Bath Iron

USS *Cythera* (PY-31) (the second of that name), 10 November 1943 (NH 93217 courtesy the Naval History & Heritage Command Photographic Dept.).

Works of Bath, Maine, in October 1930 and was notable for her state of the art sound system, "a Haynes-Griffin radio-phonograph installation.... All bulky apparatus and control equipment [is] in an alcove concealed by doors. The owner may choose either radio programs or electrically amplified music from the world's finest music recordings. The phonograph is entirely automatic in operation, playing 48 selections, or a program up to 4 hours duration, without repetition."[47] Speakers were located throughout the vessel's common spaces. Two months after her launch, the owner changed her name to *Seventeen*. The Navy commissioned her USS *Carnelian* (PY-19) precisely six months before the attack on Pearl Harbor. Her naval duty began patrolling the southeast coast and later as convoy escort between Trinidad and Recife, Brazil. *Carnelian* began the year 1945 with reassignment to the Mine Warfare Test Station at Solomons, Maryland. She was decommissioned one year later.[48]

❖ ❖ ❖ ❖

The year before *Trudione* was launched, Pusey & Jones of Wilmington, Delaware, built the diesel yacht *Lotosland* for Edward A. Deeds. "Most of the wood used was either teak or black walnut, and the fireplaces were made of Carrara marble. All of the staterooms were air-conditioned, and each had its own full-size bathtub and shower. It was the first private vessel to be outfitted with a seaplane—a five-passenger Sikorsky S-39—and a crew of more than thirty people was required for full operation."[49] This yacht's sound system needed no electronic amplification. The music room boasted a Skinner Organ Company duplexed pipe organ. The Navy purchased *Lotosland*, 16 October 1940, for 14 percent of her million-dollar cost, renamed her USS *Siren* (PY-13), the Navy's third ship of that name, and upped her complement to 89. No longer, however, when the lookouts were ordered to sing out any enemy sightings would they be accompanied by organ music. It was no fluke that Deeds' yacht carried a seaplane. He was heavily involved in aviation. An electrical engineer, he supervised the electrification of the National Cash Register Company (NCR), then went on to found the Dayton Engineering Laboratories Company (Delco), and then, with Wilbur Wright, to found the Dayton-Wright Airplane Company, which purchased Pratt & Whitney in 1917. His Moraine, Ohio, Delco plant manufactured DeHavilland DH-4 bombers during the previous world war. USS *Siren* executed her patrol duties along the Eastern Sea Frontier and was reassigned in April 1944 to the 3rd Naval District, Naval Training School (Salvage). A year later she was ordered to the 8th Naval District out of Orange, Texas, where she finished her naval service, and was struck from the Navy List 13 November 1945.[50]

❖ ❖ ❖ ❖

George Lawley & Sons of Neponset, Massachusetts, built *Athero II* for stock trader Jesse Lauriston Livermore in 1926. Renamed *Caroline* in 1928, the diesel yacht bore the eponymous name *Doctor Brinkley* when the Navy acquired her in December 1940. Converted to USS *Jade* (PY-17) the yacht was initially assigned inshore patrol in the 6th Naval District, Charleston, South Carolina, and then to the Canal Zone in May 1941. On 24 March 1943, *Jade* struck her American colors and broke out the Ecuadoran flag when she was transferred under Lend-Lease. The following January, *Jade* was back in the United States Navy in exchange for the older, but like sized and armed, converted yacht, USS *Turquoise* (PY-18).[51] *Turquoise* had been built in 1922 by the Newport News

Shipbuilding and Dry Dock Company for Edward Willys Scripps, publisher of Scripps Howard newspapers. Scripps died aboard in 1926, as the yacht lay at anchor in Monrovia Bay, Liberia. Originally named *Ohio*, the yacht went through a succession of owners and name changes before the Navy purchased *Entropy*, 21 August 1940, from Robert Van Guysling Furman of Schenectady, New York. Furman's second wife, Betty May, was an early aviatrix, member of the Ninety-Nines, an organization of female pilots, and former president of the club's southwest chapter.[52] USS *Tourmaline* (PY-20, ex–*Sylvia*) also changed her flag, though, in her case, it was after the war. Five months after her decommissioning, the Navy sold the 154-foot yacht, on 23 January 1946, to representatives of the Greek War Relief Association, who used her as the freighter *Adelphic*. Two years later, now named *Kyknos*, she became a passenger ship out of Piraeus. She went to the breakers' yard in 1979.[53]

✤ ✤ ✤ ✤

A contemporary description of USS *Ruby*'s (PY-21) original decor points out the evolution of style from the dark, ornately carved woods of the golden age of yachting to that of the "modern" age. Outside, her white hull was trimmed with gold at the peak, her topsides buff. "Decorations aboard the yacht ... are extremely severe and for the most part employ only contemporary motifs with a touch of the modernistic in the lounge. The living room is predominately gold and green against a panelled [sic] and beamed background of pure white. Fixtures are executed in old silver and the furniture is contemporary English.... Staterooms for the guests are done in variations of red, green, soft rose, tangerine, gold and green, all with mahogany furniture." Built in 1930 for Dupont vice president Harry Garner Haskell, the 191 foot, 640-ton diesel yacht *Placida* could have kept her original appellation despite, as USS *Ruby*, her armament of two 3"/50 dual purpose mounts and four 1.1" antiaircraft machine guns, fired primarily in training exercises, not in anger.[54]

✤ ✤ ✤ ✤

According to Gunner's Mate 1c Ernest Borgnine (later Academy Award winning actor and promoted to Lieutenant Commander Quinton McHale in the TV show *McHale's Navy*), the crew dreaded firing USS *Sylph*'s (PY-12) 3"/50 even in practice, fearing it would tear loose from the wood deck. At 11 knots speed *Sylph*'s roll-off depth charges were more likely to blow off the converted yacht's stern than sink a marauding U-boat. Y and K guns were added later, which provided a margin of safety by propelling her depth charges away from the ship. Despite the upgrade, in their first U-boat encounter, *Sylph* dropped 20 depth charges of which only one actually exploded. After chipping away multiple layers of paint on the charges still aboard it was revealed that they had been manufactured in 1917![55]

✤ ✤ ✤ ✤

George Lawley & Sons of Neponset, Massachusetts, built the diesel auxiliary barkentine originally named *Intrepid* for rail car inventor and cattleman Walter P. Murphy in 1929. An innovation was her hollow steel masts which also drew fresh air below deck. At 212 feet long, over all, in addition to her civilian crew of 31, she had accommodations for 14 guests, each stateroom with its own private bath. Perhaps anticipating *Intrepid*'s wartime role, there also was provision for a "well equipped armory." The Navy purchased her for one dollar on 16 July 1940 and renamed her *Sylph*, the Navy's fourth ship of that name. *Sylph* began her service, with a complement numbering 88, training reserve midshipmen in the 3rd Naval District, then graduated herself to anti-submarine patrol out of Tompkinsville, New York. In February 1942, however, *Sylph* found herself in New London, Connecticut, back training sonarmen, her primary duty for the duration. Decommissioned 19 December 1945, the War Shipping Administration sold her one year later.[56]

✦ ✦ ✦ ✦

In 1929 Pusey & Jones built the 235 foot, 1,220-ton diesel yacht *Nakhoda* for automobile body manufacturer Fred J. Fisher (as in "Body by Fisher," General Motors' first mark of excellence). *Nakhoda* was one of the larger yachts of her classification when the Navy acquired her one year before the Pearl Harbor attack. Renamed USS *Zircon* (PY-16), the converted yacht exemplified the varied duties assigned such vessels. She was first posted as an anti-aircraft gunnery school ship for officer trainees in New London, Connecticut, followed by inshore patrol from New York to Casco Bay, Maine, until fall 1941. At that time she began mail and dispatch runs between Portland, Maine, and Argentia, Newfoundland. In February 1942 she was assigned to patrol the coast off New Jersey, then to the Caribbean Sea Frontier on convoy escort between New York and Guantanamo Bay, Cuba. Next came a stint as a U.S. Coast Guard weather patrol ship out of Boston, Massachusetts. In November 1944, *Zircon* got to run with the big boys when assigned to Commander, Destroyer-Destroyer Escort Shakedown Task Group. Her final assignment came on the third anniversary of Pearl Harbor when *Zircon* was designated relief flagship Commander in Chief, Atlantic Fleet, stationed at Philadelphia. Decommissioned 10 May 1946, *Zircon* was sold a year later.[57]

✦ ✦ ✦ ✦

Although the biggest threat to U.S. and Allied shipping came from U-boats prowling the Atlantic side of the country, the Pacific Ocean could no longer be regarded as an absolute buffer against attack from the west. From 18 to 24 December 1941, nine Japanese submarines I-9, 10, 15, 17, 19, 21, 23, 25, 26, all with a range of 15,000 miles, took up position along the West Coast of the United States to attack American shipping. Though not nearly as successful as Germany's Operation Drumbeat along the east coast, the Japanese attacked eight merchantmen during that week, sinking two and damaging two. On 23 February 1942, I-17 manned its 5.5" gun to shell the Ellwood Oil Company refinery, 10 miles north of Santa Barbara, California.[58] Converted yachts had their part to play against this foe too.

USS *Isabel* (PY-10) was the greyhound of the patrol yachts, her twin Parsons steam turbines capable of driving her at 28 knots. At 245 feet, 6 inches, she also was the longest of her classification. Launched 7 June 1917 by the Bath Iron Works of Bath, Maine, she was not quite a month old before the Navy acquired her for service in the Great War as a section patrol ship (SP-521). [See appendix 4]. That war over, *Isabel* was decommissioned and laid up on 30 April 1920. Eighteen July 1921 she was back in service, with a newly installed main battery of two 3"/50s and two 3"/23s, assigned as flagship to the Yangtze Patrol, protecting American interests in the Far East from Chinese pirates. This symbol of American presence often came under sporadic sniper fire, but the shooting became seriously intense when, in October 1926, she found herself, on the Yangtze

USS *Isabel* (PY-10) at Hankow, China, dressed for the coronation of King George VI, 1937 (NH 83530 courtesy the Naval History & Heritage Command Photographic Dept.).

River, steaming through the middle of a rifle battle between opposing Chinese armies. The following March, *Isabel* played a part in resolving the Nanking Incident, during which deserting soldiers of defeated warlord Zhang Zongchang began to loot foreign properties and attack any foreigners who happened in their way. In 1928, she transferred to the Asiatic Fleet where she remained through 3 December 1941, when she was secretly tasked by President Roosevelt to scout the Japanese fleet off occupied French Indochina. *Isabel* was nearing port at Cavite Navy Yard, Philippine Islands, after receiving orders to return, when, on the morning of 7 December, U.S. time, Admiral Hart sent the Asiatic Fleet the six-word message, "Japan started hostilities. Govern yourselves accordingly." Two days later, Japanese aircraft attacked all military installations around Manila. Eight bombs, all duds, ringed *Isabel*'s fantail, and her gunners nailed one of the attackers. During the next month *Isabel* performed convoy escort in the East Indies, surviving air raids at Batavia, Palembang, and Tjilatap, escaping from several ports only days ahead of the enemy invasion forces. Seven February 1942, *Isabel* was diverted to rescue survivors from Dutch merchantman *Van Cloon* near Surabaya, Java. As she picked up survivors from the torpedoed vessel, the enemy submarine surfaced. *Isabel*'s alert gunners quickly drove the sub down and away. After the Battle of the Java Sea on 27 February 1942, *Isabel* escaped to Australia, arriving 7 March. Based at Fremantle, she took up new duties as escort and training ship for the U.S. submarines which now made that Australian port their base. Twenty-seven August 1945, she turned her bow for home, arriving San Francisco 26 October 1945. Her long service over, *Isabel* was sold for scrap 25 March 1946.[59]

✤ ✤ ✤ ✤

130   American Yachts in Naval Service

Lanikai as USS *Hermes*, Pearl Harbor, Hawaii, 1918 (NH 101785 courtesy the Naval History & Heritage Command Photographic Dept.).

The 87¼ foot, 150-ton, diesel auxiliary schooner *Lanikai* was no greyhound at a mere seven knots, but she too had a part to play in the Far East. A World War I Navy veteran as USS *Hermes* [see Chapter 5], she was in the right place when, in late November 1941, it became increasingly urgent for the U.S. Navy to know what its Japanese counterpart was up to. On 5 December 1941, the Navy chartered her from the Luzon Stevedoring Company of Manila, Philippine Islands, to investigate Japanese ship movements in the China Sea and Gulf of Siam. Lieutenant Kemp Tolley was given the command. Three days later, 7 December, Hawaiian time, before she could depart Manila, her clandestine mission was cancelled when word arrived of the Japanese attack on Pearl Harbor. Two days later *Lanikai* survived the same air raid that destroyed the Cavite Navy Yard and almost killed *Isabel*. Christmas Day she evacuated Army officers to Corregidor. Playing a deadly game of hide and seek with the Japanese war machine, *Lanikai* slowly made her way south toward Australia. She almost lost the race when a Japanese bomber straddled her with three near misses on 3 February 1942 near Surabaya, Java. Making the best of a tense situation, as soon as the airplane was gone, the crew lowered a boat and went out to gather the fish stunned to the surface by the bombs. Eighty-two days after leaving Mariveles Harbor, Luzon, *Lanikai* tied up at the dock in Fremantle, Australia. She spent the remainder of the war in the Australian Navy assigned harbor defense. Her odyssey finally ended in 1947 when a typhoon sank her in Subic Bay, Philippine Islands.[60]

✣ ✣ ✣ ✣

USS *Southern Seas* (PY-32) spent much of her service in the same general waters plied by *Isabel* and *Lanikai*. The diesel yacht began life in 1920 as the second *Lyndonia* built for Cyrus Curtis, publisher of *The Saturday Evening Post*, by the Consolidated Shipbuilding Company of New York City. Curtis mostly used her for cruising off New England. In 1939 he sold his yacht to Pan American Aviation Company. Refurbished and renamed *Southern Seas*, the 228-foot yacht became a floating luxury hotel in the South Pacific for the airline's clientele. She also ferried passengers to outlying islands not directly serviced by PanAm's Martin M-130 flying boats. The U.S. Army acquired *Southern Seas* on 30 December 1941 for use as a troop transport and survey vessel. Ironically, considering that latter task, she struck an uncharted reef 22 July 1942 in the Cook Islands, holing the hull in several places and flooding both engine rooms. Successfully raised and repaired in Auckland, New Zealand, she re-enlisted, this time in the Navy, on 23 December 1942. Her new assignment, reminiscent of her previous service with PanAm, was as a floating hotel for transient officers and officials throughout Oceania. She was at Guam 15 August 1945 when the war ended. Ordered to Okinawa on 7 September she weathered a typhoon on her arrival eight days later. A second typhoon struck Okinawa less than a month later. This time she foundered in the storm, taking 13 of her crew to the bottom with her.[61]

✣ ✣ ✣ ✣

Seven other patrol yachts also served in the Pacific, although closer to home. Publishing and utilities tycoon Ira C. Copely renamed his diesel powered yacht *Happy Days*, *Almandite* on 9 January 1942, possibly because the days weren't so happy after December 7th. Whatever his reason, the 185 foot, 705-ton *Almandite* joined the Navy 18 days later. Classified PY-24, USS *Almandite* was assigned to Pearl Harbor, Hawaii, where she patrolled the harbor entrance and performed inter-island escort and weather station duties for the duration.[62] William Mellon, financier and founder of the Gulf Oil Corporation, sold his 211 foot, 1200-ton *Vagabondia* to the Navy just two days after the Japanese attack. Commissioned USS *Azurlite* (PY-22) she joined *Almandite* at Pearl Harbor, tasked with essentially the same duties.[63] General Motors Corporation Chairman of the Board Alfred Pritchard Sloane's *Beryl* kept her name when the designation "USS" was added, and she was classified PY-23 on 17 March 1942. Similar in size and tonnage, she carried the same two 3"/50s and four .50 caliber machine guns as *Azurlite*, which she joined at Pearl Harbor on 29 June 1942, the day after *Azurlite*'s arrival.[64] USS *Crystal* (PY-25, ex–*Vida*, ex–*Cambriona*) and USS *Girasol* (PY-27, ex–*Firenza*) rounded out the Pearl Harbor patrol yacht contingent.[65] It is interesting to imagine the "regatta" if they all were in port at the same time, even in their gray Navy livery they would have made an impressive reminder of a bygone age of elegance, and, perhaps, a herald of post-war prosperity.

✤ ✤ ✤ ✤

USS *Argus* (PY-14), the second Navy ship of that name, Max C. Fleischmann's (as in Fleischmann's Yeast) diesel yacht *Haida*, spent 19 February to 17 September 1941 patrolling San Francisco Bay, after which she was transferred to the U.S. Coast and Geodetic Survey. Eight months later she was back in the Navy, resuming her original duties. *Argus*' otherwise uneventful service was interrupted 30 October 1944 when she was sent to rescue survivors of the Liberty Ship *John A. Johnson*, which had been sunk by Kaigun-chūsa (Commander) Kudo Kaneo's submarine I-12. Seventy seamen managed to abandon their sinking ship. However, only 60 remained to be rescued after Commander Kudo ordered his submarine to ram a lifeboat and rake the survivors with machine gun fire. Two weeks later USS *Ardent* and USS *Rockford* caught up with I-12 and sank the war criminal.[66]

Another Fleischmann yacht, this time for Max's brother Julius, the 225-foot, 1130-ton diesel-powered *Camargo* was built in 1928 by George Lawley & Sons of Neponset, Massachusetts. *Camargo*, bucking the trend at the time to a more vertical stem, was built with a clipper bow. Two 50-kilowatt generators provided the electricity for her lighting and refrigerated spaces. The latest Sperry Gyro Compass graced her bridge along with a fathometer which made continuous soundings of the depth under her keel. The yacht boasted an RCA wireless and radio direction finder. Six double staterooms aft, each with private bath, accommodated her guests, and the owner's suite sat on main deck in the after of the two deck houses, fore and aft of the funnel. The dining room occupied the forward one.[67]

On 7 October 1931, *Camargo* set out from New York on a yearlong around the world voyage, down the east coast into the Gulf and through the Panama Canal, across the South Pacific to Singapore, then transiting the Suez Canal into the Mediterranean to visit Egypt and Turkey, then around Europe and finally across the Atlantic back to New York.[68] The elegant, well-equipped vessel caught the eye of Dominican Republic dictator Generalisimo Rafael Trujillo, who bought her in 1938 and renamed her *Ramfis*. Later, Trujillo would also own another Navy yacht USS *Sea Cloud* (IX-99). The Navy acquired *Ramfis* on 2 February 1942, armed her with two 3"/50 dual purpose guns, two depth charge tracks and a Y-gun and commissioned her USS *Marcasite* (PY-28). Assigned to the Hawaiian Sea Frontier, she made an unsuccessful attack on a U-boat contact en route in the Caribbean. Her convoy escort duties took her as far as Midway Island. On 26 June 1943, *Marcasite* got new orders, reassigning her to patrol and weather station duties out of Seattle, Washington, which she performed until her decommissioning on 5 October 1944.[69]

✤ ✤ ✤ ✤

The Coastal Patrol Yachts (PYc) were under 200 feet in length, most under 150 feet, and generally were deployed defensively as their name suggests. An exception to that rule was USS *Captor* (PYc-40). To begin with, *Captor*, originally christened M/V *Harvard*, actually was a diesel trawler, built in 1938 by Bethlehem Steel Company of Quincy, Massachusetts, for General Sea Foods Company. The Navy purchased her on

New Years Day 1942 for conversion to a minesweeper and commissioned her USS *Eagle* (AM-132) on 5 March. *Eagle*'s defensive role lasted just over a month before she was cast in a more aggressive capacity, that of Q-ship. Armed with one 4"/50, one 20mm and two .50 caliber machine guns, the newly renamed USS *Captor* (PYc-40) went to sea posing as a helpless commercial vessel in the hope of luring a prowling U-boat to take her on with its deck gun.[70]

The idea behind the Q-ship is, in a word, deception. As far back as the beginnings of navies it was common practice to fly the flag of one's enemy, or at least that of some neutral third party. This would allow the disguised vessel to get in close and fire the first salvo to counter an opponent's speed or arms advantage. Only at the last moment would the real national flag be run up. Conversely it gave the vessel flying false colors more time to increase the distance from a formidable foe while the enemy captain pondered his next move. The Q-ship turns that doctrine on its head. In wartime any vessel not flying your or your allies' flag is fair game. Normally one tries to discourage attack by increasing an enemy's perceived or actual risk by appearing as formidable as possible, usually accomplished by protecting merchant convoys with screening warships. The Q-ship's task is to appear non-threatening, innocent, vulnerable, while hiding armament that was anything but. In the First World War, this ruse was used to some effect against U-boats. Why waste a torpedo on an easy target? Just surface and sink it with the deck gun. Only this time the U-boat found itself outgunned. The lesson from the First World War, however, had been learned, and the ploy largely was ineffective in the Second. Though *Captor* sortied into the rich sea lanes out of Boston, she never made contact and was decommissioned 4 October 1944. The only Q-ships of World War II that met with serious success were the German surface raiders, which readily changed their appearance as well as flag to prey on unsuspecting merchant ships. They might look like just another tramp steamer, but they were armed like a naval cruiser.

* * * *

An American light cruiser, USS *Vicksburg* (CL-86), wrote the final chapter to the story of one of the last palatial steam yachts, Eugene Tompkins' *Idalia*. She was built in 1899 by Delaware River Shipbuilding & Engine Works of Chester, Pennsylvania. *Idalia*'s elegant interiors were designed by no less than the studio of William Comfort Tiffany. Not knowing precisely what would be needed to fight the two ocean war the Navy now found itself in, the Department cast its net over nearly everything that could sustain itself afloat for a few weeks and that would not be required by the merchant marine. On 23 March 1942 that net caught *Idalia*, later *Malay II*, now re-christened *Palace* by her current owner William B. Baletti, who used her as a charter deep sea fishing boat. Nevertheless, not everything caught in a trawl is of use, and the Navy returned USS *Palace* (PYc-33), now deemed to be unsuitable, to her owner two months later. That was not, however, the end of the yacht's story. Having second thoughts, the Navy reacquired *Palace* on 7 August 1942, reclassified her as a Miscellaneous Auxiliary Service Craft (YAG-13) and assigned her to the Fleet Sound School at Key West, Florida. *Palace* subsequently had a couple of minor assignments until 9 September 1944 when the aforementioned light cruiser sank her as a radar gunnery target.[71]

USS *Tourist* (PYc-32) had a nearly identical career as USS *Palace*, except she survived to be sold after the war. Built in 1903 by George Lawley & Sons of Neponset, Massachusetts, the 150-foot, 185-ton steel hull steam yacht *Calumet* was the pride of Roswell Eldridge, Director of the New York & East River Ferry. Some years later, she was renamed *Kehtoh*. Between then and her enlistment in the Navy, the same day as USS *Palace*, her latest owner, Edward Baletti (of the same family of charter boat owners-captains), renamed her *Tourist*. She kept her name when commissioned, and then was also deemed unsuitable for her purpose and returned to her owner on 18 May 1942, the same day as *Palace*. Reacquired 7 August and reclassified USS YAG-14, she briefly served in the 3rd Naval District before being reassigned to join USS YAG-13 at the Fleet Sound School in Key West. The converted yacht was decommissioned on 11 August, just under a month before her comrade was sent to Davy Jones' Locker. The Circle Line Company of New York City purchased the appropriately named *Tourist* on 20 February 1945 to carry sightseers around Manhattan Island.[72]

Eight other coastal patrol yachts were immediately assigned to research or training facilities. *Jasper* (PYc-13) and *Leader* (PYc-42) went to the Navy Radio and Sound Laboratory, San Diego, California. *Sea Scout* (PYc-43) also went to San Diego, but to the West Coast Naval Training Center. *Truant* (PYc-14) got more than her share of raw recruits at Great Lakes Naval Training Station near North Chicago, Illinois. She got early retirement and was returned to her owner, Henry Ford, on 17 November 1943. *Sapphire* (PYc-2) saw duty as a support vessel at the Naval Submarine School, New London, Connecticut. *Sardonyx* (PYc-12) began her naval career with the National Defense Research Committee and then moved to the Navy Underwater Sound Laboratory in New London, after the NDRC was superseded by the Office of Scientific Research and Development on 28 June 1941. *Aquamarine* (PYc-7) did her part to win the Battle of the Atlantic against the U-boat scourge at the Naval Research Laboratory–Acoustics, and *Iolite* (PYc-41) helped train the sonarmen who would use the new underwater detection devices at the Navy Fleet Sound School in Key West, Florida.[73] Another 11 of these converted yachts began duty on inshore and coastal patrol along the Eastern Seaboard before being reassigned to training duties [see Appendix 5].

A further 27 of the coastal patrol yachts remained at their patrol stations, the majority of which were assigned to the Pacific side of the nation from San Diego, California, to Seattle, Washington. *Topaz* (PYc-10), *Sturdy* (PYc-50), *Retort* (PYc-49), *Persistent* (PYc-48), *Moonstone* (PYc-9), *Impetuous* (PYc-46) and *Agate* (PYc-4) hovered between the oceans, guarding the Panama Canal Zone [see Appendix 5].

For *Impetuous*, this was her second war. After serving as USS *Sybilla III* (SP-104) in World War I, she had been returned to her owner. Twenty-two years later she was tapped for a repeat performance. After two years on the Panama Sea Frontier, *Moonstone* was scheduled for transfer to the Ecuadoran Navy. That, however, was not to be. Off the Delaware Capes, on 16 April 1943, the four-pipe destroyer USS *Greer* (DD-145) accidentally rammed her port side and quickly sent her to the bottom. Miraculously, only one crewman was lost.[74]

✣ ✣ ✣ ✣

The 143-foot, 385-ton USS *Alabaster* (PYc-21) probably went the farthest afield of her classification. Built in 1932 for stock broker William F. Ladd by Mathis Yacht Building Company of Camden, New Jersey, the diesel yacht *Alamo* sailed under three other names, *Rellimpa*, *Ranley* and *Ronaele*, before being acquired by the Navy on 3 January 1942 and commissioned under her Navy appellation the last day of the month. Initially on inshore patrol from Delaware Bay to Chesapeake Bay, on 25 January 1944 *Alabaster* arrived at the Canal Zone to escort a tanker bound for Australia, where they arrived on St. Patrick's Day. She then proceeded to function as an anti-submarine warfare training school at Milne Bay, New Guinea, then at Seeadler Harbor, Manus, Admiralty Islands, and thence to Hollandia, New Guinea. Six February 1945 found *Alabaster* in San Pedro Bay, Leyte, where she remained through the end of the war. Her new owner, Colonel C.S. Smith, USAR, Ret., restored her and renamed her *Alamo*. For many years the yacht held title as the largest private yacht on the West Coast. From 1959 through 1960, *Alamo* served as the setting for the CBS television show, *Mr. Lucky*, starring John Vivian, Ross Martin and Piper Laurie. Sold twice more, the then *Fiesta II* burned and sank during conversion to a floating restaurant in 1982 at Puerto Vallarta, Mexico.[75]

✣ ✣ ✣ ✣

The luck of the 66-foot, British diesel motor yacht *Stephanotis* ran out on 3 December 1930. As English steamers tried to run the Union blockade of the Confederacy during the American Civil War, *Stephanotis* was attempting to run another blockade in a war called Prohibition, in the same general area off southern Georgia. That night, instead of being met by smaller speedboats to offload her 1,500 sacks of liquor, the Coast Guard caught up with her. The crew was arrested, the contraband was deep-sixed— at least that was the official report—and *Stephanotis* herself was conscripted into the United States Coast Guard, designated CG-975. On 20 June 1933, she became YP-4 under U.S. Navy command. She remained on assignment in the 1st Naval District out of Boston from then until being placed out of service 8 February 1945.[76]

✣ ✣ ✣ ✣

The designation YP, first used in 1920, stands for Naval District Yard Patrol Craft, which comprised a collection of vessels ranging from motor launches to private yachts and fishing trawlers. Although some of the fishing vessels were larger, the general run of the "Yippies" was 100 feet long, displacing 50 to 175 tons. Armament ranged from the one 3"/50 dual purpose mount plus two 20mm and two depth charge tracks carried by YP-425 (formerly USS *Brave*, PYc-34) to nothing. The initial fleet comprised five dozen Coast Guard craft no longer needed after repeal of the Volstead Act ended Prohibition. Their number increased to 650 during World War II. Although the Yippies' primary role was in training personnel and research, some of them did see combat. YP-16 (ex–CG-267), YP-17 (ex–CG-275) and YP-97 [these three not yachts] were lost in the Japanese occupation of the Philippine Islands and were struck from the Navy list 24 July 1942. At Guadalcanal, the so classified vessels were used as tugs, dispatch boats, rescue craft, troop and supply ferries and even as transports in minor amphibious assaults. YP-284 came out second best in action against a Japanese destroyer on 25 October 1942 off Lunga Point, Guadalcanal. The Japanese cruiser *Sendai* had sent YP-346 to the bottom off Guadalcanal the previous month.[77]

In 1939, Hodgdon Brothers of East Boothbay, Maine, built the 85-foot, 93-ton auxiliary sailing yacht *Imelda* for John J. Hagerty. The yacht went to a second owner, who changed her name to *Mystic*, before the Navy acquired her in 1942 and placed the machine gun and depth charge armed yacht in service as YP-357, assigned patrol off Key West, Florida. In 1945, the Navy returned her to her owner, who promptly sold the yacht. She went through three changes of ownership and name changes before, as *Irmay*, she was sold, in 1950, due to "matrimonial difficulties," to the Central Intelligence

The C.I.A.'s yacht *Juanita* (originally John H. Hagerty's yacht *Imelda*), probably at a small harbor on the Ionian Sea, c. 1951 (courtesy Hodgdon Yachts).

Agency, which outfitted her with specialized radio equipment during a clandestine refit. Under yet another new name, *Juanita* participated in Project OBOPUS/BGFIEND in the Ionian Sea off Greece, as a covert, floating propaganda radio station aimed at fomenting unrest to overthrow the Hoxha government of Albania. The racing yacht proved to be a less than optimal broadcasting platform and *Juanita* was sidelined in Piraeus, Greece. Thirteen years later, she had been sold at least three more times, but on these occasions she retained her latest name. As of this writing she is available for charter.[78]

※ ※ ※ ※

Some of the YPs were old-timers. The 1917-built steam yacht *De Grasse* (ID-217) had been deemed unsuitable after her conversion in July 1917 and was returned to her owner J.L. Redmond of New York City [see Chapter 5]. This time around she apparently passed muster and was reacquired in early 1942. Renamed USS YP-506, she was armed with a single 3-pounder cannon and one machine gun. Apparently no record remains of her wartime assignment, but she survived the war to be sold in 1946.[79] Even older was YP-200. The 76-foot, 387-ton gasoline powered motor yacht *Edithena* was built in 1914 by Charles L. Seabury Company of Morris Heights, New York, for Loring Q. White, president of Bridgewater Trust Company. She served in the First World War as USS *Edithena* (SP-624). After the war she went to the Bureau of Fisheries under the new name *Widgeon* on 21 October 1919. In 1942 the Navy once again needed her service and she was rearmed with a single 1-pounder cannon. After the war she went back to the Fish and Wildlife Service in December 1945.[80]

※ ※ ※ ※

The 97-foot diesel motor yacht *Innisfail* was built in 1939 by Mathis-Trumpy Boatbuilding Company of Camden, New Jersey, for meat packing millionaire Joseph M.

Cudahy. The Cudahy family spent much of their leisure time aboard the double-planked wood hull *Innisfail*, their second of that name, cruising the East Coast. (Cudahy's first *Innisfail*, renamed *Enticer*, can be seen in the movie *Some Like It Hot*.) In May 1942, *Innisfail* traded her name and luxury for a number and more austere accommodations and became USS YP-354. Armed with two 20mm antiaircraft guns and a single depth charge track, she spent five years patrolling the Chesapeake Bay. YP-354 was placed out of Navy service in 1947, but, restored to her former glory, she remained in government service as a secondary presidential yacht until sold in 1965.[81]

* * * *

Another 38 yachts of all sizes were converted to naval use but were placed into the Miscellaneous Unclassified (IX) category. This is a catchall which comprised, during World War II, everything from the 1798 frigate USS *Constitution* (IX-21), to the 1898 battleship USS *Illinois* (IX-15), the 1907 salvage tug-ice breaker USS *Favorite* (IX-45), to the 1921 tanker USS *Vandalia* (IX-191), the 1944 USS *Callao* (IX-205), the German Kriegsmarine armed trawler *Externsteine*, captured in 1944 off Greenland, to the 1928 passenger steamer USS *President Warfield* (IX-169). *President Warfield* was sold in late 1946 to the Potomac Shipwrecking Company of Washington, D.C. In reality, they were agents for the Jewish Haganah. In 1947, the nondescript steamer found everlasting fame as the Zionist ship *Exodus*.[82]

* * * *

The diminutive, gasoline auxiliary yawl *Wimbee* (IX-88), just under 60 feet long, was involved in her own exodus before the United States entered the war. Built in 1936 by Ernst Burmester of Bremen, Germany, as *Roland von Bremen*, the yacht was Germany's entry in the 1936 Newport, Rhode Island, to Bermuda race. The yacht finished eighth and did not fare much better in subsequent races. In 1938, Berlin Jew Leo Berson bought the yacht with the intention of fleeing the Third Reich, which he did along with the yacht's racing navigator Hanns von Lottner. After successfully arriving in the United States, Berson renamed his yacht *Condor* and later sold her to W.L. McFarland of Greenwich, Connecticut. The Navy acquired the subsequently named *Wimbee* on 30 July 1942 and placed her in service patrolling the Gulf out of Port Everglades, Florida. By 28 June 1944 *Wimbee* was no longer of value to the war effort and was struck from the Navy List and sold just over seven months later.[83]

* * * *

On the 18th anniversary of the World War I Armistice, Vadim Stefan Makaroff, son of Vice Admiral Stepan Osipovich Makarov, commander of the Russian fleet in the Russo-Japanese War (who went down with his flagship the battleship *Petropavlovsk* on 13 April 1904), donated his 70-foot main trysail ketch *Vamarie* to the United States Naval Academy for training purposes. Built in 1933 by Abeking and Rasmussen of Bremen, Germany, *Vamarie* sailed in nine blue water races between 1934 and 1936, logging over 30,000 miles. The midshipmen continued her racing tradition as the Navy's entry in the 1937 and 1939 Chesapeake Bay seasons as well as competing in the 1938 Newport, Rhode Island, to Bermuda race, coming in 29th out of 44 finishers. Makaroff's interest in aviation was apparent in his yacht's unique auxiliary propulsion system, which consisted of an airplane propeller rigged to a hub on the mizzen mast and belt driven by a gasoline engine affixed to the deck. The Navy, however, was not interested in having a wingless flying boat. They removed the propeller and reconfigured *Vamarie*'s (IX-47) power plant to a more conventional design.

In the fall of 1940 three other yachts were donated to the Naval Academy: Sterling Morton's 88-foot two-masted auxiliary schooner *Freedom* (IX-43), the late Dudley F. Wolfe's 68½-foot gasoline auxiliary sloop *Highland Light* (IX-48), and Wallace F. Lanahan's 55-foot gasoline auxiliary cutter *Spindrift* (IX-49), which he sold for one dollar.[84]

✣ ✣ ✣ ✣

Of the 38 IX classified yachts, only eight were actually commissioned, earning the USS designation. The rest were "placed in service," though this did not affect their employment in the war, and in one case a Navy commission would have been inappropriate. The 111½-foot diesel auxiliary *Geoanna* (IX-61) started her assignment on 19 February 1942 on patrol out of San Pedro, California. July second of the following year, she became a Coast Guard Training vessel, but two months later she switched services entirely, becoming a communications ship for the U.S. Army.[85]

Not counting the four yachts that went to the Naval Academy, the remaining 34 were almost evenly split between the East Coast and Gulf Sea Frontiers (18) and the West Coast and Hawaiian ones (16). Founder of Victor Talking Machine Company (later RCA Victor), Eldridge R.F. Johnson's 1934, 87 foot, 94-ton diesel auxiliary ketch *Elsie Fenimore* was renamed USS *John M. Howard* (IX-75) two weeks before her commissioning into the Navy on 1 September 1942. Her task would be conducting ordnance experiments along the Atlantic seaboard.[86] The 1930, 130 foot, 320-ton diesel motor yacht USS *Galaxy* (IX-54) spent not only her wartime service at the Underwater Sound Laboratory, Fort Trumbull, New London, Connecticut, but even after her decommissioning 2 August 1945 she was placed back in service to continue her experimental work for almost another eight months.[87]

The 1938, 92-ton wood-hull auxiliary yawl USS *Saluda* (IX-87, ex–*Odyssey*) had a similar military career in underwater sound research, first out of Miami, Florida, from June 1943 into January 1947, when she was decommissioned and placed in service at New London, Connecticut. One year later found *Saluda* stationed at San Diego, California, where she alternated doing research and competing in local sailing races. In 1968, she was reclassified YAG-87 (Miscellaneous Auxiliary Craft) and was finally struck from the Navy List on 15 April 1974. Four years later, *Saluda* was turned over to the Mount Rainier Council of the Boy Scouts of America. With her original name restored, Sea Scout Ship (SSS) *Odyssey* now serves the Sea Scouts of Tacoma, Washington, and is available for charter.[88]

The 1911, 138 foot, 141-ton gasoline motor yacht *Martha's Vineyard* (IX-97) and the 1922, 110 foot, 167-ton wood-hull diesel motor yacht *Aide de Camp* (IX-224) also served with the Underwater Sound Laboratory. The latter, however, remained at her latest owner Harvard University. *Aide de Camp* started life as *Colleen*, built by George Lawley & Sons of Neponset, Massachusetts, for yarn manufacturer Samuel Agar Salvage. The yacht's lavish appointments would serve a succession of owners before commencing her civilian wartime work for the Navy at Harvard University. Circa 1926–27 New Hampshire Governor John Gilbert Winant, whom President Franklin Roosevelt later would appoint Ambassador to the Court of St. James, purchased the yacht and renamed her *Ranger*. In 1928, her new owner H.M. Pierce renamed her *Poinsettia* and, three years later, sold her to Boston financier Frederick Henry Prince, who again changed her name, this time to *Aide de Camp*. That name stuck until 1955 when the Kennedy Marine Engine Company of Biloxi, Mississippi, acquired and renamed her *Mariner II*. *Aide de Camp* did not actually transfer to the Navy until 31 May 1945, after Germany's surrender. She continued in her research capacity, this time based at Fort Lauderdale, Florida, until placed out of service on 2 November of that year.[89]

✧ ✧ ✧ ✧

Hollywood's contribution to the war effort involved more than just making patriotic films. Three of the IX yachts had a Tinseltown connection. The 1920 106 foot, 96-ton diesel auxiliary schooner *Seaward* (IX-60) was acquired 31 January 1942 from Cecil B. DeMille Productions for patrol out of San Pedro, California, protecting the Port of Los Angeles.[90] In 1934, director John Ford purchased the 106½ foot, 147-ton wood-hull auxiliary diesel ketch *Faith* and renamed her *Araner*. That same year Ford was commissioned a lieutenant commander in the Naval Reserve. He was called up to active duty in the summer of 1941, and *Araner* (IX-57) followed him into the Navy the following January. The classic ketch, mostly under sail, patrolled the Western Sea Frontier off Guadalupe and San Clemente Islands.[91] The third of the Hollywood yachts did not actually establish her Industry connection until 1946. The 118 foot, 122 ton *Zaca* (IX-73), a 1930 wood-hull diesel auxiliary schooner, was placed in service on 19 June 1942, assigned to the Western Sea Frontier. As an airplane guard ship, she stood ready to rescue crews of downed aircraft off Northern California.[92] She diligently did her duty but was to see more action after the war than during it, albeit of a far different kind. The Navy placed *Zaca* out of service on 6 October 1944 and finally sold her the following July to Joseph Rosenberg of San Francisco. He, in turn, resold the yacht in 1946 to Hollywood heartthrob Errol Flynn, and the good times began to roll.

> The Zaca provided Flynn with the things he loved and needed most—adventure and the sea. All the while, the yacht also served as a playground for Flynn's otherwise overpowering needs. The vessel was the venue of choice for the actor's wild orgies: Flynn would arrange with his friends to escort many attractive women to the yacht, and then the men would share an abundance of booze, laughter, stories, and even their women.[93]

Flynn owned the yacht until his death in 1959.

✧ ✧ ✧ ✧

One of the oldest of the IX converted yachts, *Seven Seas* (IX-68), was also the most impressive anachronism, looking like a China Clipper of old on naval patrol. Originally named *Abraham Rydberg*, the 168 foot, 430-ton auxiliary square-rigged ship was built in 1912 by Bergsund M.V. Atkieb of Stockholm, Sweden, as a cadet training vessel for the Swedish Navy. Seventeen years later she was converted into a yacht. William S. Gubelmann, ultimately holder of over 5,000 patents for business machines, bought her in 1936. Gubelmann spent five months fitting her out to his satisfaction and renamed her *Seven Seas*. The Navy kept that name when they acquired her on 10 April 1942. For the next two years *Seven Seas* served as a station ship out of Key West, Florida. With the Battle of the Atlantic essentially won, the converted yacht was placed out of service on 22 May 1944 and was struck from the Navy List on 27 July.[94]

Though not as impressive under canvas, another set of sails against the Reich was USS *Guinevere* (IX-67), a 1921, 195 foot, 503-ton diesel-electric auxiliary schooner.

Commissioned 16 June 1942, *Guinevere* performed harbor patrol out of Boston and convoy escort past Greenland as far as the mid-ocean meeting point (MOMP), south of Iceland, where British escorts would take over. As Tom Kelly, who served aboard, described it, "We were supposed to patrol for U-boats but we stayed just out of sight of the convoys. It would have depressed the merchant sailors too much to think that all that stood between them and Hitler's navy was a sailing ship." The fun began after the MOMP hand-over when "Guinevere would shut off its engine, hoist its sails and cruise a zigzag course back 'in the general direction of Boston,' its sonar sweeping for U-boats all the while. That, Kelly said, 'was like a holiday.'"[95] *Guinevere* was decommissioned on 2 August 1945 and sold the following year.[96]

* * * *

Four-masted diesel auxiliary bark *Sea Cloud* (ex–*Hussar V*) under full sail prior to World War II (NH 76462 courtesy the Naval History & Heritage Command Photographic Dept.).

6. World War Again

The 316 foot, 2323-ton USS *Sea Cloud* (IX-99) slid down the ways at the Friederich Krupp Germaniawerft of Kiel, Germany, in 1931. She was financier Edward Francis Hutton's fifth yacht named *Hussar*. A four-masted diesel-electric auxiliary bark, she was the image of a classic tea clipper under her 32,000 square feet of canvas. After Hutton and wife Marjorie Merriweather Post divorced in 1935, her new husband, United States Ambassador to the Soviet Union Joseph E. Davies acquired title and changed the yacht's name to *Sea Cloud*. With war inevitable, Davies offered his yacht to the Navy in 1941, but was turned down. The situation changed, however, after the Japanese attack on Pearl Harbor, Hawaii. On 7 January 1942 the Navy chartered *Sea Cloud* for $1.00 per annum and then armed her with two 3"/50 dual purpose mounts, eight 20mm antiaircraft guns, four depth charge K-guns, one Mk.X Hedgehog and two depth charge tracks. With all but her main mast and associated rigging removed for the duration, only her clipper bow hinted at her full glory. After initial assignment to the Coast Guard, classified WPG-284, she was commissioned in the Navy on 9 April 1943.

It was then that USS *Sea Cloud*'s importance to naval history began, after her new captain Lieutenant Carlton Skinner, USCGR, persevered in pressing his case that the only way to effectively prepare black seamen to fill out the Navy's need for trained personnel was to have them work alongside crewmen who already knew the ropes. That meant fully integrated crews—whites and blacks working together and living together in all ratings. Although the Navy already had black sailors serving under white officers on the destroyer escort USS *Mason* (DE-529) and the submarine chaser USS PC-1264, those still were segregated crews. As a result, the men had to rely more on classroom theory and enthusiasm than the guidance of old hands. Skinner's was still a radical proposal for the time.

The second week of June 1944 Skinner's experiment was put to the ultimate test. En route from Bermuda to Argentia, Newfoundland, *Sea Cloud*'s sonar operator reported a contact to the captain, who immediately sounded General Quarters. The yacht proceeded to track the submarine, the crew ready and eager for the right moment to pounce. What followed was eight hours of dropping depth charges, searching, firing K-guns and more searching. Despite the crew's best efforts, *Sea Cloud* eventually lost contact. Skinner, having radioed their position, was ordered to proceed to his destination. Task Group 22.5, consisting of escort aircraft carrier USS *Croatan* (CVE-25) and Destroyer Escorts USS *Frost* (DE-144), *Huse* (DE-145), *Inch* (DE-146), *Snowden* (DE-246) and *Swansey* (DE-248), was ordered to take over where *Sea Cloud* left off. They regained the contact, and their attack, on 12 June, drove Oberleutnant Wilhelm Gerlach's Type XIV Milchkuh U-490 to the surface where she was sunk by gunfire. *Sea Cloud* was credited with an assist.

Though *Sea Cloud*'s attack on U-490 was not itself immediately successful, it had far-reaching consequences. It provided proof that integration was not only possible but desirable and doubtless helped President Truman's eventual decision to issue, on 26 July 1948, Executive Order 9981, which finally integrated the military. *Sea Cloud* was decommissioned on 4 November 1944 and returned to the owner's agent. Eventually, *Sea Cloud* became too expensive to maintain and Marjorie Davies offered her for sale. There were no buyers until Dominican Republic dictator Generalissimo Rafael Trujillo offered a 44-passenger Vickers Viscount turboprop airplane in exchange. The deal was struck, although the details remain sketchy. Years after Trujillo's assassination, and after serious neglect and subsequent deterioration, the yacht's current owners, Sea Cloud Cruises,

USCGC *Sea Cloud*, October 1942. Of her original rig, only her mainmast remains, with an added crow's nest (National Archives, US Coast Guard photograph 4940–42 NYBOS).

Gmb, of Hamburg, Germany, acquired her and have fully restored and upgraded her to give her passengers a taste of yachting history.[97]

✤ ✤ ✤ ✤

Another one-dollar enlistee, the 1926 diesel auxiliary schooner *Blue Dolphin* (IX-65) was purchased outright, for that amount, by the Navy from Boston businessman and amateur naturalist Amory Coolidge on 17 March 1942. She was placed in service on 6 April, assigned as a station ship at Casco Bay, Maine. Coolidge had purchased the *Dolphin* in 1933 and, essentially following in the wake Allison Vincent Armour and his yacht *Utowana*'s turn-of-the-century voyages [see Chapter 5 and Appendices 4 & 5], almost immediately set sail for the Galapagos Islands. The personal object of the voyage was adventure, the practical justification was to collect samples for the Museum of Comparative Zoology at Harvard College. Fittingly, after her naval service, *Blue Dolphin* was sold in September 1945 to David C. Nutt, then a commander, USNR, who was involved in oceanographic research, particularly in the Arctic and Greenland. On 3 April 1949, the Chief of Naval Operations (CNO) again deemed *Blue Dolphin* "suitable for use as a naval auxiliary in time of war, and authorized her to fly the Naval Reserve Yacht pennant. She was, however, never called back into service."[98]

✤ ✤ ✤ ✤

When Japanese forces bombed Pearl Harbor, the Philippines fell and Japanese soldiers occupied several of the Aleutian Islands; when German U-boats enjoyed their

"Happy Time" in the shooting gallery that was the Atlantic seaboard, the United States Navy had to grab what it could to rapidly fill in its ranks of patrol vessels. The two ocean aqueous buffer that hitherto had allowed America to go its own way no longer was proof against foreign attack. As in the past, yachts and yachtsmen, the sea-going Minutemen, stood ready to augment the nation's defense capability. Though there were numerous tactical victories, it is difficult, perhaps even impossible, to determine with certainty the strategic impact of converted yachts on the eventual outcome of the war. As Captain Samuel Eliot Morison, USN, noted in the preface to his *History of United States Naval Operations in World War II: The Battle of the Atlantic 1939–1943*, "Twelve inches' difference in the course of a torpedo, a few yards' deflection in the fall of a salvo, may make the difference between victory and defeat." Captain Morison was talking about the influence of luck in warfare, but consider for a moment that those same 12 inches and few yards were the former playthings of the wealthy turned to more serious pursuits. There also might lie the difference.

Epilogue

From the very beginnings of the United States its Navy, in time of need, has acquired civilian vessels of all types, some with a little arm twisting, most either through the owner's patriotism or financial expedience. In the two world wars, five of the converted yachts were lost to enemy action and another four went to the bottom due to collision with a vessel they were trying to protect. As of this writing, at least 16 of the World War II yachts currently are available for charter, though, apart from *Sea Cloud* and *Zaca*, under new names: USS *Beaumont* is now *Talitha G.*, USS *Dauntless* is now *Delphine*, USS *Argus* is now *Haida G.*, USS *Agate* is now *Vallarta Alegre*, USS *Amber* is now *Thea Foss*, USS *Aquamarine* is now *Miss Ann*, USS *Black Douglas* is now *El Boughaz*, USS *Leader* is now *Grace* (as in Grace Kelly, who honeymooned aboard), USS *Peridot* is now *Maha*, *El Cano* is now *Yankee Clipper*, USS *Saluda* is now *Odyssey*, *Wimbee* is now *Roland Von Bremen*, YP-354 is now *El Presidente*, and YP-357 is now *Juanita*.

In an age where a warship can stand off many hundreds of miles, her crew never physically laying eyes on their target, and lay waste to an entire city, let alone another ship, it is perhaps prophetic that *Blue Dolphin* never again was called up despite CNO's recommendation and all the wars that have followed the Second World War. The Navy's new coastal patrol craft are purpose-built, avoiding the compromises inherent in converting a yacht that was designed to pamper its owner, where the shots were served in cut-crystal glasses instead of fired from naval guns. As of this writing there are no government plans to enlist yachts in the future. That attitude, however, is nothing new. Nevertheless, yachts are unlikely to be called up except, one can speculate, for clandestine operations where they can publicly stand out without being noticed except as symbols of wealth. The super-yachts of today often carry helicopters, occasionally submarines, such as the Triton 1000/3, 10½ foot, three person mini-sub. Some super-yachts even are submarines themselves, like the Hyper-Sub $9,500,000 submersible powerboat and Russian billionaire Andrey Melnichenko's 390 foot, $350,000,000 NZ megayacht, simply named *A*. The armed yacht of the future is likely to be a super-yacht armed with military-grade surveillance and defensive measures against pirates. For now the yachtsmen's artillery is the popping champagne cork, but their floating palaces have stood ready to bear the acrid blast of cordite in support of decisive naval force, and may yet again.

> "It follows then as certain as that night succeeds the day, that without a decisive naval force we can do nothing definitive, and with it, everything honorable and glorious."
> —President George Washington writing to the Marquis de Lafayette, 15 November 1781

Appendix 1

Instructions to Commanders of Privateers

Continental Congress, April 3, 1776:

I. You may, by force of arms, attack, subdue and take all ships and other vessels belonging to the inhabitants of Great Britain, on the high seas, or between high water and low water mark, except ships and vessels bringing persons who intend to settle and reside in the United Colonies; or bringing arms, ammunition, or war-like stores, to the said colonies, for the use of such inhabitants thereof as are friends to the American cause, which you shall suffer to pass unmolested, the commanders thereof permitting a peaceable search and giving satisfactory information of the contents of the ladings and destinations of voyages.

II. You may, by force of arms, attack, subdue and take all ships and other vessels whatsoever, carrying soldiers, arms, gunpowder, ammunition, provisions, or any other contraband goods, to any of the British armies or ships of war employed against these colonies.

III. You shall bring such ships and vessels, as you shall take, with their guns, rigging, tackle, apparel, furniture, and ladings to some convenient port or ports of the United Colonies, that proceedings may thereupon be had in due form, before the courts which are or shall be appointed to hear and determine causes civil and maritime.

IV. You, or one of your chief officers, shall bring or send the master and pilot and one or more principal person or persons of the company of every ship or vessel by you taken, as soon after capture as may be, to the judge or judges of such court as aforesaid, to be examined upon oath, and make answer to the interrogatories which may be propounded, touching the interest or property of the ship or vessel and her lading; and, at the same time, you shall deliver, or cause to be delivered to the judge or judges, all passes, sea-briefs, charter-parties, bills of lading, cockets [customhouse seals], letters and other documents and writings found on board, proving the said papers by the affidavit of yourself or of some other person present at the capture, to be produced as they were received, without fraud, addition, subduction or embezzlement.

V. You shall keep and preserve every ship or vessels and cargo by you taken, until they shall, by a sentence of a court properly authorized, to be adjudged lawful prizes; not selling, spoiling, wasting, or diminishing the same, or breaking the bulk thereof, nor suffering and such thing to be done.

VI. If you, or any of your officers or crew, shall, in cold blood, kill or maim, or by torture or otherwise, cruelly, inhumanly, and contrary to common usage and the practice of civilized nations in war, treat any person or persons surprized [sic] in the ship or vessel you shall take, the offender shall be severely punished.

VII. You shall, by all convenient opportunities, send to Congress written accounts of the captures you shall make, with the number and names of the captives, copies of your journal from time to time, and intelligence of what may occur or be discovered concerning the designs of the enemy and the destination, motions and operations of their fleets and armies.

VIII. One-third, at least, of your whole company shall be landsmen. [This provision served the dual purposes of allowing the spread of the pool of available able bodied seamen among as many vessels as was possible and of apprenticing and training a new crop of sailors.]

IX. You shall not ransom any prisoners or captives, but shall dispose of them in such manner as the Congress, or, if that be not sitting, in the colony whither they shall be brought, as the general assembly, convention, or council, or committee of safety, of such colony shall direct.

X. You shall observe all such further instructions as Congress shall hereafter give in the premises, when you shall have notice thereof.

XI. If you shall do anything contrary to these instructions, or to others hereafter to be given, or willingly suffer such thing to be done, you shall not only forfeit your commission and be liable to an action for breach of the condition of your bond, but be responsible to the party grieved for damages sustained by such malversation.

Additional articles, April 7, 1781:

1. You are to pay sacred regard to the rights of neutral powers and the usage and customs of civilized nations; and on no pretence [sic] whatever, presume to take or seize any ships or vessels belonging to the subjects of princes or powers in alliance with these United Sates... [Note the change from "United Colonies" in section III to "United States" here.]

2. You shall permit all neutral vessels freely to navigate on the high seas or coasts of America except such as are employed in carrying contraband goods or soldiers to the enemies of these United States.

3. You shall not seize or capture any effects belonging to the subjects of belligerent powers on board neutral vessels, excepting contraband goods; and you are carefully to observe, that the term contraband is confined to those articles which are expressly declared to be such in the treaty of amity and commerce, of the sixth day of February, 1778, between these United States and his most Christian majesty [King Louis XVI of France], namely: arms, great guns, bombs, with their fusees and other things belonging to them, cannon-balls, gun-powder, matches, pikes, swords, lances, spears, halberts, mortars, petards, grenadoes, salt-petre, muskets, musket-ball, bucklers, helmets, breast plates, coats of mail, and the like kind of arms proper for

arming soldiers, musket rests, belts, horses with their furniture, and all other warlike instruments whatever.

From "Journals of the Continental Congress," Library of Congress, as quoted in Allen, Gardner Weld, A Naval History of the American Revolution in Two Volumes, Vol. II, Houghton Mifflin Company, Boston, 1913, Appendix III, pp. 695-698.

Appendix 2
The Trent *Affair*

In 1838 Lieutenant Charles Wilkes was given overall command of the United States Exploring Expedition (authorized in 1836) to survey the Southern Ocean. This took him to Antarctica in December 1839. In 1861, now a captain, he commanded the screw frigate USS *San Jacinto* when, on 8 November, that vessel stopped and boarded the Royal Mail packet RMS *Trent*. *Trent* was subsequently allowed to proceed to England, but not with her passengers, Confederate commissioners James Murray Mason and John Slidell and their staff. They had been sent to Europe to seek official recognition of the Confederate States of America from Great Britain and France.

While the Americans celebrated this naval coup, the British were incensed at this blatant violation of their ostensible neutrality. Her Majesty's Government demanded the immediate release of the Rebels and a formal apology. Although neither side was eager for a war, heated rhetoric threatened to tip the balance in that direction. England went so far as to dispatch military reinforcements to Canada and to strengthen her naval presence in the Western Atlantic. Technical difficulties with the transatlantic telegraph cable delayed communications sufficiently to allow time for tempers to cool.

Eventually, on 26 December, Secretary of State William H. Seward ordered Mason, Slidell et alia released and explained to Her Majesty's Government's satisfaction that Wilkes had acted on his own initiative, not under orders. Furthermore, that Wilkes had erred by seizing RMS *Trent* and libeling her to adjudication by a court of competent jurisdiction. Cooler heads prevailed, and a third war with England was avoided.

https://history.state.gov/milestones/1861-1865/trent-affair U.S. Department of State, Office of the Historian, accessed 12/04/2016

Appendix 3

Yachts Acquired for Service in the War with Spain*

USS *Aileen*
t. 192; l. 120'wl; s. 14; a. one 3-pdr
Built 1896 by John Roach & Sons of Chester, PA. Purchased 2 May 1898 from Richard Stevens for $55,000. Assigned coastal defense. Naval Militia service: New York 18 May 1899 to 18 November 1909; Rhode Island 18 November 1909. On 7 April 1917 returned to Navy for World War I service.

✣ ✣ ✣ ✣

USS *Buccaneer*
t. 160; l. 138'; b. 20'; s. ?; a. two 6-pdr, four 2-pdr, one 1-pdr
Built 1888 as *Unquowa* by Atlantic Iron Works of Boston, MA. Lent 13 June 1898 by owner William Randolph Hearst. Assigned waters around Key West. Returned 12 September 1898.

✣ ✣ ✣ ✣

USS *Dorothea*
t. 594dp; l. 178'wl; b. 23'3"; s. 14; a. four 6-pdr, two 1-pdr, two mg
Built 1897 by William Cramp & Sons of Philadelphia, PA. Purchased 21 May 1898 from Thomas McKean estate for $187,000. Assigned blockade patrol Key West, FL, to Havana, Cuba. Naval Militia service: Illinois May 1901; Ohio 1909. Returned to Navy 20 April 1917. Assigned patrol of Mexican waters. On 8 January 1918 reassigned to Havana for training Cuban naval officers. Decommissioned 23 June 1919. Sold 20 November 1919.

✣ ✣ ✣ ✣

USS *Eagle* [4th of that name] (ex–*Almy*)
t. 434dp; 177'; b. 24'; s. 12; a. two 6-pdr rapid fire
Built 1890 by Harlan & Hollingsworth of Wilmington, DE. Purchased 2 April 1898 from Frederic Gallatin for $10,000. Assigned North Atlantic Squadron blockading Cuba. Post-war Caribbean surveying duty. Patrolled off Nicaragua 1909. Landed Marines at Santiago, Cuba, 1912. Gunboat with cruiser squadron during Haiti operations July 1915 to March 1916. Patrolled around

151

Cuba during World War I. Decommissioned 23 May 1919. Sold 3 January 1920.

✧ ✧ ✧ ✧

USS *Elfrida*
t. 164dp; l. 101'6"; b. 18'; s. 10; a. one 3-pdr rapid fire, two 1-pdr rapid fire
Built 1889 by Harlan & Hollingsworth of Wilmington, DE. Purchased 15 June 1898 from W. Seward Webb for $50,000. Assigned coastal patrol off Connecticut. Naval Militia service: Connecticut 29 April 1899; New Jersey 1900; Connecticut 1902; back to Navy 27 June 1908; North Carolina 20 August 1909. Returned to Navy for World War I and designated SP-988. Assigned 5th Naval District. Decommissioned 31 March 1918. Sold 11 May 1918.

✧ ✧ ✧ ✧

USS *Free Lance*
t. 132; l. 137'; b. 20'8"; s. 14; a. two .65 cal. Gatling guns
Built 1895 by Lewis Nixon of Elizabethport, NJ. Leased 12 May 1898 from F. Augustus Schermerhorn. Assigned section patrol off New York City. Returned to owner early 1899. Leased again 19 July 1917. Assigned 3rd Naval District (NYC). Returned to owner 24 December 1918.

✧ ✧ ✧ ✧

USS *Frolic* [3rd of that name] (ex–*Comanche*)
t. 607dp; l. 165'; b. 25'; s. 11; a. two 3-pdr
Built 1892 by Globe Iron Works of Cleveland, OH. Purchased 28 May 1898 from H.M. Hanna for $115,000. Assigned mail service to North Atlantic Squadron blockading Cuba and Puerto Rico. Post war transferred to Asiatic Squadron in operations with U.S. Army to suppress the Philippine insurrection. 21 May 1909 transferred to War Department for Philippine service.

✧ ✧ ✧ ✧

USS *Gloucester* (ex–*Corsair II*)
t. 786dp; l. 240'8"; b. 27'2"; s. 17; a. four 6-pdr, four 3-pdr, two Gatling guns
Built 1891 by Neafie & Levy of Philadelphia, PA. Purchased 23 April 1898 from J. Pierpont Morgan for $225,000. Assigned North Atlantic Squadron blockading Cuba. Naval Militia service: U.S. Naval Academy 1899 to 1902; Massachusetts and New York 1905 to 1917. Recommissioned 7 April 1917. Assigned 3rd Naval District. Sold 21 November 1919.

✧ ✧ ✧ ✧

USS *Hawk* (ex–*Hermione*)
t. 545dp; l. 145'; b. 22'; s. 14; a. one 3-pdr, two 1-pdr
Built 1891 by Fleming & Ferguson of Paisley, Scotland. Purchased 2 April 1898 from Henry Lillie Pierce estate for $50,000. Assigned North Atlantic Squadron blockading Cuba. Naval Militia service: Ohio 1900 to 1909; New York

3 August 1909 to 21 May 1919 when decommissioned and placed in reserve fleet. Designated PY-2 1920. Reclassified IX-14 1 July 1921. Recommissioned 16 April 1922 to 14 February 1940. Sold for scrap 25 February 1940.

✣ ✣ ✣ ✣

USS *Hist* (ex–*Thespia*)
t. 472dp; l. 174'; b. 23'; s. 14.5; a. three 3-pdr, four 1-pdr, two mg
Built 1895 by William Cramp & Sons of Philadelphia, PA. Purchased 22 April 1898 from David Dows Jr. for $65,000. Assigned blockading fleet off Santiago, Cuba, through end of war. Out of commission early 1899 to 18 July 1902. Assigned patrol and dispatch duty in Caribbean. On 4 March 1903 posted to Long Island Sound for duty with submarine testing; 28 September 1905 assigned Training Station at Newport, RI, as tender to frigate USS *Constellation*. After another stint in the Caribbean, this time including surveying work, decommissioned 24 July 1911. Sold that November.

✣ ✣ ✣ ✣

USS *Hornet* [4th of that name] (ex–*Alicia*)
t. 301dp; l. 180'; b. 24'; s. 15; a. three 6-pdr, two 1-pdr
Built 1890 by Harlan & Hollingsworth of Wilmington, DE. Purchased 6 April 1898 from Henry M. Flagler for $117,500. Assigned North Atlantic Squadron blockading Cuba. Naval Militia service: North Carolina October 1898–1902. The tender to receiving ship *Franklin* until struck 18 March 1910. Sold 12 July 1910.

✣ ✣ ✣ ✣

USS *Huntress*
t. 82; l. 97'wl; b. 16'; s. 14; a. two 3-pdr rf
Built 1895 by Charles L. Seabury & Co. of Nyak on Hudson, NY. Purchased 7 June 1898 from Frank C. Fowler for $27,500. Assigned auxiliary gunboat off Staten Island and in Long Island Sound. Naval Militia service: New Jersey 30 December 1898 to 1907; Missouri 1907 to 1917. Struck 12 March 1917. Sold 3 December 1917.

✣ ✣ ✣ ✣

USS *Inca*
t. 120; l. 114'; b. 18'; s. 14; a. one 1-pdr
Built 1898 by George Lawley & Son of South Boston, MA. Purchased 13 June 1898 from F.B. McQuesten for $35,000. Assigned patrol and training out of Boston, MA. Decommissioned and transferred to Massachusetts Naval Militia 27 August 1898 to 1908.

✣ ✣ ✣ ✣

Ituna
t. 171gt; l. 135'6"wl; b. 19'8"; s. ?; a. (proposed armaments 6-pdr rf and mg)
Built 1886 by A. & J. Inglis Ltd. of Glasgow, Scotland. (Newspaper accounts have her acquired from Allison V. Armour and assigned dispatch duty off

Cuba.) After commercial service off Mexico and reconfiguration as fishing trawler, foundered in a gale 13 March 1920.

✤ ✤ ✤ ✤

USS *Kanawha* [2nd of that name]
t. 175; l. 114'; b. 18'; s. 14; a. one 3-pdr, three 1-pdr two mg
Built 1896 by Charles L. Seabury & Co. of Nyak, NY. Purchased 7 June 1898 from John P. Duncan for $50,000. Assigned support of U.S. occupation forces Cuba 21 August to 12 September 1898. Naval Militia service: Rhode Island 12 December 1898 12 August 1899. Subsequently transferred to War Department.

✤ ✤ ✤ ✤

Llewellyn (ex–*Marietta*)
t. 92gt; l. 118'wl; b. 16'; s. 18; a. ?
Built 1893 by Pusey & Jones Co. (hull only) of Wilmington, DE. Lent by Alfred Carr 11 May 1898 to the Second Naval Battalion, New York Naval Militia, as flagship, to patrol the lower bay, New Jersey coast and Long Island.

✤ ✤ ✤ ✤

USS *Mayflower* [2nd of that name]
t. 2,690dp; l. 273'wl; b. 36'; s. 17; a. two 5", six 6-pdr
Built 1896 by J. & G. Thomson of Clyde Bank, Scotland. Purchased 19 March 1898 from Ogden Goelet estate for $430,000. Assigned 20 April 1898 to North Atlantic Squadron blockading Twice as Admiral Dewey's flagship 1902. Cuba. Converted to Presidential Yacht 25 July 1905. Decommissioned 22 March 1929. Sold 19 October 1931. Purchased by War Shipping Administration 31 July 1942, renamed *Butte*. Commissioned in U.S. Coast Guard as *Mayflower* 19 October 1943, rearmed with one 5"/51, two 3"/50, six 20mm, two depth charge racks, four K-guns, one Hedgehog, to patrol Atlantic coast. Decommissioned 1 July 1946. Sold 8 January 1947 for use as Arctic sealer, renamed *Calanit*. Sold 1948 to agent of Aliyah Bet and carried Jewish refugees from *Exodus* back to Palestine. Scrapped 1955.

✤ ✤ ✤ ✤

USS *Oneida* [3rd of that name] (ex–*Illawara*)
t. 150; l. 111'; b. 18'6"; s. 12; a. one 3-pdr rf
Built 1896 by Bath Iron Works of Bath, ME. Purchased 22 April 1898 from Eugene Tompkins for $60,000. War service unknown. Naval Militia service: District of Columbia 1912. Served as Naval Disciplinary Barracks at Port Royal SC 1914. Sold November 1915 to Charleston, SC, Pilot's Association and renamed *Henry P. Williams*. Reacquired from them 27 June 1917 and commissioned 6 August 1917, renamed SP-509. Assigned minesweeping training and patrol. Returned to owner 26 December 1918.

✤ ✤ ✤ ✤

Yachts Acquired for Service in the War with Spain

USS *Restless* [2nd of that name]
t. 137; l. 115'6"; b. 16'; s. 13; a. six 6-pdr, two mg
Built 1887 by Houston & Woodbridge of Marcushook, PA. Purchased 22 April 1898 from Hiram W. Sidley for $29,000. Assigned section patrol Northeast Coast 14 May to 25 August 1898. Assigned to Torpedo Squadron Newport, RI, as practice minelayer 1911 to 1913. Sold 5 September 1913.

* * * *

USS *Scorpion* [4th of that name] (ex–*Sovereign*)
t. 775; l. 212'10"; b. 28'1"; s. 14; a. four 6-pdr
Built 1896 by John N. Robins of South Brooklyn NY. Purchased 7 April 1898 from M.C.D. Borden for $300,000. Assigned to Flying Squadron on blockade and escort duty off Santiago, Cuba, and in action at Daiquiri Beach, Siboney, Cuba, 22 May 1898 to 27 Nov 1898. Post-war assigned to Isthmian Canal Commission surveying proposed canal routes. Out of service for a year, next assigned hydrographic survey in Caribbean. From 4 December 1908 assisted in earthquake relief out of Constantinople, Turkey, then evacuation of Americans during first Balkan war 1912 to 1913. Interned at Constantinople for duration of WWI. Decommissioned 20 October 1927. Sold 25 June 1929.

* * * *

USS *Shearwater*
t. ?; l. 124'; b. 18'; s. ?; a. ?
Built 1887 by Hawthorne & Co. of Leith, Scotland. Purchased 9 May 1889 [*sic*–more likely 1898] from Henry R. Wolcott for $26,000. War service unknown. Naval Militia service: Pennsylvania 31 December 1898 to 24 April 1908. Sold autumn 1908.

* * * *

USS *Siren* [2nd of that name] (ex–*Eugenia*)
t. 315dp; l. 123'wl; b. 19'2"; s. 13; a. ?
Built 1897 by Hawthorne & Co. of Leith, Scotland. Purchased 9 June 1898 from J.G. Cassat for $40,000. Assigned North Atlantic Squadron on Cuban blockade. Naval Militia service: Virginia 22 June 1899. Then tender to receiving ship *Franklin*. Struck 30 August 1910.

* * * *

USS *Stranger*
t. 369dp; l. 164'7"; b. 23'7"; s. 14; a. two 3-pdr rf
Built 1880 by William Cramp & Sons of Philadelphia, PA. Purchased 9 June 1898 from Mrs. Mary Lewis (Hoagland estate) for $75,000. War service unknown. Naval Militia service: Louisiana 16 November 1898 to 23 October 1915 when struck. Sunk shortly thereafter.

* * * *

USS *Sylph* [3rd of that name] (ex-hull No. 295)
t. 152; l. 123'8"; b. 20'; s. 15; a. one 6-pdr (1905), none (1914)
Built 1890 by John Roach & Co. of Chester, PA. Purchased June 1898 from the builder for $50,000. Commissioned 18 August 1898 as Presidential Yacht. Designated PY-5 17 July 1921. Struck 29 April 1929. Sold 26 November 1929 and converted to party fishing boat.

✣ ✣ ✣ ✣

USS *Sylvia*
t. 302dp; l. 130'wl; b. 18'6"; s. 9; a. one 3-pdr rf, three 1-pdr rf, two mg
Built 1882 by A. Stephan & Sons of Glasgow, Scotland. Purchased 13 Jun 1898 from Edward M. Brown for $25,000. Assigned patrol off Key West, FL. Naval Militia service: Maryland 19 December 1898 to 6 December 1907, then to Pennsylvania until 13 September 1913, then to District of Columbia until 10 April 1917 when recommissioned in Navy for WWI. Assigned 5th Naval District. Struck 24 April 1919. Sold 20 October 1921.

✣ ✣ ✣ ✣

USS *Viking*
Built 1883 by John Roach & Co. of Chester, PA. Purchased 22 April 1898 from Horace A. Hutchins for $30,000. Assigned North Atlantic Squadron blockading Cuba from 12 July to 16 August 1898. Transferred to War Department 9 December 1899.

✣ ✣ ✣ ✣

USS *Vixen* (ex–*Josephine*)
t. 806dp; l. 182'3"; b. 28'; s. 16; a. four 6-pdr, four 1-pdr
Built 1896 by Lewis Nixon of Elizabethport, NJ. Purchased 9 April 1898 from T.A.B. Widner for $150,000. Assigned Cuban blockade 7 May 1898 to September 1898. Naval Militia service: New Jersey 6 Dec 1907 to April 1917. Post-war assigned survey, dispatch, supply and transportation services in the Caribbean 21 May 1899 to 6 December 1907. WWI assigned patrol off eastern seaboard of U.S. The station ship at St. Thomas, U.S. Virgin Islands. Classified PY-4 on 17 July 1920. Decommissioned 15 November 1922. Sold 22 June 1923.

✣ ✣ ✣ ✣

USS *Wasp* [7th of that name] (ex–*Columbia*)
t. 630dp; l. 180'wl; b. 23'; s. 16.5; a. four 6-pdr, 2 mg
Built 1893 by William Cramp & Sons of Philadelphia, PA. Purchased 26 March 1898 from J.H. Ladew for $95,000. Assigned Cuban blockade. Naval Militia service: Florida 15 December 1898 to 21 June 1899; New York 1908 to early 1917. Returned to Navy for World War I service. Decommissioned 1 December 1919. Sold 20 September 1921.

✣ ✣ ✣ ✣

USS *Yankton* (ex–*Penelope*)

t. 975dp; l. 185'wl; b. 27'6"; s. 12.5; a. six 3-pdr, two mg

Built 1893 by Ramage & Ferguson of Leith, Scotland. Purchased from H.E. Converse May 1898. Assigned North Atlantic Squadron blockading Cuba. Post-war stationed at Guantanamo Bay, Cuba, engaging in survey work. 16 December 1907 departed Hampton Roads, VA as part of the Great White Fleet. Assisted in earthquake relief at Messina, Sicily, 9–14 January 1909; 1909 to 1917 assigned tender to Atlantic Fleet. World War I assigned section patrol off New England, then convoy escort out of Gibraltar. Post WWI arrived Murmansk, Russia, 8 February 1919 as part of failed American military operations against the Bolsheviks. Decommissioned 27 February 1920. Sold 20 October 1921. Seized in New York 1923, laden with illegal rum. Scrapped 1930.

Owner is listed at time yacht purchased by Navy. Often there were one or more prior owners.

t. = Tonnage, which can be given as actual displacement (dp), in gross tons (gt) a volume measure, 10 cubic feet equal to one gross tons; in net tons (nt), also volume, subtracts non revenue producing space; or as displacement (dp), a weight measurement in long tons (2,240 pounds). If the system is not specified, the author is unsure which was used and the number only is given.

l. = Length, which can be measured at the waterline (wl), or the greatest length over all (oa). The latter can vary with the vessel's rig. If the source of the number is not specified, the author is unsure which measurement is given in the documents.

b. = Beam, which is the greatest width of the vessel.

s. = Speed, which is given in knots - nautical miles (6,080.2') per hour.

a. = Armament, which can vary during a vessel's term of service.

pdr = pounder; a gun that fires a projectile of the given weight in pounds.

rf = rapid-fire.

mg = machine gun (not always listed with other armaments).

*Compiled from Report of the Secretary of the Navy, 1898 Part 12, The Navy Department Library; the Dictionary of American Naval Fighting Ships (DANFS); The Steam Yachts: An Era of Elegance by Erik Hofman; the New York Times and other period newspapers.

Appendix 4

Yachts Over 100 Feet in World War I Naval Service, Including Shorter Vessels Named in Text

Table 4.1: Yacht Builders

Builder	Location	Code	Builder	Location	Code
Bath Iron Works	Bath, Maine	BIW	Ramage & Ferguson Ltd.	Leith, Scotland	R&F
Pusey & Jones Corporation	Wilmington, Delaware	P&J	George Lawley & Sons	Neponset, Massachusetts	GLS
John Roach & Sons	Chester, Pennsylvania	JRS	Charles L. Seabury Company	Morris Heights, New York	CLS
Fore River Shipbuilding Company	Quincy, Massachusetts	FRS	Herreshoff Manufacturing Co.	Bristol, Rhode Island	HHM
Robert Jacob Shipyards	City Island, New York	RJS	Sillit Buchanan		SLT
D. & W. Henderson & Company	Glasgow, Scotland	DWH	Camper & Nicholson	Gosport, Maine	C&N
J.M. Bayles & Sons	Port Jefferson, New York	JMB	Townsend-Downey Shipbldg. Co.	Shooter's Island, New York	TDS
Robbins Dry Dock & Repair Company	Brooklyn, New York	RDD	Matthews Boat Company	Port Clinton, Ohio	MBC
Hawthorne & Company	Leith, Scotland	H&C	W. & A. Fletcher Company	Hoboken, New Jersey	WAF
William Cramp & Sons	Philadelphia, Pennsylvania	WCS	Burlee Dry Dock Company	Staten Island, New York	BDD
Harlan & Hollingsworth	Wilmington, Delaware	H&H	Ailsa Shipbuilding Company	Troon, Scotland	ASC
Lewis Nixon (Crescent Shipyard)	Elizabethport, New Jersey	LNX	Wood & McClure	City Island, New York	WMC
Neafie & Levy Company	Philadelphia, Pennsylvania	N&L	I.L. Snow & Company	Rockland, Maine	ILS
W.F. Stone Shipbuilding Yards	Oakland, California	WFS	T.S. Marvel Shipbuilding Company	Newburgh, New York	TSM
Murray & Tregurtha Inc.	South Boston, Massachusetts	M&T	John N. Robinton & Son	Erie Basin, New York	JNR
Luders Marine Construction Company	Stamford, Connecticut	LMC	Percy Tuttle	Greenport, Long Island, New York	PRT

Yachts Over 100 Feet in World War I Naval Service

Builder	Location	Code	Builder	Location	Code
Fleming & Ferguson	Paisley, Scotland	F&F	Northern Boat Company	Port Clinton, Ohio	NBC
Laird Brothers	Birkenhead, England	LDB	Clydebank Engine & Shipbldg. Co.	Glasgow, Scotland	CES
Cook, Walton & Gimmel	Hull, England	CWG	Greenport Basin & Constr. Co.	Greenport, Long Island, New York	GBC
Cobb, Butler & Company	Rockland, Maine	CBC	Henderson & Robbins	Erie Basin, New York	H&R
A. Stephan & Sons	Glasgow, Scotland	ASS	Sam Williams	Marco, Florida	SWS
Adolph Apel	Atlantic City, New Jersey	AAP	Cleveland Shipbuilding Company	Cleveland, Ohio	CSB
John S. White & Company	Cowes, Isle of Wight, England	JSW	John Scott & Company	Kinghorn, Scotland	JSC
Samuel H. Pine	New York City	SHP	Joseph Supple	Portland, Oregon	JPP

Table 4.2: The Yachts

ABBREVIATIONS: 2-letter postal abbreviations used for states; dates given as dd/mm/yy; SP—Section Patrol rto—returned to owner; rnd—renamed; aqd—acquired; rqd—reacquired; dp—displacement; dcmd—decommissioned; USCGC—U.S. Coast Guard Cutter; mg—machine gun; gt—gross tons; dct—depth charge track; ID—identifying number; cpl—complement; a—armament; YP—District/Yard Patrol vessel; USC&GS—U.S. Coast & Geodetic Survey; PY—Patrol Yacht; pdr—pounder gun (preceded by approx. weight of projectile); SAWS—Spanish-American War service; NHO—Navy Hydrographic Office. Number after some USS ship names indicates one or more previous naval vessels of that name.

Number Acquired	Navy Name Original Name	Original Owner Acquired From	Built Speed	Type	Tons Length	Complement, Armament, Notes
SP-1370 06/10/17	USS A-1 A-1	- - - E.E. Wright	1911-SLT - - -	houseboat	6.16dp 31'2"	cpl-6, a: - - -. assigned 11th ND - San Diego CA
SP-516 26/05/17	USS Actus Halawa	E.B. Dane - - -	1907-GLS 15 knots	steam yacht	99dp 107'8"	cpl-23; a: two 3-pdr. trans War Dept. 20/07/20
- - - 07/04/17	USS Aileen Aileen	- - - - - -	1896-JRS 14 knots	steamer	192dp 120'	cpl-33; a: one 3-pdr, two 1-pdr. rqd after Span-Am War then NY and RI Naval Militias. dcmd 05/07/19
SP-1793 24/12/17	USS Akela Akela	William H. Ames Henry Alfred Bishop	1899-CLS 12 knots	steam yacht	72dp 117'6"	cpl-15; a: none. rto 15/04/19
SP-206 28/04/17	USS Alacrity Alacrity	John H. Blodgett - - -	1910-P&J 14 knots	diesel motor yacht	101dp 118'6"	cpl-16, a: 1 3-pdr, 1 1-pdr, 2 mg, 1 Y-gun. rto 28/04/19. Rnd Nedra B. aqd USCG 20/08/42 as USCGC Blanchard. Rto 20/08/43
SP-166 01/06/17	USS Alcedo Veglia	Nath'l de Rothschild George W.C. Drexel	1895-DWH 12 knots	steam aux. tops'l schooner	981dp 275'	cpl-94; a: 4 3"/50, 2 mg. sunk by U-boat 05/11/17. first U.S. warship sunk in the war
SP-317 22/04/17	USS Aloha Aloha	Arthur Curtiss James - - -	1910-FRS 12 knots	3-mast steam aux. bark	659gt 218'	cpl-79; a: 2 3"/50, 2 dct. rto 29/01/19. scrapped 1938
SP-1290 03/10/17	SP-1290 Anemone IV	- - - E.A. Sims	1899-C&N 8 knots	ketch-rigged aux. schooner	118gt 127'	cpl-24; a: 1 1-pdr. never actually commissioned. rto 04/03/19
SP-135 11/05/17	USS Aphrodite Aphrodite	Col. Oliver H. Payne - - -	1899-BIW 15 knots	3-mast steam schooner	1,500dp 302'	cpl-68; a: 4 3"/50, 2 mg. escorted first convoy U.S. troops to Europe. rto 12/07/19
SP-418 03/07/17	USS Aramis Aramis	Arthur Hudson Marks - - -	1916-RJS 13 knots	diesel motor yacht	375dp 157'6"	cpl-33; a: 2 6-pdr, 2 1-pdr, 2 mg. reclassified PY-7 17/07/20. dcmd 06/1021. struck 20/07/33
SP-577 28/05/17	USS Arcady Osceola	- - - - - -	1898-SHP 13 knots	steam yacht	167dp 140'	cpl-23; a: 1 3-pdr, 2 mg. dcmd 12/05/19

Yachts Over 100 Feet in World War I Naval Service

Number Acquired	Navy Name Original Name	Original Owner Acquired From	Built Speed	Type	Tons Length	Complement, Armament, Notes
SP-593 07/08/17	USS Artemis Cristina	- - - John L. Severence	1911-P&J 12 knots	steam yacht	456gt 177'6"	cpl-65; a: 2 3"/50, 2 mg, 8 depth charges. rnd Arcturus 20/02/18. trans U.S. Coast & Geodetic Survey 05/05/19
SP-651 10/06/17	USS Atlantic II Atlantic	Wilson Marshal - - -	1904-T&D 10 knots	3-mast steam aux. schooner	206dp 185'	cpl-66; a: 3 3"/50. won Kaiser's Cup Transatlantic Race 1905. post WWI once owned Cronelius Vanderbilt. USCG WIX-271 in WWII
ID-2640 18/06/18	USS Bayocean Bayocean	- - - - - -	1911-JPP 13 knots	triple screw diesel yacht	130dp 138'	cpl-19; a: 2 3-pdr. pre-war mostly commuting Portland to Bayocean OR. dcmd 14/03/19
SP-249 18/08/17	USS California Hauoli	- - - Clara B. Stocker	1903-RDD 19 knots	steam yacht	299dp 211'	cpl-60; a: 2 6-pdr. rnd Hauoli 18/02/18. underwater sound research w/ Thomas Edison 28/01/19. dcmd 08/10/19
SP-723 09/09/17	USS Calumet Calumet	Charles G. Emery James A. Farrell	1903-GLS 11 knots	steam yacht	153dp 147'	cpl-55; a: 2 6-pdr. dcmd 11/01/19 and rto. subsequently sold 5 times. abandoned 1936
SP-162 30/04/17	USS Christabel Christabel	A.C. Kennaard - - -	1893-DWH 12 knots	steam yacht	248dp 164'	cpl-66; a: 2 3"/50. dcmd 19/05/19
SP-1234 17/09/17	USS Cigarette Cigarette	C.A. Wood - - -	1905-GLS 22 knots	steam yacht	99dp 125'4"	cpl-21; a: 1 1-pdr. dcmd July 1919
SP-185 21/11/17	USS Clarinda Clarinda	- - - - - -	1913-MBC 14 knots	motor yacht	76dp 98'	reclassified YP-185 1920. dcmd 26/12/30
SP-813 10/06/17	USS Corona Corona	Henry Laughlin - - -	1905-H&C - - -	Steam yacht	304dp 172'	cpl-63; a: 2 3"/50. dcmd 17/05/19. capsized and sank 25/04/41
SP-159 15/05/17	USS Corsair Corsair (III)	J. Pierpont Morgan - - -	1899-WAF 19 knots	steam yacht	1,136gt 304'	cpl-146; a: 2 3"/50. rto 09/06/19. 02/01/30 USC&GS to 07/04/42 rqd as USS Natchez PG-85. rnd US Oceanographer. dcmd Sep '44
SP-575 20/10/17	USS Cythera Agawa	William L. Harkness - - -	1906-R&F 12 knots	steam yacht	1,000dp 215'	cpl-113; a: 3 3". rto 19/03/19. rqd 31/12/41 and reclassified PY-26. sunk by U-boat 02/05/42
ID-1217 07/06/17	USS De Grasse Fleet	J.L. Redmond - - -	1917-GLS 14.5 knots	steam yacht	- - - 81'2.5"	cpl-5 civilian; a: 1 3-pdr, 1 mg. placed in service, not commissioned. rto 07/11/18. rqd 1942 as YP-506. sold 1946
- - - 20/05/17	USS Dorothea Dorothea	Thomas McKean - - -	1897-WCS 14 knots	steam yacht	594dp 178'	cpl-50; a: 2 3-pdr. rqd after SAW'S Illinois & Ohio Naval Militias. dcmd 23/06/19
SP-321 02/06/17	USS Druid Druid	- - - W.W. Dwyer	1902-BDD 17 knots	steam yacht	539dp 217'	cpl-113; a: 2 3". dcmd 28/05/19. sold 10/09/19
SP-549 27/07/17	USS Edorea Monaloa	- - - - - -	1909-GLS 13 knots	steam yacht	- - - 137'4"	cpl-25; a: 1 3-pdr. rto 10/12/18

Number Acquired	Navy Name Original Name	Original Owner Acquired From	Built Speed	Type	Tons Length	Complement, Armament, Notes
SP-988 1917	USS Elfrida Elfrida	- - - W. Seward Webb	1889-H&H 10.5 knots	2-mast steam aux. schooner	164dp 101'6"	cpl- - -; a: 1 6-pdr. rqd after SAWS CT, NJ, NC Naval Militias. dcmd 31/03/18
SP-1414 24/08/17	Eliza Hayward Eliza Hayward	- - - - - -	- - - - - -	sailing sloop	- - - - - -	cpl- - -; a: - - -. rto 24/09/18
SP-175 10/06/17	USS Emiline Katoomba	Kenneth M. Clark Robert Graves	1898-ASC 10 knots	steam yacht	407dp 196'	cpl-72; a: 2 3". 1902 rnd Rivera. 1910 rnd Emeline. dcmd 19/05/19. 1920 rnd Katherine R. sunk 1935
SP-177 23/07/17	USS Emerald 2 Emrose	A.W. Rose Lt. Maxwell Wyeth	1906-P&J - - -	steam yacht	198dp 140'4"	cpl-13; a: - -. Navy Reserve Lt. Wyeth remained aboard as skipper. rto 12/12/18
SP-642 21/06/17	USS Felicia Felicia	- - - Jesse H. Metcalf	1898-RDD 14 knots	steam yacht	213gt 179'	cpl-49; a" 3 3-pdr. laid up by collision 30/08/18. sold 25/03/20
SP-173 28/04/17	USS Florence Quickstep	James W. Aiker James W. Aiker	1903-HHM 12 knots	steam yacht	104dp 124'	cpl-17; a: 1 6-pdr, 2 3-pdr. Navy Reserve Ens. Aiker remained aboard as skipper. rto 22/02/19
SP-830 19/07/17	USS Freelance Freelance	F.A. Schermerhorn F.A. Schermerhorn	1895-LNX 14 knots	steam yacht	132dp 137'	cpl-18; a: 2 3-pdr. leased from owner Spanish-American War the rto 1899. rqd from same. rto 24/12/18
SP-714 14/07/17	USS Galatea Galatea	B.L. Ford	1914-P&J 14 knots	steam yacht	367dp 192'	cpl-57; a: 3 3". dcmd 15/07/19. receiving ship Portsmouth ME Navy Yard. sold 20/12/21
SP-41 26/03/17	USS Gem Gem	William Ziegler, Jr.	1913-GLS 15 knots	steam motor yacht	201dp 146'6"	cpl-15; a: 2 3-pdr. experimental test bed. dcmd 10/01/19. rto Jan 1919
SP-579 28/06/17	USS Get There Get There	J.S. Bache & F.L. Richards	1916-WMC 28 knots	motorboat	15dp 58'1.5"	cpl-8; a: 1 1-pdr, 2 mg. rto 13/03/19
- - - April 1898	USS Gloucester Corsair II	J. Pierpont Morgan	1891-N&L 17 knots	steam yacht	786dp 240'8"	cpl-79; a: 3 3-pdr, 4 1-pdr. SAWS. 1899-1902 US Naval Academy. MA & NY Naval Militias to 1917. sold 21/11/19
SP-512 10/06/17	USS Guinevere Guinevere	Edgar Palmer	1908-GLS 10 knots	3-mast steam aux. schooner	499dp 197'6"	cpl-75; a: 4 3" .grounded and wrecked off French coast 26/01/18
SP-209 April 1917	USS Harvard Eleanor	William A. Slater George F. Baker, Jr	1894-BIW 12 knots	3-mast steam aux. bark	804dp 243'	cpl-37; a: 4 3-pdr. 1900 rnd Wacouta. rto 26/07/19
SP-210 Aug. 1917	USS Helenita Helenita	- - - Frank J. Gould	1902-CLS 16 knots	steam yacht	304dp 187'	cpl- - -; a: 2 3". rto 17/06/19

Yachts Over 100 Feet in World War I Naval Service

Number Acquired	Navy Name Original Name	Original Owner Acquired From	Built Speed	Type	Tons Length	Complement, Armament, Notes
SP-3096 19/07/18	USS Helvetia Helvetia	R.K. Snow	1905-ILS - - -	3-mast schooner	499dp 157'4"	cpl - - ; a: - - -. used as decoy Q-ship to attract enemy submarines. sold back to owner February 1919
- - - 06/04/17	USS Hermes Hermes	Jaluit GES German, confiscated	1914-WFS 7 knots	2-mast diesel aux. schooner	340dp 89'5"	cpl-31; a: none. trans Hawaian Ter. Gov't 15/09/19-Apr 1920. sold 21/10/26 Lanikai Fish Co. rnd Lanikai. in movie The Hurricane
SP-509 27/06/17	Henry P. Williams Illawara	Eugene Tompkins	1896-BIW 12 knots	2-mast steam aux. schooner	150dp 111'	cpl-6; a: none. SAWS as USS Oneida then DC Naval Militia, disciplinary barracks Port Royal SC. rto 26/12/18
SP-521 03/07/17	USS Isabel Isabel	John N. Willys	1917-BIW 26 knots	steam turbine yacht	710gt 245'3"	cpl-99; a: 4 3"/50, 4 torpedo tubes, 8 smaller guns. Asiatic Fleet between wars. escaped Philippines 1941. scrapped 1946
- - - 24/09/17	USS Isis Isis	W.S. & J.T. Spaulding	1901-TSM 15 knots	steam yacht	555dp 199'	cpl-71; a: - - -. aqd USC&GS 1915. returned 30/04/19 USC&GS. grounded and sank February 1920
SP-952 July 1917	USS Itty E Itty E	F.H. Rawson	1916-M&T 35 knots	open motor boat	- - - 25'	cpl - - -; a: - - -. scrapped 1920
SP-72 May 1917	USS Joyance Cavalier	- - - William H. Childs	1907-RJS 14 knots	steam yacht	119dp 134'8"	cpl - - -; a: 1 3-pdr. sold 05/08/19
SP-602 01/06/17	USS Juniata Josephine	Edward Shearson George W. Elkins	1911-RJS 17 knots	gasoline motor yacht	142dp 139'6"	cpl-11; a: 1 3-pdr, 1 1-pdr, 2 mg. rto 13/07/18
SP-389 May 1917	USS Kajeruna Hauoli	Frank M. Smith A.w. Gieske	1903-JNR 14 knots	steam yacht	147dp 153'	cpl - - -; a: 2 6-pdr, 1 mg. rnd Seminole then Kajeruna. rto 16/01/19
SP-130 28/04/17	USS Kanawha II Kanawha II	Henry H. Rogers John Borden	1898-CLS 20 knots	3-mast steam yacht	575dp 227'	cpl-65; a: 4 3". 1 6-pdr. sold 1915 Borden. rnd Piqua 01/03/18. rto 01/07/19. abandoned Cuba 1922 as Antonio Maceo
SP-439 08/05/17	USS Kanised Nahmeoka	- - - Louis Kann	1910-- - - 12 knots	diesel motor yacht	61dp 100'	cpl - - -; a: 2 1-pdr. rnd Tuscanola then Kanised. struck 31/03/19. sold 13/12/19
SP-415 07/10/17	USS Kemah Kemah	F.E. Lewis II	1918-LMC 13 nots	diesel motor yacht	300dp 146'	cpl-51; a: 2 3". aqd while under construction. placed out of service 03/09/19. sold 22/09/20
SP-529 02/06/17	USS Kestrel II Kestrel II	D. Herbert Hostetter	1912-PRT 12 knots	gasoline motor yacht	93dp 108'	cpl-9; a: 1 3-pdr. rto 06/01/19
SP-399 June 1917	USS Legonia II Walucia	- - - William B. Hurst	1909-P&J 13 knots	steam yacht	119dp 168'	cpl-36; a: 4 6-pdr, 2 mg. rnd Lydonia before Legonia II. reclassified YP-399 at some point. dcmd 01/08/21. ssold 30/09/21

Appendix 4

Number Acquired	Navy Name / Original Name	Original Owner / Acquired From	Built Speed	Type	Tons Length	Complement, Armament, Notes
SP-721 03/07/17	USS Linta / Linta	Walter Lutgen	1905-CLS 12 knots	steam yacht	53dp 108'	cpl-26; a: 3 6-pdr. rto 19/02/19
SP-700 21/08/17	USS Lydonia / Lydonia	William A. Lydon	1912-P&J 12 knots	motor yacht	497dp 181'	cpl-34; a: 4 3", 2 mg, w/ destroyer HMS Basilisk credit sinking submarine UB-70. dcmd 07/08/19 and trans USC&GS
SP-735 28/04/17	USS Malay / Malay	- - - Hannah P. Weld	1898-JRS 15 knots	steam yacht	173dp 150'	cpl-29; a: 2 3-pdr, 1 mg, 1 Y-gun. rto 01/03/19
SP-527 Aug 1917	USS Margaret / Eugenia	- - - - - -	1899-JRS 6 knots	steam yacht	245dp 176'	cpl- - -; a: 2 3", 2 dct. dcmd November 1918. sold for scrap 30/09/21
SP-737 02/06/17	USS Marold / Marold	L.K. Liggett	1914-NBC 20 knots	gasoline motor yacht	35dp 100'	cpl-14; a: 2 3-pdr, 2 mg. rto 09/05/19
SP-397 10/08/17	USS Mary Alice Bernice	- - - William J. Connors	1897-RDD 20 knots	steam yacht	180dp 174'	cpl-51; a: 2 3-pdr, 2 mg, rnd Oneta 1907. rnd Mary Alice 1910. sunk by collision 05/10/18
SP-164 11/08/17	USS May / May	- - - J.R. De Lamar	1891-ASC 13 knots	steam yacht	1,100dp 239'	cpl-77; a: 2 3", 2 mg. grounded 27/07/19. abandoned 28/02/20
SP-117 19/04/17	USS Mohican 3 / Lady Godiva	- - - Robert Perkins	1890-LDB 8.6 knots	steam aux. tops'l schooner	231dp 144'	cpl-48; a: 2 6-pdr, 2 mg. rnd Norseman before Navy. April 1918 rnd SP-117. dcmd 15/02/19. rto 17/02/19
SP-771 21/06/17	USS Nahma / Nahma	Robert Walton Goelet	1897-CES 22 knots	aux. topsail schooner	2,900dp 319'	cpl-162; a: 2 5", 2 3", 2 mg, after armistice refugee relief Russia and Turkey. dcmd & rto 19/07/19
SP-161 30/06/17	USS Narada / Semiramis	- - - Henry D. Walters	1889-R&F 12 knots	aux. topsail schooner	505dp 224'	cpl- - -; a: - - -. rn Margarita before Navy. experimental anti-submarine work. dcmd 13/01/19. rto 04/02/19
SP-666 04/07/17	USS Natoma / Natoma	- - - Richard Howe	1913-CLS 10 knots	diesel motor yacht	112dp 120'	cpl- - -; a: 1 3-pdr, 1 mg. trans USC&GS 04/04/19. scrapped 1935
SP-517 31/08/17	USS Naushon / Oneonta	- - - J. Shewan	1895-JRC 13 knots	steam yacht	135dp 154'3"	cpl- - -; a: 2 6-pdr, 2 mg. rnd Norman before acquisition. struck 13/06/19
SP-136 10/08/17	USS Niagara 6 / Niagara	Howard Gould	1898-H&H 12 knots	3-mast steam aux. bark	2,690dp 282'	cpl-195; a: 4 4", 2 mg, 1 Y-gun. reclassified PY-9 17/07/20. dcmd 21/04/22. to NHO 24/06/24. sold for scrap 13/09/33
SP-609 01/06/17	USS Nokomis / Nokomis II	Horace E. Dodge	1914-P&J 16 knots	steam yacht	1,265dp 243'	cpl-191; a: 4 3", 2 mg. reclassified PY-6 17/07/20. to NHO 25/07/25. struck 25/05/38. rnd Burke. aqd USCG 1943 as Bodkin

Yachts Over 100 Feet in World War I Naval Service

Number Acquired	Navy Name / Original Name	Original Owner / Acquired From	Built / Speed	Type	Tons / Length	Complement, Armament, Notes
SP-131 10/05/17	USS Noma / Noma	W.B. Leeds / William Vincent Astor	1902-BDD 19 knots	steam yacht	1,250dp 262'6"	cpl-80; a: 4 3", 4 mg. Ens. Astor stayed on as junior officer. postrt war to U.S. forces in Constantinople. tro 15/07/19
SP-311 01/08/17	USS Onward 2 / Galatea	E. Leydon Ford / - - -	1908-CLS 13.8 knots	steam yacht	157dp 140'	cpl-43; a: 2 6-pdr, 2 mg. rnd Ungava before aqd. 18/04/19–26/11/20 in USC&GS. sold 1921. wrecked rum runner April 1923
SP-167 15/06/17	USS Owera / Owera	NY Sen. Peter G. Gerry / - - -	1907-R&F 12 knots	steam yacht	426dp 195'	cpl- - - -; a: 2 6-pdr, 2 mg. rto 08/01/19
SP-671 15/08/17	USS Parthenia / Parthenia	- - - / Henry E. Converse	1903-HHM 13.5 knots	steam yacht	144dp 131'	cpl-22; a: 1 3-pdr, 1 mg. sold 17/08/20
SP-699 26/06/17	USS Pawnee 3 / Monoloa II	- - - / Gordon Dexter	1904-GLS 13 knots	steam yacht	75dp 114'	cpl-21; a: 1 3-pdr, 2 mg. used as minesweeper. rnd SP-699 in 1918. sold 12/07/21
SP-1204 30/06/17	USS Pilgrim / Pilgrim	Boston Racing Synd. / Beaufort Fish... Co.	1893-P&J 6.9 knots	2-mast racing sloop	98dp 120'	cpl-27; a: 2 1-pdr. America's Cup racer. conv. steam aux. 1894. conv. gas aux. 1913. rto 07/01/19. 6 owners before aqd
SP-179 25/05/17	USS Privateer / Privateer	Robert A. Smith / - - -	1917-CLS 22 knots	gasoline motor yacht	- - -	cpl- - - -; a: 1 6-pdr, 2 mg. reclassified YP-179 post war. trans to U.S. Shipping Board 30/06/30
- - - 07/06/17	USS Rainier / Patrol	- - - / - - -	1917-- - - 5 knots	aux. sloop	108'	cpl-41; A: 2 4", 2 mg. dcmd 28/05/19. sold 05/08/21
SP-211 16/08/17	USS Rambler / Rambler	- - - / Keneth Van Riper	1900-LNX 13 knots	steam yacht	340dp 119'9"	cpl- - - -; a: 2 3"/50, 2 mg. dcmd 09/07/19. sold 16/09/19
SP-237 22/06/17	USS Ranger 5 / Thomas Slocum	- - - / Thomas W. Slocum	1910-RJS 13 knots	steam yacht	288dp 177'	cpl-45; a: 4 6-pdr. 28/04/19 - 26/11/30 to USC&GS. sold 21/12/31
SP-157 01/06/17	USS Remlik / Candace	- - - / Willis S. Kilmer	1903-CWG 14 knots	motor yacht	149dp 133'5"	cpl-62; a: 2 3", 2 mg. Chief Bosun's Mate John MacKenzie awarded Medal of Honor. dcmd 07/11/19
SP-198 07/04/17	USS Reposo II / Sophia	- - - / - - -	1882-- - - 14 knots	steam yacht	600dp 200'	cpl-18; a: 1 3-pdr, 2 mg. rebuilt 1902-GBC. rnd Empress, Onondaga, Turbese.dcmd 24/12/18
SP-3157 25/07/18	USS Robert H. McCurdy	- - - / - - -	1903-CBC - - -	NOT A YACHT	157dp 140'	cpl-32; a: - - -. original named retained. 4-mast commercial schooner used as Q-ship. dcmd February 1919
SP-225 May 1917	USS Sabalo / Sabalo	W. Earl Dodge / - - -	1916-GLS 14 knots	gasoline motor yacht	725dp 178'	cpl-12; a: 2 3-pdr. dcmd and rto 03/03/19. sold 4 times 1921-1940 then to Royal Canadian Navy as HMCS Cougar
SP-192 03/07/17	USS Sachem 3 / Celt	- - - / Manton B. Metcalf	1902-P&J 12 knots	steam yacht	204dp 141'	cpl-49; a: 1 6-pdr, 2 3-pdr, 2 mg. rto 10/02/19. rqd 17/02/42 & rnd USS Phenakite

| | | | | | 317dp 186'3" | |

Number Acquired	Navy Name Original Name	Original Owner Acquired From	Built Speed	Type	Tons Length	Complement, Armament, Notes
SP-687 24/05/17	USS Satilla Satilla	- - - RH McCormick estate	1902-GLS 14 knots	steam yacht	106dp 128'	cpl-28; a: 1 3-pdr, 1 mg. aqd for Naval Militia. dcmd 07/11/19
SP-427 07/05/17	USS Seneca Seneca	- - - Johnson Lighterage	1888- - - 18 knots	steam yacht	157dp 150'	cpl-33; a: 2 6-pdr. rto 06/01/19
SP-915 23/05/17	USS Shirin Shirin	- - - S.T. Rhea, Jr.	1896-CLS 13.5 knots	motor yacht	59dp 110'	cpl-9; a: 2 3-pdr, 2 mg. dcmd 18/12/18. sold 29/06/21
SP-3572 31/10/18	USS Shuttle Shuttle	Nathan Strauss H.P. Davidson	1906-HHM 15 knots	steam yacht	42dp 94'6"	cpl-6; a: - - -. rnd Skipaki by Davidson. rto 28/03/19
SP-543 10/06/17	USS Sialia Sialia	Henry Ford	1914-P&J 14.5 knots	steam yacht	558dp 207'	cpl-61; a: 2 3", 2 mg. 06/10/19-06/02/20 in USC&GS sold back to Ford. rnd Yankee Clipper
SP-170 14/06/18	USS Sovereign 2 Sovereign	M.C.D. Borden his estate	1911-CLS 25.2 knots	steam turbine yacht	173dp 166'	cpl- - -; a: 2 3". struck 23/04/19. rto
SP-134 04/05/17	USS Sultana Sultana	Trenor Luther Park Mrs. E.H. Harriman	1899- H&R 12 knots	steam yacht	390dp 186'	cpl-62; a: 4 3", 2 mg. rto 17/02/19
SP-510 18/05/17	USS Suzanne Christina	Frederick C. Fletcher	1908-GLS 13 knots	gasoline motor yacht	123dp 110'	cpl-18; a: 1 3-pdr, 1 1-pdr, 1 mg. Esperanza then Jorosa before Suzanne. struck 28/12/18. rto
SP-104 14/05/17	USS Sybilla III Paragon	John F. Bettz	1915-RJS 15 knots	diesel motor yacht	103dp 120'	cpl-9; a: 1 1-pdr, 1 3-pdr, 1 mg. rto 24/12/18. rnd Arlis. rnd Impetuous for WWII service
- - - June 1898	USS Sylvia Sylvia	- - - - - -	1882-ASS 9 knots	steam yacht	302dp 130'	cpl- - -; a: 1 3-pdr,1 1-pdr, 2 mg. SAWS. then MD, PA, DC Naval Militias. rqd 10/04/17. struck 24/04/19. sold 20/10/21
SP-471 06/06/17	USS Sylvia II - - -	- - -	- - - SWS 6.9 knots	motor yacht	17dp 48'6"	cpl-8; a: 1 1-pdr, 1 mg. name canceled, number only to avoid confusion. destroyed by hurricane 09/09/19
SP-1016 16/04/17	USS Talofa Talofa	Eben H. Ellison	1910-GLS 12 knots	steam yacht	82dp 101'	cpl-19; a: 2 3-pdr. rto 24/04/19
SP-124 25/04/17	USS Tarantula 2 Tarantula	William K. Vanderbilt II	1912-GLS 14 knots	motor yacht	160dp 128'9"	cpl- - - -; a: 2 6-pdr, 2 mg. Lt(jg) Vanderbilt had command. until 01/10/17. sunk by collision 28/10/18
SP-1761 30/08/17	USS Tech Jr. Tech Jr.	- - -	1912-AAP 30.4 knots	motorboat	- - 20'	cpl- - - -; a: - - -. rto 27/11/17
SP-391 23/06/17	USS Thetis 2 Thetis	Charles H. Fuller	1901-GLS 12 knots	steam yacht	97.6dp 127'	cpl-17; a: 2 3-pdr, 2 mg. struck 31/03/19. sold 19/07/20

Yachts Over 100 Feet in World War I Naval Service

Number Acquired	Navy Name / Original Name	Original Owner / Acquired From	Built / Speed	Type	Tons / Length	Complement, Armament, Notes
SP-951 1917	USS Utowana / Utowana	Allison Vincent Armor Commonwealth Fish.	1891-N&L 10.4 knots	steam yacht	414gt 168'9"	cpl-32; a: - -, rebuilt as fishing trawler 1917. used as minesweeper. dcmd 11/09/19. sold 13/09/20
SP-163 04/05/17	USS Vedette 2 / Virginia	Isaac Stern Frederick W Vanderbilt	1899-BIW 13 knots	steam yacht	442dp 199'6"	cpl-61; a: 3 3", 2 mg, 10 mines. NOT Spanish-American Way yacht. rto 04/02/19
SP-431 04/08/17	USS Venetia / Venetia	F.W. Sykes John Diedrich Sprekles	1903-H&C 13 knots	steam yacht	589gt 226'	cpl-69; a: 4 3", 2 mg. sold 3X before to Sprekles. rto 04/04/19. 3 more owners, no further naval service. scrapped 1968
SP-519 16/04/17	USS Vergana / Vergana	E.S. Flower Charles H. Crocker	1897-TSM 12 knots	schooner rig steam yacht	128dp 145'	cpl-19; a: 2 1-pdr. dcmd 16/01/19. sold 25/02/22
- - April 1898	USS Vixen / Josephine	T.A.B. Widner	1896-LNX 16 knots	schooner rig steam yacht	806dp 182'3"	cpl-80; a: 4 6-pdr, 2 1-pdr. SAWS. NJ Naval Militia Dec 1907-Apr 1917. reclassified PY-4 17/07/20. dcmd 15/11/22. sold 22/06/23
SP-238 24/05/17	USS Waconda / Revolution	F. Augustus Heinze Charles Hayden	1901-CLS 18knots	steam turbine yacht	190gt 177'	cpl-28; a: 2 6-pdr, 2 mg. only 17' beam, designed for speed rather than sea keeping. struck 21/08/19. sold 04/06/20
SP-158 25/05/17	USS Wadena / Wadena	Jeptha Homer Wade II	1891-CSB 13 knots	schooner rig steam yacht	246gt* 176'*	* stats after lengthening 1894. cpl-66; a: 2 3", 2 mg, 10 depth charges. sold 12/07/20
SP-160 20/07/17	USS Wakiva II / Wakiva II	Lamon V. Harkness Harry Harkness	1907-R&F 15 knots	steam yacht	853gt 239'6"	cpl- - -; a: 4 3", 2 mg. c. 28/11/17 attacked and sank U-boat. sunk by collision 21/05/18
SP-132 10/06/17	USS Wanderer 3 / Kethailes	William Johnston H.A.C. Taylor	1897-R&F 12 knots	steam yacht	362gt 197'	cpl-56; a: 2 3", 2 mg. night 22-23/04/18 in harbor when ammo ship Florence H. exploded, assisted rescue. struck 24/04/19
- - Mar 1898	USS Wasp 7 / Columbia	J.H. Ladew	1893-WCS 16.5knots	steam yacht	630dp 180'	cpl-55; a: 2 3-pdr. SAWS. FL and NY Naval Militias between wars. dcmd 01/12/19. sold 20/09/21
SP-165 08/06/17	USS Wenonah / Wenonah	Walter G. Ladd	1915-GLS 12 knots	schooner rig steam yacht	470dp 163'	cpl-65; a: 2 3", 2 mg. dcmd & trans USC&GS 12/04/19. returned Navy Oct 1922. reclassified PY-11 23/09/23. sold 15/05/29
SP-221 May 1917	USS Whirlwind / Whirlwind	- - - -	1909-CLS 20 knots	3-shaft gasoline motor yacht	59dp 117'	cpl-9; a: 1 3-pdr, 1 1-pdr, 1 mg. only 12' beam, designed for speed not sea keeping. dcmd 08/12/17. training ship 1918. sold 1919

Appendix 4

Number Acquired	Navy Name / Original Name	Original Owner / Acquired From	Built / Speed	Type	Tons / Length	Complement, Armament, Notes
SP-156 30/05/17	USS Winchester / Winchester	P. Winchester Rouss	1916-BIW 31.65 knots	oil-fired steam turbine yacht	399dp 225'	cpl-40; a: 1 3", 1 6-pdr, 2 mg, 1 Y-gun. experimental minesweeping. dcmd 19/12/19. sold 24/03/21 to Cox & Stevens
SP-852 13/07/17	USS Wissahickon / Valda	Mrs. Charles Henry	1900-GLS 12 knots	steam yacht	194dp 120'	cpl-19; a: 1 3-pdr, 2 mg. rto 15/02/19
SP-581 09/08/17	USS Xarifa / Xarifa	- - - C.N. Nelson	1896-JSW 11 knots	steam aux. tops'l schooner	378dp 192'	cpl-71; a: 2 3-pdr, 2 mg. rnd Ophelie. Nelson bought 1911 & rnd Xarifa. rto 04/05/19
SP-617 29/09/17	USS Yacona / Cem	- - - Henry Clay Pierce	1898-JSC 10 knots	schooner rig steam yacht	527gt 211'	cpl-67; a: 2 3", 2 mg, 10 depth charges. rnd Amelia before Yacona. 27/07/21 trans Philippine Insular Government
- - - May 1898	USS Yankton / Penelope	- - -	1893-R&F 12.5 knots	schooner rig steam yacht	975dp 185'	cpl-86; a: 2 3-pdr (1911). SAWS. Great White Fleet 1907-09. 1919 anti Bolshevik ops Russia. sold 1921. rum runner 1923
SP-133 27/04/17	USS Zara / Solgar	- - -	1891-F&F 10 knots	steam yacht	184dp 152'	cpl-62; a: 2 6-pdr, 2 mg. struck 01/05/18. sold 13/09/19
SP-235 16/08/17	USS Zoraya / Zoraya	William Biel	1901-JMB 12 knots	steam yacht	129dp 135'	cpl-33; a: 2 3-pdr. rto 08/02/19

Primary sources to compile this table:

Dictionary of American Naval Fighting Ships at www.history.navy.mi and www.navsouce.org

Appendix 5
World War II Yachts

Table 5.1: Yacht Builders

Builder	Location	Code	Builder	Location	Code
Krupp Germaniawerft	Kiel, Germany	KGW	Ramage & Ferguson	Leith, Scotland	R&F
Great Lakes Engineering Works	Ecorse, Michigan	GLE	George Lawley & Sons	Neponset, Massachusetts	GLS
Bath Iron Works	Bath, Maine	BIW	Consolidated Shipbuilding Company pre-WWI Charles L. Seabury Co.	New York City	CSC
Pusey & Jones	Wilmington, Delaware	P&J	Defoe Boat & Motor Works	Bay City, Michigan	DBM
Newport News Shipbuilding & Dry Dock Co.	Newport News, Virginia	NNS	Mathis Yacht Building Company	Camden, New Jersey	MYB
Lake Union Dry Dock Company	Seattle, Washington	LUD	Craig Shipbuilding Company	Long Beach, California	CRG
Robert Jacob Shipyards	City Island, New York	RJS	John Samuel White	East Cowes, England	JSW
Delaware River Shipbuilding & Engine Works	Chester, Pennsylvania	DRS	Herreshoff Manufacturing	Bristol, Rhode Island	HHM
William Muller	Wilmington, California	WMR	Luders Marine Construction Co.	Stamford, Connecticut	LMC
Hodgdon Brothers	East Boothbay, Maine	HDB	Abeking & Rasmussen	Bremen, Germany	A&R
F.F. Pendleton	Wiscasset, Maine	FFP	King Shipways	Hong Kong	KSW
Arthur D. Story Shipyards	Essex, Massachusetts	ADS	Philip & Son	Dartmouth, England	P&S
Adams Company	East Boothbay, Maine	ACO	San Diego Marine Construction Company	San Diego, California	SDM
Shelburn Shipbuilding Company	Shelburn, Nova Scotia	SSC	Bergsund M.V. AB	Stockholm, Sweden	BMV
Electric Boat Company	Groton, Connecticut	EBC	Nunes Brothers Boat & Ways Company	Sausalito, California	NBB
M.M. Davis & Sons	Solomons, Maryland	MMD	T. Berlin Albury	Harbor Island, Bahamas	TBA
Jakobson & Petersen	Brooklyn, New York	J&P	Marco U. Martinolich	Lussinpiccolo, Italy	MUM

Appendix 5

Builder	Location	Code	Builder	Location	Code
Henry B. Nevins, Inc.	City Island, New York	HBN	Ernst Burmester	Bremen, Germany	EBM
Symonette Ship Building Company	Nassau, Brit. W. Indies	SSB	Bethlehem Shipbuilding Corp.	Wilmington, Delaware	BSC
Salisbury Yacht Company	Salisbury, Maryland	SYC			
Lyman James Shipyard	Essex, Massachusetts	LJS			

Table 5.2: The Yachts

ABBREVIATIONS: Patrol Gunboat—PG; Patrol Yacht—PY; Coastal Patrol Yacht—PYc; District Yard Patrol Craft—YP; Miscellaneous Unclassified—IX; Motor Torpedo Boat Tender—AGP; Coastal Minelayer—CMC; Coastal Guard Gunboat—WPG; Section Patrol—SP; Minesweeper—AM; Coastal Minesweeper—AMc; Submarine Chaser—PC; Destroyer—DD; Miscellaneous Auxiliary Service Craft—YAG; USC&GS—U.S. Coast & Geodetic Survey; F&WS—Fish & Wildlife Service; USCG—U.S. Coast Guard; aqd—acquired; dp—displacement; rnd—renamed; gt—gross tons; dcmd—decommissioned; rto—returned to owner; dct—depth charge track; dcp—depth charge projector; mg—machine gun; cpl—complement; a—armament. Dates are given as dd/mm/yy. Number after some USS ship names indicates one or more previous naval vessels of that name.

Number Acquired	Navy Name Original Name	Original Owner	Built Speed	Type	Tons Length	Notes
PG-60 23/01/42	USS Beaumont Reveler	Russell Alger	1930-KGW 15.5 knots	diesel motor yacht	1,434dp 226'	cpl-110; a: 2 3"/50, 6 mg, 2 dct, 2 dcp. 1931 rnd Chalena. 1939 rnd Carola. dcmd 19/02/46. currently Talitha G.
PG-61 21/01/42	USS Dauntless 2 Delphine	Horace Elgin Dodge	1921-GLE 16 knots	steam motor yacht	1,950dp 257'7"	cpl-135; a ; 2 3"/50. dcmd 11/05/46. currently Delphine
AGP-2 28/11/41	USS Hilo Caroline	Eldridge H. Johnson	1931-BIW 14 knots	diesel motor yacht	2,350dp 278'11"	cpl-116; a: 1 3"/50. sold 1938 William B. Leeds as Moana. originally PG-58. dcmd 03/03/46
AGP-3 06/12/40	USS Jamestown 2 Savarona (II)	Emily Roebling Cadwallader	1928-P&J 15 knots	diesel motor yacht	1,780dp 294'	cpl-259; a: 2 3"/50, 6 20mm. sold 1929 Col. William Boyce Thompson rnd Alder. originally PG-55. decomm'd 06/03/46
AGP-1 16/10/40	USS Niagara 7 Hi-Esmaro	H. Edward Manville	1929-BIW 16 knots	diesel motor yacht	1,922dp 267'	cpl-139; a: 2 3"/50. originally CMc-2, then PG-52. sunk by air attack 23/05/43
WPG-122 21/03/40	USS Nourmahal Nourmahal	William Vincent Astor	1928-KGW 15 knots	diesel motor yacht	2,250dp 263'10"	cpl-153; a: (45) 2 4"/50, 6 20mm, 8 mg, 2 dct, 4 dcp, 2 mousetrap. was WPG-72, then PG-72. laid up 18/07/46. sold for scrap 11/09/64
PG-57 04/11/41	USS Plymouth 4 Alva	William Kissam Vanderbilt II	1931-KGW 15 knots	diesel motor yacht	1,500dp 264'5"	cpl-155; a: 1 4"/50, 2 3"/50. sunk by U-boat 04/08/43
PG-54 05/12/40	USS St. Augustine Viking	George F. Baker	1929-NNS 14 knots	turbo-elec. motor yacht	1,720dp 272'2"	cpl-185; a: 2 3"/50. sold 1938 Norman B. Woolworth rnd Noparo. sunk by collision 06/01/44. 115 of crew died
PG-59 20/01/42	USS San Bernardino Vanda	Ernest B. Dane	1928-BIW 17 knots	diesel motor yacht	1,768dp 240'2"	cpl-107; a: 2 3"/50, 2 40mm. dcmd 04/01/46

Appendix 5

Number Acquired	Navy Name Original Name	Original Owner	Built Speed	Type	Tons Length	Notes
PG-53 13/11/40	USS Vixen 4 Orion	Julius Forstmann	1929-KGW 15 knots	diesel motor yacht	3,097dp 333'2"	cpl-279; a: 4 3"/50, 9 mg. flagship for 4 admirals. dcmd 24/05/46
PG-56 24/04/41	USS Williamsburg Aras II	Hugh J. Chisholm	1930-BIW 13.5 knots	diesel motor yacht	1,805dp 243'9"	cpl-81; a: 2 3"/50, 8 mg. 1945 briefly Amphibious General Communications ship (AGC-369), then presidential yacht 1945-1962
PY-24 27/01/42	USS Almandite Happy Days	Ira C. Copely	1927-KGW 12 knots	diesel motor yacht	705dp 185'4"	cpl-75; a: 1 3"/50, 4 mg, 2 dct. dcmd 22/01/46
PY-14 25/10/40	USS Argus 2 Haida	Max C. Fleischmann	1929-KGW 14.5 knots	diesel motor yacht	859dp 207'6"	cpl-59; a: 1 3"/50, 4 mg, 1 dcp, 2 dct. 17/09/41 to 18/04/42 w/ USC&GS. dcmd 15/04/46. currently Haida G.
PY-22 09/12/41	USS Azurlite Vagabondia	William L. Mellon	1928-KGW 13.5 knots	diesel motor yacht	1,200dp 210'11"	cpl-67; a: 2 3"/50, 4 mg. dcmd 22/01/46. sold 29/01/47
PY-23 13/12/41	USS Beryl Rene	Alfred Pritchard Sloane, Jr.	1930-P&J 14.2 knots	diesel motor yacht	1,220dp 225'	cpl-66; a: 2 3"/50, 4 mg, 2 dct. dcmd 25/01/46
PY-19 13/05/41	USS Carnelian Trudione	Ross W. Jusdson	1930-BIW 12 knots	diesel motor yacht	500dp 190'11"	cpl-59; a: 1 3"/50, unknown no. 20mm, 2 dct. launched October, rnd Seventeen Dec 1930. dcmd 04/01/46
PY-15 25/1140	USS Coral Sialia	James K. Stewart	1914-P&J 14 knots	steam motor yacht	790dp 214'6"	cpl-61; a: 2 3"/50, 2 mg. SP-543 in WWI. rnd Yankee Clipper by Henry Ford 1920, who owned prior to WWI. dcmd 10/09/43
PY-25 15/01/42	USS Crystal Cambriona	W.O. Biggs	1929-P&J 18 knots	diesel motor yacht	1,400dp 225'	cpl - - -; a: 2 3"/50. rnd Vida 1938. dcmd 06/03/46
PY-26 31/12/41	USS Cythera Agawa	William L. Harkness	1906-R&F 12 knots	steam motor yacht	1,000dp 215'	cpl-71; a: 3 3". SP-575 in WWI, rto 19/03/19. sunk by U-boat 02/05/42
PY-31 14/07/42	USS Cythera 2 Argosy	C.A. Stone	1931-KGW 15 knots	diesel motor yacht	800dp 205'7"	cpl-74; a: 1 3"/50. sold 1934 Sir Thomas Sopwith rnd Vita. sold1937. struck April 1946. March 1947 Palestine refugee ship SS Ben Hecht
PY-27 16/03/42	USS Girasol Firenza	- - -	1926-KGW 12 knots	diesel motor yacht	700dp 170'	cpl-55; a: 1 3"/50. dcmd 26/01/46
PY-10 03/07/13	USS Isabel Isabel	John N. Willys	1917-BIW 28 knots	steam turbine motor yacht	930dp 245'6"	cpl-103; a: 2 3"/50, 2 3"/23, 1 dcp. dcmd mid-1920 to mid-1921. SP-521 in WWI. Yangtze Patrol 1928. escaped Philippines to Australia

Number Acquired	Navy Name Original Name	Original Owner	Built Speed	Type	Tons Length	Notes
PY-17 Dec 1940	USS Jade Athero II	Jesse Lauriston Livermore	1926-GLS 14 knots	diesel motor yacht	582dp 171'	cpl-26; a: 1 3"/50, 4 mg, 2 dct. 1928 rdn Caroline. 1938 rnd Doctor Brinkley. Mar 1943 to Jan 1944 to Ecuador Navy. sunk 1948 Guam
PY-28 02/02/42	USS Marcasite Camargo	Julius Fleischmann	1928-GLS 12 knots	diesel motor yacht	1,130dp 225'2"	cpl-120; a: 2 3"/50, 2 dct, 1 Y-gun. sold 1938 Generalissimo Rafael Trujillo rnd Ramfis. dcmd 5/10/44
PY-29 16/03/42	USS Mizpah Savarona (I)	Emily Roebling Cadwallader	1926-NNS 14 knots	diesel motor yacht	607dp 174'	cpl-62; a: 2 3"/50, 3 mg, 2 dct, 2 dcp. 1927 son Richard M., Jr. rnd Sequoia. sold 1929 Eugene F. McDonald rnd Allegro, later Mizpah
PY-21 19/06/41	USS Ruby Placida	Harry Garner Haskell, Sr.	1930-BIW 13 knots	diesel motor yacht	640dp 190'11"	cpl-67; a: 2 3"/50, four 1.1"mg. dcmd 25/07/45
PY-13 16/10/40	USS Siren 3 Lotosland	Edward A. Deeds	1929-P&J 11.5 knots	diesel motor yacht	720dp 196'5"	cpl-89; a: 2 3"/50, 2 mg, 2 dct. for first month clasified Coastal Minelayer CMc-1. struck 13/11/45
PY-32 30/12/41	USS Southern Seas Lyndonia (II)	Cyrus Curtis	1920-CSC 11 knots	diesel motor yacht	1,116dp 228'	cpl-47; a: ?No. 20mm. 1939 PanAm rnd Southern Seas to be floating hotel and inter island ferry. sunk by typhoon 09/10/45
PY-12 16/07/40	USS Sylph 4 Intrepid	Walter P. Murphy	1929-GLS 11 knots	diesel aux. barkentine	850dp 212'	cpl-88; a: 1 3"/50, 6 mg, 1 dct, 1 Y-gun. often used under sail. Ernest Borgnine (McHale's Navy) served aboard. dcmd 19/12/45
PY-20 16/05/41	USS Tourmaline Sylvia	Logan Gamble Thomson	1930-BIW 13 knots	diesel motor yacht	750dp 154'	cpl-161; a: 2 3"/50, 4 mg, 2 dct. YP-71 for first 3 days. sold 1946 Greek War Relief Assoc.
PY-18 21/08/40	USS Turquoise Ohio	Edward Willys Scripps	1922-NNS - - -	diesel motor yacht	565dp 172'	cpl-60; a: 1 3"/50, 2 dct. successive owners rnd Maramichi, Walucia III, Kallisto, Entropy. 29/01/44 trans. to Ecuador
PY-16 09/12/40	USS Zircon Nakhoda	Fred J. Fisher	1929-P&J 14 knots	diesel motor yacht	1,220dp 235'4"	cpl-108; a: 2 3"/50, 6 mg, 2 dct. sold 1947. NYC pilot boat 1951
PYc-28 12/03/42	USS Ability Sylvia	Logan Gamble Thomson	1926-DBM 13 knots	diesel motor yacht	280dp 133'	cpl-43; a: 1 20mm, 2 dct. sold R.E. Olds rnd Reomar IV. dcmd 29/09/44
PYc-4 27/10/40	USS Agate Armina	W.W. Atterbury	1930-MYB 13 knots	diesel motor yacht	185dp 110'6"	cpl- - -; a: 2 3"/23, 2 mg. rnd Stella Polaris. 02/11/40 AM-78, rnd Goldcrest. 20/12/40 PYc-4 named Agate. currently Val-larta Allegre
PYc-21 03/01/42	USS Alabaster Alamo	Wiliam F. Ladd	1932-MYB 14.5 knots	diesel motor yacht	385dp 148'	cpl-48; a: 1 3", 2 mg, 2 dct. dcmd 17/12/45. used in 1960s CBS TV show "Mr. Lucky." burned and sank 1982

Appendix 5

Number Acquired	Navy Name Original Name	Original Owner	Built Speed	Type	Tons Length	Notes
PYc-6 23/12/40	USS Amber Infanta	Edward Lowe	1930-LUD 12.5 knots	diesel motor yacht	260dp 120'	cpl - -; a: 1 3"/50, 2 dct. rnd Polaris prior to Navy purchase. dcmd 18/10/44. sold back to owner 13/06/45. currently Thea Foss
PYc-3 04/11/40	USS Amethyst Samona II	- - -	1931-CRG 14.5 knots	diesel motor yacht	525dp 147'	cpl-46; a: 1 3"/50, 2 dct. trans to USCG 10/03/44 redesignated WYPc-3
PYc-11 16/03/42	USS Andradite Cameco	James E. Whitin	1927-DBM 11.7 knots	diesel motor yacht	395dp 132'6"	cpl-56; a: 1 3"/23, 2 mg, 2 dct, 1 Y-gun. originally with USC&GS named Guide. dcmd 19/12/45. burned and sank 1/07/56
PYc-7 13/01/41	USS Aquamarine Vasanta–Siele	John H. French	1926-P&J 12 knots	diesel motor yacht	215dp 124'	cpl-36; a: 2 mg. rnd Siele before completion. sold 1936 Robert H. Wolfe rnd Seawolf. dcmd 21/06/46
PYc-45 02/01/42	USS Black Douglas Grenadier	Robert C. Roebling	1930-BIW 9.5 knots	3-mast diesel aux. schooner	371dp 133'5"	cpl - -; a: 4 mg. sold 1941 F&WS, aqd rnd Black Douglas IX-55 from F&WS, returned to F&WS 04/10/44. currently El Boughaz I
PYc-38 01/04/42	USS Carolita Ripple	- - -	1923-KGW 14 knots	diesel motor yacht	236dp 133'5"	cpl - -; a: 1 3"/50. dcmd 28/04/44. sunk as gunnery target 1947
PYc-16 15/12/41	USS Chalcedony Valero III	Captain Alan Hancock	1931-CRG 11.5 knots	diesel motor yacht	1,000dp 195'1"	cpl - -; a: 1 3"/23. dcmd 10/01/46. scrapped 1946
PYc-27 05/03/42	USS Colleen Colleen	S.A. Savage	1928-P&J 14 knots	diesel motor yacht	250dp 150'	cpl-28; a: 1 3"/50. trans to U.S. Coast Guard 11/09/45 as WYPc-27
PYc-26 02/03/42	USS Cymophane Robador	Robert Law, Jr.	1926-NNS 14 knots	diesel motor yacht	523 161'	cpl-49; a: 1 3"/50. rnd Seaforth 1929. dcmd 23/08/44
PYc-1 25/10/40	USS Emerald 3 Savitar	Joseph H. Seaman	1922-CSC 14 knots	diesel motor yacht	104 96'	cpl-32; a: - - -. dcmd 11/08/42. sold 1945
PYc-35 08/04/41	USS Felicia 2 Felicia	Sen. Jesse H. Metcalfe	1931-BIW 11.5 knots	diesel motor yacht	447 147'9"	cpl-42; a: 1 20mm. from 16/12/43 cadet training ship at Harvard University
PYc-29 17/03/42	USS Gallant Viking	George F. Baker	1909-P&J 13 knots	steam yacht	350dp 177'6"	cpl - -; a: 1 3"/50, 1 20mm, 1 mg. 1937 rnd Falcon. sold North Star Excursion Corp. rnd North Star. 28/06/45 Circle Line rnd Traveler

World War II Yachts

Number Acquired	Navy Name Original Name	Original Owner	Built Speed	Type	Tons Length	Notes
PYc-15 01/12/41	USS Garnet Caritas	J.P. Bartram	1925-KGW 12 knots	diesel motor yacht	490dp 156'9"	cpl-50; a: 1 3"/50, 6 mg, 2 dct. dcmd 29/12/45. currently land-locked museum and gift shop at Ship Ashore Resort, Smith River CA
PYc-46 12/08/40	USS Impetuous Paragon	John F. Bettz	1915-RJS 16 knots	diesel motor yacht	103dp 120'	cpl-9; a6 mg. originally aqd 14/05/17 as USS Sybila III SP-104. returned 24/12/18. rnd Arlis. rqd 12/08/40. initially USS PC-454
PYc-41 04/09/42	USS Iolite Florence D	- -	1914-GLS 10 knots	diesel motor yacht	200dp 154'	cpl- -; a: - -. dcmd 17/06/44. sold 1945
PYc-13 01/07/41	USS Jasper Stranger	- -	1938-LUD 12 knots	diesel motor yacht	395dp 134'	cpl- -; a: none. out of service 14/08/47. 1955 to Scripps Institute of Oceanography. 1976 cruise ship Explorer
PYc-20 27/01/42	USS Jet Thalia	T.M. Howell	1930-DBM 12 knots	diesel motor yacht	472dp 160'	cpl- -; a: 1 3"/50. dcmd 27/08/45. scrapped 1948
PYc-31 23/03/42	USS Lash Caroline	Edward Ford	1914-RJS 14 knots	steam yacht	339dp 187'8"	cpl- -; a: 2 3". 1919 Horace Dodge estate rnd Delphine. 1922 Stella Ford Schlotman rnd Stellaris. 1940 NY Waterway Cruises rn Sylph II
PYc-42 24/10/42	USS Leader Curlew	- -	1927-JSW 13 knots	diesel motor yacht	230dp 117'	cpl-25; a: 2 20mm, 2 dct , 2 rocket launchers.sold 1947 rnd Chito. sold rnd Hyding. sold 4X rnd Paullu. now Norwegian yacht Grace
PYc-39 13/04/42	USS Marnell Marnell	Alworth Investment Corp.	1930-DSC 14 knots	diesel motor yacht	180dp 135'	cpl-45; a: - -. sold 1933 Marnell Investment Group. dcmd 21/12/45
PYc-37 09/04/42	USS Mentor Haida	Max C. Fleischmann	1941-RJS 13 knots	diesel motor yacht	182dp 127'	cpl-35; a: 1 40mm, 2 20mm, 2 dct. 29/08/46 thru 18/05/50 Woods Hole Oceanographic Inst. 14/05/52 to World Surplus Trading Co.
PYc-9 10/02/41	USS Moonstone Nancy Baker	- -	1929-KGW 12 knots	diesel motor yacht	645dp 171'9"	cpl-50; a: 1 3"/50, 2 mg, 2 dct. rnd Mona then Lone Star. 16/10/43 sunk by collision USS Greer DD-145
PYc-22 15/01/42	USS Olivin Bidou	J.A. Moffett	1930-BIW 13 knots	diesel motor yacht	120dp 124'	cpl- -; a: 1 3"/50, 2mg, 2 dct. dcmd 21/03/44. scrapped 1946
PYc-5 03/12/40	USS Onyx Janey III	- -	1924-CSC 12 knots	diesel motor yacht	190dp 118'7"	cpl- -; a: 1 3"/50, 6 mg, 2 dct. rnd Rene then Pegasus before Onyx. damaged beyond economic repair in collision Feb 1944
PYc-8 27/01/41	USS Opal Coronet (II)	Irving Tar Bush	1928-KGW 13 knots	diesel motor yacht	590dp 185'6"	cpl-50; a: 2 3", 2 dct. lent Ecuador 23/09/43, sold outright 13/05/49

Appendix 5

Number Acquired	Navy Name Original Name	Original Owner	Built Speed	Type	Tons Length	Notes
PYc-33 23/03/42	USS Palace Idalia	Eugene Tompkins	1899-DRS - -	steam yacht	195dp 163'	cpl- -; a: none. rnd Malay II then Palace. rto William B. Baletti 18/05/42. rqd 07/08/42. sunk as radar target 09/09/44
PYc-36 07/04/42	USS Paragon Paragon	Charles J. Davol	1929-BIW 14 knots	diesel motor yacht	176dp 138'2"	cpl- -; a: 1 6-pounder. dcmd 27/01/44. sold 1945. ran aground-wrecked 1949
PYc-47 20/09/40	USS Patriot 2 Katoura	A.L. Loomis	1930-HHM 18 knots	diesel motor yacht	83dp 96'6"	cpl- -; a: 1 3"/50, 2 mg, 2 dct. originally USS PC-455. struck 14/10/44
PYc-18 22/12/41	USS Peridot Bymar	B.D. Miller	1938-DBM 13 knots	diesel motor yacht	300dp 144'7"	cpl-48; a: 1 3"/50, 8 mg, 2 dct. dcmd 03/01/46. subsequently rnd Mimosan, Halimede, Zimba, Maha, Al Mojil, Matahari, Maha
PYc-44 22/01/43	USS Perseverance Gem	William Ziegler	1913-GLS 18 knots	steam yacht	190ddp 164'5"	cpl-24; a: 1 20mm, 2 dct. rnd Gypsy Jo, Athero, Carolus, Condor. aqd U.S. Coast Guard 28/07/42 as USCGC Bedford WPYc-346
PYc-48 13/08/40	USS Persistent Onwego	George L. Bourne	1931-CSC 12 knots	diesel motor yacht	110dp 120'	cpl- -; a: 4 mg, 2 dct. originally USS PC-456. dcmd 27/09/44
PYc-25 17/02/42	USS Phenakite Celt	J.R. Maxwell	1902-P&J 15 knots	steam yacht later diesel	317dp 186'3"	cpl-40; a: 1 3"/23, 4 mg, 2 dct. first aqd 03/07/17 for WWI as USS Sachem SP-192. dcmd 17/11/44. later Sightseer then Circle Line V
PYc-17 08/01/42	USS Pyrope Oceanus	John William Kiser	1923-KGW 12.5 knots	diesel motor yacht	490dp 156'4"	cpl-49; a: 1 3"/50, 1 40mm, 2 dct. dcmd 13/12/46
PYc-49 11/10/40	USS Retort Enaj IV	Thomas G. Bennett	1923-GLS 12 knots	steam yacht later diesel	164dp 120'	cpl- -; a: 1 3"/50, 6 mg, 2 dct. sold 1930 rnd Kooyang II. sold 1936 rnd Evelyn R. II. originally USS PC-458. dcmd 23/09/44
PYc-19 29/12/41	USS Rhodolite Seapine	Frank H. Goodyear	1931-BIW 11 knots	diesel motor yacht	588dp 158'	cpl-56; a: 1 3"/50, 4 mg. Goodyear died before delivery so sold to business partner Hollander rnd Yankee. dcmd 29/12/45
PYc-2 01/11/4	USS Sapphire 2 Comoco	- - -	1922-GLS 13.5 knots	diesel motor yacht	500dp 165'4"	cpl-59; a: 1 3"/50/ 1 Y-gun, 2 dct. rnd Margo then Buccaneer before aqd. dcmd 29/10/45
PYc-12 19/06/41	USS Sardonyx Queen Anne	Alexander Dallas Thayer	1928-KGW 11.5 knots	diesel motor yacht	640dp 175'4"	cpl- -; a: 4 mg, 2 dct. dcmd 03/01/44
PYc-43 24/12/42	USS Sea Scout Valero II	Captain Alan Hancock	1922-WMR - -	diesel motor yacht	195dp 125'6"	cpl- -; a: - -. aqd from U.S. Coast Guard. dcmd 15/05/44. 1945 sold original owners as original name
PYc-50 04/09/40	USS Sturdy Avalance	Anson Wales Hard, Jr.	1930-CSC 17 knots	diesel motor yacht	380dp 154'	cpl- -; a: - -. sold 1935 Arthur V. Davis rnd Elda. originally USS PC-460. dcmd 20/11/44

World War II Yachts

Number Acquired	Navy Name Original Name	Original Owner	Built Speed	Type	Tons Length	Notes
PYc-10 14/02/41	USS Topaz Doromar	- - -	1931-LMC 13 knots	diesel motor yacht	160dp 111'8"	cpl- --; a: 1 3"/50, 2 mg, 2 dct. dcmd 27/09/44
PYc-32 23/03/42	USS Tourist Calumet	Roswell Eldridge	1903-GLS - - -	steam yacht	185dp 150'	cpl-32; a: - -. 3rd sale Edward Baletti rnd Dixie. sold 3X rnd Tourist. rto Baletti 1942, rqd 1942 as USS YAG-14. dcmd 11/08/44
PYc-14 03/07/41	USS Truant Truant	Helen H. Newberry	1892-HHM 10 knots	steam yacht	375dp 138'	cpl- --; a: 2 3"/50. sold 1936 Henry Ford. 17/11/43 rto
PYc-30 23/03/42	USS Vagrant Vagrant	Harold Stirling Vanderbilt	1941-BIW 12 knots	diesel motor yacht	425dp 117'7"	cpl-14; a: 2 mg. originally USS YP-258. dcmd 29/12/43. rto 1947
PYc-51 07/10/40	USS Valiant 2 Vara	Harold Stirling Vanderbilt	1929-HHM 15 knots	diesel motor yacht	190dp 150'	cpl- --; a: 1 3"/50. originally USS PC-509. dcmd Sep 1944
PYc-52 27/12/41	USS Venture 2 Vixen	Adolph M. Bick	1931-CSC 17 knots	wood hull diesel yacht	138dp 110'	cpl-24; a: 2 mg, 4 depth charges. originally USS PC-826. dcmd 25/09/43 then in service training. struck 1945. later sold at least 4X
IX-43 10/09/40	Freedom Freedom	Sterling Morton	1931-GLE - - -	2-mast gas aux. schooner	- - - 88'8"	gift to Naval Academy. served in non-commissioned status into 1962
IX-47 11/11/36	Vamarie Vamarie	Vadim S. Makaroff	1933-A&R - - -	2-mast gas aux. schooner	45gt 72'	gift to Naval Academy. non-commissioned status. destroyed in storm 1954
IX-48 26/10/40	Highland Light Highland Light	Dudley A. Wolfe	1931-GLS - - -	gasoline aux. sloop	32gt 68'7"	gift of estate to Naval Academy. non-commissioned status into 1965
IX-49 23/10/40	Spindrift Spindrift	Wallace W. Lanahan	1928-FFP - - -	gasoline aux. cutter	17gt 54'9"	sold $1.00 to Naval Academy. non-commissioned status. placed in reserve 1947. struck 1952
IX-50 22/05/41	USS Bowdoin Bowdoin	- - -	1921-HDB - - -	2-mast diesel aux. schooner	66dp 88'	South Greenland patrol. struck May 1944. sold 1945
IX-52 14/07/41	Cheng Ho Cheng Ho	Anne Archbold	1939-KSW - - -	diesel aux. junk	175 94'	cpl- --; a: 1 3"/50, 2 mg. Pearl Harbor picket patrol. there on 07/12/41
IX-54 08/09/41	USS Galaxy Gallaxy	Bernard W. Doyle	1930-P&J 11.4 knots	diesel motor yacht	320dp 130'	cpl-27; a: none. underwater sound experiments. struck 01/05/46
IX-55 02/01/42	USS Black Douglas Grenadier	Robert C. Roebling	1930-BIW 9.5 knots	3-mast diesel aux. schooner	371dp 133'5"	cpl- --; a: 1 4", 4 mg. aqd from F&WS which aqd in Sep 1941. see also PYc-45. struck 14/10/44

Appendix 5

Number Acquired	Navy Name Original Name	Original Owner	Built Speed	Type	Tons Length	Notes
IX-57 27/01/42	Araner Faith	acquired from John Ford	1926-ADS 8 knots	diesel aux. ketch	147dp 106'5"	cpl- -; a: - -. returned to Mrs. Ford 12/07/44. rnd Faith then Windjammer circa 1975
IX-58 19/02/42	Dwyn Wen Dwyn Wen	- -	1906-P&S - -	diesel aux. schooner	160dp 128'	cpl- -; a: - -. struck 18/07/44
IX-59 02/02/42	Volador Volador	- -	1926-WMR 7 knots	diesel aux. schooner	114dp 110'	cpl- -; a: - -. 17/08/43 trans to Army
IX-60 31/01/42	Seaward Seaward	Cecil B. DeMille	1920-ACO 7 knots	diesel aux. schooner	96 106'	cpl-6; a: - -. struck 18/07/44
IX-61 01/02/42	Geoanna Geoanna	- -	1934-CSC 8 knots	2-mast diesel aux. schooner	- - 111'6"	cpl- -; a: - -. trans to Army 03/09/43 as communications ship TP-249
IX-62 23/12/41	Vileehi Vileehi	acquired from Hiram T. Horton	1930-SDM 7 knots	gasoline aux. ketch	54 80'	cpl- -; a: - -. rto 27/09/45
IX-63 13/02/42	Zahma Zahma	John H. Cromwell	1915-GLS 8 knots	diesel aux. ketch	157dp 93'	cpl-6; a: - -. out of service 13/04/43. rejected for WWI service
IX-65 17/03/42	Blue Dolphin Blue Dolphin	acquired from Amory Coolidge	1926-SSC 8 knots	2-mast diesel aux. schooner	91dp 99'8"	cpl-12; a: - -. 03/04/49 designated "suitable for use as a naval auxiliary in time of war"
IX-66 21/03/42	USS Migrant Migrant	acquired from Carl Tucker	1929-GLS 11 knots	3-mast diesel aux. sloop	661dp 223'3"	cpl- -; a: 1 3"/50, 4 20mm, 2 dct. dcmd 03/08/45. struck 13/08/45
IX-67 24/03/42	USS Guinevere 2 Guinevere	acquired from Edgar Palmer	1921-GLS - -	3-mast diesel-elec schooner	503dp 195'	cpl- -; a: - -. struck 1945. sold 1946
IX-68 10/04/42	Seven Seas Abraham Rydberg	acquired from W.S. Gubelmann	1912-BMV 14 knots	3-mast full-rigged ship	430dp 168'	cpl- -; a: - -. originally Swedish Navy training ship. struck 29/07/44
IX-69 03/05/42	Puritan 4 Puritan	acquired from Harry J. Bauer	1931-EBC 8 knots	diesel aux. schooner	101dp 102'9"	cpl- -; a: - -. rto 18/11/44
IX-70 1/05/42	USS Gloria Dalton Gloria Dalton	- -	1925-CSC - -	diesel aux. schooner	86dp 87'	cpl- -; a: - -. laid up for repairs 16/11/42
IX-73 12/06/42	Zaca 2 Zaca	Templeton Cracker	1930-NBB 9 knots	2-mast diesel aux. schooner	122gt 118'	cpl-10; a: - -. sold 1946 Errol Flynn's floating pleasure palace. currently Zaca

World War II Yachts

Number Acquired	Navy Name / Original Name	Original Owner	Built / Speed	Type	Tons / Length	Notes
IX-75 02/07/42	USS John M. Howard / Elsie Fenimore	Eldridge Reeves Fenimore Johnson	1934-MYB 9 knots	diesel aux. ketch	94dp 87'	cpl- - ; a: - - . dcmd 09/05/45. in service thru 16/11/45. disposal 24/01/46
IX-76 15/07/42	Ramona Ohnkara	acquired from S.M. Spalding	1920-HHM - -	gasoline aux. schooner	126dp 109'	cpl- - ; a: - - . rto 05/08/44
IX-77 20/07/42	Juniata 3 Etak	acquired from W.H. Rohl	1930-KGW 11 knots	2-mast diesel aux. schooner	242dp 134'	cpl- - ; a: - - . rnd Vega 1938. sold 04/06/45
IX-79 27/07/42	El Cano Cressida	acquired from George Vanderbilt	1927-KGW 7.5 knots	aux. topsail schooner	464dp 172'	cpl-25; a: - - . Vanderbilt rnd Crimper 1938. rnd Pioneer 1939. rto Vanderbilt post war
IX-82 21/07/42	Luster Ko-Asa	- - -	1936-MMD 8 knots	diesel aux. ketch	68dp 82'6"	cpl-4; a: - - . placed out of service 26/06/44. trans to War Shipping Admin. 20/12/44
IX-83 29/07/42	Ashley Winslow	from Adavondach School, Florida	1937-TBA 7.5 knots	aux. schooner	41dp 65'	cpl-12; a: - - . actual duties and disposition remain a mystery
IX-84 11/08/42	Congaree Wakiva	Harkness Edwards	1938-J&P 7.5 knots	diesel aux. yawl	35gt 70'3"	cpl-11; a: - - . sold 1947
IX-85 18/08/42	Euhaw Nurmah	John H. Cromwell	1910-GLS 9 knots	gasoline aux. yawl	59dp 84'	cpl-12; a: - - . renamed Mayhap prior to acquisition. sold 01/11/44
IX-86 18/08/42	Pocotagligo Lynx	acquired from Charles D. Wiman	1926-MUM 12 knots	diesel aux. schooner	60dp 96'	cpl-12; a: - - . aqd by Maritime Commission then trans to Navy as Marpatcha. resold to owner 14/03/45
IX-87 31/07/42	USS Saluda Odyssey	acquired from Mrs. Barklie Henry	1938-HBN 9 knots	diesel aux. yawl	92dp 88'7"	cpl-10; a: - - . Navy Electronics Lab San Diego post war. reclassified YAG-87 1968. struck 1974. now SSS Odyssey w/ Sea Scouts
IX-88 30/07/42	Wimbee Roland von Bremen	acquired from W.L. MacFarland	1936-EBM 7 knots	gasoline aux. yawl	22dp 59'9"	cpl- - ; a: - - . sold 1938 Leo Berson rnd Condor after used to escape Nazi Germany
IX-89 18/08/42	Romain Merida	- - -	1937-SSB - -	diesel Aux. Schooner	66gt 84'	cpl-10; a: - - . struck 1947
IX-90 19/08/42	Forbes Doerello III	acquired from Pond School	1927-MUM - -	diesel aux. schooner	110dp 98'	cpl-14; a: - - . rnd Morning Star before aqd. struck 12/08/43
IX-91 23/09/42	Palomas Goodwill	acquired from Keith Spaulding	1922-BSC 10 knots	diesel aux. schooner	312dp 161'	cpl- - ; a: - - . struck 1946

Number Acquired	Navy Name / Original Name	Original Owner	Built / Speed	Type	Tons / Length	Notes
IX-97 11/01/43	Martha's Vineyard / Thelma	- - -	1911-CSC - - -	gasoline motor yacht	141gt 138'	cpl-11; a: - - -. 06/09/46 to War Shipping Admin. for to
IX-99 07/01/42	USS Sea Cloud / Hussar (V)	Joseph E. Davies	1931-KGW 14 knots	4-mast diesel aux. bark	2,323dp 316'	cpl-187; a: 2 3"/50, 8 20mm, 4 K-gun, hedgehog, 2 dct.32,000 sq.ft sails. 1st fully integrated Navy ship. ex-USCG WPG-284. 04/11/44 rto
IX-175 01/10/40	Kestrel / Chanco	acquired from Chanco Corp.	1938-SYC 11 knots	diesel motor yacht	219dp 98'10"	xcpl-19; a: 2 mg. riginally AMc-5. 29/10/45 to War Shipping Admin. for disposal
IX-224 31/05/45	Aide De Camp / Colleen	Samuel Agar Salvage	1922-GLS 15 knots	diesel motor yacht	167dp 110'	cpl- - -; a: none. 1927 rnd Ranger. 1928 rnd Poinsettia.1931 rnd Aide De Camp. at Harvard Underwater Sound Lab entire war. sold 1946

Records are mostly incomplete for the District Patrol Craft. The Navy created the classification when taking over around sixty Coast Guard vessels no longer needed after repeal of the Volstead Act (05/12/33) ended Prohibition. Additions in WWII increased this fleet to nearly 650 vessels of all types. After the war, all were struck from the Navy List and sold.

Number Acquired	Navy Name / Original Name	Original Owner	Built / Speed	Type	Tons / Length	Notes
YP-4 20/06/33	YP-4 / Stephanotis	U.S. Coast Guard	1909 - - - - - -	diesel motor yacht	49gt 66'	British rum runner captured 03/12/30. originally in Coast Guard service as CG-975. out of service 08/02/45
YP-109 21/10/41	YP-109 / Elvida	- - -	- - - - - -	diesel motor yacht	86dp 107'5"	at Pearl Harbor during attack 07/12/41. struck 03/01/46
YP-200 1942	YP-200 / Edithena	acquired Bureau of Fisheries	1914-CSC 12 knots	gasoline motor yacht	38dp 76'	originally acquired ??/06/17 USS Edithena SP-624. 21/10/19 to Bureau of Fisheries as Widgeon. returned to Bureau Dec 1945
YP-249 14/03/42	YP-249 / Althea	C. Hayward Murphy	1930-BIW - - -	diesel motor yacht	148dp 106'	placed out of service 1945
YP-261 19/01/42	USS Sard / Alida	Bertram Harold Borden	1922-GLS 15 knots	diesel motor yacht	212dp 135'	1927 rn Victoria May. 1935 rn All Alone. in Dept. of Commerce 1938 rn Navigation. laid up 21/06/44
YP-284	- - -	- - -	- - - - - -	diesel trawler	- - - - - -	Sunk by Japanese destroyer Guadalcanal 25/10/42
YP-346	- - -	- - -	- - - - - -	diesel trawler	- - - 97'	Sunk by Japanese cruiser Guadalcanal 09/09/42
YP-354 15/04/42	YP-354 / Innisfail	J.M. Cudahy	1935-MYB - - -	diesel motor yacht	- - - - - -	placed out of service 1947 but remained in use as presidential yacht into 1965. renamed El Presidente 1965
YP-357 1942	YP-357 / Imelda	John M. Hagerty	1939-HDB - - -	diesel motor yacht	93dp 85'	rto 1945. sold several times & renamed. 1950 sold CIA for covert operations off Greece & Albania rnd Jane or Juanita
YP-391 1942	YP-391 / Bluebird	- - -	1938 - - - - - -	motor yacht	115dp - - -	

World War II Yachts

Number Acquired	Navy Name Original Name	Original Owner	Built Speed	Type	Tons Length	Notes
YP-403 09/05/42	YP-403 Chanticleer	- -	1941-MYB - - -	diesel motor yacht	115dp 60'1"	struck 15/11/45
YP-407 09/05/42	YP-407 Maid Marian II	- -	1931-MYB - - -	diesel motor yacht	97dp 101'8"	struck 07/02/46
YP-425 05/04/42	YP-425 Rose B.	- -	1930-DBM 16 knots	diesel motor yacht	194dp 138'11"	a: 1 3"/50, 2 20mm, 2 dct. originally rnd USS Brave PYc-34. placed out of service 28/11/45
YP-454 1942	YP-454 Souris	- -	1930-HBN - - -	- -	- - 107'	originally Iolite PYc-24. reclassified 23/06/42 to avoid confusion with USS Iolite PYc-41
YP-455 22/06/42	YP-455 Alura	- -	1922-CSC - - -	diesel motor yacht	124dp 120'3"	struck 26/02/46
YP-506 1942	YP-506 Fleet	J.L. Redmond	1917-GLS 14.5 knots	steam yacht	- - 81'2.5"	cpl-5 civilian; a: 1 3-pounder, 1 mg. rnd De Grasse ID-1217 aqd 07/06/17. rto 07/11/18. sold 1946
YP-521 - -	YP-521 - -	- -	- - - - -	- -	- - - -	
YP-552 07/09/42	YP-552 Taormina	- -	1924 - - - - - -	diesel motor yacht	- - 113'4"	struck 11/10/45
YP-559 13/09/42	YP-559 Kyma	- -	1928 - - - - - -	diesel motor yacht	- - 99'9"	
YP-603 1942	YP-603 Shiawassee	- -	1933 - - - - - -	- -	- - 105'	trans to Maritime Admin for disposal 1946
YP-608 - -	YP-608 - -	- -	- - - - -	diesel motor yacht	- - - -	

Primary sources to compile this table:
Dictionary of American Naval Fighting Ships *at www.history.navy.mil and www.navsource.org and www.shipscribe.com/usnaux.*

Chapter Notes

[For all chapters: unless otherwise noted, all access to Naval History and Heritage Command entries from the *Dictionary of American Naval Fighting Ships*, and to NavSource Naval History was verified as of March 15, 2017.]

Chapter 1

1. Gardiner, R. and B. Lavery, *The Line of Battle: The Sailing Warship 1650–1840* (London: Conway, 1992; 2004 ed.), 68–70.
2. Robinson, John, and George Francis Dow, *The Sailing Ships of New England 1607–1907* (Salem, MA: Marine Research Society, Salem, 1922), 34.
3. *Ibid.*
4. The Joseph Bucklin Society. "First Navy." Accessed November 15, 2011. http://www.bucklinsociety.net/first_navy.htm.
5. Allen, Gardner Weld, *A Naval History of the American Revolution in Two Volumes*, Vol. I (Boston: Houghton Mifflin Company, 1913), 40–41.
6. Paullin, Charles Oscar, *The Navy of the American Revolution: Its Administration, Its Policy and Its Achievements* (Cleveland: The Burrows Brothers Company, 1906), 80.
7. Griffin, Martin I.J., "The Commodores of the Navy of the United Colonies." *Appleton's Booklovers Magazine*, Vol. VI (July–December, 1905), New York: D. Appleton and Company, 1905, 575.
8. Naval History and Heritage Command. "History of the Department of the Navy." Accessed November 10, 2011. http://www.history.navy.mil/faqs/faq31-1.htm.
9. *Ibid.*
10. Chapelle, Howard I., *The American Sailing Navy: The Ships and Their Development* (New York: Konecky & Konecky, 1949), 53–54.
11. *Naval Documents of the American Revolution*, Vol. 2, "American Theatre, part 3 of 9, Sept. 3, 1775–Oct. 31, 1775, " (Washington, D.C.: U.S. Government Printing Office, 1966), 442, accessed February 27, 2017, http://ibiblio.org/anrs/docs/E/E3/ndar_v02p03.pdf.
12. Maclay, Edgar Stanton, *A History of the United States Navy From 1775 to 1894*, Vol. I (New York: D. Appleton and Company, 1895), 44.
13. *Ibid.*
14. Advertisement from *The Boston Gazette*, 13 November 1780, in Angus Konstam, *Privateers & Pirates 1730–1830* (Oxford: Osprey Publishing, 2001), 19.
15. Maclay, Edgar Stanton, *A History of American Privateers* (New York: D. Appleton and Company, 1899), 259, accessed March 7, 2017.
16. Letter from Master-Commandant Arthur Sinclair in Maclay, *A History of American Privateers*, xxiv–xxv.
17. Private letter quoted in Maclay, *A History of the United States Navy From 1775 to 1894*, Vol. I, 71.
18. Records of Parliament, Vol. XIX, 707–711, in *A History of the United States Navy...*, Vol. I, 101–102.
19. Allen, Vol.1, 43–44.
20. Maclay, *A History of the United States Navy...*, Vol. I, 139–140, 188.
21. Letter to the President of Congress dated 18 February 1782, in *Ibid.*, 139.
22. Maclay, *A History of American Privateers*, 373.
23. Maclay, *A History of the United States Navy...*, Vol.1, 151.
24. *Ibid.*, 87–88.
25. *Ibid.*, 157.
26. *Ibid.*
27. Lord Palmerston's defense of Treaty of Adrianople in the House of Commons, March 1, 1848, in *Hansard's Parliamentary Debates. 3rd Series, Commencing with the Accession of William IV*, Vol. XCVII (London: G. Woodfall and Son et alia, 1848), 79-column 122.
28. Maclay, *A History of the United States Navy...*, Vol.1, 308.
29. Maclay, *A History of American Privateers*, 225.
30. Maclay, *A History of the United States Navy...*, Vol.1, 319.
31. "Hornet and Brig Argus," in *The Weekly Register: Containing Documents, Essays and Facts; Together with Notices of the Arts and Manufactures, and a Record of the Events of the Times*, Vol. II, March 1812 to September 1812, No. 45, July 11,

1812, Hezekiah Niles, ed. (Baltimore: H. Niles, 1812), 319.
  32. *Ibid.*, 334.
  33. Crowninshield, Francis B., *The Story of George Crowninshield's Yacht Cleopatra's Barge on a Voyage of Pleasure to the Western Islands and the Mediterranean 1816–1817* (Boston: privately printed, 1913), 12.
  34. *Ibid.*, 15.
  35. Maclay, *A History of American Privateers*, 506.

Chapter 2

  1. Maclay, Edgar Stanton, *A History of the United States Navy From 1775 to 1901*, Vol. II (New York: D. Appleton and Company, 1906), 62.
  2. Smedley, Rev. Edward, Rev. Hugh James Rose, and Rev. Henry John Rose, eds., "Naval Architecture," *Encyclopedia Metropolitana; or Universal Dictionary of Knowledge*, Vol. VI (London: B. Fellowes; F. and J. Rivington; Duncan and Malcolm, et alia, 1845), 343 (footnote).
  3. Naval History and Heritage Command. "Wave I," in *Dictionary of American Naval Fighting Ships*. [*DANFS*] Accessed March 15, 2017. http://www.history.navy.mil/danfs/w4/wave-i.htm.
  4. Slave Ship Trouvadore. "Identifying the Remains of Onkahye." Accessed December 23, 2011. http://slaveshiptrouvadore.org/antipiracy-antislavery-patrols/us-schooner-onkahye/indentifying- the-remains-of-onkahye/
  5. Naval History and Heritage Command. "Onkahye," in *DANFS*. Accessed March 15, 2017. http://www.history.navy.mil/danfs/o3/onkahye.htm.
  6. Peverelly, Charles A., ed., *The Book of American Pastimes, Containing a History of the Principal Base Ball, Cricket, Rowing, and Yachting Clubs of the United States* (New York: published by the author, 1866), 15.
  7. "The New York Yacht Club: Its Organization, Founders and its First Cruise. Annual Regattas and Winning Yachts–Yachts Now Belonging to the Club–Charter of the Club–Rules and Regulations–Honorary Members–Coming Regattas. Officers. Yachts of the Club. Charter of the Club. Rules and Regulations. Honorary Members. The Ensuing Regatta, Etc." *The New York Times*, June 3, 1865, accessed December 20, 2011, http://www.nytimes.com/1865/06/03/news/new-york-yacht-club-its-organization-founders-its-first-cruise-annual-regattas.html?pagewanted=all *New York Times*, 3 June 1865. "New York Yacht Club..."
  8. Naval History and Heritage Command. "Onkahye," in *DANFS*.
  9. *Reports from the Court of Claims Submitted to the House of Representatives, The Third Session of the Thirty-fourth Congress 1856-'57*, In One Volume, "O.H. Berryman and Others vs. The United States" (Washington: Cornelius Wendell, 1857) 61–62.
  10. *Ibid.*, 73.
  11. Sanger, George P., ed., *The Statutes at Large and Proclamations of the United States of America, from March 1871 to March 1873, and Treaties and Postal Conventions*, Vol. XVII (Boston: Little, Brown, and Company, 1873), 665.
  12. Thompson, Winfield M. "Historic American Yachts: The Slave Yacht Wanderer." *The Rudder*, Vol. XV, No. 2, February 1904, 53.
  13. Peverelly, *The Book of American Pastimes...*, 45.
  14. *Ibid.*, 54.
  15. *Ibid.*, 44.
  16. *Ibid.*, 54.
  17. Spears, John R., *The American Slave-Trade: An Account of Its Origin, Growth and Suppression* (New York: Charles Scribner's Sons, 1900), 195.
  18. Thompson, *The Rudder*, Vol. XV, No. 2, 56.
  19. Spears, 197.
  20. Peverelly, *The Book of American Pastimes...*, 45.
  21. National Archives and Records Administration, Southeast Region. "The Wanderer: A finding aid, U.S. District Court, Savannah, Georgia, Mixed Cases, 1790–1860," 2. Accessed January 22, 2012. http://www.archives.gov/southeast/finding-aids/wanderer.pdf.
  22. Spears, 205.
  23. Naval History and Heritage Command. "Wanderer I," in *DANFS*.
  24. Peverelly, Charles A., ed. "Yachting Foam," *Brentano's Aquatic Monthly and Sporting Gazetteer*, Volume I, April to September 1879, 468.
  25. "Revenue Cutters After Smugglers of Chinese," *The New York Times*, October 1, 1906. Accessed January 24, 2012. http://query.nytimes.com/gst/abstract.html?res=FA0713FC355F13718DDDA80894D8415B868CF1D3.
  26. *Ibid.*
  27. "The Frolic Discovered." *The Gazette*, Montreal, Vol. CXXXV, No. 244, October 11, 1906, 12. Accessed March 1, 2017. https://news.google.com/newspapers?nid=Fr8DH2VBP9sC&dat=19061011&printsec=frontpage&hl=en.
  28. "District Court, D. Rhode Island, November 15, 1906, No. 1,132," *The Federal Reporter, Volume 148, Cases Argued and Determined in the Circuit Courts of Appeals and Circuit and District Courts of the United States, December, 1906–February, 1907* (St. Paul MN: West Publishing Co., 1907), 920.

Chapter 3

  1. Stark, Francis Raymond, *The Abolition of Privateering and the Declaration of Paris. Studies in History, Economics and Public Law*, Vol. VIII, No. 3 (New York: Columbia University Press, 1897), 141.
  2. *Ibid.*, 147–8.
  3. Scharf, J. Thomas, *History of the Confederate States Navy from Its Organization to the Surrender*

of Its Last Vessel (New York: Rogers & Sherwood, 1887, 53–54.
   4. Stark, 155–156.
   5. *Appendix to the Congressional Globe, for the First Session, Thirtieth Congress: Containing Speeches and Important State Papers, New Series 1847–8* (Washington: Blair and Rives, 1848), 94.
   6. "Representative Men of the Republican Party." *The Old Guard, A Monthly Journal Devoted to the Principles of 1776 and 1787*, Vol. II, issue 7, C. Chauncy Burr, ed. (New York: Van Evrie, Horton & Co., 1864), 156.
   7. Scharf, 33.
   8. *Ibid.*, 41.
   9. *Ibid.*, 60.
   10. *Congressional Globe, 1861-'62, 3325, 3335.* "Piracy and Privateering," (Lawrence's Wheaton (1863), 643), in *Index to the Miscellaneous Documents of the Senate of the United States for the First Session of the Forty-Ninth Congress* (in 13 volumes) Chapter XX, Section 385 (Washington, D.C.: U.S. Government Printing Office, 1886), 492.
   11. Scharf, 67.
   12. United States Naval War Records Office, *Official Records of the Union and Confederate Navies in the War of the Rebellion*, Series II—Vol. 1 (Washington, D.C.: U.S. Government Printing Office, 1921), 266, 346.
   13. Robinson, William Morrison, *The Confederate Privateers* (New Haven, CT: Yale University Press, 1928), 125–127.
   14. Naval History and Heritage Command. "Jefferson Davis," in *DANFS*; Walsh, George Ethelbert. "Privateers," *Lippincott's Monthly Magazine: Popular Journal of General Literature, Science, and Politics*, Vol. LXII, July to December 1898, 228; "The Schooner, 'S.J. Waring." *Harper's Weekly.* August 3, 1861, 485.Accessed August 30, 2014. http://www.sonofthesouth.net/leefoundation/civil-war/1861/august/schooner-waring.htm.
   15. "The Sea and Sea Power as a factor in the History of the United States, Address of the Hon. H.A. Herbert, Secretary of the Navy, Before the Class at the U.S. Naval War College, Newport R.I., August 10, 1896." *United States Naval Institute Proceedings*, Vol. XXII, No. 3, 1896, H.G. Dressel, ed., 568. Annapolis, MD: United States Naval Institute, 1896.
   16. Boynton, Charles Brandon, *The History of the Navy During the Rebellion*, Vol. I (New York: D. Appleton and Company, 1867), 89.
   17. *Ibid.*, 108.
   18. Civil War Trust. "This Day in the Civil War." Accessed April 12, 2016. http://www.civilwar.org/150th-anniversary/this-day-in-the-civil-war.html#1861.
   19. United States Coast Guard. "Hope, 1861." Accessed September 22, 2014. http://www.uscg.mil/history/webcutters/Hope1861.pdf; *Record of Movements Vessels of the United States Coast Guard 1790—December 31, 1933*, Department of Transportation, United States Coast Guard (Washington: Reprinted by the Coast Guard Historian's Office, A Bicentennial Publication, U.S. Coast Guard Headquarters, 1989), 420; Bartlett, John Russell, *Memoirs of Rhode Island Officers Who Were Engaged in the Service of Their Country During the Great Rebellion of the South* (Providence RI: Sidney S. Rider & Brother, 1867); *Official Records of the Union and Confederate Navies...*, Series II, Vol. 1, 103.
   20. Naval History and Heritage Command. "Hope," in *DANFS Official Records of the Union and Confederate Navies...*, Series II, Vol. 1, 103.
   21. New York Yacht Club. "James Gordon Bennett, I Presume." Accessed September 9, 2014. http://www.nyyc.org/about/history-heritage/931-james-gordon-bennett-i-presume.
   22. Lincoln, Abraham. "Letter to Salmon P. Chase," in *1809–1865, Collected Works of Abraham Lincoln*, Vol. 4 (Ann Arbor: University of Michigan Digital Library Production Services, 2001), accessed September 12, 2014. http://quod.lib.umich.edu/cgi/t/text/text-idx?c=lincoln;rgn=div1;view=text;idno=lincoln4;node=lincoln4%3A589.
   23. United States Coast Guard. "U.S. Revenue Cutters and Lighthouse Service in the Civil War," 4–6. Accessed September 9, 2014. https://www.uscg.mil/history/uscghist/USRMCivilWarChronology.pdf.
   24. Wallace, William N., *The Macmillan Book of Boating* (New York: The Macmillan Company, 1964), 47, 48, 51.
   25. Marryat, Captain Frederick, R.N., *The Pirate*, and *The Three Cutters* (London: Henry G. Bohn, 1854), 206.
   26. Marine Harbor. "Regattas." Accessed April 14, 2013. http://harbor.passchristian.net/regattas.htm.
   27. *Ibid.*
   28. "The Southern Yacht Club of New Orleans," *Outing, An Illustrated Monthly Magazine of Sport, Travel and Recreation*, Vol. XXXI, October, 1897—March 1898, 555, James H. Worman and Ben J. Worman, eds.
   29. Scheib, Flora K., *History of the Southern Yacht Club* (Gretna, LA: Pelican Publishing Company, 1986), 21.
   30. MacTaggart, Ross, *The Golden Century: Classic Motor Yachts, 1830–1930* (New York: W.W. Norton & Company, 2001), 15.
   31. Stephens, W.P., "Steam Yachting in America," *The Book of Sport*, William Patten, ed. (New York: J. E. Taylor & Company, 1901), 394.
   32. "Federal Rights Violated; Seizure of Coast Survey Vessels in Florida and South Carolina. List of Vessels in that Service Their Position and Commanders," *The New York Times.* January 24, 1861. Accessed January 31, 2012. http://www.nytimes.com/1861/01/24/news/federal-rights-violated-seizure-coast-survey-vessels-florida-south-carolina-list.html.
   33. *Record of Movements...*, 35, 37.
   34. United States Coast Guard. "Harriet Lane, 1858." Accessed September 7, 2014. http://www.uscg.mil/history/webcutters/harrietlane1858.pdf.

35. Tucker, Philip C., III. "The United States Gunboat Harriet Lane." *The Southwestern Historical Quarterly*. Vol. 21, April 1, 1918, 360.
36. United States Coast Guard. "Harriet Lane, 1858."
37. *Ibid.*
38. Tucker, 360.
39. United States Coast Guard. "Harriet Lane, 1858."
40. Tucker, 361.
41. United States Coast Guard. "Harriet Lane, 1858."
42. Tucker, p. 371.
43. Texas State Historical Association. "Harriet Lane." Accessed September 8, 2014. http://www.tshaonline.org/handbook/online/articles/qth01
44. The Clyde Built Ships. "Lady Marchant." Accessed September 9, 2014. http://www.clydeships.co.uk/view.php?year_built=&builder=&ref=21936&vessel=LADY+LE+MARCHANT; "Arthur Leary Is Dead," *The New York Times*, February 24, 1893, accessed 09 September 2014, http://query.nytimes.com/mem/archive-free/pdf?res=9803E6DB1F3FEF33A25757C2A9649C94629ED7CF; United States Coast Guard. "Miami, 1862." Accessed September 10, 2014. http://www.uscg.mil/history/webcutters/Miami_1862.pdf; *Prince Edward Island Register*, "Passengers Arriving from Other Ports in the Maritimes," May 21, 1855 to December 1, 1856, accessed September 9, 2014, http://www.islandregister.com/maritimepass.html.
45. United States Coast Guard. "U.S. Revenue Cutters and Lighthouse Service in the Civil War." Accessed September 9, 2014. https://www.uscg.mil/history/uscghist/USRMCivilWarChronology.pdf.
46. Mindell, David A., *Iron Coffin: War, Technology, and Experience Aboard the USS Monitor* (Baltimore: The Johns Hopkins University Press, 2000), 79, 80.
47. United States Coast Guard. "U.S. Revenue Cutters and Lighthouse Service in the Civil War."
48. Littlefield, Francis L., "The Capture of the Chesapeake," in *Collections of the Maine Historical Society*, Third Series, Vol. II (Portland, ME: Published by the Society, 1906), 285–307.
49. United States Coast Guard. "Miami, 1862."
50. United States Naval War Records Office, *Official records of the Union and Confederate Navies in the War of the Rebellion*. Series I—Vol. 4. "Operations in the Gulf of Mexico, November 15, 1860—June 7, 1861; Operations on the Atlantic Coast, January 1, 1861—May 13, 1861; Operations on the Potomac and Rappahannock Rivers, January 5, 1861—December 7, 1861" (Washington, D.C.: U.S. Government Printing Office, 1896), 169.
51. Naval History and Heritage Command. "Wanderer 1," in *DANFS*. *Official Records of the Union and Confederate Navies...*, Series II, Vol. 1, 235–236.
52. United States Naval War Records Office, *Official Records of the Union and Confederate Navies in the War of the Rebellion*, Series I—Vol. 16. "South Atlantic Blockading Squadron from October 1, 1864, to August 8, 1865; Gulf Blockading Squadron from June 7 to December 15, 1861" (Washington, D.C.: U.S. Government Printing Office, 1903), 797–800.
53. Naval History and Heritage Command. "Wanderer 1," in *DANFS*.
54. Thompson, *The Rudder*, Vol. XV, No. 2, 141.
55. Sanger, George P., ed., *The Statutes at Large, Treaties, and Proclamations of the United States of America, from December 1863, to December 1865*, Vol. XIII (Boston: Little, Brown and Company, 1866), 401–402.
56. Naval History and Heritage Command. "Gertrude," in *DANFS*.
57. *Official Records of the Union and Confederate Navies...*, Series II, Vol. 1, 230.
58. Stiles, T.J. "The Commodore's Civil War." *Vanderbilt University Magazine*. Accessed September 23, 2014. http://www.vanderbilt.edu/magazines/vanderbilt-magazine/2011/04/the-commodores-civil-war/.
59. *Ibid.*
60. Naval History and Heritage Command. "Gertrude," in *DANFS*.
61. Choules, Rev. John Overton, *The Cruise of the Steam Yacht North Star; a Narrative of the Excursion of Mr. Vanderbilt's Party to England, Russia, Denmark, France, Spain, Italy, Malta, Turkey, Madeira, Etc.* (Boston: Gould and Lincoln, 1854), 19–22.
62. Naval History and Heritage Command. "Gertrude," in *DANFS*.
63. Semmes, Admiral Rafael, *Memoirs of Service Afloat During the War Between the States* (Baltimore: Kelly, Piet & Co., 1869), 665, 733.
64. Open Jurist. "72 U.S. 28—The Peterhoff," in *United States Supreme Court, December Term, 1866*. Accessed September 20, 2014. http://openjurist.org/72/us/28.
65. Dickens, Charles, ed., "Narrative of Accident and Disaster," in *The Household Narrative of Current Events (for the year 1850), Being a Monthly Supplement to Household Words* (London: Office, 16, Wellington Street North, 1850), 253; "Monthly Notes—Recovery of the Peterhoff Steam Yacht," *The Practical Mechanic's Journal*, Vol. IV (April, 1851–March, 1852): 118; *The Peterhoff, Argument of E. Delafield Smith, United states District Attorney, Addressed to the United States Court at New York, In the Case of the Prize Steamer Peterhoff, July 10, 1863 Printed for the Use of the Court, from a Stenographic Report by A.F. Warburton, Esq., and Revised by the District Attorney* (New York: John W. Amerman, 1863), 7–8.
66. *Hansard's Parliamentary Debates. 3rd Series, Commencing with the Accession of William IV*. Volume CLXX, Comprising the Period from the Twenty-seventh Day of March 1863, to the twenty-eighth Day of May 1863, Second Volume of the Session (London: Cornelius Buck, 1863), Column 78–79.
67. "American Affairs in England.; British Indig-

nation Pressure for War The American Minister Giving Passports to British Merchantmen Cotton and Commerce Ireland France Poland," *The New York Times*, April 18, 1863. Accessed September 29, 2014. http://www.nytimes.com/1863/05/04/news/american-affairs-england-british-indignation-pressure-for-war-american-minister.html?pagewanted=1.

68. United States Naval War Records Office, *Official Records of the Union and Confederate Navies in the War of the Rebellion*, Series I—Vol. 2. "The Operations of the Cruisers, from January 1, 1863, to March 31, 1864" (Washington, D.C.: U.S. Government Printing Office, 1895), 176.

69. Open Jurist. "72 U.S. 28."

70. History Central. "Peterhoff," Accessed February 25, 2017. http://historycentral.com/navy/Steamer/peterhoff.html.

71. *Official Records of the Union and Confederate Navies...*, Series I, Vol. 2, 159; *Official Records of the Union and Confederate Navies...*, Series II, Vol. 1, 95; Naval History and Heritage Command. "Gertrude," in *DANFS*.

72. *Official Records of the Union and Confederate Navies...*, Series I, Vol. 2, 448.

73. United States House of Representatives, *Executive Documents Printed by Order of The House of Representatives During the Second Session of the Thirty-Eighth Congress, 1864–'65*, in Fifteen Volumes. "Papers Relating to Foreign Affairs, Great Britain, Case of the Seizure of the Bark Saxon, Enclosure 2 in No. 1" (Washington, D.C.: U.S. Government Printing Office, 1865), 259; Tucker, Spencer, ed., *American Civil War: The Definitive Encyclopedia and Document Collection* (Santa Barbara, CA: ABC-CLIO, Inc., 2013), 1716.

74. *The American Journal of International Law, Supplement to*, Vol. 10, 1916, Official Documents (New York: Baker, Voorhis & Company, 1916), 145.

75. Naval History and Heritage Command. "Gertrude," in *DANFS*.

76. *Official Records of the Union and Confederate Navies...*, Series I, Vol. 16, 695.

77. *Ibid.*, 575–7, 630, 687, 688, 694–695; Naval History and Heritage Command. "Dart 1," in *DANFS*; *Official Records of the Union and Confederate Navies...*, Series II, Vol. 1, 72.

78. Boynton, Charles Brandon, *The History of the Navy During the Rebellion*, Vol. II (New York: D. Appleton and Company, 1868), 278.

79. Maclay, Edgar Stanton, *A History of the United States Navy From 1775 to 1901*, Vol. II (New York: D. Appleton and Company, 1906), 496.

80. Naval History and Heritage Command. "Corypheus," in *DANFS*.

81. "A Trip in the Yacht Teazer from the Wight to the West Indies, in 1852." *Hunt's Yachting Magazine*, Volume the First (London: Hunt and Son, 1852), 149.

82. "The Cruise of the Viking," *Lippincott's Magazine of Popular Literature and Science*. Old Series Vol. XXX (November 1882), 426.

83. "Types of Cruising Yachts," *The Art Journal*. New Series, Vol. 38 (London: J.S. Virtue & Co. Ltd., 1886), 270.

84. Young, A., *Digest of Maritime Law Cases from 1837 to 1860* (London: Horace Cox, 1865), 62.

85. Walker, Edward A., *Our First Year of Army Life: An Anniversary Address Delivered by the First Regiment of the Connecticut Volunteer Heavy Artillery at Their Camp Near Gaines Mills, VA, June 1862, by the Chaplain of the Regiment* (New Haven: Thomas H. Pease, 1862), 79.

86. Naval History and Heritage Command. "Teaser," in *DANFS*.

87. Scheib, 18.

88. *Official Records of the Union and Confederate Navies...*, Series I, Vol. 16, 822.

89. Chaffin, Tom, *The H.L. Hunley: The Secret Hope of the Confederacy* (New York: Hill and Wang, 2008), 15–17.

90. Savage, Thomas, "Letter to Secretary of State William Seward, 2 September 1861." *Message of the President of the United States to the Two Houses of Congress at the Commencement of the Second Session of the Thirty-Seventh Congress*, Vol. I (Washington, D.C.: U.S. Government Printing Office, 1861), 281.

91. *Official Records ... Navies*, Series I, Vol. 17, pp. 21, 22.

92. Law Resource. Betts, Samuel Rossiter, District Judge of United States District Court for the Southern District of New York. *Case No. 5,456, March 1862, The Gipsey.* Accessed September 15, 2014. https://law.resource.org/pub/us/case/reporter/F.Cas/0010.f.cas/0010.f.cas.0436.1.pdf.

93. "Intercourse of the British at Nassau with the Rebel States, from *The Nassau Guardian*," *The New York Times*, April 28, 1862, accessed August 12, 2014, http://www.nytimes.com/1862/04/28/news/intercourse-of-the-british-at-nassau-with-the-rebel-states.html.

94. Wise, George D. "Report to Accompany bill H.R. 6839. Report No. 1728—William G. Ford, claimant," in *Index to the Reports of Committees of the House of Representatives for the First Session of the Forty-Seventh Congress, 1881-'82*, Vol. 6 (Washington: Government Printing Office, 1882), 339–340.

95. *Ibid.*

96. The Historical Society of Pennsylvania. "Vaux Family Papers, 1739–1923" (collection 684) Accessed October 21, 2014. http://www2.hsp.org/collections/manuscripts/v/vaux684.xml.

97. United States Naval War Records Office, *Official Records of the Union and Confederate Navies in the War pf the Rebellion*. Series I, Vol. 5, "Operations on the Potomac and Rappahannock Rivers from December 7, 1861, to July 31, 1865," (Washington, D.C.: U.S. Government Printing Office, 1897), 289.

98. Welles, Gideon, *Report of the Secretary of the Navy with an Appendix Containing Reports from Officers*, December 1865 (Washington, D.C.: U.S. Government Printing Office, 1865), 515.

99. Library and Archives of Canada. "Ship

Registrations, 1787–1966, Item 75607: Sylphide." Accessed March 3, 2017. http://www.bac-lac.gc.ca/eng/discover/ship-registration-index-1787-1966/Pages/item.aspx?IdNumber=75607&DotsIdNumber=.

100. Naval History and Heritage Command. "Virginia 3," in *DANFS* .

101. United States Naval War Records Office. *Official records of the Union and Confederate Navies in the War of the Rebellion*. Series I, Vol. 21, "Operations of the West Gulf Blockading Squadron from January 1 to December 31, 1864," (Washington, D.C.: U.S. Government Printing Office, 1906), 132.

102. "From New-Orleans; United States District Court, New-Orleans Industry of Judge Durell Prize Cases Before the Court Confiscation Cases Prizes Condemned Prizes Released Large Amounts Involved," *The New York Times*, July 31, 1865. Accessed October 22, 2014. http://www.nytimes.com/1865/07/31/news/new-orleans-united-states-district-court-new-orleans-industry-judge-durell-prize.html.

103. *Official Records of the Union and Confederate Navies...*, Series II, Vol. 1, 78.

104. Stillé, Charles J., *History of the United States Sanitary Commission, Being the General Report of its Work During the War of the Rebellion* (Philadelphia: J.B. Lippincott & Co., 1866), 65.

105. Stillé, Charles J., *Memorial of the Great Central Fair for the U.S. Sanitary Commission, Held at Philadelphia June 1864* (Philadelphia: United States Sanitary Commission, 1864), 55–56.

106. *Official Records of the Union and Confederate Navies...*, Series II, Vol. 1, 78.

107. Loubat, J.F., ed., *A Yachtsman's Scrapbook, or the Ups and Downs of Yacht Racing* (New York: Brentano Brothers, 1887), 5.

108. Brown, Harry, *The History of American Yachts and Yachtsmen* (New York: The Spirit of the Times Publishing Company, 1901), 18.

109. Loubat, 15.

110. Robinson, Bill, "Great Moments in the America's Cup," *Yachting*, Vol. 154, No. 3, September 1983, 84–85.

111. Jenrich, Charles H., "The Checkered Career of a Gallant Lady," *Popular Boating*, Vol.12, No. 3, September 1962, 53.

112. *Ibid.*, 112; Naval History and Heritage Command. "America 1," in *DANFS*. Accessed March 15, 2017. http://www.history.navy.mil/danfs/a8/america-i.htm.

113. *Official Records of the Union and Confederate Navies...*, Series I, Vol. 5, 735.

114. United States Naval War Records Office. *Official Records of the Union and Confederate Navies in the War of the Rebellion*, Series I, Vol. 12, North Atlantic Blockading Squadron, February 2, 1865–August 3, 1865; South Atlantic Blockading Squadron, October 29, 1861—May 13, 1862 (Washington, D.C.: U.S. Government Printing Office, 1901), 643; Naval History and Heritage Command, "America 1," in *DANFS*.

115. *Official Records of the Union and Confederate Navies...*, Series II, Vol. 1, 34.

116. Naval History and Heritage Command. "America 1," in *DANFS*.

117. "Famous Old Yacht America Gets Ovation As She Leaves Boston on Final Journey," *The New York Times*, September 11, 1921, accessed October 23, 2014, http://query.nytimes.com/mem/archive-free/pdf?res=9F0CE7DE153EEE3ABC4952DFBF66838A639EDE; Naval History and Heritage Command. "America 1," in *DANFS*.

118. Military History Encyclopedia on the Web. "American Civil War: The Blockade and the War at Sea." Accessed April 12, 2016. http://www.historyofwar.org/articles/wars_american_civil_war09_waratsea.html.

119. Civil War Trust. "Blockade." Accessed April 12, 2016. http://www.civilwar.org/education/history/navy-hub/navy-history/blockade.html.

Chapter 4

1. National Park Service. "Maritime History of Massachusetts: U.S. Navy." Accessed December 30, 2014. http://www.nps.gov/nr/travel/maritime/navy.htm.

2. Welles, Gideon, *Report of the Secretary of the Navy with an Appendix Containing Reports from Officers, December 1865* (Washington, D.C.: U.S. Government Printing Office, 1865), xiii.

3. *Ibid.*, xxix.

4. *Ibid.*, v.

5. Barrett, Joseph H., *Life of Abraham Lincoln: Presenting His Early History, Political Career, and Speeches In and Out of Congress; Also a General View of His Policy as President of the United States; with His Messages, Proclamations, Letters, Etc., and a Concise History of the War* (Cincinnati: Moore, Wilstach & Baldwin, 1864), 84.

6. Welles, Gideon, *Report of the Secretary of the Navy with an Appendix Containing Bureau Reports, etc. December 1867* (Washington: Government Printing Office, 1867), 1.

7. *Report of the Secretary of the Navy Being Part of the Message and Documents Communicated to the Two Houses of Congress at the Beginning of the Second Session of the Forty-Seventh Congress* (in Three Volumes) Vol. I (Washington, D.C.: U.S. Government Printing Office, 1882), 6.

8. Dewey, George, *Autobiography of George Dewey, Admiral of the Navy* (New York: Charles Scribner's Sons, 1913), 154.

9. *Navy Yearbook, Embracing All Acts Authorizing the Construction of Ships of the "New Navy" and Resume of Annual Naval Appropriation Laws from 1883 to 1920, Inclusive*, "Increase of the Navy" (Washington, D.C.: U.S. Government Printing Office, 1921), 15.

10. Naval History and Heritage Command. "Dolphin 4," "Boston 5," "Atlanta 2," "Chicago 1" in *DANFS*.

11. Mahan, Captain Alfred Thayer, USN, *Naval*

Strategy Compared with the Principles and Practice of Military Operations on Land (Boston: Little, Brown, and Company, 1911), 101.

12. Wharton, Francis, ed., *A Digest of the International Law of the United States: Taken from Documents Issued by Presidents and Secretaries of State, and from Decisions of Federal Courts and Opinions of Attorneys-general*, Vol. 1 (Washington, D.C.: U.S. Government Printing Office, 1887), 361.

13. "A Century of Quarrels with Spain." *Self Culture: A Magazine of Knowledge*, Vol. III, No. 2, May 1896. (Chicago: The Werner Company, 1896), 104; History of Cuba.com. "Full Text of the Ostend Manifesto." Accessed March 1, 2017. http://www.historyofcuba.com/history/havana/Ostend2.htm.

14. Lee, Fitzhugh, and Joseph Wheeler, *Cuba's Struggle Against Spain with the Causes for American Intervention and a Full Account of the Spanish-American War, Including Final Peace Negotiations* (New York: The American Historical Press, 1899), 149.

15. Maclay, Edgar Stanton, *A History of the United States Navy from 1775 to 1902*, Vol. III (New York: D. Appleton and Company, 1907), 40–41.

16. The American Presidency Project. Washington, George, *Eighth Annual Address to the House and the Senate, 7 December 1796*. Accessed January 12, 2015. http://www.presidency.ucsb.edu/ws/?pid=29438.

17. Cooke, Captain A.P., USN, "Our Naval Reserve and the Necessity for Its Organization," *Proceedings of the United States Naval Institute*. George W. Tyler, Charles R. Miles and W.F. Worthington, eds. Vol. XIV, 1888, 179, 186.

18. Gardner, William. "The Steam Yacht as a Naval Auxiliary in Time of War," *Transactions of the Society of Naval Architects and Marine Engineers*, Vol. I, 1893, 221–222.

19. McAdoo, William. "The Yacht as Naval Auxiliary," *The North American Review*. Lloyd Bryce, ed. Vol. 161, No. 465, 1895, 172.

20. "Navy Yard Busier Than Since 1865." *The Brooklyn Daily Eagle*. April 3, 1898, 5. Accessed January 14, 2015. https://www.newspapers.com/image/50465152/.

21. "Our Auxiliary Navy," *The Chicago Daily Tribune*, October 11, 1897, 6, accessed January 14, 2015. http://archives.chicagotribune.com/1897/10/11/; Naval History and Heritage Command. "Yale 1," "Harvard 1," "St. Paul 1," "St. Louis 3," in *DANFS*.

22. Fulton, Robert I., and Thomas C. Trueblood, eds., *Patriotic Eloquence Relating to the Spanish-American War and Its Issues* (New York: Charles Scribner's Sons, 1900), 91.

23. PBS. "Crucible of Empire." Accessed January 3, 2015. http://www.pbs.org/crucible/frames/_film.html.

24. Fulton, 86–87.

25. Stone, Herbert S., ed., *The Spanish-American War: The Events of the War Described by Eye Witnesses* (New York: Herbert S. Stone & Company, 1899), 9.

26. historyofcuba.com. "Teller Amendment." Accessed January 15, 2015. http://www.historyofcuba.com/history/teller.htm.

27. "Naval Auxiliary Board: Seven Yachts, Recommended for Second-Class Gunboats, to be Purchased," *The New York Times*, April 20, 1898, accessed January 15, 2015, http://query.nytimes.com/gst/abstract.html?res=9E06E5DE1139E433A25753C2A9629C94699ED7CF.

28. Strouse, Jean, *Morgan: American Financier*, "letter from Jack Morgan to his mother after the maiden voyage of Corsair II in October 1891" (London: Harville Press, 1999), 290.

29. Chernow, Ron, *The House of Morgan: An American Banking Dynasty and the Rise of Modern Finance* (New York: Touchstone, Simon & Schuster Inc., 1990), 80.

30. Naval History and Heritage Command. "Gloucester 1" in *DANFS*.

31. Creelman, James, *On the Great Highway, the Wanderings and Adventures of Special Correspondent* (Boston: Lothrop, Lee & Shepard Co., Boston, 1901), 188.

32. *Ibid.*, 190.

33. Trask, David F., *The War with Spain* (New York: Simon and Schuster, 1981; Bison Books ed. 1991, 271).

34. Proctor, Ben, *William Randolph Hearst: The Early Years, 1863–1910* (New York: Oxford University Press, 1998), 122–123; Whyte, Kenneth, *The Uncrowned King: The Sensational Rise of William Randolph Hearst* (Berkeley CA: Counterpoint Press, 2009), 401.

35. Tucker, Spencer, ed., *The Encyclopedia of the Spanish-American and Philippine-American Wars: A Political, Social, and Military History* (Santa Barbara, CA: ABC-CLIO, 2009), 786.

36. Campbell, W. Joseph, *The Year That Defined American Journalism: 1887 and the Clash of Paradigms* (New York: Routledge, 2013), 189.

37. Haze Gray and Underway. "Buccaneer," in *DANFS*; Brigantine Antiques. "Unquowa." Accessed January 25, 2015. http://brigantineantiques.com/Unquowa.htm; Maritime History of the Great Lakes. Accessed January 25, 2015. http://images.maritimehistoryofthegreatlakes.ca/23001/data?n=47.

38. Hofman, Erik, *The Steam Yachts: An Era of Elegance* (Tuckahoe, NY: John de Graff, Inc., 1970), 116–117.

39. Digital History Project. Blanchard, Frank Leroy, "Yacht of a Millionaire," *The Metropolitan Magazine*. Vol.VIII, No. 4, October 1898. Accessed February 27, 2017. http://www.digitalhistoryproject.com/2011/09/millionaire-howard-gould-steam-yacht.html.

40. Naval History and Heritage Command. "Sylph 3" in *DANFS*.

41. Hofman, 16.

42. *Ibid.*, 54–55.

43. "Outing's Monthly Review of Amateur

Sports and Pastimes: Yachting." *Outing, An Illustrated Monthly Magazine of Sport, Travel and Recreation*, James H.Worman and Ben J. Worman, eds., Vol. XXXII, April—September, 1898, 83; Naval History and Heritage Command. "Dorothea," in *DANFS*.

44. The California Military Museum. Denger, Mark J. "The Genesis of the Naval Reserve." Accessed June 6, 2015. http://californiamilitaryhistory.org/NavRes.html.

45. "Naval Militia." *The Americana: A Universal Reference Library Comprising the Arts and Sciences, Literature, History, Biography, Geography, Commerce, Etc., of the World* Vol. 10, Frederick Converse Beach, ed. (New York: Scientific American Compiling Department, 1903), 774.

46. *Annual Report of the Operations of the Naval Militia for the Years 1908 and 1909*, Office of the Assistant Secretary [of the Navy] (Washington, D.C.: U.S. Government Printing Office, 1910), 4.

47. "The Steam Yacht 'Hermione' from Gourock to New York, Calls Here According to Arrangement," *The Evening Telegram*, St. John's, Newfoundland: July 3, 1895, 4, accessed June 20, 2015. http://news.google.com/newspapers?nid=35&dat=18950703&id=SqNEAAAAIBAJ&sjid=GDkDAAAAIBAJ&pg=5942,320024.

48. Naval History and Heritage Command. "Hawk 1," in *DANFS*.

49. Naval History and Heritage Command. "Siren 2," in *DANFS*.

50. Naval History and Heritage Command. "Viking 1," in *DANFS*.

51. Flagler Museum. "The Amazing Story of Henry Flagler's Yacht *Alicia*." Accessed January 21, 2015. http://www.flaglermuseum.us/history/flaglers-yacht-alicia; Naval History and Heritage Command. "Hornet 6," in *DANFS*.

52. Library of Congress. "Chronology of Cuba in the Spanish-American War." Accessed June 20, 2015. http://www.loc.gov/rr/hispanic/1898/chroncuba.html; Naval History and Heritage Command. "Hist," in *DANFS*.

53. Naval History and Heritage Command. "Wasp 7," in *DANFS*.

54. Naval History and Heritage Command. "Eagle 4," in *DANFS*.

55. "Launch of the Sovereign," *The New York Times*, May 19, 1896, accessed June 20, 2015. http://query.nytimes.com/mem/archive-free/pdf?res=9A03E4DF133EE333A2575AC1A9639C94679ED7CF.

56. Naval History and Heritage Command. "Scorpion 4," in *DANFS*.

57. "Ogden Goelet is Dead," *The New York Times*, August 28, 1897, accessed June 20, 2015. http://query.nytimes.com/mem/archive-free/pdf?res=9D02E2D71638E733A2575BC2A96E9C94669ED7CF.

58. "The U.S.S. *Mayflower*," *Marine Engineering/log*, Vol. 6, No. 7, July 1901 (New York: Simmons-Boardman Publishing Company, 1901), 278.

59. Haze Gray and Underway; "Mayflower," in *DANFS*; "The U.S.S. *Mayflower*," *Marine Engineering/log*, Vol. 6, No. 7, 278; Clyde Built Ships. "Mayflower." http://clydeships.co.uk/view.php?official_number=&imo=&builder=&builder_eng=&year_built=&launch_after=&launch_before=&role=&type_ref1=&propulsion=&category=&owner=&port=&flag=&disposal=&lost=&ref=4479&vessel=MAYFLOWER; Coast Guard Modeling. "Notable, Interesting or Unique Cutters." Accessed June 14, 2015. http://old.coastguardmodeling.com/01C_Famous.html; Spanish American War Centennial Website. "Alfonso XII." Accessed June 20, 2015. http://www.spanamwar.com/AlfonsoXii.htm; "Ogden Goelet is Dead," *The New York Times*; "Navy Yard Busier Than Since 1865." *Brooklyn Daily Eagle*, 5.

60. "Cuba Buys Steam Yacht," *The New York Times*, May 21, 1907, accessed February 23, 2015, http://query.nytimes.com/mem/archive-free/pdf?res=9400E6DA143EE733A25752C2A9639C946697D6CF.

61. Fulton, *Patriotic Eloquence*, 279.

62. Ibid., 91.

Chapter 5

1. Fulton, Robert I. and Thomas C. Trueblood, eds., *Patriotic Eloquence Relating to the Spanish-American War and Its Issues* (New York: Charles Scribner's Sons, 1900), 171–172.

2. Ibid., 117.

3. Ibid., 201.

4. Ibid., 27.

5. Ibid., 49.

6. Ibid., 171–2.

7. *Public Opinion: a Comprehensive Summary of the Press Throughout the World on All Important Current Topics*, Volume XXV, July, 1898-December, 1898, "Foreign Affairs" (New York: The Public Opinion Company, 1898), 298.

8. Ibid., 300.

9. Ibid., 300.

10. Carnegie Endowment for International Peace, *Publication No. 17, American Foreign Policy*, 2nd ed. (Washington, D.C.: Carnegie Endowment, 1920), 45–46.

11. Ibid., 63.

12. Mahan, Captain Alfred Thayer, USN, "The Battle of the Sea of Japan" *Collier's: The National Weekly* Vol. XXXV, No. 12, June 17, 1905, 12–13.

13. Fiske, Commander Bradley A., USN. "Compromiseless Ships," *The Proceedings of the United States Naval Institute*, Vol. XXXI, No. 3, September 1905, 549–553.

14. Republican Congressional Committee 1908, *Republican Campaign Textbook*. (Philadelphia: Dunlap Printing Co., 1908), 364.

15. Lougheed, Victor, *Vehicles of the Air* (Chicago: The Reilly and Britton Company, 1909, 3d ed.), 37–38.

16. Daniels, Josephus, *Our Navy at War* (New York: George H. Doran Company, 1922.), 11.
17. *Hearings Before the Committee on Naval Affairs, House of Representatives, Sixty-Fourth Congress, First Session, On Estimates Submitted by the Secretary of the Navy*, Vol. 2, Section 23 (Washington: Government Printing Office, 1916), 1879–1880.
18. "Urgent Need of Ships For Coast Defense is Outlined." *Official Bulletin, United States Committee on Public Information*. Vol. 1, No. 3, May 12, 1917 (Washington, D.C.: U.S. Government Printing Office, 1917), 1.
19. "Yale to Form Naval Unit; Mosquito Fleet Growing," *The Brooklyn Daily Eagle*, February 26, 1917, 24.
20. "Mosquito Fleet Growing" *The Brooklyn Daily Eagle*, February 26, 1917, 24.
21. "Miss Morgan's Wedding; J. Pierpont Morgan's Eldest Daughter Married to H.L. Satterlee," *The New York Times*, November 16, 1900, accessed June 20, 2015, http://query.nytimes.com/mem/archive-free/pdf?res=9E00EFDE143FE433A25755C1A9679D946197D6CF.
22. PBS, "The American Experience: The Idle Rich." Accessed July 2, 2015. http://www.pbs.org/wgbh/amex/1900/peopleevents/pande28.html;Digital History Project. "The Rise of Big Business." Accessed July 2, 2015. http://www.digitalhistory.uh.edu/disp_textbook.cfm?smtID=2&psid=3165.
23. Ibid.
24. PBS, "The American Experience."
25. Hughes, Tyler. "The Gilded Age Era." Accessed September 12, 2015. http://thegildedageera.blogspot.com/2012/07/stuyvesant-fish-mansion-new-york-city.html.
26. Long, Clarence D., ed., "Wages and Earnings in the United States, 1860–1890," in *National Bureau of Economic Research* (Princeton, NJ: Princeton University Press, 1960), 39–49, accessed September 12, 2015. http://www.nber.org/chapters/c2497.pdf.
27. Tripp, Rhoda Thomas, ed., *The International Thesaurus of Quotations* (New York: Thomas Y. Crowell Company, 1970), 104.
28. MacTaggart, Ross, *Millionaires, Mansions, and Motor Yachts: An Era of Opulence* (New York: W.W. Norton & Company, 2004), 14.
29. Matthews, Scott J., "Development of the Motor Yacht," *Motor Boating*, Vol. 12, No. 6, December 1913, 9.
30. Chris Caswell, "Passionate Heritage," *Yachting Magazine*. Accessed September 12, 2015. http://www.yachtingmagazine.com/passionate-heritage.
31. "Yacht With 32-Knot Speed," *The New York Times*, May 16, 1912, accessed September 29, 2015, http://query.nytimes.com/mem/archive-free/pdf?res=9F07E1DB153CE633A25755C1A9639C946396D6CF.
32. Woodrow Wilson. "State of the Union Address, December 7, 1915." Infoplease. Accessed September 30, 2015. http://www.infoplease.com/t/hist/state-of-the-union/127.html.
33. Daniels, *Our Navy at War*, 301.
34. "Yacht Scout Fleet Sought By Daniels," *The New York Times*, May 3, 1916, accessed September 29, 2015, http://query.nytimes.com/mem/archive-free/pdf?res=9C0DE4DC113FE233A25750C0A9639C946796D6CF.
35. Daniels, *Our Navy at War*, 299.
36. Naval History and Heritage Command. "Alcedo," in *DANFS*.
37. "Yachts in War Dress," *The Brooklyn Daily Eagle*, April 23, 1917, accessed July 20, 2015. https://www.newspapers.com/image/54337141/.
38. "Yacht Scout Fleet Sought By Daniels," *New York Times*.
39. Vessel information compiled from *DANFS* from Naval History and Heritage Command at www.history.navy.mil and NavSource Naval History at www.navsource.org.
40. Ibid.
41. Naval History and Heritage Command. "De Grasse I," in *DANFS*.
42. NavSource Naval History. "Hermes/Lanikai." Accessed March 15, 2017. http://www.navsource.org/archives/12/130096.htm; Naval History and Heritage Command; "Hermes," in *DANFS*.
43. Thomas, Lowell, *Raiders of the Deep* (Annapolis, MD: Naval Institute Press, 1994), 292–333.
44. The Naval Districts in 1918 were: 1-Boston MA, 2-Newport RI, 3-New York NY, 4-Philadelphia PA, 5-Norfolk VA, 6-Charleston SC, 7-Jacksonville/Miami FL, 8-New Orleans LA, 9-Great Lakes IL, 10-San Juan PR, 11-San Diego CA, 12-San Francisco CA, 13-Seattle WA, 14-Pearl Harbor HI, 15-Cristobal Canal Zone, 16-Philippine Islands, 17-Kodiak AK, and Naval District Washington DC.
45. Naval History and Heritage Command. "Pawnee 3," "Elfrida," in *DANFS* [see also Appendix 4]; NavSource Naval History. "Pawnee." Accessed March 15, 2017. http://www.navsource.org/archives/12/170699.htm; "Seneca." http://www.navsource.org/archives/12/170427.htm; "Sylvia." http://www.navsource.org/archives/12/130087.htm [see also Appendix 4].
46. NavSource. "Rainier." http://www.navsource.org/archives/12/179935.htm; "Bayocean." http://www.navsource.org/archives/12/172640.htm; "Vergana." http://www.navsource.org/archives/12/170519.htm; Naval History and Heritage Command. "Rainier I," "Bayocean I," "Vergana," in *DANFS*.
47. NavSource. "Mohican." http://www.navsource.org/archives/12/170117.htm; Naval History and Heritage Command. "Mohican III," in *DANFS*.
48. D'Amico, Angela and Richard Pittenger, "A Brief History of Active Sonar," digitized by Woods Hole Oceanographic Institution from *Aquatic Mammals*, Vol. 35, Issue 4, September 24, 2010 (Macomb, IL: Document & Publication Services at Western Illinois University, 2010), 1, accessed

March 7, 2017, http://csi.whoi.edu/sites/default/files/literature/Full%20Text.pdf.

49. Naval History and Heritage Command. "Hauoli," in *DANFS*.

50. Naval History and Heritage Command. "Aramis," in *DANFS*.

51. Naval History and Heritage Command. "Gem," in *DANFS*.

52. NavSource. "Florence." http://www.navsource.org/archives/12/170173.htm; Naval History and Heritage Command. "Florence," in *DANFS*.

53. NavSource. "Emerald." http://www.navsource.org/archives/12/170177.htm; Naval History and Heritage Command; "Emerald II," in *DANFS*; Stringer, Harry R., *The Navy Book of Distinguished Service: An Official Compendium of the Names and Citations of the Men of the United States Navy, Marine Corps, Army and Foreign Governments Who Were Decorated by the Navy Department for Extraordinary Gallantry and Conspicuous Service Above and Beyond the call of Duty in the World War* (Washington, D.C.: Fassett Publishing Company, 1921), 147.

54. Mead, Frederick S. ed., *Harvard's Military Record in the World War* (Boston: The Harvard Alumni Association, 1921), 968; Naval History and Heritage Command. "Tarantula II," in *DANFS*.

55. NavSource. "Mary Alice." http://www.navsource.org/archives/12/170397.htm; Naval History and Heritage Command. "Mary Alice," in *DANFS*.

56. Brown, Harry, *The History of American Yachts and Yachtsmen* (New York: The Spirit of the Times Publishing Company, 1901), 70; Naval History and Heritage Command. "Felicia I," in *DANFS*.

57. NavSource. "Pilgrim." http://www.navsource.org/archives/12/171204.htm; Floating Hospital for Children at Tufts Medical Center. "History of Floating Hospital for Children." Accessed August 17, 2015. http://www.floatinghospital.org/About-Us/History.aspx

58. FindaGrave. "Lieutenant Wilson Marshall, Jr." Accessed October 13, 2015. http://www.findagrave.com/cgi-bin/fg.cgi?page=gr&GRid=103910506; Yacht Pals "Schooner *Atlantic*." Accessed February 4, 2015. http://www.yachtpals.com/schooner-atlantic-yacht-9173; "Kaiser's Gold Trophy Proves to be Pewter," *The New York Times*, June 9, 1918, accessed February 4, 2015, http://query.nytimes.com/mem/archive-free/pdf?res=9A0DE5D9103BEE3ABC4153DFB0668383609EDE.

59. "Consigned to the Sea: Trenor L. Park's Palatial Yacht Sultana Successfully Launched," *The New York Times*, December 19, 1919, accessed August 20, 2015, http://query.nytimes.com/mem/archive-free/pdf?res=9E02E4D81F3EEF33A2575AC1A9649D94689FD7CF; Naval History and Heritage Command. "Sultana," in *DANFS*.

60. "Notes of Clubs and Craft," *Outing: An Illustrated Monthly Magazine of Sport, Travel and Recreation*, James H. Worman, ed., Vol. XXIV, April 1894–September 1894, 63; "Maritime History of the Great Lakes," *The Maritime Review*. January 28, 1892. Accessed August 24, 2015. http://images.maritimehistoryofthegreatlakes.ca/26804/data; Naval History and Heritage Command. "Wadena," in *DANFS*.

61. Naval History and Heritage Command. "Isabel," in *DANFS*; Hofman, 222–223; Cressman, Robert J., "Historic Fleets: A Fine Little Vessel," *Naval History*, Vol. 22, No. 6, December 6, 2008, 60–61.

62. "The Road to France: The Transportation of Troops and Military Supplies 1917–1918" in Benedict Crowell and Robert Forrest Wilson, *How America Went to War; An Account From Official Sources of the Nation's War Activities 1917–1920*, Vol. II (New Haven, CT: Yale University Press, 1921), 397; Naval History and Heritage Command. "Aphrodite," "Corsair I," in *DANFS*.

63. Naval History and Heritage Command. "Voyage from U.S. to Azores by Converted Yachts." https://www.history.navy.mil/our-collections/photography/wars-and-events/world-war-i/incidents--1917/voyage-from-the-us-to-the-azores-by-uss-margaret-and-other-conve.html.

64. Naval History and Heritage Command. "May, SP-164," "Helenita I," in *DANFS*; Stringer, 47, 146; NavSource. "Helenita." http://www.navsource.org/archives/12/170210.htm.

65. NavSource. "Margaret." http://www.navsource.org/archives/12/170527.htm; "Rambler." http://www.navsource.org/archives/12/170211.htm; Naval History and Heritage Command. "Rambler," in *DANFS*.

66. Naval History and Heritage Command. "Lydonia," "Wenonah I, in *DANFS*; NavSource. "Lydonia." http://www.navsource.org/archives/12/170700.htm;"Wenonah I." http://www.navsource.org/archives/12/170165.htm; Stringer, 30.

67. Naval History and Heritage Command. "Cythera (SP-575)," in *DANFS*; Blair, Clay, *Hitler's U-Boat War: The Hunters, 1939–1942* (New York: Random House, 1996), 544.

68. Wreck Site. "SS Maizar." Accessed October 28, 2015. http://wrecksite.eu/wreck.aspx?31320; NavSource. "Artemis/Arcturus." http://www.navsource.org/archives/12/170593.htm; Naval History and Heritage Command. "Artemis," in *DANFS*.

69. Naval History and Heritage Command. "Wakiva II," in *DANFS*; NavSource. "Wakiva II." http://www.navsource.org/archives/12/170160.htm.

70. Naval History and Heritage Command. "Nokomis I," in *DANFS*; NavSource. "Nokomis." http://www.navsource.org/archives/12/1306.htm.

71. Stringer, 55.

72. Hofman, 226–227.

73. Stringer, 14.

74. Naval History and Heritage Command. "Remlick," in *DANFS*; *Military Times*.

"John MacKenzie." Accessed March 15, 2017. http://valor.militarytimes.com/recipient.php?recipientid=1770.

75. Abbatiello, John J., *Anti-Submarine Warfare in World War I: British Naval Aviation and the Defeat of the U-boat* (New York: Routledge, 2006), 37; Rössler, Eberhard, trans. by Harold Erenberg, *The U-boat: The Evolution and Technical History of German Submarines* (Annapolis, MD: Naval Institute Press, 1981), 33.

76. Husband, Joseph, Ens. U.S.N.R.F., *On the Coast of France: The Story of the United States Naval Forces in French Waters* (Chicago: A.C. McClurg & Co., 1919), 10–11.

77. Naval History and Heritage Command. "Vedette I," in *DANFS*.

78. Naval History and Heritage Command. "Venetia," in *DANFS*; NavSource. "Venetia." http://www.navsource.org/archives/12/170431.htm; Daniels, *Our Navy at War*, "U.S.S. Venetia," 22–23.

79. Naval History and Heritage Command. "Noma," "U-117," in *DANFS*; NavSource. "Noma." http://www.navsource.org/archives/12/170131.htm; U-Boat Net. "U-117." Accessed October 29, 2015. http://uboat.net:8080/wwi/boats/index.html?boat=117; Mead, 46.

80. Lighthouse Friends. "North Dumpling, New York." Accessed August 12, 2015. http://www.lighthousefriends.com/light.asp?ID=740.

81. Naval History and Heritage Command. "Yankton," in *DANFS*; NavSource. "Yankton." http://www.navsource.org/archives/12/130088.htm.

82. Connecticut History. Vivian Zoë, "The Slaters Go Round the World," Accessed April 15, 2016. http://connecticuthistory.org/the-slaters-go-round-the-world/.

83. "Pleasure Craft for Navy Use," *The New Country Life*, Vol. XXXII (New York: Doubleday, Page & Company, 1917), 65; NavSource. "Harvard." http://www.navsource.org/archives/12/170209.htm.

84. Hofman, 86–87; Crawford, Richard, "The Venetia," *San Diego Union-Tribune*, September 9, 2010, C2, accessed March 7, 2017, http://www.sandiegoyesterday.com/wp-content/uploads/2010/09/Venetia.pdf; Daniels, *Our Navy at War*, "U.S.S. Venetia," 22–23.

Chapter 6

1. "The Motor Boating Market Place," *Motor Boating*, Vol. XIV, No. 3, September 1919, 61.

2. *Annual Reports of the Navy Department for the Fiscal Year 1920* (Washington, D.C.: U.S. Government Printing Office, 1921), 1088.

3. *Ships' Data U.S. Naval Vessels, July 1, 1935* (Washington, D.C.: U.S. Government Printing Office, 1935), 5.

4. American Presidency Project. "Calvin Coolidge, Address Before the American Legion Convention in Omaha, Nebraska, October 6, 1925." Accessed November 20, 2015, http://www.presidency.ucsb.edu/ws/index.php?pid=438.

5. Smith, Michael A., "Passing Power, 90th Anniversary," *Yachting*, Vol. 181, No. 5, May 1997, 52.

6. United States Coast Guard Auxiliary. C. Kay Larson. "Bravo Zero: The Coast Guard Auxiliary in World War II." Accessed February 9, 2016. wow.uscgaux.info/content.php?unit=1-DEPT&category=auxhistory

7. "Editorial," *Motor Boat*, Vol. XVII, No. 7, April 10, 1920, 42.

8. BBC. "Industry and Social Change." Accessed November 27, 2015. http://www.bbc.co.uk/schools/gcsebitesize/history/mwh/usa/boomrev1.shtml.

9. "Biggest, Most Luxurious Private Yacht in the World," *The American Weekly Inc.* (Sunday Supplement to *The Milwaukee Sentinel*), November 24, 1929, 43.

10. "The Golden Age of Yachts," *Motor Boating & Sailing*, Vol. 136, No. 6, December 1975, 28, 29, 67.

11. BBC. "Industry and Social Change."

12. U.S. Department of Labor. Bernstein, Irving, "Americans in Depression and War." Accessed November 28, 2015. http://www.dol.gov/dol/aboutdol/history/chapter5.htm.

13. Roosevelt, Franklin D., "The Genesis of the New Deal, 1928–32," *The Public Papers and Addresses of Franklin D. Roosevelt*, Vol. 1 (New York: Random House, 1938), 624.

14. "The Forgotten Man," *Motor Boating*, Vol. 1, No. 2, August 1932, 21.

15. Legal Information Institute. "46 U.S. Code § 57105—Acquisition of Vessels for Essential Services, Routes, or Lines." Accessed November 24, 2015; https://www.law.cornell.edu/uscode/text/46/57105.

16. Furer, Rear Admiral Julius Augustus, USN ret., *Administration of the Navy Department in World War II* (Washington, D.C.: U.S. Government Printing Office, 1959), 56–57.

17. "Congress Considers New Laws to Govern Motor Craft," *Motor Boating*, Vol. LXI, No. 4, April 1938, 116.

18. Larson, "Bravo Zero..."

19. *Ibid*.

20. "Navy Buys More Boats; Sea Train Almost Finished," *The Chicago Sunday Tribune*, Vol. XCIX, No. 46, Part 1, November 17, 1940, 12, accessed February 28, 2017, http://archives.chicagotribune.com/1940/11/17/page/12/article/navy-buys-more-boats-sea-train-almost-finished.

21. *Annual Report of the Secretary of the Navy for the Fiscal Year 1941* (Washington, D.C.: U.S. Government Printing Office, 1941), 2.

22. Gannon, Michael, *Operation Drumbeat* (New York: Harper & Row Publishers, 1990), 214–215.

23. Noble, Dennis L., "The Beach Patrol and Corsair Fleet," *The U.S. Coast Guard in World*

War II (Washington, D.C.: Coast Guard Historian's Office, 1992), 4.

24. Albon, Christopher, "The Hooligan Navy," U.S. Naval Institute blog, accessed February 16, 2016, blog.usni.org/2010/02/11/the-hooligan-navy.

25. National Sailing Hall of Fame documentary film, *The Hooligan Navy (The Corsair Fleet)* accessed January 29, 2016, http://nshof.org/index.php?option=com_content&view=article&id=314&Itemid=28; Shipbuilding History. "George S. Lawley & Sons, Neponset MA." Accessed April 16, 2016. http://www.shipbuildinghistory.com/history/shipyards/6yachtsmall/lawley.htm.

26. Noble, 5.

27. Morison, Samuel Eliot, *History of United States Naval Operations in World War II: The Battle of the Atlantic* (Edison, NJ: Castle Books, 1947, 2001 ed.), 275; Classic Yacht Info. "Yacht: Black Watch." Accessed March 7, 2017 classicyachtinfo.com/yachts/black-watch/

28. NavWeaps. Accessed February 19, 2016. www.navweaps.com/Weapons/WNUS_4-50_mk9.htm; www.navweaps.com/Weapons/WNUS_3-50_mk10-22.htm.

29. Naval History and Heritage Command. "Beaumont I." in *DANFS*; NavSource. "Beaumont." Accessed March 15, 2017. http://www.navsource.org/archives/12/09060.htm.

30. Naval History and Heritage Command. "San Bernardino I," in *DANFS*.

31. Naval History and Heritage Command. "Nourmahal," in *DANFS*; NavSource. "Nourmahal." http://www.navsource.org/archives/12/09072.htm; United States Coast Guard Historian's Office. "Nourmahal." Accessed January 19, 2016. https://www.uscg.mil/history/webcutters/Nourmahal_PG72.pdf; BR/Sulzer. "Nourmahal." Accessed December 5, 2015. http://www.derbysulzers.com/shipnourmahal.html.

32. Naval History and Heritage Command. "Vixen VI," in *DANFS*.

33. Naval History and Heritage Command. "Dauntless II." http://www.history.navy.mil/research/histories/ship-histories/danfs/d/-dauntless-ii.html; NavSource. "Dauntless." http://www.navsource.org/archives/12/09061.htm; Mac-Taggart, Ross, *The Golden Century: Classic Motor Yachts, 1830–1930* (New York: W.W. Norton & Company, 2001), 105–107.

34. MacTaggart, *The Golden Century* 145.

35. Naval History and Heritage Command. "Williamsburg," in *DANFS*; NavSource. "Williamsburg." http://www.navsource.org/archives/12/09056.htm.

36. Naval History and Heritage Command. "Hilo," in *DANFS*; NavSource. "Hilo." http://www.navsource.org/archives/12/09058.htm.

37. Naval History and Heritage Command. "Niagara VII," in *DANFS*; NavSource. "Niagara." http://www.navsource.org/archives/12/09052.htm.

38. CharterWorld. "Motor Yacht Savarona." Accessed December 5, 2015. http://www.charterworld.com/index.html?sub=yacht-charter&charter=savarona-1860.

39. Naval History and Heritage Command. "Jamestown II," in *DANFS*.

40. U-Boat Net. "U-566." Accessed January 20, 2016. http://uboat.net/boats/u566.htm; Naval History and Heritage Command. "Plymouth IV," in *DANFS*; NavSource. "Plymouth." http://www.navsource.org/archives/12/09057.htm.

41. "Vanderbilt's Yacht Sunk," *The New York Times*, July 25, 1892, accessed February 24, 2015, http://query.nytimes.com/mem/archive-free/pdf?res=9807E6DF1731E033A25756C2A9619C94639ED7CF.

42. Naval History and Heritage Command. "St. Augustin," in *DANFS*.

43. NavSource. "Mizpah." http://www.navsource.org/archives/12/1329.htm; Naval History and Heritage Command. "Mizpah," in *DANFS*; *State of New York, Supreme Court, Appellate Division—First Judicial Department, No. 637*, "John Green, Plaintiff-Appellant, against Eugene F. McDonald, Jr., and Herman Hessberg, Sheriff of the County of Kings, Defendants-Respondents" (New York: Libman's Law Printery, 1929), 35, § 104; "Former Yachts," *Panama Canal Review*, Official Panama Canal Publication. Balboa Heights, Canal Zone, January 1964, Vol. 14, No. 6, 16.

44. Naval History and Heritage Command. "Coral," in *DANFS*; Bryan, Ford R., *Friends, Families & Forays: Scenes From the Life and Times of Henry Ford* (Detroit: Wayne State University Press, 2002), 363.

45. Naval History and Heritage Command. "Cythera II," in *DANFS*; NavSource. "Cythera." http://www.navsource.org/archives/12/1331.htm.

46. "The S.S. *Ben Hecht*: A Jewish refugee ship that changed history." The Free Library. Accessed December 8, 2015. http://www.thefreelibrary.com/The+S.S.+Ben+Hecht%3A+a+Jewish+refugee+ship+that+changed+history.-a0189831885.

47. "Haynes-Griffin advertisement," *Motor Boating*, Vol. XLVIII, No. 4, October 1931, 108.

48. Naval History and Heritage Command. "Carnelian." http://www.history.navy.mil/research/histories/ship-histories/danfs/c/carnelian.html; NavSource. "Carnelian." http://www.navsource.org/archives/12/1319.htm.

49. New York City Chapter of the American Guild of Organists. "Yacht Organ." Accessed December 11, 2015. http://www.nycago.org/Organs/NYC/html/ResDeedsEA.html.

50. Naval History and Heritage Command. "Siren III," in *DANFS*; NavSource. "Siren." http://www.navsource.org/archives/12/1313.htm.

51. Naval History and Heritage Command. "Jade," in *DANFS*; NavSource. "Jade." http://www.navsource.org/archives/12/1317.htm.

52. Naval History and Heritage Command. "Turquoise," in *DANFS*; Grems-Doolittle Library Collections. "Female Aviators in the Godfrey Collection." Accessed April 18, 2016. http://

gremsdoolittlelibrary.blogspot.com/2011/06/female-aviators-in-godfrey-collection.html.

53. NavSource. "Tourmaline." http://www.navsource.org/archives/12/1320.htm; Naval History and Heritage Command. "Tourmaline," in *DANFS*.

54. "Placida—A Clipper Stem Yacht," *Motor Boating*, Vol. XLVII, No. 2, February 1931, 94–95; Naval History and Heritage Command. "Ruby," in *DANFS*; NavSource. "Ruby." http://www.navsource.org/archives/12/1321.htm.

55. Schultz, Fred L.," 'It Made A Man Out of Me,' An Interview With Ernest Borgnine," *Naval History*, Vol. 12, No. 1, February 1998, 18–20.

56. Naval History and Heritage Command. "Sylph IV," in *DANFS*; NavSource. "Sylph." http://www.navsource.org/archives/12/1312.htm; "Million-dollar Visitor Here," *Sausalito News*, Vol XLVIII, No. 15, April 12, 1935, 5, accessed March 6, 2017, https://cdnc.ucr.edu/cgi-bin/cdnc?a=d&d=SN19350412.2.78&e=-------en--20--1--txt-txIN--------1.

57. Naval History and Heritage Command. "Zircon," in *DANFS*.

58. History Net. Donald J. Young, "Japanese Submarines Prowl the U.S. Pacific Coastline in 1941." Accessed February 27, 2016. http://www.historynet.com/japanese-submarines-prowl-the-us- pacific-coastline-in-1941.htm.

59. Naval History and Heritage Command. "Isabel," in *DANFS*; NavSource. "Isabel." http://www.navsource.org/archives/12/1310.htm.

60. NavSource. "Lanikai/Hermes." http://www.navsource.org/archives/12/130096.htm; Naval History and Heritage Command. "Lanikai," in *DANFS*.

61. Naval History and Heritage Command. "Southern Seas," in *DANFS*; NavSource. "Southern seas." http://www.navsource.org/archives/12/1332.htm.

62. Naval History and Heritage Command. "Almandite," in *DANFS*.

63. Naval History and Heritage Command. "Azurlite," in *DANFS*.

64. Naval History and Heritage Command. "Beryl I," in *DANFS*.

65. Naval History and Heritage Command. "Crystal," "Girasol," in *DANFS*; NavSource. "Crystal." http://www.navsource.org/archives/12/1325.htm.

66. Naval History and Heritage Command. "Argus II," in *DANFS*; NavSource. "Argus/Pioneer." http://www.navsource.org/archives/12/1314.htm; Nihon, Kaigun. "Sensuikan!" Accessed February 25, 2016. http://www.combinedfleet.com/I-12.htm.

67. "The Clipper Yacht Camargo," *Motor Boating*, Vol. XLII, No. 1, July 1928, 32–33.

68. Welch, Vince, "Beyond the Horizon 1930–1949," in *The Last Voyageur: Amos Burg and the Rivers of the West* (Seattle, WA: Mountaineers Books, 2012).

69. Naval History and Heritage Command. "Marcasite," in *DANFS*; NavSource. "Marcasite." http://www.navsource.org/archives/12/1328.htm.

70. Naval History and Heritage Command. "Captor," in *DANFS*; NavSource. "Captor/ex-Eagle." http://www.navsource.org/archives/12/1440.htm.

71. MacTaggart, Ross, *Millionaires, Mansions, and Motor Yachts: An Era of Opulence* (New York: W.W. Norton & Company, 2004), 35; Naval History and Heritage Command. "Palace," in *DANFS*; NavSource. "YAG-13." http://www.navsource.org/archives/12/1433.htm.

72. Naval History and Heritage Command. "Tourist," in *DANFS*; NavSource. "YAG-14." http://www.navsource.org/archives/12/1432.htm.

73. Individual vessels pages are at these websites. Accessed February 2016; Naval History and Heritage Command. http://www.history.navy.mil/research/histories/ship-histories.html; NavSource. http://www.navsource.org/archives/12/14idx.htm.

74. Naval History and Heritage Command. "Moonstone," in *DANFS*.

75. Naval History and Heritage Command. "Alabaster," in *DANFS*; NavSource. "Alabaster." http://www.navsource.org/archives/12/1421.htm.

76. NavSource. "YP-4." http://www.navsource.org/archives/14/31004.htm.

77. Morison, Samuel Eliot, *History of United States Naval Operations in World War II: The Struggle for Guadalcanal* (Edison, NJ: Castle Books, 1949; 2001 ed.), 114-footnote; Chesapeake Maritime Heritage Foundation, Inc. "Part Boat, Part Ship; The U.S. Navy YP." Accessed March 5, 2016. http://chesapeakenavalheritagefoundation.blogspot.com/2009/09/part-boat-part-ship-us-navy-yp.html; Shipbuilding History. "Patrol and Training Craft." Accessed 5 March 2016. http://www.shipbuildinghistory.com/history/smallships/yp.htm; NavSource. "YP-16." http://www.navsource.org/archives/14/31016.htm; "YP-17." http://www.navsource.org/archives/14/31017.htm; "YP-97." http://www.navsource.org/archives/14/31097.htm; "YP-425." http://www.navsource.org/archives/12/1434.htm; "YP-346." http://www.navsource.org/archives/14/31346.htm; "YP-284." http://www.navsource.org/archives/14/31284.htm; Naval History and Heritage Command. "Seminole III," in *DANFS*; "Casualties: U.S. Navy and Coast Guard Vessels, Sunk or Damaged Beyond Repair During World War II, 7 December 1941–1 October 1945. http://www.history.navy.mil/research/histories/ship-histories/casualties-navy-and-coast-guard-ships.html.

78. "Juanita." *Boat International Magazine*. Accessed March 8, 2016. http://www.boatinternational.com/yachts/the-superyacht-directory/juanita--46329; NavSource. "YP-357." http://www.navsource.org/archives/14/31357.htm; Central Intelligence Agency, Project OBOPUS. BGFIEND, vol. 12_0030 and 0031.

79. NavSource. "YP-506." http://www.navsource.org/archives/12/171217.htm.

80. Williams, Greg H., *World War II U.S. Navy Vessels in Private Hands: The Boats and Ships Sold*

and Registered for Commercial and Recreational Purposes Under the American Flag (Jefferson, NC: McFarland, 2013), 120; NavSource. "YP-200." http://www.navsource.org/archives/12/170624.htm.

81. Yacht Forums. "Trumpy: El Presidente." Accessed January 18, 2016. http://www.yachtforums.com/feature/trumpy-el-presidente.2408/; NavSource. "YP-354." http://www.navsource.org/archives/14/31354.htm; Shipbuilding History. "Mathis Yachts." Accessed January 18, 2016. http://www.shipbuildinghistory.com/history/shipyards/6yachtsmall/trumpynj.htm; Big Old Houses. "Something Completely Different." Accessed January 18, 2016. http://bigoldhouses.blogspot.com/2012/06/something-completely-different.html.

82. NavSource. "Miscellaneous Unclassified (IX) Index." http://www.navsource.org/archives/09/46/46idx.htm.

83. Williams, 196; Shipscribe. "Small IX: Auxiliary Schooners etc. (4)" Accessed January 11, 2016. http://www.shipscribe.com/usnaux/IX3/IX082.html; Naval History and Heritage Command. "Vamarie," in *DANFS*.

84. Shipscribe. "Small IX: Naval Academy Yachts." Accessed January 11, 2016. http://www.shipscribe.com/usnaux/IX3/IX043.html; Valenza, Samuel W., Jr., *The Secret Casino at Red Men's Hall* (Bloomington, IN: iUniverse, 2014), 488.

85. NavSource. "Geoanna (IX-61)." http://www.navsource.org/archives/09/46/46061.htm; Shipscribe. "Small IX: Auxiliary Schooners etc. (1)" http://www.shipscribe.com/usnaux/IX3/IX055.html.

86. Shipscribe. "Small IX: Auxiliary Schooners etc. (3)" http://www.shipscribe.com/usnaux/IX3/IX073.html; Naval History and Heritage Command. "John M. Howard IX-75," in *DANFS*.

87. Naval History and Heritage Command. "Galaxy," in *DANFS*.

88. Naval History and Heritage Command. "Saluda," in *DANFS*.

89. Naval History and Heritage Command. "Aide de Camp," in *DANFS*.

90. NavSource. "IX-60 Seaward." http://www.navsource.org/archives/09/46/46060.htm.

91. Naval History and Heritage Command. "Araner I," in *DANFS*.

92. Naval History and Heritage Command. "Zaca II," in *DANFS*.

93. Jordan, Stephen C., *Hollywood's Original Rat Pack: The Bards of Bundy Drive* (Lanham, MD: The Scarecrow Press, 2008), 67.

94. "Life on the American Newsfront: Seven Seas Races to Bermuda for Dinner," *Life*, Vol. 3, No. 10, September 6, 1937, 26; Naval History and Heritage Command. "Seven Seas," in *DANFS*.

95. Ringle, Ken, "The Last Man of War," *The Washington Post*, June 17, 2001, F01, accessed November 9, 2015, https://www.washingtonpost.com/archive/lifestyle/2001/06/17/the-last-man-of-war/7cd89c0a-5bc7-45b2-9b0e-ac112ca81436/.

96. Naval History and Heritage Command. "Guinevere II," in *DANFS*.

97. United States Coast Guard Historian's Office. Commander Carlton Skinner, USCGR (ret), "U.S.S. Sea Cloud, IX-99, Racial Integration for Naval Efficiency." Accessed January 19, 2016. http://www.uscg.mil/history/articles/Carlton_Skinner.asp; United States Coast Guard Historian's Office. "USS Sea Cloud, 1942." accessed January 19, 2016. http://www.uscg.mil/history/webcutters/Sea_Cloud_IX99.asp; Desausa.org. "Sinking of U-490 by Task Group 22.5." Accessed January 19, 2016. http://www.desausa.org/sinking_of_u_490.htm; U-Boat Net. "U-490." Accessed January 19, 2016. http://uboat.net/boats/u490.htm; Grobecker, Kurt, and Peter Neumann, *Sea Cloud: A Living Legend* (Bradley Lodge, Kemble, UK: Collectors' Books Ltd., 1991), 86–91.

98. Woram, John. "Human and Cartographic History of the Galápagos Islands: A Partial List of Ships That Have Visited the Galápagos Islands." Accessed March 14, 2016. http://www.galapagos.to/SHIPS/INDEX.php; *Annual Report of the Director of the Museum of Comparative Zoölogy at Harvard College for 1932–1933* (Cambridge MA: Printed for the Museum, 1933), 27; Millspaugh, Charles Frederick, *Plantæ Utowanæ: Plants Collected in Bermuda, Porto Rico, St. Thomas, Culebras, Santo Domingo, Jamaica, Cuba, The Caymans, Cozumel, Yucatan and the Alacran Shoals Dec. 1898 to Mar. 1899, The Antillean Cruise of the Yacht Utowana* (Chicago: Field Columbian Museum Publication 43, Botanical Series, Vol. II, No. 1, 1900), 3–13; Naval History and Heritage Command. "Blue Dolphin I," in *DANFS*.

Bibliography

Primary Sources

Abbatiello, John J. *Anti-Submarine Warfare in World War I: British Naval Aviation and the Defeat of the U-boat.* New York: Routledge, 2006.

"American Affairs in England; British Indignation Pressure for War The American Minister Giving Passports to British Merchantmen Cotton and Commerce Ireland France Poland." *The New York Times,* April 18, 1863. Accessed September 29, 2014. http://www.nytimes.com/1863/05/04/news/american-affairs-england-british-indignation-pressure-for-war-american-minister.html?pagewanted=1.

The American Journal of International Law, Supplement to Vol. 10. "1916, Official Documents." New York: Baker, Voorhis & Company, 1916.

Annual Report of the Director of the Museum of Comparative Zoölogy at Harvard College for 1932–1933. Cambridge, MA: Printed for the Museum, 1933.

Annual Report of the Operations of the Naval Militia for the Years 1908 and 1909. Office of the Assistant Secretary [of the Navy]. Washington, D.C.: U.S. Government Printing Office, 1910.

Annual Report of the Secretary of the Navy for the Fiscal Year 1941. Washington, D.C.: U.S. Government Printing Office, 1941.

Annual Reports of the Navy Department for the Fiscal Year 1920. Washington, D.C.: U.S. Government Printing Office, 1921.

Appendix to the Congressional Globe, for the First Session, Thirtieth Congress: Containing Speeches and Important State Papers, New Series 1847–8. Washington, D.C.: Blair and Rives, 1848.

"Arthur Leary Is Dead." *The New York Times,* February 24, 1893. Accessed 09 Sptember 2014. http://query.nytimes.com/mem/archive-free/pdf?res=9803E6DB1F3FEF33A25757C2A9649C94629ED7CF.

Barrett, Joseph H. *Life of Abraham Lincoln: Presenting His Early History, Political Career, and Speeches In and Out of Congress; Also a General View of His Policy as President of the United States; with His Messages, Proclamations, Letters, Etc., and a Concise History of the War.* Cincinnati: Moore, Wilstach & Baldwin, 1864.

Bartlett, John Russell. *Memoirs of Rhode Island Officers Who Were Engaged in the Service of Their Country During the Great Rebellion of the South.* Providence, RI: Sidney S. Rider & Brother, 1867.

"Biggest, Most Luxurious Private Yacht in the World." *The American Weekly Inc.* (Sunday Supplement to *The Milwaukee Sentinel*), November 24, 1929. Accessed February 15, 2015.

Blanchard, Frank Leroy. "Yacht of a Millionaire." *The Metropolitan Magazine.* Vol.VIII, No. 4 (October 1898). New York: Metropolitan Magazine Company, 1898.

Boynton, Charles Brandon. *The History of the Navy During the Rebellion,* Vol. I. New York: D. Appleton and Company, 1867.

———. *The History of the Navy During the Rebellion,* Vol. II. New York: D. Appleton and Company, 1868.

Brown, J.H., ed. *The Mercantile Navy List and Annual Appendage to the Commercial Code of Signals for All Nations.* London: Bradbury and Evans, 1861.

Bushnell, David. "General Principles and Construction of a Submarine Vessel." *Transactions of the American Philosophical Society, Held at Philadelphia, for Promoting Useful Knowledge,* Vol. IV, Article No. XXXVII. Philadelphia: 1799.

Carnegie Endowment for International Peace. *Publication No. 17, American Foreign Policy,* 2nd ed. Washington, D.C.: Carnegie, 1920.

Central Intelligence Agency, Project OBOPUS/BGFIEND, Vol. 12_0031 and 0031, declassified 2007.

"A Century of Quarrels with Spain." *Self Culture: A Magazine of Knowledge.* Vol. III, No. 2, May 1896. Chicago: The Werner Company, 1896.

Choules, Rev. John Overton. *The Cruise of the Steam Yacht North Star; a Narrative of the Excursion of Mr. Vanderbilt's Party to England, Russia, Denmark, France, Spain, Italy, Malta, Turkey, Madeira, Etc.* Boston: Gould and Lincoln, 1854.

"The Clipper Yacht Camargo." *Motor Boating.* Vol. XLII, No. 1, July 1928.

Coggeshall, George. *History of the American Privateers, and Letter-of-Marque, during our war with England in the years 1812, '13, and '14, interspersed with Several Naval Battles Between American and British Ships-of-War.* New York: George Coggeshall, 1856.

Congressional Globe, for the First Session, Thirtieth Congress: Containing Speeches and Important State Papers, Appendix to. New Series 1847–8. City of Washington, D.C.: Blair and Rives, 1848.

"Consigned to the Sea: Trenor L. Park's Palatial Yacht Sultana Successfully Launched." *The New York Times*, December 19, 1919. Accessed August 20, 2015. http://query.nytimes.com/mem/archive-free/pdf?res=9E02E4D81F3EEF33A2575AC1A9649D94689FD7CF.

Cooke, Captain A.P., USN. "Our Naval Reserve and the Necessity for Its Organization." *Proceedings of the United States Naval Institute*, Vol. XIV, George W. Tyler, Charles R. Miles, W.F. Worthington, eds. Annapolis: Naval Institute, 1888.

Coolidge, Calvin. "Calvin Coolidge, Address Before the American Legion Convention in Omaha, Nebraska, October 6, 1925." *The American Presidency Project.* Accessed November 20, 2015, http://www.presidency.ucsb.edu/ws/index.php?pid=438.

Creelman, James. *On the Great Highway, the Wanderings and Adventures of Special Correspondent.* Boston: Lothrop, Lee & Shepard Co., Boston, 1901.

Crowninshield, Francis B. *The Story of George Crowninshield's Yacht Cleopatra's Barge on a Voyage of Pleasure to the Western Islands and the Mediterranean 1816–1817.* Boston: privately printed, 1913.

"The Cruise of the Viking." *Lippincott's Magazine of Popular Literature and Science.* Old Series Vol. XXX, November 1882.

"Cuba Buys Steam Yacht." *The New York Times*, May 21, 1907. Accessed February 23, 2015. http://query.nytimes.com/mem/archive-free/pdf?res=9400E6DA143EE733A25752C2A9639C946697D6CF.

Daniels, Josephus. *Our Navy at War.* New York: George H. Doran Company, 1922.

Desausa.org. "Sinking of U-490 by Task Group 22.5." Accessed January 19, 2016. http://www.desausa.org/sinking_of_u_490.htm.

Dewey, George. *Autobiography of George Dewey, Admiral of the Navy.* New York: Charles Scribner's Sons, 1913.

"Famous Old Yacht America Gets Ovation As She Leaves Boston on Final Journey." *The New York Times*, September 11, 1921. Accessed October 23, 2014. http://query.nytimes.com/mem/archive-free/pdf?res=9F0CE7DE153EEE3ABC4952DFBF66838A639EDE.

The Federal Reporter, Volume 148, Cases Argued and Determined in the Circuit Courts of Appeals and Circuit and District Courts of the United States, December, 1906—February, 1907. District Court, D. Rhode Island, November 15, 1906, No. 1,132. St. Paul, MN: West Publishing Co., 1907.

"Federal Rights Violated; Seizure of Coast Survey Vessels in Florida and South Carolina. List of Vessels in that Service Their Position and Commanders." *The New York Times*, January 24, 1861. Accessed January 31, 2012. http://www.nytimes.com/1861/01/24/news/federal-rights-violated-seizure-coast-survey-vessels-florida-south-carolina-list.html.

Fiske, Commander Bradley A., USN. "Compromiseless Ships." *The Proceedings of the United States Naval Institute.* Vol. XXXI, No. 3, September 1905. Annapolis, MD: U.S. Naval Institute, 1905.

"Foreign Affairs." *Public Opinion: a Comprehensive Summary of the Press Throughout the World on All Important Current Topics*, Volume XXV, July, 1898-December, 1898. New York: The Public Opinion Company, 1898.

"The Forgotten Man." *Motor Boating.* Vol. 1, No. 2, August 1932.

"Former Yachts." *Panama Canal Review.* Official Panama Canal Publication. Balboa Heights, Canal Zone, January 1964. vol. 14, no. 6.

"The Frolic Discovered." *The Gazette, Montreal*, Vol. CXXXV, No. 244, October 11, 1906. Accessed March 1, 2017. https://news.google.com/newspapers?nid=Fr8DH2VBP9sC&dat=19061011&printsec=frontpage&hl=en.

"From New-Orleans; United States District Court, New-Orleans Industry of Judge Durell Prize Cases Before the Court Confiscation Cases Prizes Condemned Prizes Released Large Amounts Involved." *The New York Times*, July 31, 1865. Accessed October 22, 2014. http://www.nytimes.com/1865/07/31/news/new-orleans-united-states-district-court-new-orleans-industry-judge-durell-prize.html.

Fulton, Robert I., and Thomas C. Trueblood, eds. *Patriotic Eloquence Relating to the Spanish-American War and Its Issues.* New York: Charles Scribner's Sons, 1900.

Gardner, William. "The Steam Yacht as a Naval Auxiliary in Time of War." *Transactions of the Society of Naval Architects and Marine Engineers.* Vol. I. New York: the society, 1893.

Hansard's Parliamentary Debates. 3rd Series, Commencing with the Accession of William IV, vol. XCVII, col. 122. [Lord Palmerston—defense of Treaty of Adrianople in House of Commons, March 1, 1848.] London: G. Woodfall and Son et alia, 1848.

Hansard's Parliamentary Debates. 3rd Series, Commencing with the Accession of William IV. Volume CLXX (Comprising the Period from the Twenty-seventh Day of March 1863, to the twenty-eighth Day of May 1863) Second Volume of the Session. London: Cornelius Buck, 1863.

"Haynes-Griffin advertisement." *Motor Boating.* Vol. XLVIII, No. 4, October 1931.

Hearings Before the Committee on Naval Affairs, House of Representatives, Sixty-Fourth Con-

gress, First Session, On Estimates Submitted by the Secretary of the Navy. Vol. 2, Section 23. Washington, D.C.: U.S. Government Printing Office, 1916.

Herbert, H.A. "The Sea and Sea Power as a factor in the History of the United States, Address of the Hon. H.A. Herbert, Secretary of the Navy, Before the Class at the U.S. Naval War College, Newport R.I., August 10, 1896." *United States Naval Institute Proceedings*, Vol. XXII, No. 3. H.G. Dressel, ed. Annapolis, MD: United States Naval Institute, 1896.

The Historical Society of Pennsylvania. "Vaux Family Papers, 1739–1923" (collection 684). Accessed October 21, 2014. http://www2.hsp.org/collections/manuscripts/v/vaux684.xml.

History of Cuba. "Full Text of the Ostend Manifesto." Accessed March 1, 2017. http://www.historyofcuba.com/history/havana/Ostend2.htm.

"Hornet and Brig Argus." Hezekiah Niles, ed. *The Weekly Register: Containing Documents, Essays and Facts; Together with Notices of the Arts and Manufactures, and a Record of the Events of the Times*, Vol. II, March 1812 to September 1812. Vol. II, No. 45, July 11, 1812. Baltimore: H. Niles, 1812.

Hunt's Yachting Magazine, Volume the First. London: Hunt and Son, 1852.

"Increase of the Navy." *Navy Yearbook, Embracing All Acts Authorizing the Construction of Ships of the "New Navy" and Resume of Annual Naval Appropriation Laws from 1883 to 1920, Inclusive.* Washington, D.C.: U.S. Government Printing Office, 1921, 15.

"Intercourse of the British at Nassau with the Rebel States." *The New York Times*, April 28, 1862. Accessed August 12, 2014. http://www.nytimes.com/1862/04/28/news/intercourse-of-the-british-at-nassau-with-the-rebel-states.html.

Jenrich, Charles H. "The Checkered Career of a Gallant Lady." *Popular Boating*, Vol. 12, No. 3, September 1962.

"John Green, Plaintiff-Appellant, against Eugene F. McDonald, Jr., and Herman Hessberg, Sheriff of the County of Kings, Defendants-Respondents." *State of New York, Supreme Court, Appellate Division—First Judicial Department, No. 637.* New York: Libman's Law Printery, 1929.

"Kaiser's Gold Trophy Proves to be Pewter." *The New York Times*, June 9, 1918. Accessed February 4, 2015. http://query.nytimes.com/mem/archive-free/pdf?res=9A0DE5D9103BEE3ABC4153DFB0668383609EDE.

Konstam, Angus. *Privateers & Pirates 1730–1830*. Oxford: Osprey Publishing, 2001. (Advertisement from *Boston Gazette*, 13 November 1780. Reproduced on p.19.)

"Launch of the Sovereign." *The New York Times*, May 19, 1896. Accessed June 20, 2015. http://query.nytimes.com/mem/archive-free/pdf?res=9A03E4DF133EE333A2575AC1A9639C94679ED7CF.

Law Resource. Samuel Rossiter Betts, District Judge of United States District Court for the Southern District of New York. *Case No. 5,456, March 1862, The Gipsey.* Accessed September 15, 2014. https://law.resource.org/pub/us/case/reporter/F.Cas/0010.f.cas/0010.f.cas.0436.1.pdf.

Lee, Fitzhugh, and Joseph Wheeler. *Cuba's Struggle Against Spain with the Causes for American Intervention and a Full Account of the Spanish-American War, Including Final Peace Negotiations.* New York: The American Historical Press, 1899.

Legal Information Institute. "46 U.S. Code § 57105 - Acquisition of Vessels for Essential Services, Routes, or Lines." Accessed November 24, 2015. https://www.law.cornell.edu/uscode/text/46/57105.

Library and Archives of Canada. "Ship Registrations, 1787–1966, Item 75607: Sylphide." Accessed March 3, 2017. http://www.bac-lac.gc.ca/eng/discover/ship-registration-index-1787-1966/Pages/item.aspx?IdNumber=75607&DotsIdNumber=.

"Life on the American Newsfront: Seven Seas Races to Bermuda for Dinner." *Life*, Vol. 3, No. 10, September 6, 1937.

Lincoln, Abraham. "Letter to Salmon P. Chase" *1809–1865, Collected Works of Abraham Lincoln*, Vol. 4. Ann Arbor: University of Michigan Digital Library Production Services, 2001. Accessed September 12, 2014. http://quod.lib.umich.edu/cgi/t/text/text-idx?c=lincoln;rgn=div1;view=text;idno=lincoln4;node=lincoln4%3A589.

Littlefield, Francis L. "The Capture of the Chesapeake." *Collections of the Maine Historical Society*, Third Series, Vol. II. Portland, ME: Published by the Society, 1906.

Loubat, J.F., ed. *A Yachtsman's Scrapbook, or the Ups and Downs of Yacht Racing.* New York: Brentano Brothers, 1887.

Lougheed, Victor. *Vehicles of the Air.* Chicago: The Reilly and Britton Company, 1909. 3rd ed.

Mahan, Captain Alfred Thayer, USN. "The Battle of the Sea of Japan." *Collier's: The National Weekly.* Vol. XXXV, No. 12, 17 June 1905.

_____. *Naval Strategy Compared with the Principles and Practice of Military Operations on Land.* Boston: Little, Brown, and Company, 1911.

"Maritime History of the Great Lakes." *The Maritime Review.* January 28, 1892. Accessed August 24, 2015. http://images.maritimehistoryofthegreatlakes.ca/26804/data.

McAdoo, William. "The Yacht as Naval Auxiliary." *The North American Review.* Vol. 161, No. 465, Lloyd Bryce, ed. New York: North American Review Pub. Co., 1895.

Mead, Frederick S., ed. *Harvard's Military Record in the World War.* Boston: The Harvard Alumni Association, 1921.

"Million-dollar Visitor Here." *Sausalito News*, Vol XLVIII, No. 15, April 12, 1935. Accessed March 6, 2017. https://cdnc.ucr.edu/cgi-bin/

cdnc?a=d&d=SN19350412.2.78&e=-------en--20--1--txt-txIN--------1.

Millspaugh, Charles Frederick. *Plantæ Utowanæ: Plants Collected in Bermuda, Porto Rico, St. Thomas, Culebras, Santo Domingo, Jamaica, Cuba, The Caymans, Cozumel, Yucatan and the Alacran Shoals Dec. 1898 to Mar. 1899, The Antillean Cruise of the Yacht Utowana*. Chicago: Field Columbian Museum Publication 43, Botanical Series, Vol. II, No. 1, 1900.

"Miss Morgan's Wedding; J. Pierpont Morgan's Eldest Daughter Married to H.L. Satterlee." *The New York Times*, November 16, 1900. Accessed June 20, 2015. http://query.nytimes.com/mem/archive-free/pdf?res=9E00EFDE143FE433A25755C1A9679D946197D6CF.

"Monthly Notes—Recovery of the Peterhoff Steam Yacht." *The Practical Mechanic's Journal*, Vol. IV, April, 1851–March, 1852. London: George Hebert, 1852.

"The Motor Boating Market Place." *Motor Boating*. Vol. XIV, No. 3, September 1919.

"Narrative of Accident and Disaster." *The Household Narrative of Current Events (for the year 1850), Being a Monthly Supplement to Household Words*. Charles Dickens, ed. London: Office, 16, Wellington Street North, 1850.

"Naval Architecture," footnote p. 343. Rev. Edward Smedley, Rev. Hugh James Rose and Rev. Henry John Rose, eds. *Encyclopedia Metropolitana; or Universal Dictionary of Knowledge*. Vol. VI. London: B. Fellowes; F. and J. Rivington; Duncan and Malcolm, et alia, 1845.

"Naval Auxiliary Board: Seven Yachts, Recommended for Second-Class Gunboats, to be Purchased." *The New York Times*, April 20, 1898. Accessed January 15, 2015. http://query.nytimes.com/gst/abstract.html?res=9E06E5DE1139E433A25753C2A9629C94699ED7CF.

Naval Documents of the American Revolution, Vol. 2. "American Theatre: Sept. 3, 1775-Oct. 31, 1775." (part 3 of 9). Washington, D.C.: U.S. Government Printing Office, 1966.

"Navy Buys More Boats; Sea Train Almost Finished." *The Chicago Sunday Tribune*. Vol. XCIX, No. 46, Part 1, November 17, 1940. Accessed February 28, 2017. http://archives.chicagotribune.com/1940/11/17/page/12/article/navy-buys-more-boats-sea-train-almost-finished.

"Navy Yard Busier Than Since 1865." *The Brooklyn Daily Eagle*. April 3, 1898. Accessed January 14, 2015. https://www.newspapers.com/image/50465152/.

"The New York Yacht Club: Its Organization, Founders and its First Cruise. Annual Regattas and Winning Yachts–Yachts Now Belonging to the Club–Charter of the Club–Rules and Regulations–Honorary Members–Coming Regattas. Officers. Yachts of the Club. Charter of the Club. Rules and Regulations. Honorary Members. The Ensuing Regatta, Etc." *The New York Times*, June 3, 1865. Accessed December 20, 2011. http://www.nytimes.com/1865/06/03/news/new-york-yacht-club-its-organization-founders-its-first-cruise-annual-regattas.html?pagewanted=all.

"Ogden Goelet is Dead." *The New York Times*, August 28, 1897. Accessed June 20, 2015. http://query.nytimes.com/ mem/archive-free/pdf?res=9D02E2D71638E733A2575BC2A96E-9C94669ED7CF.

"O.H. Berryman and Others vs. The United States." *Reports from the Court of Claims Submitted to the House of Representatives, The Third Session of the Thirty-fourth Congress 1856-'57*. In One Volume. Washington, D.C.: Cornelius Wendell, 1857.

Open Jurist. "72 U.S. 28––The Peterhoff," in *United States Supreme Court, December Term, 1866*. Accessed September 20, 2014. http://openjurist.org/72/us/28.

"Our Auxiliary Navy." *The Chicago Daily Tribune*. October 11, 1897. Accessed January 14, 2015. http://archives.chicagotribune.com/1897/10/11/.

"Papers Relating to Foreign Affairs, Great Britain, Case of the Seizure of the Bark Saxon, Enclosure 2 in No. 1." United States House of Representatives. *Executive Documents Printed by Order of The House of Representatives During the Second Session of the Thirty-Eighth Congress, 1864–'65*, in Fifteen Volumes. Washington, D.C.: U.S. Government Printing Office, 1865.

"Passengers Arriving from Other Ports in the Maritimes." *Prince Edward Island Register*, The Examiner, May 21, 1855 to December 1, 1856. Accessed September 9, 2014. http://www.islandregister.com/maritimepass.html.

The Peterhoff, Argument of E. Delafield Smith, United states District Attorney, Addressed to the United States Court at New York, In the Case of the Prize Steamer Peterhoff, July 10, 1863 Printed for the Use of the Court, from a Stenographic Report by A.F. Warburto, Esq., and Revised by the District Attorney. New York: John W. Amerman, 1863.

Peverelly, Charles A., ed. *The Book of American Pastimes, Containing a History of the Principal Base Ball, Cricket, Rowing, and Yachting Clubs of the United States*. New York: published by the author, 1866.

_____ "Yachting Foam." *Brentano's Aquatic Monthly and Sporting Gazetteer*, Vol. I, April to September 1879. New York: August Brentano, Jr., 1879.

"Piracy and Privateering." *Congressional Globe, 1861-'62, 3325, 3335*. see Lawrence's Wheaton (ed. 1863), p.643, in *Index to the Miscellaneous Documents of the Senate of the United States for the First Session of the Forty-Ninth Congress* (in 13 volumes) Chapter XX, Section 385. Washington, D.C.: U.S. Government Printing Office, 1886.

"Placida—A Clipper Stem Yacht." *Motor Boating*. Vol. XLVII, No. 2, February 1931.

"Pleasure Craft for Navy Use." *The New Country

Life. Vol. XXXII. New York: Doubleday, Page & Company, 1917.

Record of Movements Vessels of the United States Coast Guard 1790—December 31, 1933, Department of Transportation, United States Coast Guard. Washington, D.C.: Reprinted by the Coast Guard Historian's Office, A Bicentennial Publication, U.S. Coast Guard Headquarters, 1989.

Report of the Secretary of the Navy Being Part of the Message and Documents Communicated to the Two Houses of Congress at the Beginning of the Second Session of the Forty-Seventh Congress. (in Three Volumes) Vol. I. Washington, D.C.: U.S. Government Printing Office, 1882.

"Representative Men of the Republican Party." *The Old Guard, A Monthly Journal Devoted to the Principles of 1776 and 1787,* Vol. II, issue 7. C. Chauncy Burr, ed. New York: Van Evrie, Horton & Co., 1864.

Republican Campaign Textbook. Republican Congressional Committee and Republican National Campaign Contributors. Philadelphia: Republican Congressional Committee, 1908. Philadelphia: Dunlap Printing Co., 1908.

"Revenue Cutters After Smugglers of Chinese." *The New York Times,* October 1, 1906. Accessed January 24, 2012. http://query.nytimes.com/gst/abstract.html?res=FA0713FC355F13718DDDA80894D8415B868CF1D3.

Ringle, Ken. "The Last Man of War." *The Washington Post,* June 17, 2001. Accessed November 9, 2015. https://www.washingtonpost.com/archive/lifestyle/2001/06/17/the-last-man-of-war/7cd89c0a-5bc7-45b2-9b0e-ac112ca81436/.

Roosevelt, Franklin D. "The Genesis of the New Deal, 1928–32." *The Public Papers and Addresses of Franklin D. Roosevelt.* Vol. 1. New York: Random House, 1938.

Sanger, George P., ed. *The Statutes at Large and Proclamations of the United States of America, from March 1871 to March 1873, and Treaties and Postal Conventions,* Vol. XVII. Boston: Little, Brown, and Company, 1873.

_____. *The Statutes at Large, Treaties, and Proclamations of the United States of America, from December 1863, to December 1865.* Vol. XIII. Boston: Little, Brown and Company, 1866.

Savage, Thomas. "Letter to Secretary of State William Seward, 2 September 1861." *Message of the President of the United States to the Two Houses of Congress at the Commencement of the Second Session of the Thirty-Seventh Congress,* Vol. I. Washington, D.C.: U.S. Government Printing Office, 1861.

Scharf, J. Thomas, *History of the Confederate States Navy from Its Organization to the Surrender of Its Last Vessel.* New York: Rogers & Sherwood, 1887.

"The Schooner, 'S.J. Waring.'" *Harper's Weekly,* August 3, 1861. Accessed August 30, 2014. http://www.sonofthesouth.net/leefoundation/civil-war/1861/august/schooner-waring.htm.

Schultz, Fred L. "'It Made A Man Out of Me,' An Interview With Ernest Borgnine." *Naval History.* Vol. 12, No. 1, February 1998.

Semmes, Admiral Rafael. *Memoirs of Service Afloat During the War Between the States.* Baltimore: Kelly, Piet & Co., 1869.

Ships' Data U.S. Naval Vessels. July 1, 1935. Washington, D.C.: U.S. Government Printing Office, 1935.

Skinner, Commander Carlton, USCGR (ret.). "U.S.S. *Sea Cloud,* IX-99, Racial Integration for Naval Efficiency." *United States Coast Guard Historian's Office.* Accessed January 19 2016. http://www.uscg.mil/history/articles/Carlton_Skinner.asp.

"The Steam Yacht 'Hermione' from Gourock to New York, Calls Here According to Arrangement." *The Evening Telegram,* St. John's, Newfoundland, July 3, 1895. Accessed June 20, 2015. http://news.google.com/newspapers?nid=35&dat=18950703&id=SqNEAAAAIBAJ&sjid=GDkDAAAAIBAJ&pg=5942,320024.

Stephens, W.P. "Steam Yachting in America." *The Book of Sport.* William Patten, ed. New York: J. E. Taylor & Company, 1901.

Stone, Herbert S., ed. *The Spanish-American War: The Events of the War Described by Eye Witnesses.* New York: Herbert S. Stone & Company, 1899.

Stringer, Harry R. *The Navy Book of Distinguished Service: An Official Compendium of the Names and Citations of the Men of the United States Navy, Marine Corps, Army and Foreign Governments Who Were Decorated by the Navy Department for Extraordinary Gallantry and Conspicuous Service Above and Beyond the call of Duty in the World War.* Washington, D.C.: Fassett Publishing Company, 1921.

Strouse, Jean. *Morgan: American Financier.* (Letter from Jack Morgan to his mother after the maiden voyage of Corsair II in October 1891.) London: Harville Press, 1999.

Tenney, William Jewett, *The Military and Naval History of the Rebellion with Biographical Sketches of Deceased Officers.* New York: D. Appleton & Company, 1865.

Thompson, Winfield M. "Historic American Yachts: The Slave Yacht *Wanderer.*" *The Rudder.* Vol. XV, No. 2, February 1904.

"Types of Cruising Yachts." *The Art Journal.* New Series, Volume 38. London: J.S. Virtue & Co. Ltd., 1886.

United States Coast Guard Historians Office. "Nourmahal." https://www.uscg.mil/history/webcutters/Nourmahal_PG72.pdf.

_____. "USS Sea Cloud, 1942." Accessed January 19, 2016. http://www.uscg.mil/history/webcutters/Sea_Cloud_IX99.asp.

United States Naval War Records Office. *Official Records of the Union and Confederate Navies in the War of the Rebellion,* Series I, Vol. 2. "The Operations of the Cruisers, from January 1,

1863, to March 31, 1864." Washington, D.C.: U.S. Government Printing Office, 1895.

___. *Official Records of the Union and Confederate Navies in the War of the Rebellion,* Series I, Vol. 16. "South Atlantic Blockading Squadron from October 1, 1864, to August 8, 1865; Gulf Blockading Squadron from June 7 t December 15, 1861." Washington, D.C.: U.S. Government Printing Office, 1903.

___. *Official Records of the Union and Confederate Navies in the War of the Rebellion,* Series II, Vol. 1. Washington, D.C.: U.S. Government Printing Office, 1921.

___. *Official records of the Union and Confederate Navies in the War of the Rebellion.* Series I - Vol. 4. "Operations in the Gulf of Mexico, November 15, 1860–June 7, 1861; Operations on the Atlantic Coast, January 1, 1861–May 13, 1861; Operations on the Potomac and Rappahannock Rivers, January 5, 1861–December 7, 1861." Washington, D.C.: U.S. Government Printing Office, 1896.

___. *Official records of the Union and Confederate Navies in the War of the Rebellion.* Series I, Vol. 12. "North Atlantic Blockading Squadron, February 2, 1865–August 3, 1865; South Atlantic Blockading Squadron, October 29, 1861–May 13, 1862." Washington, D.C.: U.S. Government Printing Office, 1901.

___. *Official records of the Union and Confederate Navies in the War of the Rebellion.* Series I - Vol. 17. "Gulf Blockading Squadron, December 16, 1861–February 21, 1862; East Gulf Blockading Squadron, December 22, 1862–July 17, 1865." Washington, D.C.: U.S. Government Printing Office, 1903.

___. *Official records of the Union and Confederate Navies in the War of the Rebellion.* Series I, Vol. 21. "Operations of the West Gulf Blockading Squadron from January 1 to December 31, 1864." Washington, D.C.: U.S. Government Printing Office, 1906.

___. *Official Records of the Union and Confederate Navies in the War of the Rebellion.* Series I, Vol. 5. "Operations on the Potomac and Rappahannock Rivers from December 7, 1861, to July 31, 1865." Washington, D.C.: U.S. Government Printing Office, 1897.

"Urgent Need of Ships for Coast Defense is Outlined." *Official Bulletin, United States Committee on Public Information.* Vol. 1, No. 3, May 12, 1917. Washington, D.C.: U.S. Government Printing Office, 1917.

"The U.S.S. Mayflower." *Marine Engineering/log.* Vol. 6, No. 7, July 1901. New York: Simmons-Boardman Publishing Company, 1901.

"U.S.S. Venetia." *Our Navy: the Standard Publication of the United States Navy.* Vol. XIII, No. 7, November 1919. New York: Our Navy Publishing Company, 1919.

"Vanderbilt's Yacht Sunk." *The New York Times,* July 25, 1892. Accessed February 24, 2015. http://query.nytimes.com/mem/archive-free/pdf?res=9807E6DF1731E033A25756C2A9619C94639ED7CF.

Walker, Edward A. *Our First Year of Army Life: An Anniversary Address Delivered by the First Regiment of the Connecticut Volunteer Heavy Artillery at Their Camp Near Gaines Mills, VA, June 1862, by the Chaplain of the Regiment."* New Haven, CT: Thomas H. Pease, 1862.

Walsh, George Ethelbert. "Privateers." *Lippincott's Monthly Magazine: Popular Journal of General Literature, Science, and Politics.* Vol. LXII, July to December 1898.

Washington, George. *Eighth Annual Address to the House and the Senate, December 1796.* Accessed 12 January 2015. http://www.presidency.ucsb.edu/ws/?pid=29438.

Welles, Gideon. *Report of the Secretary of the Navy with an Appendix Containing Bureau Reports, etc. December 1867.* Washington, D.C.: U.S. Government Printing Office, 1867.

___. *Report of the Secretary of the Navy with an Appendix Containing Reports from Officers, December 1865.* Washington, D.C.: U.S. Government Printing Office, 1865.

Wharton, Francis, ed. *A Digest of the International Law of the United States: Taken from Documents Issued by Presidents and Secretaries of State, and from Decisions of Federal Courts and Opinions of Attorneys-general.* Vol. 1. Washington, D.C.: U.S. Government Printing Office, 1887.

Wilson, Woodrow. "State of the Union Address, December 7, 1915." Accessed September 30, 2015. http://www.infoplease.com/t/hist/state-of-the-union/127.html.

Wise, George D. "Report to Accompany bill H.R. 6839. Report No. 1728." (William G. Ford, claimant). *Index to the Reports of Committees of the House of Representatives for the First Session of the Forty-Seventh Congress, 1881-'82,* Vol. 6. Washington, D.C.: U.S. Government Printing Office, 1882.

Worman, James H., and Ben J. Worman, eds. "Outing's Monthly Review of Amateur Sports and Pastimes: Yachting." James H. Worman and Ben J. Worman, eds. *Outing, An Illustrated Monthly Magazine of Sport, Travel and Recreation* Vol. XXXII, April–September, 1898. New York: The Outing Publishing Company, 1898.

___. "The Southern Yacht Club of New Orleans." *Outing, An Illustrated Monthly Magazine of Sport, Travel and Recreation,* Vol. XXXI, October, 1897–March 1898. New York: The Outing Publishing Company, 1898.

Worman, James H., ed. "Notes of Clubs and Craft." *Outing: An Illustrated Monthly Magazine of Sport, Travel and Recreation.* Vol. XXIV, April 1894–September 1894. New York: The Outing Company, Ltd., 1894.

"Yacht Scout Fleet Sought By Daniels." *The New York Times,* May 3, 1916. accessed September 29, 2015. http://query.nytimes.com/mem/archive-free/pdf?res=9C0DE4DC113FE233A25750C0A9639C946796D6CF.

"Yacht With 32-Knot Speed." *The New York Times*, May 16, 1912. Accessed September 29, 2015. http://query.nytimes.com/mem/archive-free/pdf?res=9F07E1DB153CE633A25755C1A9639C946396D6CF.

"Yachts in War Dress." *The Brooklyn Daily Eagle*. April 23, 1917. Accessed July 20, 2015. https://www.newspapers.com/image/54337141/.

"Yale to Form Naval Unit; Mosquito Fleet Growing." *The Brooklyn Daily Eagle*. February 26, 1917. Accessed 20 June 2015. https://www.newspapers.com/image/54451112/.

Young, A. *Digest of Maritime Law Cases from 1837 to 1860*. London: Horace Cox, 1865.

Secondary Sources

Albon, Christopher. "The Hooligan Navy." U.S. Naval Institute blog. Accessed February 16, 2016. blog.usni.org/2010/02/11/the-hooligan-navy.

Allen, Gardner Weld. *A Naval History of the American Revolution*, Vols. I & II. Boston: Houghton Mifflin Company, 1913.

BBC. "Industry and Social Change." Accessed November 27, 2015. http://www.bbc.co.uk/schools/gcsebitesize/history/mwh/usa/boomrev1.shtml.

Beach, Frederick Converse, ed. "Naval Militia." *The Americana: A Universal Reference Library Comprising the Arts and Sciences, Literature, History, Biography, Geography, Commerce, Etc., of the World*. Vol. 10. New York: Scientific American Compiling Department, 1903.

Bernstein, Irving. "Americans in Depression and War." U.S. Department of Labor. Accessed November 28, 2015. http://www.dol.gov/dol/aboutdol/history/chapter5.htm.

Big Old Houses. "Something Completely Different." Accessed January 18, 2016. http://bigoldhouses.blogspot.com/2012/06/something-completely-different.html.

Blair, Clay. *Hitler's U-Boat War: The Hunters, 1939–1942*. New York: Random House, 1996.

BR/Sulzer. "Nourmahal." Accessed December 5, 2015. http://www.derbysulzers.com/shipnourmahal.html.

Brigantine Antiques. "Unquowa." Accessed January 25, 2015. http://brigantineantiques.com/Unquowa.htm.

Brown, Harry. *The History of American Yachts and Yachtsmen*. New York: The Spirit of the Times Publishing Company, 1901.

Bryan, Ford R. *Friends, Families & Forays: Scenes From the Life and Times of Henry Ford*. Detroit, MI: Wayne State University Press, 2002.

Campbell, W. Joseph. *The Year That Defined American Journalism: 1887 and the Clash of Paradigms*. New York: Routledge, 2013.

Caswell, Chris. "Passionate Heritage." *Yachting Magazine*. Accessed September 12, 2015. http://www.yachtingmagazine.com/passionate-heritage.

Chaffin, Tom. *The H.L. Hunley: The Secret Hope of the Confederacy*. New York: Hill and Wang, 2008.

Chapelle, Howard I. *The American Sailing Navy: The Ships and Their Development*. New York: Konecky & Konecky, 1949.

CharterWorld. "Motor Yacht Savarona." Accessed December 5, 2015. http://www.charterworld.com/index.html?sub=yacht-charter&charter=-savarona-1860.

Chernow, Ron. *The House of Morgan: An American Banking Dynasty and the Rise of Modern Finance*. New York: Touchstone, Simon & Schuster Inc., 1990.

Chesapeake Maritime Heritage Foundation, Inc. "Part Boat, Part Ship; The U.S. Navy YP." Accessed March 5, 2016. http://chesapeakenavalheritagefoundation.blogspot.com/2009/09/part-boat-part-ship-us-navy-yp.html.

Civil War Trust. "Blockade." Accessed April 12, 2016. http://www.civilwar.org/education/history/navy-hub/navy-history/blockade.html.

____. "This Day in the Civil War." Accessed April 12, 2016. http://www.civilwar.org/150th-anniversary/this-day-in-the-civil-war.html#1861.

Classic Yacht Info. "Yacht: Black Watch." Accessed March 7, 2017. classicyachtinfo.com/yachts/black-watch/.

The Clyde Built Ships. "Lady Marchant." Accessed September 9, 2014. http://www.clydeships.co.uk/view.php?year_built=&builder=&ref=21936&vessel=LADY+LE+MARCHANT.

____ "Mayflower." Accessed June 12, 2015. http://clydeships.co.uk/view.php?official_number=&imo=&builder=&builder_eng=&year_built=&launch_after=&launch_before=&role=&type_ref1=&propulsion=&category=&owner=&port=&flag=&disposal=&lost=&ref=4479&vessel=MAYFLOWER.

Coast Guard Modeling. "Notable, Interesting or Unique Cutters." Accessed June 14, 2015. http://old.coastguardmodeling.com/01C_Famous.html.

"Congress Considers New Laws to Govern Motor Craft." *Motor Boating*. Vol. LXI, No. 4, April 1938.

Crawford, Richard. "The Venetia." *San Diego Union-Tribune*. September 9, 2010. Accessed March 7, 2017. http://www.sandiegoyesterday.com/wp-content/uploads/2010/09/Venetia.pdf.

Cressman, Robert J. "Historic Fleets: A Fine Little Vessel." *Naval History*, Vol. 22, No. 6, December 6, 2008.

Crowell, Benedict, and Robert Forrest Wilson. *How America Went to War; An Account From Official Sources of the Nation's War Activities 1917–1920*. Vol. II, "The Transportation of Troops and Military Supplies 1917–1918. New Haven, CT: Yale University Press, 1921.

D'Amico, Angela, and Richard Pittenger. "A Brief History of Active Sonar." Digitized by Woods Hole Oceanographic Institution from *Aquatic*

Mammals. Vol. 35, Issue 4, September 24, 2010. Macomb, IL: Document & Publication Services at Western Illinois University, 2010. Accessed March 7, 2017. http://csi.whoi.edu/sites/default/files/literature/Full%20Text.pdf.

Denger, Mark J. "The Genesis of the Naval Reserve." The California Military Museum. Accessed June 6, 2015. http://californiamilitaryhistory.org/NavRes.html.

Digital History. "The Rise of Big Business." Accessed July 2, 2015. http://www.digitalhistory.uh.edu/disp_textbook.cfm?smtID=2&psid=3165.

"Editorial." *Motor Boat.* Vol. XVII, No. 7, April 10, 1920.

Find a Grave. "Charles Dabney." Accessed September 3, 2014. http://www.findagrave.com/cgi-bin/fg.cgi?page=gr&GRid=12765059.

_____. "Lieutenant Wilson Marshall, Jr." Accessed October 13, 2015. http://www.findagrave.com/cgi-bin/fg.cgi?page=gr&GRid=103910506.

Flagler Museum. "The Amazing Story of Henry Flagler's Yacht *Alicia*." Accessed January 21, 2015. http://www.flaglermuseum.us/history/flaglers-yacht-alicia.

Floating Hospital for Children at Tufts Medical Center. "History of Floating Hospital for Children." Accessed August 17, 2015. http://www.floatinghospital.org/About-Us/History.aspx.

Furer, Rear Admiral Julius Augustus, USN ret. *Administration of the Navy Department in World War II.* Washington, D.C.: U.S. Government Printing Office, 1959. Digitized by Hyperwar Foundation. Accessed November 21, 2015. http://ibiblio.org/hyperwar/USN/Admin-Hist/USN-Admin/USN-Admin-2.html.

Gannon, Michael. *Operation Drumbeat.* New York: Harper & Row Publishers, 1990.

Gardiner, R., and B. Lavery. *The Line of Battle: The Sailing Warship 1650–1840.* London: Conway, 1992 (2004 ed.).

"The Golden Age of Yachts." *Motor Boating & Sailing.* Vol. 136, No. 6, December 1975.

Grems-Doolittle Library Collections. "Female Aviators in the Godfrey Collection." Accessed April 18, 2016. http://gremsdoolittlelibrary.blogspot.com/2011/06/female-aviators-in-godfrey-collection.html.

Griffin, Martin I.J. "The Commodores of the Navy of the United Colonies." *Appleton's Booklovers Magazine*, Vol. VI, July-December, 1905. New York: D. Appleton and Company, 1905.

Grobecker, Kurt, and Peter Neumann. *Sea Cloud: A Living Legend.* Bradley Lodge, Kemble, UK: Collectors' Books Ltd., 1991.

Haze Gray and Underway (Naval History and Photography). "Bucaneer." http://www.hazegray.org/danfs/patrol/bucaneer.htm.

_____. *Dictionary of American Navy Fighting Ships.* Accessed June 20, 2015.

_____. "Eagle IV." http://www.hazegray.org/danfs/patrol/eagle4.htm.

_____. "Mayflower." http://www.hazegray.org/danfs/patrol/py1.htm.

History Central. "Peterhoff." Accessed February 25 2017. http://historycentral.com/navy/Steamer/peterhoff.html.

historyofcuba.com "The Teller Amendment." Accessed January 15, 2015. http://www.historyofcuba.com/history/teller.htm.

Hofman, Erik. *The Steam Yachts: An Era of Elegance.* Tuckahoe, NY: John de Graff, Inc., 1970.

The Hooligan Navy (The Corsair Fleet). National Sailing Hall of Fame documentary film. Accessed January 29, 2016. http://nshof.org/index.php?option=com_content&view=article&id=314&Itemid=28.

Hughes, Tyler. "The Gilded Age Era." Accessed September 12, 2015. http://thegildedageera.blogspot.com/2012/07/stuyvesant-fish-mansion-new-york-city.html.

Husband, Joseph, Ens. U.S.N.R.F. *On the Coast of France: The Story of the United States Naval Forces in French Waters.* Chicago: A.C. McClurg & Co., 1919.

"Juniata." *Boat International Magazine.* Accessed March 8, 2016. http://www.boatinternational.com/yachts/the-superyacht-directory/juanita--46329.

Jordan, Stephen C. *Hollywood's Original Rat Pack: The Bards of Bundy Drive.* Lanham, MD: Scarecrow Press, 2008.

The Joseph Bucklin Society. "First Navy." Accessed November 15, 2011. http://www.bucklinsociety.net/first_navy.htm.

Larson, C. Kay. "Bravo Zero: The Coast Guard Auxiliary in World War II." United States Coast Guard Auxiliary. Accessed February 9, 2016. wow.uscgaux.info/content.php?unit=1-DEPT&category=auxhistory.

Lefkowitz, Arthur S. *Bushnell's Submarine.* New York: Scholastic, 2006.

The Lehrman Institute. "James Gordon Bennett (1795–1872)." *Mr. Lincoln and New York.* Accessed September 10, 2014. http://www.mrlincolnandnewyork.org/content_inside.asp?ID=32&subjectID=3.

Library of Congress. "Chronology of Cuba in the Spanish-American War." Accessed June 20, 2015. http://www.loc.gov/rr/hispanic/1898/chroncuba.html.

Lighthouse Friends. "North Dumpling, New York." Accessed August 12, 2015. http://www.lighthousefriends.com/light.asp?ID=740.

The Lincoln Log. "A Daily Chronology of the Life of Abraham Lincoln." Accessed September 9, 2014. http://www.thelincolnlog.org/Home.aspx.

Long, Clarence D., ed. "Wages and Earnings in the United States, 1860–1890." *National Bureau of Economic Research.* Princeton NJ: Princeton University Press, 1960.

Maclay, Edgar Stanton. *A History of American Privateers.* New York: D. Appleton and Company, 1899.

_____. *A History of the United States Navy From 1775 to 1894,* Vol. I. New York: D. Appleton and Company, 1895.

_____. *A History of the United States Navy From 1775 to 1901*, Vol. II. New York: D. Appleton and Company, 1906. Accessed March 7, 2017. https://archive.org/stream/historyofunited02macl#page/n7/mode/2up.

_____. *A History of the United States Navy from 1775 to 1902*, Vol. III. New York: D. Appleton and Company, 1907.

MacTaggart, Ross. *The Golden Century: Classic Motor Yachts, 1830–1930*. New York: W.W. Norton & Company, 2001.

_____*Millionaires, Mansions, and Motor Yachts: An Era of Opulence*. New York: W.W. Norton & Company, 2004.

Marine Harbor. "Regattas." Accessed April 14, 2013. http://harbor.passchristian.net/regattas.htm.

Maritime History of the Great Lakes. Accessed January 25, 2015. http://images.maritimehistoryofthegreatlakes.ca/23001/data?n=47.

Marryat, Captain Frederick, R.N. *The Pirate; The Three Cutters* (in one volume). London: Henry G. Bohn, 1854.

Matthews, Scott J. "Development of the Motor Yacht." *Motor Boating*, Vol. 12, No. 6, December 1913.

Military History Encyclopedia on the Web. "American Civil War: The Blockade and the War at Sea." Accessed April 12, 2016. http://www.historyofwar.org/articles/wars_american_civil_war09_waratsea.html.

Military Times. "Hall of Valor." Accessed August 18, 2015. http://valor.militarytimes.com/recipient.php?recipientid=1770.

Mindell, David A. *Iron Coffin: War, Technology, and Experience Aboard the USS Monitor*. Baltimore MD: The Johns Hopkins University Press, 2000.

Missall, John, and Mary Lou Missall. *The Seminole Wars: America's Longest Indian Conflict*. Gainesville: University Press of Florida, 2004.

Morison, Samuel Eliot. *History of United States Naval Operations in World War II: The Battle of the Atlantic*. Edison, NJ: Castle Books, 1947; 2001 ed.

_____. *History of United States Naval Operations in World War II: The Struggle for Guadalcanal*. Edison, NJ: Castle Books edition, 1949; 2001 ed.

National Archives and Records Administration, Southeast Region. "The Wanderer: A finding aid, U. S. District Court, Savannah, Georgia, Mixed Cases, 1790–1860." Accessed January 22, 2012. http://www.archives.gov/southeast/finding-aids/wanderer.pdf.

National Park Service. "Maritime History of Massachusetts: U.S. Navy." Accessed December 30, 2014. http://www.nps.gov/nr/travel/maritime/navy.htm.

Naval History and Heritage Command. *Dictionary of American Naval Fighting Ships*. [DANFS] Accessed 2011 through 2017. [Searched by vessel name and/or classification.] http://www.history.navy.mil//.

_____. History of the Department of the Navy." Accessed November 10, 2011. http://www.history.navy.mil/faqs/faq31-1.htm.

_____. "Jefferson Davis." Accessed August 30, 2014. http://www.history.navy.mil/danfs/cfa5/jefferson_davis.htm.

_____. "Voyage from U.S. to Azores by Converted Yachts." Accessed July 27, 2015. https://www.history.navy.mil/our-collections/photography/wars-and-events/world-war-i/incidents--1917/voyage-from-the-us-to-the-azores-by-uss-margaret-and-other-conve.html.

NavSource Naval History [mostly mirror and photo supplement to DANFS]. Accessed 2015 through 2017. [Searched by vessel name and/or classification.] www.navsource.org.

NavWeaps. "4"/50 (10.2 cm) Marks 7, 8, 9 and 10." Accessed February 19, 2016. www.navweaps.com/Weapons/WNUS_4-50_mk9.htm.

_____. "3"/50 (7.62 cm) Mark 10, 17, 18, 19, 20, 21 and 22." www.navweaps.com/Weapons/WNUS_3-50_mk10-22.htm.

New York City Chapter of the American Guild of Organists. Accessed December 11, 2015. http://www.nycago.org/Organs/NYC/html/ResDeedsEA.html.

New York Yacht Club. "James Gordon Bennett, I Presume." Accessed September 9, 2014. http://www.nyyc.org/about/history-heritage/931-james-gordon-bennett-i-presume.

Nihon, Kaigun. "Sensuikan!" Accessed February 25, 2016. http://www.combinedfleet.com/I-12.htm.

Noble, Dennis L. "The Beach Patrol and Corsair Fleet." *The U.S. Coast Guard in World War II*. Washington, D.C.: Coast Guard Historian's Office, 1992.

Paullin, Charles Oscar. *The Navy of the American Revolution: Its Administration, Its Policy and Its Achievements*. Cleveland: The Burrows Brothers Company, 1906.

PBS. "The American Experience: The Idle Rich." Accessed July 2, 2015. http://www.pbs.org/wgbh/amex/1900/peopleevents/pande28.html.

_____. "Crucible of Empire." Accessed January 3, 2015. http://www.pbs.org/crucible/frames/_film.html.

Proctor, Ben. *William Randolph Hearst: The Early Years, 1863–1910*. New York: Oxford University Press, 1998.

Robinson, Bill. "Great Moments in the America's Cup." *Yachting*, Vol. 154, No. 3, September 1983.

Robinson, John, and George Francis Dow. *The Sailing Ships of New England 1607–1907*. Salem, MA: Marine Research Society, Salem, 1922.

Robinson, William Morrison. *The Confederate Privateers*. New Haven, CT: Yale University Press, 1928.

Rössler, Eberhard, trans. by Harold Erenberg *The U-boat: The Evolution and Technical History of German Submarines*. Annapolis, MD: Naval Institute Press, 1981.

Scheib, Flora K. *History of the Southern Yacht Club*. Gretna, LA: Pelican Publishing Company, 1986.

Shaw, David W. *America's Victory: The Heroic Story of a Team of Ordinary Americans—and How They Won the Greatest Yacht Race Ever.* Dobbs Ferry, NY: Sheridan House, Inc., 2002.

Shipbuilding History. "George S. Lawley & Sons, Neponset MA." Accessed 16 April 2016. http://www.shipbuildinghistory.com/history/shipyards/6yachtsmall/lawley.htm.

_____. "Mathis Yachts." Accessed January 18, 2016. http://www.shipbuildinghistory.com/history/shipyards/6yachtsmall/trumpynj.htm.

_____. "Patrol and Training Craft." Accessed March 5, 2016. http://www.shipbuildinghistory.com/history/smallships/yp.htm.

Shipscribe. Accessed January 11, 2016.

_____. "Small IX: Auxiliary Schooners etc. (1)" http://www.shipscribe.com/usnaux/IX3/IX055.html.

_____. "Small IX: Auxiliary Schooners etc. (3)" http://www.shipscribe.com/usnaux/IX3/IX073.html.

_____. "Small IX: Auxiliary Schooners etc. (4)" http://www.shipscribe.com/usnaux/IX3/IX082.html.

_____. "Small IX: Naval Academy Yachts" http://www.shipscribe.com/usnaux/IX3/IX043.html.

Slave Ship Trouvadore. "Identifying the Remains of Onkahye." Accessed December 23, 2011. http://slaveshiptrouvadore.org/antipiracy-antislavery-patrols/us-schooner-onkahye/indentifying-the-remains-of-onkahye/.

Smith, Michael A. "Passing Power, 90th Anniversary." *Yachting.* Vol. 181, No. 5, May 1997.

Southern Yacht Club. "A Brief History." Accessed May 9, 2016. http://www.southernyachtclub.org/Default.aspx?p=DynamicModule&pageid=384486&ssid=303396&vnf=1.

The Spanish American War Centennial Website. "Alfonso XII." Accessed June 20, 2015. http://www.spanamwar.com/AlfonsoXii.htm.

Spears, John R. *The American Slave-Trade: An Account of Its Origin, Growth and Suppression.* New York: Charles Scribner's Sons, 1900.

"The S.S. *Ben Hecht*: A Jewish Refugee Ship that Changed History." The Free Library. Accessed December 8, 2015. http://www.thefreelibrary.com/The+S.S.+Ben+Hecht%3A+a+Jewish+refugee+ship+that+changed+history.-a0189831885.

Stark, Francis Raymond. *The Abolition of Privateering and the Declaration of Paris.* Studies in History, Economics and Public Law. Vol. VIII, No. 3. New York: Columbia University, 1897.

Stiles, T.J. "The Commodore's Civil War." *Vanderbilt University Magazine.* Accessed September 23, 2014. http://www.vanderbilt.edu/magazines/vanderbilt-magazine/2011/04/the-commodores-civil-war/.

Stillé, Charles J. *History of the United States Sanitary Commission, Being the General Report of its Work During the War of the Rebellion.* Philadelphia: J.B. Lippincott & Co., 1866.

_____. *Memorial of the Great Central Fair for the U.S. Sanitary Commission, Held at Philadelphia June 1864.* Philadelphia: United States Sanitary Commission, 1864.

Texas State Historical Association. "Harriet Lane." Accessed September 8, 2014. http://www.tshaonline.org/handbook/online/articles/qth01.

Thomas, Lowell. *Raiders of the Deep.* Annapolis, MD: Naval Institute Press, 1994.

Toll, Ian W. *Six Frigates.* New York: W.W. Norton, 2006.

Trask, David F. *The War with Spain.* New York: Simon & Schuster, 1981; Bison Books ed. 1991.

Tripp, Rhoda Thomas, ed. *The International Thesaurus of Quotations.* New York: Thomas Y. Crowell Company, 1970.

Tucker, Philip C., III. "The United States Gunboat Harriet Lane." *The Southwestern Historical Quarterly.* Vol. 21, April 1, 1918.

Tucker, Spencer, ed. *American Civil War: The Definitive Encyclopedia and Document Collection.* Santa Barbara, CA: ABC-CLIO, Inc., 2013.

_____. *The Encyclopedia of the Spanish-American and Philippine-American Wars: A Political, Social, and Military History.* Santa Barbara, CA: ABC-CLIO, LLC, 2009.

U-Boat Net. "U-117." Accessed October 29, 2015. http://uboat.net:8080/wwi/boats/index.html?boat=117.

_____. "U-490." Accessed January 19, 2016. http://uboat.net/boats/u490.htm.

_____. "U-566." Accessed January 20, 2016. http://uboat.net/boats/u566.htm.

United States Coast Guard. "Harriet Lane, 1858." Accessed September 7, 2014. http://www.uscg.mil/history/webcutters/harrietlane1858.pdf.

_____. "Hope, 1861." Accessed September 22, 2014. http://www.uscg.mil/history/webcutters/Hope1861.pdf.

_____. "Miami, 1862." accessed September 10, 2014. http://www.uscg.mil/history/webcutters/Miami_1862.pdf.

_____. "Nourmahal." Accessed December 5, 2015. https://www.uscg.mil/history/webcutters/Nourmahal_PG72.pdf.

_____. "U.S. Revenue Cutters and Lighthouse Service in the Civil War." Accessed September 9, 2014. https://www.uscg.mil/history/uscghist/USRMCivilWarChronology.pdf.

Urefsky, Melvin I. *Louis D. Brandeis: A Life.* New York: Random House, 2009.

Valenza, Samuel W., Jr. *The Secret Casino at Red Men's Hall.* Bloomington IN: iUniverse, 2014.

Waddell, J.H. *The Dartmoor Massacre.* New York: W. Abbatt, 1815.

Wallace, William N. *The Macmillan Book of Boating.* New York: The Macmillan Company, 1964.

Welch, Vince. *The Last Voyageur: Amos Burg and the Rivers of the West.* Seattle: Mountaineers Books, 2012.

Whyte, Kenneth. *The Uncrowned King: The Sensational Rise of William Randolph Hearst.* Berkeley, CA: Counterpoint Press, 2009.

Williams, Greg H. *World War II U.S. Navy Vessels in Private Hands: The Boats and Ships Sold and Registered for Commercial and Recreational Purposes Under the American Flag.* Jefferson, NC: McFarland, 2013.

Woram, John. "Human and Cartographic History of the Galápagos Islands." Accessed March 14, 2016. http://www.galapagos.to/SHIPS/INDEX.php.

Wreck Site. "SS *Maizar*." Accessed October 28, 2015. http://wrecksite.eu/wreck.aspx?31320.

Yacht Forums. "Trumpy: El Presidente." Accessed January 18, 2016. http://www.yachtforums.com/feature/trumpy-el-presidente.2408/.

Yacht Pals. "Schooner *Atlantic*." Accessed February 4, 2015. http://www.yachtpals.com/schooner-atlantic-yacht-9173.

Young, Donald J. "Japanese Submarines Prowl the U.S. Pacific Coastline in 1941." History Net. Accessed February 27, 2016. http://www.historynet.com/japanese-submarines-prowl-the-us-pacific-coastline-in-1941.htm.

Zoë, Vivian. "The Slaters Go Round the World." *Connecticut History.* Accessed April 15, 2016. http://connecticuthistory.org/the-slaters-go-round-the-world/.

Index

Numbers in **_bold italics_** indicate pages with illustrations

A (diesel megayacht) 145
USS *A-1* (houseboat) 92, 160
A. Stephan & Sons (builder) 94, 156, 158, 166
Abbott, Mather, professor 87
ABCD naval expansion program 60, 62
Abeking and Rasmussen (builder) 137, 169, 177
abolition of privateering 30, 65; Congress of Paris (1856) 27; *see also* Declaration of Paris
Abraham Rydberg (aux, full-rigged ship) see *Seven Seas*
Abril (diesel yacht) *see* USS *Cythera* (2nd)
An Act for Encouraging the Fixing out of Armed Vessels... 11
An Act for the Better Government of the Navy 21
Adams, Charles Francis, III 57
Adams, John 7, 8, 9, 15
Adams, Secy. of Navy John 58
Adams, John Quincy 61
Adams, Samuel 5
Adams Company (builder) 169, 178
Adela (Confederate schooner) 51
Adelphic (diesel yacht) *see* USS *Tourmaline*
Admiraliteits Jacht **_6_**
CSS *Advance* (blockade runner) **_30_**
USS *Agate* (diesel yacht) 134, 145, 173
Aid (Union sloop) *see Dart*
Aide de Camp (diesel motor yacht) 138, **_138_**, 180
USRC *Aiken see Petrel*
Aker, James W. 97
CSS *Alabama* 2, 32, 44, **_45_**, 46; *see also* USS *Vanderbilt*
USS *Alabama* 2

USS *Alabaster* (diesel yacht) 134, 135, 173
Alamo (diesel yacht) *see* USS *Alabaster*
USS *Albatross* 32, 173
USS *Alcedo* (steam yacht) **_90_**, 91, 160
Alcyon (schooner) 52
Alden, Cdr. James *see* USS *South Carolina*
Alder (diesel yacht) *see* USS *Jamestown*
Alicia (steam yacht) *see* USS *Hornet*
Allan, James 74
Allan, Richard 74
Allen, Charles H. 68
Allen, LCdr. Ezra Griffin *see* USS *Wakiva II*
USS *Almandite* (diesel yacht) 131, 172
Almy (steam yacht) *see* USS *Eagle* (4th)
Alphonso XII (Spanish cruiser) 81
Alphonso XII (Spanish freighter) 75
Alvarado (bark) 32
Amber (cable ship) 104
USS *Amber* (diesel yacht) 145, 174
America (privateer ship) **_16_**, 17
America (racing schooner yacht) 1, 20, 54–56, **_57_**, 58
American Anti-Slavery Convention 29
American Expeditionary Force convoy Group No. 1 101
American Expeditionary Force convoy Group No. 2 101
American imperialism: Beveridge, Albert J., Sen. 83; Bryan, William Jennings 83–84; Cousins, Rep. Robert G. 63–64; Depew, Sen. Chauncey Mitchell 83; Ire-

land, Archbishop John 83; Lodge, Sen. Henry Cabot 83; Schurz, Carl 82
American privateersmen, British treatment of 12
American Yacht List of 1896 2
America's Cup 20, 56, 57, 77, 99, 165
"Anaconda Plan" 58
Andrew Doria (Continental brig) 11
USS *Anemone IV* (aux. schooner yacht) 92
Anglesey, Lord (re. yacht *America*) 55
USS *Annapolis* (gunboat) 78
Annie B. (schooner) 41
Annual List of Merchant Vessels of the U.S., 1858 and 1860 2
Antelope (British blockade runner) 57
Anton Brunn (diesel yacht) *see* USS *Williamsburg*
USS *Aphrodite* (steam yacht) 101, 109, 160
Araner, (diesel aux. yacht) 139, 178
USS *Aramis* (diesel yacht) 96, 160
Aras II (diesel yacht) *see* USS *Williamsburg*
USS *Arcturus see* USS *Artemis* (steam yacht)
USS *Ardent* 132
Argosy (diesel yacht) *see* USS *Cythera* (2nd)
USS *Argus* (diesel yacht) 132, 145, 172
USS *Artemis* (steam yacht) 102–104, 161
USS *Arthur see Corypheus*
Arthur, Pres. Chester Alan 60
ASDIC 96
Ashkhabad (Soviet tanker) 103
Aspinwall, William H. 37

209

Astor, William Vincent 108, 109, 118, 119, 165, 171
Athero II (diesel yacht) *see* USS *Jade*
USS *Atlantic II* (steam aux. yacht) **99**, 100, 161
Atlantic Iron Works (builder) 68, 151
Au Revoir (steam yacht) 66
auxiliary cruisers conversion (1897) 63, 66, 73
USS *Azurlite* (diesel yacht) 131, 172

Baker, George F. 123, 171, 174
Baker, George F., Jr. 109, 162
Baker, Capt. T. Harrison *see Savannah* (privateer)
Baldwin, Cdr. Charles H. *see* USS *Vanderbilt*
Baletti, Edward 134, 177
Baletti, William B. 133, 176
Balkan wars 80, 155
Bamberg (British merchantman) 51
Barbary pirates 13, 14
Bath Iron Works (builder) 82, 121, 125, 128, 154, 158, 160, 162, 163, 167–169, 171–177, 180
HMS *Basilisk* 103, 164
Battle of Santiago, Cuba 66, 77, 87
battleship debate 85
USS *Bayocean* (diesel yacht) **95**, 161
Beary, RAdm. Donald B. *see* USS *Williamsburg*
Beaufort Fish Scrap and Oil Co. 99, 165
USS *Beaumont* (diesel yacht) 117, 145, 171
Beauregard, Pierre G.T., Brig-Gen. 28
SS *Ben Hecht* 125, 172; *see also* USS *Cythera* (2nd)
Bennett, James Gordon 33, 34
Bennett, James Gordon, Jr. 34, 35
Benson, LCdr. Howard H.J. *see* USS *Noma*
Bergson Group 125
Bergsund M.V. Atkieb (builder) 139, 169, 178
Bernice (steam yacht) *see* USS *Mary Alice*
Berryman, Lt. Otway H. 20, 21; *see also Onkahye*
Berson, Leo 137, 178
Betts, Samuel R., Judge 46, 47, 52
Bigelow, Albert S. 82
Biological Survey Commission 93

Black Douglas (diesel aux. yacht) 145, 174, 176
Black Warrior (American packet) 62
Blanchard, Frank Leroy 69
Bland, Schuyler Otis, Rep. 115
Blau, Lt. Thomas, USNRF 102
blockade requirement 27, 32, 46
blockade results, Civil War 58
Blue Dolphin (diesel aux. yacht) 142, 145, 178
Blue Water (steam yacht) *see* USS *Wenonah*
Boniland, James *see Peterhoff*
Bonita (schooner yacht) 25
Borden, Matthew Chaloner Durfee 72, 79, 155, 166
Borgnine, GM 1c. Ernest 127, 173
Boston Floating Hospital 99
Boston Tea Party 5–6
Bowlin, James B., U.S. Special Commissioner 37
Breton Patrol Squadron 103, 104
Brezen (Norwegian ship) 76
British and American naval strength, 1776 9
British Tea Act 5
Broadfoot Iron Works 81
USS *Brooklyn* (battleship) 68
Brown, Capt. Dick *see America* (racing schooner yacht)
Brown, John 28
Brown, Rhode Island District Judge 26
Browning, Acting Volunteer Lt. Charles H. *see* USS *Virginia*
USS *Buccaneer* (steam yacht) 68, 69, 151
Buchanan, Pres. James 27, 37, 62
Burnham, Lamont G., Esq. 99
Burriel, Juan, Gen. 62
USS *Bushnell* 109
Bushnell, David 3, 12, 85
Butler, Benjamin F., MajGen. 35, 52, 53, 57
USS *Butte see* USS *Mayflower* (steam yacht)
"buy a motor boat" 113

Cadwallader, Emily Roebling 114, 122, 124, 171, 173
USS *Calhoun see Corypheus*
USS *California* (steam yacht) *see* USS *Hauoli*
Calumet see USS *Tourist* (steam yacht)
Camargo (diesel yacht) 132, 173
Camas Meadows (tanker) 123

Cambriona (diesel yacht) *see* USS *Crystal*
Cameron, Secy. of War Simon 54
Camilla see America (racing schooner yacht)
Canaris, KptLt. Wilhelm *see* SM U-34
Candace (steam yacht) *see* USS *Remlik*
Capes, William (builder) 19, 20
USS *Captor* (diesel trawler) 132, 133
USS *Carnelian* (diesel yacht) 126, 172
Carola (diesel yacht) *see* USS *Beaumont*
Caroline (diesel yacht) *see* USS *Hilo*
Cassatt, Joseph Gardner 25, 75
Cecil B. DeMille Productions 139, 178
Cecilia see Dart
Central Intelligence Agency 135, 136
HM Frigate *Cerberus* 13
Chalena (diesel yacht) *see* USS *Beaumont*
Chandler, Secy. of Navy William E. 59, 60
Charles L. Seabury Co. (builder) 72, 136, 151, 154, 158, 160, 162–167, 169
Charter Oak (schooner) 22
Chase, M.S., Acting Master *see* USS *Hope*
Chase, Secy. of Treasury Salmon P. 34, 39
Chase, Samuel 8
Chastain, E. Artimas, CCM. *see* USS *Nokomis*
Chesapeake (screw steamer) 40
US Frigate *Chesapeake* and HMS *Leopard* incident 15
HMS *Chieftan* 125
Chinese smuggling 25, 26
Chisholm, Hugh J. 120, 172
Chris-Craft (builder) 112
USS *Christabel* (steam yacht) 105, 108, 161
C.J. Mare & Co. (builder) 45
Clarendon, Lord 27
Cleveland Shipbuilding Co. 100, 159, 167
Coast Guard Reserve 112, 115
coastal patrol yacht (PYc) 117, 132, 134
Coastal Picket Patrol 115, 117
Cohan, George M. 100
Colby, Herbert F. 25, 26
Colleen (diesel yacht) *see* USS *Aide de Camp*

Index

Columbia (sail racing yacht) 66
Columbia (steam yacht) *see* USS *Wasp* (7th)
Condor (gasoline aux. yacht) *see* *Wimbee*
Confederate commerce raiders 32
Congress of Paris 27
Continental Navy, proposed creation of: Adams, John 7, 8, 9; Chase, Samuel 8; Deane, Silas 8, 9; Gadsden, Christopher 8; Langdon, John 9; Rutledge, John 7; Ward, Samuel 7
Cooke, Capt. A.P. 62, 63
Cooke, Gov. Nicholas 7
Coolidge, Amory 142, 178
Coolidge, Pres. Calvin 111
Cooper, Oliver P., CGM. *see* USS *Wakiva II*
Copely, Ira C. 131, 172
USS *Coral* (diesel yacht) 124, 172
Corrie, William C. 22–24
USS *Corsair* (steam yacht) *see* *Corsair III*
Corsair Fleet 115
Corsair II (steam yacht) 66, **67**; *see also* USS *Gloucester*
Corsair III (steam yacht) 101
Corsair IV (turbo-electric yacht) 114
Corypheus (schooner yacht) 2, 48, 49
Court of Claims 21, 110
Cousins, Robert G. 63, 64, 82
Coxetter, Louis M. 31, 32
Cramp's Shipyards 55
Craven, Lt. Tunis Augustus *see* USS *Crusader*
Creelman, James 66, 68
Cristina (steam yacht) *see* USS *Artemis*
Crocker, Charles H. 96, 167
Crown Colony of Rhode Island and Providence Plantations 6, 7
Crowninshield family 16–17, 58
Crucis (tug) 104
USS *Crusader* 40, 41
Cudahy, Joseph M. 2, 136–137, 180
Curtis, Cyrus 131, 160, 173
USS *Crystal* (diesel yacht) 124, 131, 172
USS *Cythera* (1st) (steam yacht) 102, 103, **104**, 124, 161, 172
USS *Cythera* (2nd) (diesel yacht) 124, **125**, 172

Dabney, Thomas Smith 35
Daniels, Secy. of Navy Josephus 86, 92; aboard USS *Sylph* **89**
Dart (schooner yacht) 48
"Dartmoor Massacre" 12
USS *Dauntless* (steam yacht) 119, 120, 145, 171
David Crockett (blockade runner) 56
Davidson, H.P. 166
Davies, Joseph E. 141, 180
Davis, Confederate Pres. Jefferson 28
Day, Thomas Fleming 88
Deane (privateer ship) 9
Deane, Silas 8, 9
de Blaquiere, Lord John 56
Decie, Henry Edward 56
Decker, Karl 68
Declaration of Independence, naval strength at 9
Declaration of Paris (Congress of Paris) 27, 28–29, 46, 65
Deeds, Edward A. 126, 173
de Graff, Johannes (governor of Dutch Antilles) 11
USS *De Grasse* (steam turbine yacht) 93, 136, 161, 181
de la Cámara, Spanish Adm. Manuel 68
Delphine (steam yacht) 119, 175; *see also* USS *Dauntless*
Denbigh (blockade runner) *see* *Gertrude*
Denison, Acting Collector of Customs George S. 53
depth charge 103, 105, 106, **107**, 108, 116–118, 127, 141
destruction of Confederate privateer *Petrel* **31**
Dewey, Cdr. George 60, 68
Diggs, Lt. John T. *see* *Lanikai*
Diver (sail racing yacht) 20
Doctor Brinkley (diesel yacht) *see* USS *Jade*
Dodge, Anna 119
Dodge, Horace Elgin 105, 119, 164, 171, 175
dog's birthday dinner *see* "The Gilded Age"
USS *Dolphin* 32
USS *Dolphin* (2nd) 60
Don Jorge Juan (Spanish cruiser) 78
Dorchester Heights 6
Dorothea (steam yacht) 73, 151, 161
Dows, David, Jr. 77, 153
drawbacks of yacht conversion 103, 127
Drexel, George W.C. 91, 160
Durell, Judge 54

HMS *Eagle* (3rd rate ship-of-the-line) 12, 85
USS *Eagle* (4th) 79, 151
USS *Eagle* (7th) *see* USS *Captor* (diesel trawler, Q-ship)
Earhart, Amelia 119
East Gulf Blockading Squadron 41
Eco (blockade runner) *see* *Gertrude*
economy between the world wars 87, 112–114
Echo see Jefferson Davis (Confederate brig)
Edison, Thomas Alva 96, 161
USS *Edithena* (gasoline yacht) 136, 180
Edlu II (Coast Guard yawl) 117
Edwards, RAdm. Richard S. *see* USS *Vixen*
El Boughaz (diesel aux. schooner) *see* *Black Douglas*
Eldridge, Roswell 134, 177
Eleanor (steam aux. yacht) 109, 162
USS *Elfrida* (steam yacht) 94, 152, 162
USS *Ella and Annie* (gunboat) 40
Ellen (schooner) *see* *Gertrude*
Elliot Richie *see* *Harriet Lane*
El Presidente (diesel yacht) 145, 180; *see also Innisfail* (2nd)
Elsie Fenimore (diesel aux. yatch) *see* USS *John M. Howard*
Eliza Hayward (sailing sloop) 92, 162
Elverson, James, Jr. 124
USS *Emerald* (steam yacht) *see* *Fairie*
USS *Emerald* (2nd) (steam yacht) 97, 162
Emma Tuttle (schooner) 33
Emrose (steam yacht) *see* USS *Emerald* (2nd)
Enchantress (schooner) 32
Entropy (diesel yacht) *see* USS *Turquoise*
envoys to Paris: Gerry, Marshall, Pinckney (1796) 15
Eugenia (steam yacht) *see* USS *Siren* (2nd)
Eugenia (steam yacht) *see* USS *Margaret*
Ex-German Submarine Expeditionary Force 109
SS *Exodus* 81, 137, 154
Ezilda (schooner) 41

Fairie (steam yacht) 54, 55
Faith (diesel aux. yacht) *see* *Araner*
Farragut, RAdm. David G. 2, 38, 48, 53

feint against Adm. de la Cámara's Spanish fleet 68
USS *Felicia* (steam yacht) 98, 99, 162
Fessenden, Reginald A. 96
Fiesta II (diesel yacht) *see* USS *Alabaster*
Firefly (steam yacht) 37
Firenza (diesel yacht) *see* USS *Girasol*
Fish, Marion "Mamie" Graves Anton 87, 88
Fisher, Fred J. 128, 173
Fiske, Cdr. Bradley A. 85
Flagler, Henry Morrison 77, 153
Fleetwing (sailing yacht) 35
Fleischmann, Julius 132, 173
Fleischmann, Max C. 132, 172, 174
Fleming and Ferguson (builder) 74, 152, 159, 168
Fletcher, LCdr. Frank Jack *see* USS *Margaret*
USS *Florence* (steam yacht) 97, 162
CSS *Florida* 32
Flying Squadron 44, 80, 155
Flynn, Errol 139, 178
Fontleroy, Lieutenant *see* *Firefly*
Foote, Commodore 33
Ford, Henry 112, 124, 134, 166, 172, 177
Ford, John 139, 178
Ford, William G. 53
The Forgotten Man 114
Forstmann, Julius 113, 119, 172
Fort Gadsden 18
Fort Sumter 28, 30, 33, 38, 40, 56, 59
Foster, Charles Henry Wheelwright 57, 58
Fowler, F.S. 96, 167
Franklin (Continental schooner) **8**
Franklin (Norwegian freighter) 76
USS *Free Lance* (steam yacht) **75**, 152; petty officers with Gatling gun **76**
Freedom (gasoline aux. schooner) 138, 177
SS *Frisia* 98
Frolic (schooner yacht) 25, 26, 152
USS *Frolic II* (ex–CSS *Advance*) **30**
Furman, Betty May 127
Furman, Robert van Guysling 127

Gadsden, Christopher 8
USS *Galaxy* (diesel yacht) 138, 177

Gallatin, Frederic 79, 151
Gardner, William (naval ready reserve) 63
Garrick, Jacob 32
Gaspé (British armed schooner) 7
USS *Gem* (steam yacht) 96, 162, 176
General Worth (schooner) 52
Geoanna (diesel aux. yacht) 138, 178
George Lawley and Son (builder) 93, 126, 127, 132, 133, 138, 153, 158, 160–162, 165, 168, 169, 173, 175–181
Georgiana (British blockade runner) 56
Gerlach, OLt. Wilhelm *see* U-490
Gertrude (British blockade runner) 47
USS *Get There* (58' motor boat) **92, 93**, 162
"The Gilded Age" 87, 88
Gimcrack (sail racing yacht) 20, **21**
Gipsey (also *Gypsy*) (schooner yacht) 2, 50, 52
USS *Girasol* (diesel yacht) 131, 172
Glair, Frank B. 71
USS *Gloucester* 66, **67**, 152, 162; *see also* *Corsair II*
Goelet, Ogden 80, 154; start of Goelet Cup Race **61**
Goldsborough, Commodore Louis *see* USS *Vanderbilt*
Goldsborough, Lt. J.R. *see* *Wave*
Gould, Howard 69, 164
Grace (diesel yacht) 145; *see also* USS *Leader*
Grean, Charlie, soundman 116, 117
Great Lakes Engine Works (builder) 119, 169, 171, 176, 177
Great White Fleet 109, 157, 168
Greek War Relief Association 127, 173
USS *Greer* (destroyer) 134, 175
Gubelmann, William S. 139, 178
USS *Guinevere* (diesel-electric aux. schooner) 139, 140, 178
Gulf Blockading Squadron 41, 48, 52
SS *Gussie* (troop ship) 78

Hagerty, John J. 135
Haida G. (diesel yacht) *see* USS *Argus*
Happy Days (diesel yacht) *see* USS *Almandite*

Haralton, Lt., USN 29
Hardegen, KptLt. Reinhard *see* U-123
Hardi Biaou (diesel aux. schooner) *see* *Valor*
Harkness, Lamon Vanderburgh 104, 167
Harkness, William L. 103, 161, 172
Harlan & Hollingsworth (builder) 69, 77, 94, 151–153, 158, 162, 164
USRC *Harriet Lane* (side-wheel steamer) 22, 37, **38**, 39, 48
Harriman, Mary 100, 166
Hartford Convention 29
Hatuey (steam yacht) *see* *Pantooset*
M/V *Harvard* *see* USS *Captor* (diesel trawler)
USS *Harvard* *see* *Eleanor* (steam aux. yacht)
Haskell, Harry Garner 127, 173
USS *Hauoli* (steam yacht) 96, 161, 163
USS *Hawk* **74**, 75, 152; *see also* *Hermione* (steam yacht)
Hawkins, Thomas 22
Hawthorne, Nathaniel 5
Hawthorne and Co. (builder) 75, 155, 158
Hay, Secy. of State John 84
Hazard, LCdr. Stanton L. *see* USS *Artemis*
Hearst, William Randolph 60, 66, 68, 69, 151
Hecht, Ben 125
Helm, Lt. James M. *see* USS *Hornet*
Helvetia (3-mast schooner) 92, 163
Hemingway, Ernest 116
USRC *Henrietta* (sailing yacht) **34**, 35
USS *Hermes* *see* *Lanikai* (diesel aux. yacht)
Hermione (steam yacht) **74**, 152; *see also* USS *Hawk*
Herreshoff, N.G. (builder) 72, 158, 162, 165, 166, 169, 176, 177, 179
SS *H.F. Dimock* 123
HM Submarine *H-4* 108
Hiawatha (steam yacht) 66
Hi-Esmare (diesel yacht) *see* USS *Niagara*
Highland Light (gasoline aux. sloop) 138, 177
USS *Hilo* 117, 121, 171
Hinman, Elisha, Esq. 9
USS *Hist* (steam yacht) **65**, 77, 153; gunner at 37mm gun **78**

Index

CSS *H.L. Hunley* 51, 85
Hodgdon Brothers (builder) 135, 169, 177, 180
Hood, Lt. J. *see* USS *Hawk*
"Hooligan Navy" 16, 115, ***116***, 117
Hoover, Pres. Herbert 58, 81, 111
USRC (also USS) *Hope* (sailing yacht) 33
Hope (British transport) 7, 8
Hopkinson, Francis 13
USS *Hornet* (4th) (steam yacht) 77, 153
Hornkohl, KptLt. Hans *see* U-566
USS *Housatonic* 85
Howell, 1st Lt. Charles Frederick *see* USS *Artemis*
Hull No. 295 (steam yacht) *see* USS *Sylph*
SS *Hundvaago* 107
Hunley, Horace Lawson 51, 85
USS *Huntsville* 48
Hussar V (diesel aux. yacht) *see* *Sea Cloud*
Hutchins, Horace A. 76, 156
Hutton, Edward Francis 1, 114, 141
hydrophones 91, 117, 122; K-Tubes 96
Hyper-Sub (diesel submarine yacht) 145

I-12 (Japanese submarine) 132
I-17 (Japanese submarine) 128
Idalia (steam yacht) *see* USS *Palace*
Illawarra (steam yacht) 66, 154, 163
Imelda (diesel aux. yacht) ***136***
USS *Impetuous* (diesel yacht) 134, 166, 175
Indiana Salvage Company 75
Ingersoll, Adm. Royal E. *see* USS *Vixen*
SS *Ingleside* 103
Ingram, Adm. Jonas H. *see* USS *Vixen*
Innisfail (2nd) (diesel yacht) 2, 136, 137, 180
internal combustion propulsion 88
USS *Iowa* (battleship) 68
Irmay (diesel aux. yacht) *see* *Imelda*
USS *Isabel* (steam turbine yacht) 101, 111, 124, 128, ***129***, 130, 131, 163, 172
USS *Itty E* (25' motor boat) 92, 163
Ituna (steam yacht) 66, 153
Ives, Thomas P. 33

J. & G. Thomson (builder) 80, 154
jacht schepen 1, 5, ***6***
Jackson, Pres. Andrew 19
USS *Jade* (diesel yacht) 126, 173
Jaluit Gesellschaft 93, 163
USS *Jamestown* (sloop-of-war) 32
USS *Jamestown* (2nd) (diesel yacht) 121, 122, ***123***, 171
Jarman, Stephen *see* *Peterhoff*
Jay Treaty (1794) 14
Jefferson (privateer yacht) 17
Jefferson Davis (Confederate brig) 31, 32
Jeremiah Simonson (builder) 43
Joanna Ward (Confederate schooner) 38
John A. Johnson (Liberty Ship) 132
John Carver (US Army ship) 32
USS *John M. Howard* (diesel aux. ketch) 138, 179
John N. Robbins (builder) 79
John Roach & Co. (builder) 71, 76, 151, 156, 158, 160, 164
John Welsh (brig) 32
Johnson, Pres. Andrew 73
Johnson, Col. John D. 22
Johnson, Eldridge H. 121, 171
Johnson, Eldridge R.F. 138, 179
Johnson, LCdr. L.C. *see* USS *Remlik*
Jones, Hugh C. 99
Joseph (civilian brig) 31
Juanita (CIA yacht) *see* *Imelda*
Judson, Ross W. 125
USS *Juniata* (sloop-of-war) 60
Junkins, E.A. 26

Kaiser Cup scandal 99, 100, 161
Karl Decker incident 68
Kaufman, RAdm. James L. *see* USS *Williamsburg*
USS *Kearsarge* (sloop-of-war) 45
Kehew, Capt. John *see* *Jefferson* (privateer yacht)
Kehtoh (steam yacht) *see* USS *Tourist*
Kellogg-Briand Pact 114
Kelly, Tom 140
Kennedy, Cdr. Duncan *see* USS *Mayflower*
Kennedy Marine Engine Co. 139
King, Adm. Ernest J. *see* USS *Vixen*
Kirkpatrick, EM 2c Charles E. 105

Kittredge, Lt. J.W. *see* *Corypheus*
Knox, General 5
Krupp Germaniawerft (builder) 118, 122, 141, 169, 171, 172, 174–176, 179, 180
Kudo, Cdr. Kaneo *see* I-12 (Japanese submarine)
Kyknos (diesel yacht) *see* USS *Tourmaline*

Ladd, William F. 134, 173
Ladew, Joseeph Harvey, Sr. 77, 78, 156, 167
Lady Godiva (steam yacht) *see* USS *Mohican*
Lady Marchant (steam yacht) 39; *see also* USRC *Miami*
Laird Brothers (builder) 96, 159, 164
Lamar, Charles A. L. 22–25
Lanahan, Wallace F. 138, 177
Langdon, John 9
Langevin, Paul 96
Lanikai (diesel aux. yacht) 93, 94, ***130***, 131, 163
Lanikai Fish Company 93
Launburg, OLtzS. 108
Laurens, slaver barque (also *Lawrence*) 20, 21
Laverock (British racing yacht) 55, 56
Lavinia *see* *Harriet Lane*
Lawrence, William, Bishop *see* "The Gilded Age"
Lea, LCdr. Edward 38
USS *Leader* (diesel yacht) 145, 175
Leary, Arthur 39
Lee, Sgt. Ezra *see* *Turtle*
Leeds, Willam B. 121, 165, 171
Lehnmann, John C. 25–26
Letters of Marque and Reprisal 9, 10, 28, 30, 31; drawbacks 10; effectiveness 10, 11, 17
USS *Leyden* (tug) 78
Lincoln, Pres. Abraham: aboard USS *Monitor* 39; calls up troops 28; ends privateering 30; modernizing and expanding the Navy 32–33, 34, 40, 43, 54; on rebellion (1848) 29
Livermore, Jesse Lauriston 126, 173
Long, Secy. of Navy John Davis 68
Lopez, Carlos Antonio 37
Lorillard, Pierre, Jr. 35
Lotosland (diesel yacht) *see* USS *Siren* (3rd)
Lougheed, Victor 85
RMS *Lusitania* 85

Luzon Stevedoring Company 94, 130
USS *Lydonia* (steam yacht) 102, 103, 163, 164
Lyndonia (diesel yacht) *see* USS *Southern Seas*
Lyons, Lord Richard 41, 47

MacKenzie, CBM. John 106, 165
MacKenzie, Cdr. M.R.S *see* USS *Mayflower*
Maclay, William, Senator against a standing navy 13
Maennale, Lt. Frederick William *see* USS *Artemis*
Maha (diesel yacht) *see* USS *Peridot*
Mahan, Capt. Alfred Thayer: battleship debate 85; importance of Cuba and Panama 60, 61
USS *Maine* (armored cruiser) 60, 63, 66, 81
SS *Maizar* 103
Makaroff, Vadim Stefan 137, 177
Malay II (steam yacht) *see* USS *Palace*
SS *Malla* (steam yacht) *see* USS *Mayflower*
Mallory, Confederate Secy. of Navy Stephen R. 29
Malloy, RAdm. Thomas, USCG 115
Manville, Mrs. H. Edward 122
USS *Maratanza see* CSS *Teaser*
USS *Marcasite* (diesel yacht) *see Camargo*
Marcy, Secy. of State William L. 27; plan to annex Cuba 62
USS *Margaret* (steam yacht) 101, *102*, 103, 164
Maria (sail racing yacht) 20
Marietta (yacht) 66, 154
Mariner II (diesel yacht) *see Aide de Camp*
Marix, LCdr. Adolph *see* USS *Scorpion*
Marjorie (steam yacht) *see* USS *Margaret*
Marks, Arthur Hudson 96, 160
Marryat, Capt. Frederick, RN 35, 36
Marshall, Wilson 99, 100
Martha's Vineyard (gasoline motor yacht) 138, 180
USS *Mary Alice* (steam yacht) 98, 164
Mary Baker (sloop yacht) 52
Mary E. Thompson (brig) 32
Mary Goodell (ship) 32

USS *Mason* (destroyer) 141
Mason, Hobbs & Co. 40
Massachusetts Government Act 6
Mathis-Trumpy Boatbuilding Co. 136
Mathis Yacht Building Co. 134, 169
USS *May* (steam yacht) 102, 164
Mayflower (British freighter) 81
USS *Mayflower* (steam yacht) *64*, 81, 111, 154; President T. Roosevelt aboard *72*
McCullough, LCdr. R.P. *see* USS *Lydonia*
McCully, RAdm. N.A. *see* USS *Yankton*
McDonald, Eugene F., Jr. 124, 173
McFarland, W.L. 137
McKean, Flag Officer William W. *see* USS *Niagara* (screw frigate)
McKean, Thomas 73, 151, 161
McKinley, William 64, 65, 68, 71
Medal of Honor 105–106, 165
Medford (blockade runner) 57
HMS *Medusa* (paddle steamer) 23
Mellon, William 131, 172
Melville, Wilbert 96
USS *Merrimac see* CSS *Virginia*
Mervine, Flag Officer William *see* USS *South Carolina*
SS *Messidor* 103
USRC *Miami* 2, 39, 40; *see also Lady Marchant*
USS *Miami* 2, 36, 37
mine warfare 12, 13, 94, 109, 126
Minett, Lt. Henry *see* USS *Viking*
miscellaneous unclassified (IX) 117, 137
Miss Ann (diesel yacht) *see* USS *Aquamarine*
Mitchel, Lt. Ormsby M. *see* USS *Plymouth*
Mizpah, USS (diesel yacht) 124, 173
Moana (diesel yacht) *see* USS *Hilo*
USS *Mohican* (steam yacht) 96, 164
USS *Monitor* 39, 43
Monroe Doctrine 61
Montgomery, R.H. 35
USS *Monticello see Peterhoff*
USS *Moonstone* (diesel yacht) 134, 175

Moore, Harrison B. 66
INS *Mooz see* USS *Cythera* (2nd)
Morgan, J. Pierpont 2, 66, 87, 101, 114, 152, 161, 162
Morgan/Satterlee wedding 87
Morison, Capt. Samuel Eliot 143
Mortar Flotilla at Key West 38
Morton, Sterling 138, 177
Mosquito Fleet (1812) 16
motor boats for general public 112, 114
Mount Rainier Council of the Boy Scouts 138
Mugford, Capt. James *8*
Muravieff, Count 84
Murphy, Walter P. 127, 173
Mystic (diesel aux. yacht) *see* USS *Imelda*

Nakhoda (diesel yacht) *see* USS *Zircon*
Naparo (turbo-electric yacht) *see* USS *St. Augustine*
Nashville (merchant steamer) 38
Naval Appropriations Act: August 1916 89; March 1883 60; May 1916 90
Naval Coast Defense Reserve 86, 87
naval contraction 59, 60
naval expansion 59, 88, 89, 114, 115
naval militia 73, 74
Naval Reserve 62, 63, 73
Navy Cross 97, 102, 103, 105
Navy, state of in 1830 19
Neafie and Levy (builder) 55, 66, 152, 158, 162, 167
need for speed 112
USS *New London* (screw steamer) 52
New York Yacht Club 5, 20, 23, *24*, 25, 33, 55, 88
Newport News Shipbuilding & Dry Dock Co. 123, 169, 171, 173, 174
USS *Niagara* (diesel yacht) 121, 122, 171
USS *Niagara* (screw frigate) 48, 52
USS *Niagara* (steam aux. yacht) *69*, 70, 164; Welte Philharmonic pipe organ *71*
Nickels, Lt. J.F. *see* USS *Ella and Annie*
Nimitz, LCdr. Chester W. *see* USS *Aramis*
Niobe (British sloop of war) 62
Noe-Daquy (blockade ruunner) *see* USS *Virginia*

Index

USS *Nokomis* (steam yacht) 105, *106*, 111, 164
USS *Noma* (steam yacht) *107*, 108, 165
North Atlantic Squadron Blockading Cuba 46, 75, 76, 77, 79, 80, 81, 151- 157
North Star (steam yacht) 43, 44
Northern secession movement (1814–1859) 29
Norton, Surveyor of the Port S.S. 22
USS *Nourmahal* (diesel yacht) 117, *118*, 119, 171
Nutt, Cdr. David C. 142

USS O-13 98
SSS *Odyssey* (diesel aux. yawl) *see* USS *Saluda*
Ohio (diesel yacht) *see* USS *Turquoise*
Olson, Thomas, CBM. 105
Oneta (steam yacht) *see* USS *Mary Alice*
Onkahye (sailing yacht) 18, 19, 20, 21, 22
USS *Onward* (steam yacht) 109, 165
Operation Drumbeat 115, 128
USS *Oregon* (armored cruiser) 68
Orion (diesel yacht) *see* USS *Vixen*
Osgood, Franklin 35
Osgood, George 35
Ostend Manifesto (1854) 62
USS *Ottawa* 56

Pacific Squadron, Commodore John Roberts 47
Packer & Watson 41
USS *Palace* (steam yacht) 133, 134, 176
Palmerston, Lord 14, 46
USS *Panay* (gunboat) 114
Pantooset (steam yacht) 82
Paragon (diesel yacht) *see* USS *Impetuous*
Parish, Frank P. 81
Park, Trenor Luther 100
Pass Christian Hotel 35
Patrol (steam aux. yacht) *see* USS *Rainier*
patrol gunboat (PG) 117
patrol yacht (PY) 124
USS *Pawnee* (steam yacht) 94, 165
Payne, Col. Oliver Hazard 101, 160
USS PC-1264 141
Penelope (steam yacht) *see* USS *Yankton*

USS *Peridot* 145, 176
Perkins, Robert 96, 164
Perry (USN brig) 31
Perry, CSA Capt. William 31
Peterhoff (side-wheel steamer) 44, 45, *46*
Peterhoff Affair 45–47
Petrel (privateer schooner) *31*, 37
Picket (US steamer) 33
Pierce, Pres. Franklin 27, 62
Pierce, Henry Lillie 74, 152
Pierce, H.M. 138
Pilar (cabin cruiser) 116
Pilgrim (sloop yacht) 50, *98*, 99, 165
Pitcher, Henry Sotheby 56
Placida (diesel yacht) *see* USS *Ruby*
USS *Plymouth* (diesel yacht) 117, 122–123
Poinsettia (diesel yacht) *see* *Aide de Camp*
Pompey see *America* (privateer)
Porter, Capt. David Dixon 38
Porterfield, Cdr. Lewis B. *see* USS *Venetia*
Post, Marjorie Merriweather 141
post Great War economy: boom 87, 88, 112, 113; bust 113, 114
USS *Potomac* (presidential yacht) *see* USS *Williamsburg*
Price, Cdr. Cicero *see* USS *Huntsville*
USS *Primrose* 3, 53
Prince, Frederick Henry 139
Princess Royal (blockade runner) 56
privateer ship *Deane* 9
Providence see sloop *Katy*
Pulitzer, Joseph 60, 66
Pusey & Jones (builder) 105, 122, 124, 126, 128, 154, 158, 160–166, 169, 171–174, 176, 177

Q-Ship *91*, 133, 163, 165
Quadruple Alliance (1823) 61
quasi war with France (1798) 15
Quickstep (steam yacht) *see* USS *Florence*

Racer (sloop) 33
USS *Rainier* (steam aux. yacht) 95, 165
USS *Rambler* (steam yacht) 2, 101, 103, 165
Ramfis (diesel yacht) *see* *Camargo*

Ranger (diesel yacht) *see* *Aide de Camp*
Ranger (sloop) 41
Ranley (diesel yacht) *see* USS *Alabaster*
Ratsey's yard (builder) 2
Read, Lieutenant, USN *see* USS *New London*
Rebecca (racing sloop) 33, 34
recognition of American Flag: *Andrew Doria* (brig) 11; Sultan of Morocco 11; Treaty of Amity and Commerce, and Treaty of Alliance 12
Redmond, J.L. 93, 136, 161, 181
Regina Maris *see* USS *Vixen*
USS *Reid* (destroyer) 101
Rellimpa (diesel yacht) *see* USS *Alabaster*
USS *Remlik* (steam yacht) 106, 107
Republican Party platform, 1908 (re: Navy) 85
Resolute (racing yacht) 57
Restless (steam yacht) 66, 155
Reveler (diesel yacht) *see* USS *Beaumont*
Richard Vaux (sloop yacht) 3, 53
Robert H. McCurdy (4-mast schooner) *91*, 92, 165
Robert Steele & Co. (builder) 39
SS *Robin Moor* 115
Robinson, John G. 50–53
Robinson, Lt. John M. *see* USS *Siren* (2nd) (steam yacht)
USS *Rockford* 132
Rockwood, Capt. 50
Roland von Bremen (gasoline aux. yacht) *see* *Wimbee*
Ronaele (diesel yacht) *see* USS *Alabaster*
Roosevelt, Elliott 125
Roosevelt, Pres. Franklin Delano 86, 114, 119, 129, 138
Roosevelt, Kermit 119
Roosevelt, Pres. Theodore 64, 71, *72*, 81, 87
HM Frigate *Rose* 6
Rose, KpLt. Hans *see* U-53
Rosenberg, Joseph 139
Rouss, Peter Winchester 88, 168
Rowland, W.J. 22
USS *Ruby* (diesel yacht) 127, 173
rum running 109, 135, 180
Rust, Cdr. Armistead *see* USS *Hist*
SS *Rutherglen* 103
Rutledge, John 7–8
Rynders, U.S. Marshall Isaiah 22

USS *Sachem* (screw steamer) 48, 165, 176
USS *St. Augustine* (turbo-electric yacht) 123, 171
St. Lawrence (US Frigate) *31*
USS *Saluda* (diesel aux. yacht) 138, 145, 179
Salvage, Samuel Agar 138, 180
Sampson, RAdm. William T. 68, 75, 81
USS *San Bernardino* (diesel yacht) 118, 171
Santa Clara (brig) 32
Santa Maria del Mare (diesel yacht) *see* USS *Cythera* (2nd)
Santiago Apostal (Spanish sloop) 81
Santo Domingo (Spanish freighter) 79
CSS *Savannah* (ironclad) 37
Savannah (privateer) *28*, 31
Savarona (diesel yacht) *see* USS *Mizpah*
Savarona II (diesel yacht) *see* USS *Jamestown*
Savarona III (diesel yacht) 114
Saxon Affair *see* USS *Vanderbilt*
Scattergood, S.S. 41
USS *Scorpion* (steam yacht) *79*, 80, 155; *see also Sovereign*
Scott, LtGen. Winfield 58
Scripps, Edward Willys 127, 173, 175
USS *Sea Cloud* (diesel aux. yacht) 1, 114, 132, ***140***, 141, ***142***, 145, 180
Seaward (diesel aux. yacht) 139, 178
Seminole Wars 18, 19
Semmes, Capt. Rafael *see* CSS *Alabama*
Sendai (Japanese cruiser) 135
USS *Seneca* (steam yacht)
Seven Seas (aux. full-rigged ship) 139, 178
Seventeen (diesel yacht) *see* USS *Carnelian*
Seward, Secy. of State William H. 28, 34, 41, 150
Shackford, W.G. 69
Shark (Union sloop) *see Dart*
CSS *Shenandoah* 32
Shoemaker, LCdr. Harry E. *see* USS *Isabel*
Shortland, Captain 12
Shuttle (motor boat) 92, 166
Sialia (steam yacht) *see* USS *Coral*
Sims, VAdm. William Sowden 89
USS *Siren* (2nd) (steam yacht) 75, 76, 155

USS *Siren* (3rd) (diesel yacht) 126, 173
S.J. Waring (schooner) 32
Skinner, Lt. Carlton, USCGR *see* USS *Sea Cloud*
Slater, William 109, 162
slavers, interdiction of 18, 20–24
Sloane, Alfred Pritchard 131, 172
sloop *Katy* (renamed *Providence*) 7, ***14***
Smith, Alonzo (yacht builder) 25
Smith, MM 1c. Charles A.A. 105
Smith, Christopher Columbus (boat builder) ***112***
Smith, Col. C.S., USAR, Ret. 135
Smith & Dimon (builder) 37
Soley, Asst. Secy. of Navy James Russell 29
Sopwith, Thomas O.M. 124, 172
South Atlantic Blockading Squadron 33, 56
USS *South Carolina* (screw steamer) 48
Southerland, Lt. W.H.H. *see* USS *Eagle* (3rd)
USS *Southern Seas* (diesel yacht) 131, 173
Southern Yacht Club 35, ***36***, 50, 52
Sovereign (steam yacht) *79*, 155; *see also* USS *Scorpion*
Spear, Alden T., Acting Master *see Corypheus*
speed over opulence 36, 49, 55, 72, 88, 99, 112
Spence, Joseph *see Peterhoff*
Sperry, Elmer A. 96, 132
Spindrift (gasoline aux. yacht) 138, 177
Spotts, Lt. James H. *see Wanderer*
Spreckels, John Diedrich 110
Sproats, David 12
Stanford, Alfred 115
Stanton, Secy. of War Edwin 39, 43
Stanton, William Frederick, letter to wife re: Lincoln 39
Steers, George (naval architect) 55
Steers, Henry (builder) 33
Steindorff, OLtzS Ernst *see* UC-71
Stephanotis (British diesel yacht) 135, 180
Sterns, N.S. 77
Stevens, C.E. 25

Stevens, John Cox (yachtsman, designer) 19, 20, 55, 56
Stevens, William Picard (naval architect) 36
Stewart, James K. 124, 172
USS *Stiletto* (steam turbine yacht) 72, 73
Stirling, Major 2
Stoker, Clara B. 96
Stone, C.A. 124, 172
Stranger (steam yacht) *see* USS *Wenonah*
Street, William T., Acting Master *see* USS *Primrose*
Stribling, RAdm. Cornelius K. 41, 54
Stringham, Flag Officer S.H. (memo to Gideon Welles) 56
submarine chasers 101, 111
submarine volunteer counterforce: Civilian Coastal Picket Patrol 115, 117; Corsair Fleet 115; Daniels, Josephus 86, 90; junior navy 91; "Mosquito Fleet" 87; Roosevelt, Franklin D. 86; Yale University 87
Sullivan, Ens. Daniel A.J. 105, 106
USS *Sultana* (steam aux. yacht) 100, 108, 166
super yachts *see A* (diesel megayacht); *Hussar V* (later *Sea Cloud*) (diesel aux. yacht); *Hyper-Sub* (diesel submarine yacht); *Orion* (diesel yacht); *Savarona II* (diesel yacht); *Savarona III* (diesel yacht)
Supply (storeship) *see Gipsey*
USS *Surveyor* 104
SS *Susette Fraisinette* 108
USS *Sybilla III* (diesel yacht) *see* USS *Impetuous*
USS *Sylph* (3rd) (steam yacht) 71, ***89***, 156
USS *Sylph* (4th) (diesel aux. yacht) 127–128, 173
Sylphide (schooner yacht) 53, 54
Sylvia (diesel yacht) *see* USS *Tourmaline*
USS *Sylvia* (steam yacht) 94, ***95***, 156, 166
Symons, Capt. J. *see* HM Frigate *Cerberus*

CSS *Tacony* (commerce raider) 57
Talitha G. *see* USS *Beaumont* (diesel yacht)
USS *Tarantula* (steam yacht) ***97***, 98, 166
Task Group 22.5 141

Index

CSS *Teaser* (screw steam tug) 50, *51*, 96
Teazer (yacht) 49, 50
USS *Tech Jr.* (24' motor boat) 92
Telegraph (British schooner) 41
Teller Amendment to war declaration 65
Templeton, 2nd Viscount 56
Thea Foss (diesel yacht) *see* USS *Amber*
Thelma Phoebe (steam yacht) *see* USS *Onward*
Thespia (steam yacht) *see* USS *Hist*
Thompson, Lt. W.D. *see* *Harriet Lane*
Thompson, William Boyce 122, 171
Three Brothers (3-masted clipper) *see* USS *Vanderbilt*
Thurmond, Sophia Dabney 35
Tillman, William 32
Tobey, the Rev. Rufus B. 99
Tolley, Lt. Kemp *see* *Lanikai*
Tompkins, Eugene 133, 154, 163, 176
USS *Topeka* (gunboat) 78
Tornado (Spanish gunboat) 62
USS *Tourist* (steam yacht) 133, 134, 177
USS *Tourmaline* (diesel yacht) 127, 173
Transport Group No. 1 (June1917) 101
Transport Group No. 2 (June 1917) 101
Treaty of Alliance 12
Treaty of Amity and Commerce 12, 15, 148
Treaty of Ghent 12, 17, 18
Treaty of Mortefontaine 15
Treaty of Paris (1783) 13, 14
Treaty of Paris (1898) 82
Trent Affair 45, 150
Trouble (sailing yacht) 19, 20
Trudione *see* USS *Carnelian*
Trujillo, Rafael, Generalissimo 132
USS *Turquoise* (diesel yacht) 126, 127, 173
Turtle (submarine) 12, 13

SM U-20 85
SM U-34 103
SM U-53 85, *86*
U-69 115
SM U-117 109
U-123 115
SM U-151 (ex-*Deutschland*) 94
U-402 103
U-490 141
U-566 123

SM UB-52 108
SM UB-70 103
SM UB-88 109
SM UB-148 109
SM UC-71 109
SM UC-97 109
U.S. Naval Academy 57, 58, 66, 122, 137, 138, 152, 162, 177
U.S. Navy: established 13; state of prior to Spanish war 59, 60
U.S. Sanitary Commission 54, 55, *54*
Unquowa (steam yacht) *see* USS *Buccaneer*
Upton, Henry Montagu *see* Templeton, 2nd Viscount

Vagabondia *see* USS *Azurlite*
Valkyrie (British racing yacht) 99
Vallarta Alegre *see* USS *Agate*
Valor (Coast Guard diesel aux. schooner) 116, 117
Vamarie (gasoline aux. yacht) 137, 138, 177
SS *Van Cloon* 129
Vanda (diesel yacht) *see* USS *San Bernardino*
Vandalia (US sloop-of-war) 19
USS *Vandalia* (tanker) 137
USS *Vanderbilt* 2, *42*, 43–45; *Peterhoff* Affair 44–46; *Saxon* Affair 47
Vanderbilt, Cornelius 2, 43, 161; Congressional resolution 42
Vanderbilt, Lt. William Kissam, II (jg) 97, 122, 166, 171; *see also* USS *Tarantula*
Vaux, James 53
Vaux, Richard 53
Veblen, Thorstein *see* "The Gilded Age"
USS *Vedette* (steam yacht) 107, 108, 167
Veglia (steam yacht) *see* USS *Alcedo*
USS *Venetia* (steam yacht) 107, *108*, 110, 167
USS *Vergana* (steam aux. yacht) 96
vessel naming confusion 2, 36, 37, 53
Vesta (sailing yacht) 35
Vida (diesel yacht) *see* USS *Crystal*
Vigilant (racing yacht) 99
USS *Viking* (steam yacht) *65*, 76, 156
Viking (turbo-electric yacht) *see* USS *St. Augustine*
Villard, Henry 33, 34

USS *Vincennes* (sloop-of-war) 23
CSS *Virginia* (ex–USS *Merrimac*) 39, 40, 43
USS *Virginia* (captured steamer) 53, 54
Virginia (steam yacht) *see* USS *Vedette*
Virginius Incident (1873) 62
Vita (diesel yacht) *see* USS *Cythera* (2nd)
USS *Vixen* (diesel yacht) 117, 119, *120*, 172
Volunteer Coast Guard Reserve 115
von Forstner, Siegfried Freiherr, KKpt. *see* U-402
von Lottner, Hans *see* Berson, Leo
von Nostitz und Jänckendorff, Heinrich, KKpt. *see* SM U-151 (ex–*Deutschland*)

SS *Wabash* 105
Wacouta (steam aux. yacht) *see* *Eleanor*
Wade, Jeptha Homer, II 100, 167
USS *Wadena* (schooner-rigged steam yacht) 100, 101, 167
Wainwright, Cdr. Jonathan Mayhew, II *see* *Harriet Lane*
Wainwright, LCdr. Richard *see* USS *Gloucester*
USS *Wakiva II* (steam yacht) 104, 105, 167
Walewski, Count 27
Wallabout Bay 12
Wanderer (sailing yacht) 22, 23, *23*, 24, 25, 40, 41
War of 1812: naval forces at onset 15; privateers commissioned 17
War with Spain: declaration of war 65; justification 64, 65; Teller Amendment re. Cuba 65, 66
Ward, Lt. Aaron *see* USS *Wasp*
Ward, Samuel 7
warfare, ending of 84, 114
Warrior (blockade runner) *see* *Gertrude*
USS *Wasp* (7th) (steam yacht) 66, 77, 78, 156, 167
Washington, George 6, 12, 53, 145; 8th message to Congress 62; four schooners 8
Water Witch (blockade runner) 49
USS *Water Witch* (gunboat) 37
Watson, George L. (designer, builder) 74
Wave (sail racing yacht) 18, 19, 20

Index

Welles, Secy. of Navy Gideon 32–33, 42, 59; letters to 40–41, 52, 56
USS *Wenonah* (steam yacht) 101, 102, 103, 167; in heavy seas ***102***
West Gulf Squadron 38
SS *Westward Ho* 102
W.F. Stone Shipbuilding Yards 93, 158, 163
Wheeler, William M., Master's Mate *see Dart*
Whipple, Commodore Abraham 7
White, Herbert H. 25, 26
White, Loring Q. 136
Whitthorne, Washington Curran, Sen. 73
Widgeon (gasoline yacht) *see* USS *Edithena*
Wilkes, RAdm. Charles 44, 45, 150; comment by M.P. Seymour Fitzgerald 45, 46
William Capes (builder) 19, 20
William Cramp & Sons (builder) 55, 73, 77, 153, 155, 156, 158, 161, 167

William H. Brown (builder) 55
USS *Williamsburg* (diesel yacht) 120, ***121***, 172
Willys, Edward 127, 173
Willys, John N. 101, 163, 172
Wilson, Pres. Woodrow 71, 86, 88, 89, 111
Wimbee (gasoline aux. yacht) 137, 145, 179
Winant, Gov. John Gilbert 138
Winchester (turbine yacht) 88, 168
Windsor, LCdr. Charles Clifford *see* USS *May*
Windsor Forest (British mechantman) 50, 51
Windward (schooner) 32
HMCS *Wolf* (steam yacht) *see* USS *Wenonah*
Wolfe, Dudley F. 138, 177
USS *Wompatuk* (armed tug) 77
Woolworth, Norman B. 123, 171
Wyeth, Lt. Maxwell, USNRF *see* USS *Emerald* (2nd)

yacht, early development and acceptance 1, 5, ***6***, 20

yacht opulence 66, 69, 70, ***71***, 74, 98, 100, 101, 109, 113, 125–127, 132
yachts as naval auxiliaries: Gardner, William 63; McAdoo, Secy. of Navy William 63; U.S. Code 46, §57105 (29 June 1936) 114
Yankee Clipper (steam yacht) *see* USS *Coral*
Yankee Clipper 145; *see also El Cano* 175 (Appendix 5)
USS *Yankton* (steam yacht) 109, 157, 168
yard patrol craft (YP) 135
Yarrow Yard (builder) 88

Zaca (diesel aux. yacht) 139, 145, 178
Zahn, KptLt. Wilhelm *see* U-69
Zangara, Giuseppe 119
Zavala (schooner) 45
Ziegler, William, Jr. 97, 162
USS *Zircon* (diesel yacht) 128, 173

www.ingramcontent.com/pod-product-compliance
Lightning Source LLC
Chambersburg PA
CBHW060342010526
44117CB00017B/2932